For Fred & Dno,

Thanks for the memories,

Barry

August 2020

RISK TAKER, SPY MAKER

Tales of a CIA Case Officer

BARRY MICHAEL BROMAN

CASEMATE

Philadelphia & Oxford

Published in the United States of America and Great Britain in 2020 by
CASEMATE PUBLISHERS
1950 Lawrence Road, Havertown, PA 19083, USA
and
The Old Music Hall, 106–108 Cowley Road, Oxford OX4 1JE, UK

Hardcover Edition: ISBN 978-1-61200-896-7
Digital Edition: ISBN 978-1-61200-897-4

A CIP record for this book is available from the British Library

Broman, Barry Michael: CIA's Publication Review Board comments.
This does not constitute an official release of CIA information. All statements of fact, opinion, or analysis expressed are those of the author and do not reflect the official positions or views of the Central Intelligence Agency (CIA) or any other U.S. Government agency. Nothing in the contents should be construed as asserting or implying U.S. Government authentication of information or CIA endorsement of the author's views. This material has been reviewed solely for classification.

Maps by Seth Broman
All images by the author unless otherwise indicated

Printed and bound in the United States of America by Sheridan

Typeset by Versatile PreMedia Services (P) Ltd

For a complete list of Casemate titles, please contact:

CASEMATE PUBLISHERS (US)
Telephone (610) 853-9131
Fax (610) 853-9146
Email: casemate@casematepublishers.com
www.casematepublishers.com

CASEMATE PUBLISHERS (UK)
Telephone (01865) 241249
Email: casemate-uk@casematepublishers.co.uk
www.casematepublishers.co.uk

Contents

Foreword by Daniel C. Arnold   v
Acknowledgments   vii
Preface   ix

1   Early Years   1
2   Photographer   9
3   Marine   34
4   Spy   77
5   Latter Years   230

For BJ, the better half

Foreword

Growing up on a farm during the Depression, well before the advent of television, I happily read any adventure book that I could get my hands on. This book beats all of them. It is a true American success story. For anyone who wants to viscerally experience a series of contemporary true-life adventure stories, in war and peace, this book has it all. The author has lived and written an engaging story of his professional life's experiences in a series of interesting and, at times, amusing short stories.

Barry's professional work experience began in Southeast Asia as a teenage wire service photographer. After college and graduate school, he returned to Vietnam as a Marine infantry officer in combat. Barry then spent a quarter of a century traveling the world recruiting and handling agents for the Central Intelligence Agency during much of the Cold War.

I can personally attest that he was one of the best. Barry was a recruiting "headhunter," a unique type of intelligence operations officer with more than 40 recruitments under his belt. He had an unerring ability to assess promising potential assets and to recruit and handle such clandestine agents. To do so successfully over an extended period is no mean feat. In addition, he demonstrated management skills, serving as a CIA deputy chief of station, multiple assignments as chief of station, and running a successful clandestine paramilitary project.

Since retirement from the CIA, Barry has written and photographed many books, produced numerous documentary films, and is still going strong. Mention must be made of his lovely wife, "BJ" or "Betty Jane," who is a beautiful and talented complement to this extraordinary American.

Daniel C. Arnold
Retired Senior CIA Clandestine Service officer

Acknowledgments

Many people have assisted with this project and I want to thank them. Unfortunately, all cannot be named for reasons of security.

First, I want to thank the late John Stevenson and Victoria Butler for their encouragement to write this book and for providing much-needed editing help.

I want to thank Daniel Clay Arnold, my friend and mentor, for writing the forward.

I also want to thank the following people: Peter Arnett, John Whalen, Sunda Khin, Claudia Saw Lwin Robert, Robert Walsh, Daniel Sternheimer, Neil Hollander, Georges Hoffman, Bob Peterson, Colonel Andrew Finlayson, USMC (Ret), Billy Huff, Anthony Marengo, Colonel John McKay, USMC (Ret), Cottrell Fox, Ronald Drez, Denis Gray, Ambassador Timothy Carney, Fred Kroll, Colonel Michael Eiland, USA (Ret), Ken Conboy, Robert Griffin, Colonel Alan Armstrong, USA (Ret), Jay Peterson, William Shawcross, Cletus Foote, Michael Duckworth, Nate Thayer, John McCarthy, George Taylor, Steve Russell, and the late U Ye Htoon "Roland."

Thanks to the team at Casemate Publishers under difficult conditions, especially David Farnsworth, Ruth Sheppard, Isobel Fulton, and Ting Baker.

Most of all, I want to thank my wife, BJ, for putting up with me for more than half a century and for providing guidance and support for the book.

He who will not risk cannot win

JOHN PAUL JONES

Preface

For much of my working life I was employed by three organizations that are easily identified by their initials: AP, USMC, and CIA. I was a photographer for the Associated Press in Thailand, Vietnam, and Cambodia and a photo editor in Chicago and New York. I served in the 5th Regiment of the Marine Corps in Vietnam and then as a liaison officer in Thailand. After two weeks as a civilian, I entered the Clandestine Service of the Central Intelligence Agency, which kept me busy for the next 25 years, mostly in Southeast Asia. It was certainly my good fortune to have been associated with these challenging and iconic organizations but my greatest luck was to have met and married a Hawaiian lady, Betty Jane (BJ) Apilado. During my career with CIA I was chief of station twice, deputy chief of station once, branch chief twice, and managed a large international paramilitary project.

This memoir is largely a collection of stories about the people I encountered along the way. Unfortunately, not all the people can be identified. Some of the best stories cannot even be told. When I retired from the CIA in 1996 I signed a secrecy agreement, which I will honor. The text of this book has been read and approved by the Publication Review Board of the CIA. I never kept notes or a diary. Thus, these stories are all from memory, and I hope they are accurate.

Why write this book? If the CIA is a secret organization, why talk about it? I think the American people have a right to know, within limits, what the Clandestine Service of the CIA really does, and how it operates. A senior retired Agency officer I respect once told me that he wrote a memoir at the urging of a former director of central intelligence, Richard Helms, also a reluctant memoir writer, who reasoned that there was no one better able to tell what the Agency really does than someone from the Agency. I believe also that there is a lot of misunderstanding by the public about what the CIA does. This is not a kiss-and-tell book. I very much enjoyed my years in the Agency, especially those spent in the field, which in my case were 19 years out of 25, a ratio I am proud of. Every good case officer I know wants to be in the field and not at headquarters. It is the same with newsmen and also Marines. You want to be where the action is. In my case the action was in Southeast Asia, and I turned down jobs in other places to stay in the part of the world that I loved. As my old friend and colleague, known to his friends as the Bear, remarked in Southeast Asia in the late 1970s, "They paid us to live here." I nodded in agreement.

In addition to discussing my career in the CIA, I want to share some stories as a teenage wire service photographer in Thailand, Cambodia, and South Vietnam in the early 1960s, a time when Americans were just beginning to read regularly about these remote places. After college, I went back to Asia, this time as a Marine lieutenant in combat. Like all veterans of the Vietnam War, I have war stories. I also have tales from my service as a liaison officer for the R&R program in Thailand, a little known offshoot of the shooting war and a lot more amusing.

While in graduate school at the University of Washington, my favorite professor asked what I planned to do after my four years' service in the Marine Corps. I said I didn't know, but thought of the Foreign Service. He asked if I had considered the CIA. I said no. He suggested I give it some thought and offered an introduction to a CIA recruiter, which I accepted. Hearing that I had already worked in Indochina as a newsman and that I was earning a master's degree in Southeast Asian Studies with Thai as my grad school language, the recruiter said I was the kind of person the Agency was looking for. I survived the war, contacted the recruiter, and went from the frying pan of the Marine Corps to the fire of the Agency.

The last section of the book deals with events in my post-government years, when I had the opportunity and time to return to writing and photography, resulting in over a dozen books and a lesser number of documentary films, which I produced. In places the book takes the form of a travelogue of new and usually rarely visited areas that I was allowed into, usually for filmmaking. An example was a film I produced on the heroin trade in the forbidden hills of northeastern Burma known as the Golden Triangle.

The book is presented chronologically, providing some insights of life—and sometimes death—in various wars and other dangerous enterprises. It also includes anecdotes about some of the more entertaining and always interesting people and places I had the great fortune to meet and visit.

For reasons of national security, the Publication Review Board has asked me to take out some place names and dates. Some names have been changed or removed.

CHAPTER I

Early Years

During World War II my father was a glider pilot and saw action in Europe when he crossed the Rhine in the largest glider operation in history. He didn't talk about it much but over the years I heard stories about the short and brutal lives of glider pilots. The family photo album included a small black and white snapshot of young pilots with a baby seated in front with a bottle of beer between his legs. Pappy, his nickname from his wartime years when most of his men were usually a decade younger, and the name he liked me to use, would point to the young pilots in the photo saying:

> He was killed in the Normandy landings. He died in Holland in the Arnhem assault. He was killed on Operation *Varsity*, crossing the Rhine in 1945 not far from me. That's Henry Palmer. He was famous for rescuing survivors of an airplane crash in New Guinea. Henry and I are the only survivors from that group. That's me. The baby is Barry.

Like most Americans, the Bromans were immigrants, in this case from Sweden. My grandfather, Frank Broman, arrived from Eskilstuna early in the 20th century. He was a custom tailor, traveled widely in the West, and prospered. He married my grandmother, Lillian Wallenberg, an American girl of Swedish extraction who was born during the "great blizzard" of March 1888 in Minneapolis. Lily met Frank in California sometime after she survived the San Francisco earthquake in 1906. They married and settled in Los Angeles, where my father, Harry, was born a year later.

Eventually, the Bromans settled in Seattle where Harry graduated from Broadway High School and entered the University of Washington. As a freshman he played baseball and was coxswain of the frosh crew. When he was accepted into the school of architecture, he had to give up sports. An only child, Pappy joined Kappa Sigma fraternity where he immediately had brothers, some of whom engaged in the illegal but popular pursuit of manufacturing bath tub gin during the era of Prohibition. Despite the rigors of the school of architecture, Pappy was active in the Army's Reserve Officer Training Corps and was captain of the rifle team. He was commissioned a second lieutenant in 1935.

While still in college, Pappy met and married a cute Canadian girl, Hilda Foley, who immigrated to the United States at the age of 18. On her father's side, she was Irish. The family left County Waterford in the 18th century bound for New Waterford on the west coast of Prince Edward Island, Canada, a little Erin unfettered by English tyranny. My great grandfather, Thomas Foley, led the family west to Vancouver, where he later owned an outfitting company for the Yukon gold rush. Tom had eight children, one of whom was Thomas Edward Foley, my grandfather. Young Tom farmed in the Fraser River valley town of Dudney and gained local fame for once going three rounds in an exhibition bout with world heavyweight boxing champion Tommy Burns in Nanaimo, BC. Tom married Regina Marquette of Mission, BC, whose father was the local constable (sheriff). They had two sons and five daughters, one of whom was Hilda, my mother. Regina died young of tuberculosis and Tom drowned in a boating accident, making orphans of the children. All the girls immigrated to the United States as soon as they turned 18 to begin new lives.

Pappy found work as an architect for Edwin J. Ivy in Seattle for the princely sum of $30 per week. The depression was in full spate and he was lucky to get the job. He never suffered though. His father was well off and Pappy drove a Stutz Bearcat sports car. He and Mom lived a happy life as war clouds were gathering. In 1941, Pappy left his architecture practice and turned down an offer to join the Army Corps of Engineers. He wanted to fly. He volunteered to be a fighter pilot but was too old. The same with bombers. He was 32 and learned that the age limit for glider pilots was 35 so he signed up. He didn't know what he was in for. War correspondent Walter Cronkite wrote in his foreword to a book about the glider corps: "I'll tell you straight out. If you've to go into combat, don't go by glider. Walk, crawl, parachute, swim, float—anything. But don't go by glider." Cronkite knew what he was talking about. He rode a glider into battle in the ill-fated Operation *Market Garden*, British General Montgomery's "bridge too far" in Holland in 1944.

Much of Pappy's glider training took place in desolate parts of Texas, largely unhampered by trees or other glider-unfriendly obstacles. Once, during a night landing, Pappy lost sight of his wingman and the little light on his wingtips. He turned his CG-4A glider sharply away and landed safely. His wingman had flown into the side of a freight train crossing the Texas prairie, killing the pilot and co-pilot. Another time he also lost sight of his wingman in the dark and guided his plane, *The Hilda B*, to a safe landing. His wingman had hit the only farmhouse in 10 miles, killing the pilot and co-pilot. The farmer survived.

While their husbands were away trying to fly fragile aircraft with no engines, a hardy group of wives followed their husbands to dry, dusty Texas towns with names like La Mesa and Dalhart. The young war brides were on their own. They had no government support and were not allowed on base. The wives stayed in small hotels, sometimes four to a room, seeing their husbands on weekends. This is where my mother learned to play bridge. About once a week, the bridge games would be interrupted when an Air Corps officer would arrive and inform a wife that she was now a widow. Glider training came at a high cost. The bridge games would stop, the girls helped the new widow pack her things and put her on a bus or train. The bridge games then resumed.

I was born in Kentucky in 1943 while my father was assigned to Bowman Field near Louisville. I suffered from colic, which earned me a prescription for Kentucky bourbon whiskey, which solved the problem. I shared the bottle with Pappy, the first of many. Pappy shipped out in 1944, first to England and then to France. He got into the war in the spring of 1945 when he participated in Operation *Varsity*, the crossing of the Rhine River into Germany, the largest glider operation in history. As a captain he led a flight of 16 gliders into action behind German lines to secure a beachhead for British forces crossing the river in boats. His glider was hit by fire from an anti-aircraft gun, killing all the infantrymen in the back. A high-tension wire slowed the plane's descent, taking off part of the nose of the aircraft. For the next two days Pappy and his co-pilot hunkered down in a destroyed farmhouse until British soldiers broke through and rescued them. More glider pilots were killed crossing the Rhine than at the D-Day landings in Normandy. Gliders and airborne parachutists went in first, in the dark, behind German lines.

Back at his base in Melun, not far from Paris, Pappy was preparing for another glider assault in Germany but after crossing the Rhine, resistance was slight and the Allies moved fast heading for Berlin. The drop was cancelled and on May 8 Pappy was visiting Rheims Cathedral with a few buddies when senior German officers, also in Rheims, signed the official surrender to the Allies. Pappy's war was over.

Released from the Air Corps in 1945, Pappy returned to architecture in Seattle where he was made a partner in his firm and stayed in the reserves. My sister, Jennifer, joined the family in 1947 and Pappy settled down for a quiet career as an architect in Seattle. Fate intervened. He was recalled to active service for the Berlin Airlift crisis of 1948 and released after a year, only to be called up again for the Korean War in 1950. In 1954, when he was about to be released from the Air Force, he was offered any assignment in the world to keep him in uniform. He had to make a hard decision. He opted to stay in the military and took the job of base engineer at RAF Manston, a Battle of Britain fighter base on the English Channel near Dover. During the war it was the closest Allied base to occupied Europe. Although it was a Royal Air Force base, its only aircraft were American F-86 Sabre jets and some air/sea rescue helicopters. Pappy was going back to England and we were going with him.

***

Pappy flew to England before us in mid-1954. My mother, younger sister Jennifer, and I followed in December. My first airplane ride was from Seattle to Minneapolis to see my grandmother en route to England. The four-engine aircraft encountered heavy turbulence over the Rockies. My mother sat with my sister. I sat in front of them next to a young Marine who looked like he had never flown before either. As the stewardess carried a tray of coffee and soft drinks down the aisle, the plane hit a downdraft. The beverages went flying over passengers just as many of them lost their lunch. But not me or the Marine. I thought this was how all flights were, so it just needed getting used to. We flew on to an air base in Connecticut a few days later, then on to Prestwick, Scotland, via a USAF C-54 aircraft without incident. After a chilly night in Ayrshire, we caught *The Flying Scotsman*, Scotland's finest steam train, to London.

Pappy met the train. For our first dinner in London after our arduous journey from Seattle, Pappy took us to one of his favorite wartime haunts, The Brompton Road Bar and Grill in Knightsbridge. It was hot, noisy, and smoky from grilling at tables, but the beef was good. The smoke was getting to me so I asked to be excused, pleading a need to visit the toilet. Instead, I went outside into the crisp night air and went for a short walk. I promptly got lost. By luck I spotted a London policeman, a bobby, and told him my problem. After I described the smoky bistro, the bobby figured out where I belonged and walked me to the grill. I thanked him for his help, returned to our table, and never mentioned my foray outside or my first English friend.

As a result of his wartime experience in England and his rescue by the British Army in Germany after he evaded German capture for three days in the Rhine-crossing operation, Pappy was a dedicated anglophile. With a pencil moustache, he even looked the part. RAF Manston was perfect for us. Located near Dover in Kent, an hour from London by train, its Spitfires saw heavy service during the Battle of Britain in 1940 as they fought to stop German bombers heading for London. Later in the war, the runway was lengthened to accommodate crippled bombers trying to make it back to England. As a result, Manston had the longest runway in Britain.

We lived in a 19th-century country home called "Deepdene" in Herne Bay, 18 miles from the base. Instead of sending me to an American boarding school near London, Pappy opted to put me in a private English school in Herne Bay. I was the only American at Eddington House Boys' Preparatory School. It was a boarding school, but also accepted dayboys such as me. Many of the boarders were boys from families overseas, such as Malaya, Kenya, and Cyprus, where wars were raging that required the evacuation of children. I commuted by bicycle less than a mile from our house on the Canterbury Road, a two-lane road originally built by Romans two thousand years ago.

Our headmaster was G. E. Hunt, a Cambridge graduate who wore his black robes daily. He was a fellow of the Royal Geographic Society and had the head of a mounted wild boar outside his office with a small plaque saying Gambia 1935. He was an affable fellow and presided over morning assembly and prayers before school started. I enjoyed school despite having to attend on Saturday mornings, with sports in the afternoon, and suffering occasional beatings of "six of the best." These were strokes of a cane or sometimes a tennis shoe across the bottom of the miscreant inflicted for various minor infractions. Slipping sheets of blotting paper down the backs of trousers reduced pain. We wore uniforms with the school badge on the jacket and at age 11 I was introduced to Latin, French, Shakespeare, and the history of the British Empire. We played cricket, field hockey, and football (soccer) depending on the season. We were a prep school that prepared boys for public school, which was actually a private high school. Most boys went on to King's School, Canterbury, which claimed to be the oldest continuously operated school in the world, founded in the year 597. Once I got the hang of the lingo—Churchill once remarked that America and Britain were two countries separated by a common language—I loved the place.

My favorite subject was English, which consisted mainly of poetry, Dickens, and Shakespeare. The English master, Mr. Troughton, was my own Mr. Chips, the best teacher I ever had. He was large and hairy and from Northumberland. He spoke in a deep, resonating voice and never smiled. He chain-smoked cheap cigarettes and his fingertips and teeth were a deep shade of brown. His mission, he said, was to make every boy, "Except you, Broman," speak the Queen's English without any regional or working-class accent. The mark of an educated Englishman, he explained, was to be unable to tell where he was from.

Eddington House Boys' Preparatory School cricket team, Herne Bay, Kent, England 1956. B. Broman, front row, left. Slow-spin bowler.

My best sport was cricket, which I enjoyed without ever understanding the nuances of the game, such as how you can fight for a draw in a match. I was a slow-spin bowler and a fair batsman for the First Eleven of the school team. At first I had the vexing habit of throwing my bat when hitting the ball, as is done in baseball. Not in cricket. We played matches with other prep schools in east Kent. One day we were playing a school near Dover and to my great surprise my father showed up to watch. We were in the field when my father walked up in uniform to watch the match with other parents. I was bowling at the time.

The headmaster of the school welcomed him and asked how it was that an American air force major should be interested in a prep school cricket match. "That's my boy pitching," Pappy explained. "We call that bowling," the headmaster explained politely and offered a cup of tea. My cricket experience put me in good stead years later when I played for the Seattle Cricket Club and then the Royal Bangkok Sports Club, the only American on either team.

A rare moment of academic glory came my way when Mr. Troughton included me in a team to compete against other schools at King's School in Canterbury, seven miles away, dealing with an aspect of the English language. I was entered to represent the school in "sight reading," a term I had never heard before. It meant I had to read a passage from a book without any preparation. Some boys recited scenes from Shakespeare plays. Little Pugh, with an incredible singing voice, from Wales, played Portia in *The Merchant of Venice* with great emotion and effect. When it was my turn to perform, I stepped up to the lectern, where a grim-faced master handed me an open book and wished me luck. It was *Huckleberry Finn* and I had to read a passage of Huck talking to his black friend Jim. Not a problem for me, I even slipped into Jim's Negro accent. In for a penny, in for a pound, I reckoned. In the end, I won, and went up on the stage to receive my thimble-sized cup, which was awarded by an elderly academic from King's.

"Excellent American accent, Mr. Broman" he announced.

"Thank you, sir," I replied. His smile disappeared.

"Are you American?" he asked in a low voice.

"Yes, sir," I replied with a touch of pride. He was clearly not amused but mercifully did not ask for the trophy back. As I walked off the stage I saw Mr. Troughton in the audience give me a "thumbs up." It was the only time I ever saw him smile.

My elective at Eddington House was riding. My father ponied up for jodhpurs and a black riding hat and I joined five other boys, all of whom had their own horses at home. Every Thursday the school van drove us to stables in Whitstable, where a brawny young woman of Kent put us through our paces on horseback. It was great fun, usually ending with a galloping race across a lush meadow with visions of the doomed Light Brigade at Balaclava in our minds. One day, for a treat, we rode down to the ocean at Whitstable, famous for its oysters and the oldest golf club house in the world. We galloped across the hard sand at low tide until the horses and our instructor told us to stop. A few weeks later a young day-tripper down from London found something sticking up from the sands where we had ridden. It turned out to be a prong from a sea mine from World War II. Army engineers were called in and uncovered a string of six mines that had broken loose and drifted ashore. They were exploded by rifle fire. No more beach riding for us.

"Deepdene" was a charming mini manor on two acres, with trees, a lawn, fruit orchard, and a large vegetable garden. The house had four bedrooms, a sitting room, a dining room, and a huge ballroom with French doors opening on to the formal garden. The skylight over the ballroom had been painted black during the war so that German bombers couldn't use it as a landmark. We had a gardener, old Fred Hufham, two days a week. Fred had lost an eye in a childhood accident but was drafted anyway into the British Army in 1916 at the age of 15. When a sergeant saw him at the recruit depot in Dover, he sent him home saying, "The King don't need you yet lad." Fred had never been to London. He told me he saw a film once, a silent film. When I offered to take him to the local Odeon where I was a regular, he demurred, "Already seen one, ain't I?" During World War II, Fred served in the Home Guard, going out at night armed with shotguns and pitchforks to round up German aircrews brought down by the RAF. Business was brisk.

The house was the scene of dinner parties on Fridays that usually ended with a walk in the grounds at first light on Saturday mornings. I sometimes served as bartender and perfected the art of making an old fashioned (bourbon-based cocktail). The house had only one drawback; there was no central heating. Each room had a fireplace. It was my job to light fires daily in the sitting room and dining room and to keep the kitchen-stove fire running all the time. There was no heat at all in the bedrooms. We had to make do with hot water bottles. What do you expect for $95 a month?

I joined the Herne Bay troop of Boy Scouts and had a chance to meet working-class boys who were every bit as nice (often nicer) than the upper-class boys at my prep school. I was not required to pledge allegiance to the Queen as my troop mates were. We were a convivial group under the guidance of our scoutmaster, Colin Clissold from Rhondda Valley in Wales. One year I attended a world jamboree of scouts in Sutton Coldfield, where I helped interpret between American and British scouts. My favorite merit badge was the Bookman badge, which involved presenting a reading list to my examiner, the Canterbury librarian. My books invariably dealt with World War II and were almost evenly divided between escape stories of Britons captured by Germans and tales of the Royal Air Force in the Battle of Britain. After a rigorous but friendly inquisition, I passed, and my examiner invited me for a cup of tea. "I suspect your classmates don't know the history of the air war over Kent as well as you, Yank." I took it as a compliment. He went on to tell me that during the war he was in Canterbury, which was heavily bombed. One day he saw a German bomber in flames coming down very close to him. Just before the plane crashed the rear gunner waved goodbye to him. Today, when you visit Canterbury Cathedral, make a point to inspect the beautiful stained glass window. All of the original windows were blown out by German bombing, but the cathedral itself still stands. The new window features an RAF Spitfire climbing for altitude to meet the Hun. It was probably based at Manston.

A requirement in earning the First Class badge in British scouting is to undertake a 20-mile hike in a 24-hour period and write a log along the way. As second of the Springbok Patrol, I accompanied my patrol leader, Reggie, on his hike. The route followed a 20-mile segment of the Pilgrim's Way to Canterbury from Watling Street in London as described by Chaucer in *The Canterbury Tales*. Our walk ended at Canterbury Cathedral and the shrine of Thomas Becket, who was canonized there in 1173. I hope the path is still intact. Reggie didn't need a map, just a copy of Chaucer.

CHAPTER 2

Photographer

After England, Pappy was assigned to Wright-Patterson Air Force Base near Springfield, Ohio, where he attended the Air Force Institute of Technology and earned an MA in civil engineering. One of the foreign officers attending the same course was a young Royal Thai Air Force captain, Sudhi Lekhyananda. Sudhi was a Tufts University graduate and an elementary school classmate of Prince Bhumibol Adulyadej, the future King of Thailand. Sudhi's father was Thailand's first graduate of Harvard Law School and a fellow student of Prince Mahidol Adulyadej, Bhumibol's father. He was later a Minister of Justice following World War II. Sudhi was smart and easy-going; he always had a smile on his face. He quickly became Pappy's buddy and soon they would be working together in Thailand. He would become our first, and best, Thai friend.

The following year took us to Scott Air Force Base near St. Louis where an Air Force sergeant working for the Military Air Transport Service (MATS) introduced me to photography, which was to become my passion. In the summer of 1959 I worked as an attendant at the officers' club swimming pool on base. By chance, I met Technical Sergeant Lloyd Borguss one day after work. He was part of an elite team of photographers and offered to teach me photography after work and took me under this wing. I had to work my passage. He started by teaching me how to wash and dry photographs. I started at the bottom. Then I learned how to develop and print black and white film. Finally, I got to handle a camera and learned composition and techniques of photo-journalism. Lloyd was a good teacher, in addition to being a top Air Force photographer. This helped me in high school, where I became the school newspaper's photographer. My first published photo was of Senator John F. Kennedy when he was on a visit to Belleville, Illinois, in 1960 campaigning for president.

My future in photography made a move forward when I went to college. In 1961 I received a four-year academic scholarship to the University of Illinois. I joined a fraternity, Chi Phi, where I was a pledge brother of a freshman of Lithuanian descent from Chicago named Dick Butkus. Dick, a witty and friendly fellow, was on the football team. He went on to a very successful career in professional football and later as a comedian in a television series. Today the Butkus Award is given to the best football linebackers in the country at the high school, college, and professional levels.

Each pledge had to have an "activity." Mine was joining the staff of the *Daily Illini*, the school newspaper, as a photographer. I was disappointed to learn that they didn't use the elegant 35mm Nikon cameras that I had learned to use from Sergeant Borguss. The *Daily Illini* used bulky, slow-to-use 4 × 5 Speed Graphics that had been around for decades. Using the relics did teach one thing: fire discipline. On a typical assignment I was given one film holder, which means I had to get the shot with only two frames available. With a Nikon and a small roll of film, I had at least 20 chances. I gained a lot of experience in my year at the University of Illinois, and enjoyed working with an editor, Roger Ebert, who went on to a distinguished career as a film critic, first for the *Chicago Sun-Times* newspaper and then on television. He was a lot of fun to work with. Unless you missed the shot.

In 1962 my father was assigned as a civil engineer advisor to the Royal Thai Air Force (RTAF). The Vietnam War was heating up. There were US advisors in the country and helicopters to support the South Vietnamese Army (ARVN). Plans were already afoot to build air bases in Thailand to support operations in Vietnam. That was where Pappy came in, working with his friend Captain Sudhi of the RTAF.

To my surprise, Pappy offered to let me drop out of the University of Illinois, give up my scholarship, and live for one year in Thailand to give me some experience of the Far East. It didn't take me long to accept. It was a decision that changed my life.

Bangkok in 1962 was a quiet city despite a population of several million. Traffic was not a problem, although most streets were two lanes. Canals or *klongs* flanked many streets, giving Bangkok the name "Venice of the East." Wireless Road, for instance, where the American embassy is located, was a tree-lined two-lane road with *klongs* on both sides. Sathorn Road, nearby, where my father worked at the Joint United States Military Advisory Group (JUSMAG) was also a two-lane road with two large *klongs*. We lived in the north end of town closer to Don Muang Air Base, where Pappy spent much of his time. We had a large house with a staff of cook, maid, and gardener. The only drawback was the lack of air conditioning and the prevalence of cobras and other venomous snakes, especially when the rains brought them out.

Life in Bangkok in the summer of 1962 was good for a college drop out. My early days were mainly spent playing tennis at the Royal Bangkok Sports Club, an oasis in the heart of Bangkok complete with an 18-hole golf course, lawn tennis courts, and an air-conditioned billiard room (no ladies please). The covered verandah offered excellent inexpensive food and draft Singha beer. The club was founded in 1901 by King Chulalongkorn, largely for the pleasure of Siam's growing foreign population. It had Thailand's first golf course, a challenging course with lots of water hazards. Golfers employed fore caddies here, men who went before the golfers to retrieve balls lost in water.

After a hard day of lawn tennis with breaks in the Olympic-size swimming pool, my evenings usually featured attendance at parties hosted by American military or diplomatic dependents in town. As a military brat with years spent moving around the world, I made friends fast. We couldn't believe our good fortune at being in Thailand where the people were friendly, the food was great, and the weather was hot. A bowl of noodles with barbequed pork cost about 15 cents, the same as a heaped plate of shrimp fried rice. For transportation we used the sporty, open-aired, vehicles known as *tuk tuks*. These three-wheeled death traps could carry three passengers and were great fun until it rained or they had a close encounter with a Bangkok bus. There were no meters to report the cost of a ride. Each trip needed to be negotiated with the driver. This required some knowledge of Thai language. A ride anywhere in town could be had for two packs of Salem cigarettes, which cost 10 cents each at the American military PX.

This idyll came to a screeching halt after a month of tennis by day and partying by night. My father took me aside one evening as I was preparing to go out. "This isn't what I had in mind," he said, "when I let you drop out of school for a year. We now have a new rule. You have to get a job. If you don't, plan on returning to the University of Illinois in the fall." Finding a job was easier said than done, although the idea was fine with me. There weren't many jobs available for 18-year-old boys who spoke very little Thai and had few marketable skills.

Armed with a sheaf of my clippings from the *Daily Illini*, I made my way one morning in August 1962 to the offices of the *Bangkok World*, one of two English-language daily newspapers in Bangkok. Its editor, Darrell Berrigan, was a true old Asia hand. Berry had been a war correspondent for United Press in Burma and China in World War II. He looked at my clippings and said he would be happy to give me a job at the *World* but he would have to pay me the same rate he paid his Thai photographers, $40 a month. I asked if he had any idea where I could make more money. He suggested I try United Press International, his alma mater, and gave me their address on Patpong Road. He said to mention his name to the bureau chief, Bob Udick, and wished me luck. At the UPI office I was told that Mr. Udick was out of town. They suggested I try Associated Press down the street.

In those days Patpong was not the center of nightlife it became a couple of decades later. It was a respectable business center. Air France, Air Vietnam, and ESSO were there; also the United States Information Service library. A short and privately owned street, Patpong was closed down every year for the Patpong fair that raised money for a leprosarium in northern Thailand. There were good restaurants. Mizu's Kitchen, owned by a Japanese soldier who declined to return to Japan after the war, was a favorite of the foreign press corps. My favorite spot was the Red Door, a classy bar and restaurant that served Bangkok's finest Shanghai fried noodles. The owner, Suzy, let me run a tab.

With not much hope for success, I walked up to the AP offices at 103 Patpong Road. The bureau chief, Tony Escoda, was in. A Filipino with degrees from Yale and Columbia, Tony was polite, looked at my tear sheets, and asked one question, "Can you start tomorrow?" I said yes. He needed an English-speaking photographer to cover the US Army presence that was coming to Thailand. The day rate of $10 per day wasn't much better than the *Bangkok World* was offering but this was the AP, America's leading wire service. Tony quickly pointed out that this was only the starting wage; there were other perks such as travel and all expenses paid. Did I want the job? I did.

The darkroom was a challenge. It was essentially a closet, and had electricity but no air conditioning. Daytime temperatures exceeded 100 Fahrenheit. To cool my chemicals for developing and printing photos I would have a block of ice delivered in the morning. It sat in a metal basin with an electric fan behind it to lower the room temperature. When I needed chemicals cooled, I would chip ice off the block and it drop into the developer. When the temperature hit 70 degrees, I would take out the ice and put in the film. Wet negatives would still be wet two days later if left alone, so I dried them with a ladies' electric hair dryer.

This was truly starting at the bottom. The good news was that Tony was a great guy who hated dealing with photos. In short order, he put me in charge of photos, including the administrative details of dealing with Tokyo Photos from where all AP Asian photos were managed. Here, I fell under the command of Harold "Hal" Buell, the Asian photo editor, who became a mentor and lifelong friend. Hal also "gave the bride away" at my wedding in 1968. He appreciated having someone in Bangkok with initiative who loved taking photos for the AP. I was not a staff employee but a "stringer," paid only when working. I was delighted. I not only had a job, I could stay in Bangkok for a year.

My first assignment upcountry was to drive to Korat, a city northeast of Bangkok, to photograph the arrival of US Army troops as a show of force against a perceived communist threat. The AP hired a jovial fellow named Noon and his car to drive me. Noon picked me up at the office at 6AM the next morning to beat the traffic. We stopped for breakfast at Noon's favorite noodle house, an open-air stall at Rangsit, a truck stop just north of the airport. Noon ordered two big bowls of noodles for us.

I was still a neophyte to Thai food and trusted Noon to keep me healthy. The noodle soup was delicious; egg noodles, barbequed pork and spiced with fish sauce and peppers mixed with fresh vegetables. Then I saw it, a large cockroach, feet up in the bottom of my bowl. I almost retched. I had a thought. Maybe this is a delicacy in Thailand. I didn't want to offend Noon. I ate around the cockroach until it was the only thing left in the bowl.

Then I asked myself if I was supposed to eat the creature. The Thai are fond of things like fried scorpions and lesser bugs and insects. I didn't want to commit a social *faux pas*. I had to ask. I gestured to the bottom of my bowl.

"Do I eat this, Noon?" He peered into my bowl and screamed at the owner who ran to the table. Maybe Noon hadn't been given a cockroach, I thought, and had missed a treat. The owner, abashed, said something to Noon.

"What did he say?" I asked.

"Do Americans eat roaches?"

"No, we hate them."

"Thai hate them too," Noon said. "You get next bowl free." There was no next time. I avoided that noodle shop ever after. Every time we passed Rangsit, Noon would point to the shop and remind me of my close encounter with a cockroach. I am sure he regaled his buddies with the story. I regaled mine.

***

Although my boss in Bangkok was AP bureau chief Tony Escoda, the senior AP staff photographer in Southeast Asia was a West German national, Horst Faas, assigned to the Saigon bureau. Horst was already gaining fame as a war photographer, having covered combat in the Congo and Algeria. He was in Saigon photographing the war years before American ground troops arrived, and was still there when the Americans went home. He was wounded numerous times and earned two Pulitzer Prizes.

Horst would visit Bangkok from time to time, sometimes just to get away from the war. In those days he was in the field often with South Vietnamese troops and had many close calls. By the time American ground forces arrived in 1965, Horst was already an old Vietnam hand. He spent more time in harm's way than any American soldier or Marine. The first time I met Horst he was appalled at the meager day rate that AP was paying me. He had a short chat with Tony and my salary was raised three hundred percent. Horst informed me that whenever he was in town I was automatically on the clock to assist him. He became a mentor to me, and, among many other things, taught me how to prepare an expense account, a critical skill for any journalist, print or photo.

Horst tasked me to look for interesting feature stories that he could photograph when he was in Thailand. We would do these stories together and had the full approval of Tony, who maintained his hands-off policy when it came to photos. This gave me a chance to learn from the master who was extremely generous with his time and guidance.

During my search for feature photo stories, I heard of an old Chinese medicine man who had a stall on Sundays at a market in the Chinese part of town. He sold fresh cobra livers to clients to increase their virility. The liver was eaten raw, on the spot, chasing the bloody organ down with a shot of rice whiskey. I thought this would make a good photo, and so did Horst. After some effort we found the old fellow in the corner space he rented at the outdoor market. He showed us a sack

Eating a raw cobra liver in Bangkok in 1963 to illustrate a story for the Associated Press. There were no clients buying cobra livers that morning, so my boss suggested I eat one. (Photo by Horst Faas)

full of live cobras. He carefully brought each snake out of the bag and hung it by its neck on a line. He was open for business. We waited for customers. It was a slow day for cobra liver enthusiasts. After an hour of no business, Horst said, "We can't wait all day. You eat one and I will make photos."

This was not what I had anticipated, but did not want to let the team down and agreed. By this time we had attracted a small crowd. It became animated when I told the old fellow in my shaky Thai that I would buy a liver. OK, that will be 40 baht up front. Two dollars. It must have been a special price for the first buyer of the day. I selected a writhing cobra for my breakfast snack. Horst put us in the best light for photos. The old gentleman killed the snake with a quick knife slice into its neck and extricated the liver, along with the gall sack, from the bloody mess. With a flourish in front of the gathered crowd, he dropped the small liver into my open mouth as Horst snapped with his Leica. The secret to eating a raw cobra liver successfully is not to bite, just swallow. Which I did, aided by the fiery liquor that took my mind off what I had just ingested. The gathered throng broke into a cheer. One onlooker came over and expressed his sympathy. I asked what for. He explained that the average age of the liver eaters exceeded seventy. He pitied the poor American teenager who had to seek out cobra livers to improve his sex life.

I explained that I did it for the photo. He nodded politely and tried to make me think he believed me.

I only covered one boxing tournament in my life, and it was a world title bout. "Fighting" Harada of Japan defended his world flyweight title in Bangkok on January 12, 1962 against the local hero Pone Kingpetch. Boxing is a major sport in both Thailand and Japan, and Pone was a national hero. The AP made a big effort to cover the fight, as did our main rival, UPI. Horst came from Saigon to lead the photo team. Karsten Prager from Kuala Lumpur came up to assist on the news side. UPI had promised their Japanese clients that they would dominate photo coverage of the fight and assemble their own A-Team. We went to extraordinary lengths to get the photos out fast. AP set up a darkroom at the Post and Telegraph office, from where we would transmit wire photos around the world, but mainly to Tokyo where there was intense interest in the fight.

Horst and I were at ringside on opposite sides. He gave me a few pointers on covering a fight. Before the fight even started there was a riot. Fake tickets had been sold and hundreds of seats were taken by the time their rightful owners arrived. Dozens of fight fans were injured in the melee and our first four photos of the evening were of casualties being evacuated. His Majesty King Bhumibol arrived for the bout but due to the rioting no one noticed his arrival. As the fight was about to start, Karsten, at ringside, felt someone under the ring touch his feet. Checking, we found a UPI staffer looking for our telephone line, knife in hand. We hauled him out and asked for an explanation. It seems their phone was broken and he had been dispatched to even the handicap. He was sent back minus his knife.

In broiling Bangkok heat under the lights, the fight went the full 15 rounds. Every three rounds Horst would throw his film to me across the ring. I would caption both our film and send it off with a runner to the waiting darkroom man at the PTT. In the end, Pone dethroned Harada in a 2 to 1 decision. He was Thailand's first world boxing champion. AP bested UPI 12 to 1 in the Tokyo dailies the next morning.

In June 1963 I was with Horst and AP newsman Peter Arnett covering Southeast Asia Treaty Organization (SEATO) war games at Lopburi, an army center north of Bangkok. Peter was a New Zealander from Bluff, the southernmost city in the world. He started his international press career with the *Bangkok World* and moved up to the AP. He and Horst became a team, working together in Saigon for virtually the entire Vietnam War. For his battlefield coverage he won a Pulitzer Prize. Peter was a scrappy little Kiwi with a broken nose, a souvenir of his early boxing days.

One evening the assembled foreign press corps, about seven of us, were drinking at a Lopburi open-air bar when someone suggested a contest. Whoever was judged to have had the best "lead" in his journalistic career would drink for free. A "lead" is the first sentence of a story. It is meant to grab your attention. The rules stipulated that it had to have been published, not just submitted to an editor. After numerous offerings were rejected, the winner was a UPI veteran who swore that he wrote the following lead while covering Charlie Chaplin's paternity suit some years before: "Charlie Chaplin walked out of Los Angeles superior court today, acquitted in his paternity suit, smiling, and cocksure."

Later that night, news reached us that on June 11 a Vietnamese monk named Thich Quang Duc had burned himself to death in Saigon. This tragic event was recorded by AP's bureau chief in Saigon, Malcolm Browne, who had been advised to be at the site of the self-immolation and to bring a camera. The stunning photos that Browne made focused world attention on Vietnam and the growing struggle of the Buddhist majority against the Roman Catholic regime of Ngo Dinh Diem, which ended with Diem's ousting and death in November. Horst was despondent as he packed to return to Saigon. He missed the photo.

In August, anti-government demonstrations took place at the Xa Loi Pagoda in Saigon. More than four hundred Buddhist monks and nuns were arrested in the protest against the Diem regime. The AP needed to send a radiophoto machine immediately. Bangkok had a machine, and I was tapped to carry it to Vietnam. I thought this might be my chance to see some action. In those days a transmitter weighed more than 60 pounds and was very delicate. I bought two seats for my Air Vietnam flight, one for me, and one for the bulky transmitter in the first-class seat next to mine. Normally, AP staffers don't fly first class. But radiophoto machines do, so I was in luck. Horst was on hand at Tan Son Nhut airport with a jeep to carry the transmitter and me into town.

Saigon was quiet for the moment and Horst let me savor my visit, promising to take me to the "field" on a photo shoot. I stayed at the Majestic Hotel at the end of Tu Do Street, formerly Rue Catinat under the French, and since 1975, the Gai Phong (Liberation). It was a charming old colonial-style hotel but its wrought iron elevator was out of order. A Viet Cong bomb had exploded in the hotel and parts were on order. The city was beautiful with tree-lined streets, elegant old colonial buildings, and sidewalk cafés. It was a Graham Greene kind of town, where one sipped café au lait on the terrace of the Hotel Continental in the morning, reading the *Saigon Post*, eating hot baguettes and drinking café crème. Schoolgirls in flowing white silk *ao dai* dresses rode by on bikes wearing conical straw hats. This was the Asia I was looking for, and the presence of barbed wire and sand bags gave the place a hint of danger and excitement. Horst and Arnett had their own favorite place, the old Hotel Royal, a rundown French hotel with a rundown Corsican proprietor. The restaurant featured simple French fare, ceiling fans, and fading framed pictures on the wall of the shoulder patches worn by French Air Force escadrilles stationed in Vietnam before the French called it a war in 1954 and went home.

The assignment Horst had in mind was to drive outside Saigon and photograph the aircraft carrier USS *Card* that was bringing a load of helicopters to Vietnam. There were thousands of American advisors and aviation helicopter support units in country to give the Army of the Republic of Vietnam (ARVN) better mobility.

The morning of the ship's arrival we left Saigon early and drove parallel to the Saigon River through lush rice paddies. Horst assured me that there were no main force Viet Cong (VC) units in the area but we should keep our eyes open. He promised we would be back in Saigon by dark. He stopped the jeep in sight of the river next to an old French army watchtower. The twisted, rusted, metal suggested it had taken a direct hit some years before. Then we waited for the aircraft carrier to come up the river. Horst thought we would have a better angle shooting from the tower. Because I weighed approximately half Horst's weight, I was elected to photograph from the tower. Horst showed me how to operate his Leica with its 400mm lens and sent me up. I gingerly climbed the tower. From this angle, about 25 feet above the rice paddies, I had an excellent view. Finally, the escort carrier came into view and I began snapping photos. From my perspective it looked as if the carrier, with helicopters on the flight deck, was passing through the rice fields, as the river was obscured.

Suddenly, there was a loud sound of metal hitting metal very close to me. I leaned down and asked Horst what it was. "Probably just a sniper," he said. "They aren't very good shots so don't worry." But I did worry, and, feeling that we had enough photos, I moved down the ladder faster that I had climbed up. The ride back to Saigon was without incident.

***

Among my favorite assignments were opportunities to photograph the King and Queen of Thailand, usually on formal occasions involving state ceremonies or greeting foreign VIPs. King Bhumibol was born in Cambridge, Massachusetts, in 1927, when his father was studying at Harvard University. He was educated in Switzerland and became king upon the death of his brother, Ananda, in 1946. At the time of his death, in 2016, he was the longest reigning monarch in the world.

The first time I photographed the king I noticed that all the other photographers, all of them Thai newsmen, were in a group. I thought another angle would be better. When I took up my position the king noticed me. By hand gestures he moved me over to the other photographers and we all got our photos. In 1948 the king was involved in a serious automobile accident in Switzerland, which left him sightless in his right eye. He did not want to be photographed from that side. Everyone there knew it but me. I never repeated that mistake.

In 1963 the US Army participated in a major military exercise in northeastern Thailand, Operation *Thanarat*, named after Thai prime minister Field Marshal Sarit Thanarat, under the auspices of the Southeast Asia Treaty Organization (SEATO), involving more than 25,000 troops from the United States and Thailand. As part of the exercise, the American 173rd Airborne Brigade flew directly from their base in Okinawa and parachuted into Mahasarakham, a poor province in Thailand's

Thai King Bumiphol Adulyadej speaking with villagers in rural Thailand in 1963. I had a "scoop" at this event, the only photographer present and the photos got huge "play" in Thai papers in Bangkok.

northeast. It was the largest parachute operation ever in Southeast Asia. I was on the ground with an advance team and photographed the airdrop.

The highlight of the military exercise was a visit from King Bhumibol to remote Mahasarakham. The king's trip to the impoverished region was a major event for the local farmers, who revered their monarch. For days, thousands of rural Thai hiked to the dusty field, where the king would meet with them. His Majesty was a quiet, almost frail, man who lived for the welfare of his people. About thirty thousand people were there; some had walked for three days. They were mostly dressed in the indigo blue cotton shirts and trousers favored by the farmers. The crowd waited patiently in the hot dry heat for their king. Finally he arrived. Many had small gifts of flowers or cotton sarongs. I was one of the few photographers recording this emotional scene. King Bhumibol, disregarding security, walked through the throng, many of whom were prostrate as they offered their gifts. My photos ran in eight columns on the front pages of Bangkok daily newspapers the next day.

After the drop, the brigade commander was nervous over the idea of meeting His Majesty. That he had just made the largest airborne drop in the history of Southeast Asia was forgotten; he had never met a king and he was worried. Taking the general aside, I told him that the king liked to be photographed from his "good" side, and arrangements were made accordingly. I said that the king was born in the US and that his English was good. I also let the officer know that the prime minister, who accompanied the king, was a military man from the northeast who would appreciate being offered Mekong whiskey to drink. It was quickly arranged. The presentation went off without a hitch and the grateful general let me fly my film out to Bangkok on his personal aircraft. Another scoop for the AP.

After lengthy negotiations, the Associated Press received approval for an exclusive interview with the queen by AP writer Doris Klein as part of a series of interviews she was doing with first ladies around the world. I was tapped to be the photographer. Doris and I went to Chitlada Palace, the royal residence, to photograph Her Majesty and her four children. The queen's son is now King Rama X. The shoot went smoothly. Afterwards, the queen invited us to accompany her to Chulalongkorn University Hospital for a visit to the maternity ward. At the end of the shoot I posted myself outside the hospital for the queen's departure in her yellow Rolls-Royce. The driveway was lined with young nurses on hand for the royal visit. The car moved slowly. Each nurse bowed as the queen's car passed. The car stopped in front of me. Her Majesty rolled down a window and extended her hand to thank me. I assured her the pleasure was all mine and I shook the royal hand. The window went up and the car moved on.

It was always a pleasure to photograph Queen Sirikit, a lovely and gracious woman. She was a cousin of the king and the daughter of the Thai ambassador to France when Bhumibol had his car accident in Switzerland. She helped nurse him back to health and they fell in love. She gave up her dream of being a concert pianist to become the queen of Thailand.

Marlon Brando afforded me the opportunity to photograph the king and queen together with him when they all attended the world premiere of Brando's film *The Ugly American*, which was filmed largely in Thailand. At the request of AP's Hollywood Bureau, I photographed Brando's arrival in Bangkok where pretty Thai girls in silk gowns presented him with flowers. I thought the snaps were good, called Marlon at his hotel, and asked if he would like copies. He said yes, and invited me for drinks. He appreciated the photos and even autographed a couple of them. What he really wanted was a briefing on the political situation in Bangkok and the region. I was immediately impressed with the knowledge he had of the politics of Thailand and the growing communist threat in Southeast Asia. His interest was spurred on by the film he was launching in Bangkok. Fortunately, I had been in country for a while and had given similar briefings to numerous visiting journalists.

The film's premiere was a gala occasion. I wore my best clothes, a white dinner jacket with black trousers and was underdressed. The only other Western photographer was Larry Burrows, covering for *LIFE* magazine. It was my only opportunity to work with Larry, a legendary British photographer who was killed in action in Laos in 1971 when his helicopter was shot down. Queen Sirikit stole the show at the premiere. She was the most beautiful woman in attendance and everyone, especially Marlon, knew it. Her Majesty wore a stunning designer gown of Thai silk. Also in attendance was the Thai royal Mom Rachawong Kukrit Pramoj. He played the role of the prime minister in the film. In a case of reality follows fiction, Kukrit became the prime minister of Thailand in 1975. An Oxford graduate, Kukrit was a leading journalist and man of letters in Thailand. We were both members of the Foreign Correspondents' Club of Thailand, which was tiny in those days. Years later he graciously wrote the foreword of my first book, *Old Homes of Bangkok: Fragile Link*, in which his home and garden are featured.

A royal visitor to Thailand was young Princess Beatrix, later Queen Beatrix, of the Netherlands. I covered her visit, which included a stop at the Allied cemetery near the bridge over the River Kwai where more than three hundred Dutch prisoners of the Japanese are buried. The princess also visited the Pasteur Institute's snake farm in Bangkok, where thousands of poisonous reptiles were raised to provide antidotes for lethal snakebites. There were several large, round, sunken pits in which the reptiles were kept. One containing several hundred deadly kraits was chosen to show the princess. A keeper, in white smock and speaking excellent English, climbed the steps down into the pit surrounded by the lethargic snakes under the Bangkok noonday sun. He gave his briefing to the amazed visitors, including me, and casually picked up a few snakes to show how harmless they could be.

A Dutch cameraman was poised at the top of the ladder leading down into the snake pit. From there he could film Princess Beatrix and then pan to the snake expert giving his vivid talk. Unbeknownst to anyone, a krait had quietly crawled onto the ladder and was slowly climbing it, until it came to the leg of the cameraman. Someone, perhaps the princess herself, noticed the snake and reported it to the snake man. The cameraman looked down, saw the krait, and froze. The snake-farm fellow dropped the snakes he was holding, stopped his lecture, and made his way gingerly through the reptiles all around him to the ladder. He then deftly picked up the wandering krait by the tail and flung it back into the pit. The danger passed. He announced that the cameraman had done exactly the right thing; he had not moved. Then he said, "It's OK now, the snake is gone, you can move." But the man couldn't move. He was frozen in place. It took a few people to remove him from his perch above the snake pit and lay him quietly on the ground where he finally could relax. No snake antidote was required.

Another VIP visiting Thailand during my watch was Indonesian President Sukarno who passed through Bangkok briefly in 1963 en route to Jakarta after medical treatment in Europe. I was at Don Muang airport to document the event. While waiting for the plane to land, I was approached by a very unhappy Indonesian embassy official, who told me that their photographer was absent and asked if I could provide him with photos of the president's visit. I said I would be happy to, and asked what photos he needed. He said he needed only two shots. One would be Sukarno being greeted by the Indonesian ambassador. The second shot would be a little more difficult. The president would walk down the red carpet lined with the leading Indonesian citizens living in Thailand. Sukarno would stop at some point and shake hands with a woman. "No problem," I said, "which woman?" "We don't know. We have found the prettiest women we could find and the one the president shakes hands with is the one we put in his hotel room." The president was well known as a ladies' man. I tracked Sukarno's slow progress along the red carpet leading to the airport terminal as he greeted his greeters. Then he slowed and extended a hand to a very attractive young lady who shook hands with the president. Click. I had the photo. The young woman had a date.

There was one Soviet journalist working in Bangkok, Sergei Sverin, the correspondent for TASS, the Soviet News Agency. Tony Escoda pointed him out to me while we were at Don Muang airport covering Sukarno's visit. "Be careful around Sergei," Tony whispered. "He works for the KGB." Tony was right but I didn't ask how he knew. Sergei came up to Tony and offered him a ride back to Bangkok. Tony introduced me and I was included in the offer. Sergei drove a dilapidated Soviet car, a Moskvitch, an unattractive, dumpy little vehicle. While driving to Bangkok, Sergei regaled us with a story about a recent Soviet visitor to Bangkok who made the mistake of drinking water from the tap resulting in a nasty case of diarrhea. "So I gave him Thai beef with hot chilies. He was cured." When Sergei dropped us at the AP office on Pat Pong Road, the door handle came off in Tony's hand. He apologized and handed the broken handle to Sergei. "This is terrible," Sergei said. "It is last car running. We have cannibalized all the others for parts. I hope we have a handle that works." I saw Sergei at numerous social events but always kept my distance.

***

As a "stringer" I was free to work for anyone, except the competition UPI. *Time* magazine gave me an assignment to photograph the American stockpile of weapons located in Korat, a major city in the northeast about 150 miles from Bangkok. I coordinated the trip with the US military in Bangkok and was booked to fly up on a New Zealand Air Force Bristol freighter. When we landed at the Korat air base I ran into the US base commander who was getting on the plane. I had met him before and told him about my assignment for *Time* magazine. The colonel said, "No problem. We have a jeep and driver for you." I thanked him, and he boarded the Bristol freighter, bound for Bangkok.

A young US Army sergeant with a jeep from the office of public affairs greeted me. I explained that I had a tight deadline and needed to get my film to Tokyo the next day. He quickly drove me to the 9th Logistics Command compound. We drove around and I decided to photograph an array of trucks, part of the forward positioning of war material that would be in place when we needed to speed troops to the area. I stood on the hood of the jeep and started taking photos.

The arrival of another jeep disrupted the photo shoot. An army major jumped out, pulled a .45 pistol and pointed it at me.

"What are you doing?" I asked.

"Arresting you," said the major.

"For what?"

He said, "Espionage."

My driver looked worried and explained that I had permission to take photos. "Not from me," he said. The major was a reservist from Hawaii on a temporary assignment as a security officer. He took his job very seriously and Public Affairs had not cleared my visit with security.

I tried to explain my assignment for *Time* magazine and described the warm welcome the US commander has just given me. It fell on deaf ears. The major ordered the sergeant to drive me to his office. I had my photos and needed to get back to Bangkok. I told the major I was entitled to make a phone call. "To who?" he asked. "To Major General Ernest Easterbook, Commanding General of all US military personnel in Thailand."

I had met the general and photographed him a few times. A tough old combat veteran of China and Burma in World War II, he had also commanded a regiment in Korea. He was the son-in-law of General Joseph "Vinegar Joe" Stilwell. I doubted he would recall my name. Nevertheless, I pulled out my AP note pad, which contained a list of important phone numbers, including Easterbrook's. The major now looked a little worried, but let me make the call.

The general came on the line.

"General," I said, "This is Barry Broman from the AP."

"What can I do for you?" the general asked.

"I am sorry to bother you, general, but I am in Korat on an assignment and a US Army major has arrested me for espionage. I have permission to photograph from the base commander but the major has me in custody, and I need to get back to Bangkok immediately."

The general said, "Let me talk to the major."

"It's for you," I said as I passed the phone.

"Yes, sir," said the major, "right away, sir," and hung up.

"Get the fuck out of here," the chastened officer said to me.

"I need a ride to Korat town right now," I said. "Or do I need to make another phone call?

I got the ride, and caught a train that took all night to reach Bangkok. I got off at the Don Muang station and put the film on a plane to Tokyo making my deadline from *Time* magazine.

The story isn't quite over.

A few months later I returned to photograph the air arrival of American army infantry. A lot of press, including Peter Kalischer from CBS with a film crew, were on hand to greet the troops, who were part of a US military buildup in Thailand. We filmed the arrival without incident and spent the night on base in VIP quarters, which meant the rooms were air-conditioned. After dinner the journalists were invited to the officers' club for drinks. All bases in Thailand belonged to the Thai army, navy, or air force. There were no US bases. Wherever our troops were stationed, they were guests of the Thai. That night several senior Thai officers, including Royal Thai Army Lieutenant General Krit Sivara, commander of the Second Military Region in which Korat was located, were mingling with the press.

Someone suggested a friendly game of poker. Peter and I joined in. All went well until the major who had recently arrested me walked into the club. He spotted me at once but didn't say anything at first. He sat at the bar nursing a drink and keeping an eye on me. After a few drinks he walked over to our table.

"How old are you?" he asked.

"Nineteen," I answered, sipping my gin and tonic.

"You are under age," he said, "and will have to leave."

The room was suddenly very quiet. Peter came to my defense as General Krit, whom I had never met, walked over to our table and said with some authority, "Not a problem major, this journalist is my guest." The major remonstrated, "I'm sorry general, this is an American officers' club and this journalist is under age." That was absolutely the wrong thing to say. General Krit looked grim and suddenly much taller than his five feet three inches. In a low, cold voice he stared at the major and said, "This is a Royal Thai Army base and I say who can drink or not. He can." The general pointed at me.

At that point the senior American officer present asked to have a quiet word with the major. The card game resumed and I ended the evening a little ahead. The major flew home to Hawaii in the morning.

My biggest AP assignment was to cover the state visit of Chinese President Liu Shaoqi to Cambodia. Normally, the story would have been handled by Horst Faas out of the Saigon bureau but Horst was occupied elsewhere and I was tapped. AP did not have a bureau in Cambodia but it did have a Cambodian stringer named Seng Meakely who met my plane and took me to my hotel. There was a lot of press on hand for the event but no other Americans. Mal Browne, the Saigon bureau chief, was coming to write the story but was delayed.

The ruins at Angkor Wat were the featured attraction of the visit where Head of State Prince Norodom Sihanouk personally acted as tour guide for President Liu. He also cancelled all tourist reservations in Seam Reap to make room for his Chinese guests. Except for Sihanouk and the Chinese, the site was devoid of tourists. I was the only Western photographer covering the story and had trouble from the outset from Chinese security thugs who did their best to prevent me from getting too close to the VIPs from Beijing, which included Foreign Minister, Marshal Chen Yi, a burly fellow who looked like he could take care of himself. Things got dicey as we climbed steep and uneven steps up a tower at Angkor. As I struggled to keep ahead of the VIPs to get my photos, it seemed the Chinese guards had other ideas. There was little room to maneuver at the top and just as I leaned into make a photo of Sihanouk and Liu; a guard gave me a shove. Seeing me off balance and possibly heading for a serious fall, the portly Prince Sihanouk, leaned over and grabbed me, hardly breaking his running commentary on the history of Cambodia. I don't know if it is correct to say that Sihanouk saved my life but it is entirely possible.

I was the lone AP man at Angkor Wat, which meant I would have to write the story as well as photograph it. It was the only time in my AP career that I filed a story. Mal soon arrived from Saigon and took over, to my relief. Seeing a virtually deserted Angkor with the man in charge of the country leading the tour was a special treat. But the pressure to get the photos I needed, and eventually got, prevented me from fully enjoying the occasion

Another stop was in Kompong Cham on the Mekong River to witness boat races on the river. Again, the tireless Sihanouk, surrounded by bowing courtiers, supervised the event. One of my missions from Tokyo Photos was to get headshots of the Chinese visitors for file purposes. Given my ongoing difficulties with Chinese security officers, this was hard to do. My chance came at Kompong Cham when they were all lined up at the beginning of the boat race and the Cambodian National Anthem was playing. As everyone stood at attention, I walked down the row of VIPs stopping to take headshot photos of each one. As I approached Chen Yi, a security guard leaned forward to stop me and in so doing knocked Madame Chen off the podium. I escaped in the scramble of guards helping the petite and attractive lady to her feet. I changed film fast in case my camera was seized. It wasn't but I took no chances.

The finale of the state visit was a performance of the Royal Khmer Ballet in the Grand Palace in Phnom Penh. It was a grand spectacle. I was smitten by the young and beautiful dancer who led the ballet. Mel Browne, a Pulitzer Prize-winning correspondent, noticed my infatuation with the young princess took me aside and informed me that she was Princess Bopha Devi, Sihanouk's favorite daughter.

Many years later, Princess Bopha Devi, then serving as Minister of Culture, gave me special permission to photograph the national museum and parts of the Grand Palace where photographs are normally forbidden. She kindly attended the launch of my resulting book *Cambodia: The Land and its People* in Phnom Penh in 2009.

***

One day we received a telex from AP Hollywood informing us that a Tarzan film was going to be made in Thailand and AP wanted photos. I was put in touch with the production people and when the crew came to Bangkok to shoot some actions scenes on the canals of Thonburi across the Chao Phraya River from Bangkok, I was invited to come and take pictures. I spent two days photographing Tarzan fighting bad guys in a high-speed chase on the photogenic canals famous for their floating market. It was great fun and yielded some good snaps that made AP Hollywood happy. As a result of my time on the Tarzan set, the film's producer, Sy Weintraub, asked if I would like to work on the film as the stills photographer. They were off to Chiang Mai for ten weeks and he offered a very substantial raise above my AP day rate. With Tony Escoda's permission and the understanding that if AP needed me I would come back, he loaned me the office Rolleiflex camera and I left for the beautiful, bucolic, and ancient city of Chiang Mai in northern Thailand to take pictures of Tarzan.

Don't ask how Tarzan got to Thailand, I was never told. All I know is that Tarzan parachutes into Thailand in his jungle wardrobe to assist a young prince to escape the clutches of bad men. The plot was laughable but the film, especially the forest fire scenes, were quite remarkable, thanks to the very high quality of the British crew, some of whom had Oscars. Tarzan was played by American Jacques O'Mahoney whose stage name was Jock Mahony but he went by the nickname Jocko. Jock was a great guy. He was a Marine pilot in World War II and after the war worked in Hollywood as a stunt man where he doubled for John Wayne, Gregory Peck, and Errol Flynn among many others. Later, he became an actor and starred in the television series *The Range Rider* and *Yancy Derringer*, both of which I remembered from my youth. Jock was easy going, totally unaffected, and on a first-name basis with everyone in the crew including me, the lowest man on the totem pole. There were a few American actors including Woody Strode, a former UCLA and professional football player whom I remembered vividly for his skill with a bow and arrow in the film *The Professionals* with Burt Lancaster The young prince was played by Ricky Der, a quiet and pleasant American-Chinese about 10 years old. We also had a well-known Egyptian actor who played the lead villain, a part that really suited him. He was so obnoxious that the shooting schedule was changed so as to get him off the picture as soon as possible. For his last scene he was being chased through a forest fire (we were allowed to burn two thousand hectares of scrub jungle for the film). At the end of the chase he was to roll down a mountainside in desperation as Tarzan caught up with him. The director was not satisfied with the performance; he wanted more terror. After 18 takes, the makeup man said they couldn't disguise his cuts and abrasions any further. "OK," said the director, "Use the first take." The battered villain was on the next plane to Cairo.

We rented a few horses from the Thai cavalry for the villains and somehow rented a baby elephant because it was so cute, but totally untrained and a constant problem. Shooting in the jungle north of Chiang Mai one day, the elephant gave a cry of alarm that spooked the horses, which stampeded down the narrow trail that Jock and I were walking up, me in front. The horses galloped toward us and Jock grabbed me from behind and held on until they were very close. Then he threw me off the trail into the jungle and jumped on the lead horse and brought them all to a stop. I wish they had it on film but it wasn't part of the film. It was Jock being Jock and I am sure he saved my life.

In another scene, Jock is supposed to rescue the young prince as a forest fire advances toward them. We built a shrine at the edge of the jungle where the prince is praying to an image of the Buddha as the fire advances. Jock was waiting for the word "Action" from the director to dash down and rescue the prince. But the fresh shellac on the roof of the shrine burst into flames from the nearby forest fire and with cameras rolling, but without any direction, Jock ran down the hill and picked up Ricky, actually saving him. With Jock on the set we didn't need many stunt men.

We filmed for days at Wat Suan Dok, a beautiful and ancient Buddhist temple in Chiang Mai near the 13th-century city walls. One day, during a break in shooting Jock and I were walked to the nearby Thai-style house of Swiss artist Theo Meier who was probably Chiang Mai's most famous foreign resident, although he would certainly deny the charge. Theo came east in his youth to escape middle-class Basel and installed himself in Bali in the 1930s and 1940s where he gained renown as one of the original Western artists who made their lives in the tropical paradise that was Bali. As a Swiss neutral he was little touched by the Japanese occupation of Indonesia while most Westerners either fled or were interned. Theo stayed on after independence, accumulating a large following of clients and two Balinese wives. In the 1950s he was persuaded to visit Thailand by Thai Prince Sanidh Rangsit, the son of a regent of Thailand.

Theo was a true artist in the footsteps of Gauguin whose style he somewhat adapted, although he would always deny it. In those days Theo lived very frugally in a small wooden house in a grove of kapok trees that Sanidh found for him. He drank one bottle of Thai Mekhong whiskey a day on average and smoked foul Burmese cheroots wrapped with a piece of string that cost 15 cents per hundred. When the string burned through the cheroot exploded in sparks, which is why all of Theo's Balinese shirts were full of tiny holes. Theo and I became friends and he employed me to photograph his nude models. He paid me in sketches and paintings, most of which I still have.

There were few tourists in Chiang Mai in those days. The only taxis were three-wheeled *cyclos* called samlors with the driver in front. A ride anywhere in town cost about 5 cents. During filming we hired dozens of samlor drivers to play monks in the film. As a result, the lack of drivers caused the price of samlors to go up, briefly.

Toward the end of my sojourn on *Tarzan's Three Challenges*, which was never shown in Thailand due to the unfortunate and accidental burning of the Buddhist shrine that we built but did not intend to burn, I was offered two jobs on films about to be made in the region. One was *Lord Jim* with Peter O'Toole to be made in Cambodia. The other was *Seventh Dawn* with William Holden in Malaysia. I had to turn down both offers. I promised my father that I would return to university in the fall of 1963 and time was passing fast. My time on the film was truncated when I received a call from Tony one day that I was needed back in Bangkok. I said goodbye to my film friends, to Theo, and to the lovely city that Chiang Mai was in those days.

***

I would have been happy to stay in Thailand as my year there neared its end. My career with AP was going well. I had been given raises, foreign assignments, and considerable responsibility. Tony Escoda had two dislikes that I was aware of: Tokyo Photos and the Japanese. He was a writer and a good one. A graduate of Andover Prep and Yale University, Tony was from an old Spanish-Filipino family; his father had been the editor of a Manila newspaper. The Japanese killed both his parents during the occupation of the Philippines in World War II. That explained why he disliked the Japanese. Tony put me in charge of Bangkok photos and gave me a free hand in working with the Asia photo editor, Hal Buell, in Tokyo.

Tony asked if I was interested in a career in journalism. I said I wasn't sure. He lent me his battered copy of *Kansas City Milkman*. It was a gritty account of the downside of working for a wire service. In it the author, Reynolds Packard, a former UPI correspondent describes the low pay, long hours, and rampant alcoholism associated with the profession. I read the book but wasn't ready to give up on the AP. However, my year was up and I had made a deal with Pappy so I prepared to return to college in the fall of 1963. I had no inclination of returning to the University of Illinois where I had been interested in Latin American studies. That interest died after a couple of weeks in Thailand. I opted instead for the University of Washington in my home state, where they had a fine school of East Asian studies. I opted for a double major: political science and Far Eastern studies.

I joined a good fraternity, Delta Tau Delta, where I learned how to study and made new friends. The Navy welcomed me back to the NROTC (Navy Reserve Officers Training Corps) ranks and I signed up as a photographer for the school newspaper, the University of Washington's *Daily*. There, I met Bob Peterson and we soon became lifelong friends. Bob was the top photographer on campus and was selling his photos to *Sports Illustrated*. We would photograph Husky football together and established a tradition of having lunch before each home game at the Congo Room on Capitol Hill. To fortify us through the cold, wet, football games kneeling in the mud on the sidelines of Husky stadium, we fortified ourselves with small metal cans that 35mm film came in. We filled our film cans with Cognac.

Tuition in those days was $115 per quarter for a resident. With my savings from AP service and money the university paid me to photograph football for them, I put myself through college. Pappy kindly gave me a 1962 Corvair for transportation with instructions to take the car to the Madison Park Garage for servicing. The

Hatfield brothers owned the company, old high school friends of Pappy. When it came time to change the oil, I took the car in and identified myself to one of the Hatfields. "Broman" he said, "any relation to Harry Broman?" "That's my father," I replied. "Hey," he shouted to his brother working a car. "Beast Broman's son is here." The brother came out, wiped his hands on a rag, and introduced himself. Neither brother nor my father ever explained how he became known as "Beast" Broman.

On a sunny spring day, when the cherry blossoms were in bloom on the quad, I saw a pretty Asian girl hurrying to class. I snapped a few photos of her, introduced myself as a *Daily* photographer, and obtained caption data from the girl including her phone number. She was Betty Jane "BJ" Apilado, a freshman from Pepeekeo, Hawaii, a small town on the Hamakua coast of the Big Island. Ethnically half Japanese and half Filipina, she was smart as well as cute. We started dating and eventually moved into a houseboat together on Lake Union. We had a roommate, Neil Hollander, who was working for a PhD in Communications. Neil was a world traveler and had taught at the International School of Bangkok when I was working for the AP. We paid $80 per month for the aging (and listing) boat, split three ways. It had three bedrooms and an outside moorage that looked out across the lake to Seattle's Space Needle. The only downside of the houseboat was that the boat had been condemned by the city of Seattle because it listed in one corner and the roof leaked. The fraternity came to my aid by giving me old mattresses, which we put in the attic to absorb rain. It was cozy. The décor was Southeast Asian, thanks in large part to the temple rubbings that Neil acquired in Cambodia during his travels.

Bob Peterson was a six-foot-three Swede with the look and good humor of Falstaff. Among Bob's many talents were cooking and its corollary, eating. One day, we invited Bob to the houseboat for dinner. BJ, an equally good cook of both Asian and Western cuisines, made a simple but elegant meal of grilled salmon on a hibachi, miso soup, and steamed pork potstickers, lots of them. Bob brought along a half gallon of Japanese sake. As we began eating, Bob started offering toasts and keeping our little sake cups filled. BJ does not drink.

At length, I declared that I had had enough to drink. Bob disagreed and refilled my little earthenware cup with the toast, "Here's to the Corps!" A cheap shot, perhaps, but harmless. I drank and reminded Bob that I was full. Undeterred, he refilled my cup with hot sake, and lifting his cup said, "Here's to Chesty Puller." Now this was low. Chesty Puller was the greatest living Marine; the only man to win five Navy Cross medals, second only to the Medal of Honor and much loved by all Marines. Of course I drank, but assured Bob this had to be the last. Perhaps not hearing, Bob filled my cup again. I said, "There is no way you are going to make me drink that sake." Bob said only, "Here's to your mom." What could I do? Bob had played his last card. I said nothing and drank to my mom. Bob refilled my cup. "No more for me, Bob." All he said was, "Here's to *my* mom." I drank.

In the summers I worked for the AP, thanks to Hal Buell, who left his job in Tokyo to become the deputy director of AP Photos in New York. In 1964, Hal offered me a job as photo editor in Chicago. My father had finished his posting to Thailand and was again back at Scott Air Force Base in Illinois. I worked for a seasoned redheaded photo editor, Fred Wright, affectionately known to his colleagues as "Red Fright." The two senior AP photographers, Harry Hall and Paul Cannon, took me under their wings. Harry, I was told, was the only newsman in Chicago who could call Mayor Richard Daley by his first name. They went way back together. Harry would take me to his favorite watering hole after work and introduced me as "his boss." No one ever checked my ID. I was 20 years old but looked younger. One day, on my day off, Harry took me to a Chicago Cubs day baseball game. He was working. I was sent along as his caption writer and enjoyed the massive buffet that was offered to the press. Before the game, Harry took me to town to the field where the players were warming up. One of them was the great Willie Mays, center fielder of the San Francisco Giants. I told Harry that Willie was my father's favorite ball player and asked if he thought I could get Willie's autograph. Harry picked up a baseball and walked over to Willie who was warming up.

"Willie," said Harry, "this kid is my boss and he wants your autograph for his father," and handed Willie the baseball.

Willie turned to me and asked, "What's your father's name son?"

"Harry," I answered.

"Jeez, Harry, if you want an autograph, just ask."

Harry remonstrated, "It's not for me, it's for the kid's dad."

Willie laughed, signed "For Harry, Willie Mays," and gave me the ball.

Pappy treasured the ball and kept it on his desk until the day he died.

I learned a lot about editing photos in the summer of 1964. Fred Wright was a good teacher and Chicago was a good place to learn. Hal Buell then offered me my chance at the Big Apple, two summers (1966 and 1967) in New York as a photo editor at AP headquarters in the AP building in Rockefeller Center. I was being groomed for a career as a photo editor. Neil Hollander found a room for me through a friend in *The New York Times* at 400 Riverside Drive for $50 a month.

One summer I worked on the Foreign Photo desk under Jack Bodkin, sending and receiving photos from our overseas offices. It was a high pressure job with little time to make decisions on which photos to accept and which to reject. But Jack made it look easy. He was most famous in the AP for his service in the Pacific in World War II. At the battle for Iwo Jima in 1945, AP photographer Joe Rosenthal took the iconic photo of Marines raising the American flag over Mt. Suribachi. Jack Bodkin, back on board ship, developed that negative.

Bob Peterson was in New York at the time, working as a contract photographer for *LIFE* magazine nearby. He would drop by the AP at lunchtime and suggest

In front of the Associated Press building at Rockefeller Center in New York when working as a photo editor there in 1966. The photo is by Pulitzer Prize-winning photographer Eddie Adams.

a Japanese lunch with Hal and me. Hal was number two in AP Photos. We would disappear while other photo editors watched jealously. They knew I had worked for Hal when I was in Bangkok. They also knew Hal was grooming me for a career with AP, most likely including a shot at becoming the Asia photo editor based in Tokyo. I was told that my initials, BMB, were said to stand for Buell's My Buddy.

Although my job was largely limited to moving photos around the world fast from a desk, I did have a couple of chances to take photos. Miss Universe of 1965 was a Thai, Apasara Hongsakula. Her father was a colonel in the Royal Thai Air Force and had worked closely with Pappy. I persuaded AP to let me do a feature story on Apasara when she came to New York to hand over her crown in 1966. Hal agreed. The Thai ambassador to the UN offered me his car and driver to show Apasara and the Thai entrant for 1966, Cheranand Savetanand, New York. We went to the UN, the top of the Empire State Building, and a boat tour around Manhattan. The girls were charming, the photos appealing, and AP made money on the little project through its commercial outlet Wide World Photos.

Another time, I was given a press pass to see the Rolling Stones when they appeared in New York in their American tour in the summer of 1966. With me was Mineo

With Miss Universe 1965, Apasara Hongsakula from Thailand in New York, 1966, left. I was doing a feature story on Apasara for the Associated Press. At right is Cheranand Savetanand, Miss Thailand 1966. My father worked with Apasara's father, a Royal Thai Air Force colonel, in the early 1960s. I was working as a photo editor for the Associated Press in New York and was on assignment to photograph the ladies during the Miss Universe pageant.

Mizukami of AP Tokyo who was in the States for a one-year stint to learn how AP photos operated. Mizu and I were close friends, both protégés of Hal Buell. We were off duty but brought cameras along to the sold-out event. AP had a working photographer present. The concert ended prematurely as fans stormed the stage and the Stones were airlifted out of the Forest Hills venue by helicopter. I had photos of the riot and called the AP office to make sure our photographer also had them. It turned out that the photographer took some photos of the concert and didn't stay for the riot. Mizu and I then rushed to Manhattan just as the AP photo network was closing down for the night. As my negatives were being developed, AP held the network until a few photos could be transmitted. It was a scoop for AP.

The photographer I became friends with in New York was Eddie Adams, a Marine combat photographer in the Korean War and a top AP shooter. He had already finished one tour covering the Vietnam War and narrowly escaped death several times. We hung out in New York and did one assignment together. Eddie returned to Vietnam and is most remembered for his iconic photograph of a South Vietnamese police general executing a Viet Cong prisoner on the streets of Saigon during the Tet Offensive of 1968.

In San Blas, Mexico, during the Christmas break in 1966 to escape the rain of Seattle. (Photo by Neil Hollander)

In the summer of 1967, while I was working in New York, BJ was working as a Senate intern for Senator Warren G. Magnuson (D-Wash) in Washington DC. She came to New York for a weekend. For the occasion, BJ made a Vietnamese dress, traditional *ao dai* with a turquoise blue, white lined tunic over a pair of white silk pants. It was stunning and looked elegant on BJ. For this special occasion, I splurged and took BJ to Trader Vic's Polynesian restaurant in Manhattan. Usually a teetotaler, BJ took a sip of my Mai Tai and when we walked out into the hot night air after dinner she felt tipsy. I should have sprung for a taxi but took the cheap route and descended into the subway. Big mistake, the stifling heat underground caused BJ to faint. So, holding her inert body in my arms, I carried her and her flowing dress onto the northbound subway until we got to my stop at 110th Street and Broadway. Being in New York, no one noticed or at least pretended not to notice. I carried her up to Broadway and the relatively cooler air revived BJ.

I was commissioned as a second lieutenant in the Marine Corps in 1967 shortly after graduating from the University of Washington in 1967. The Corps deferred my going on active duty to let me get a master's degree in Southeast Asian Studies at the University of Washington. While in grad school I lived on the houseboat with BJ and wrote a thesis on the origins of Thai political institutions.

CHAPTER 3

Marine

As a Navy ROTC midshipman I could be commissioned in the Navy or Marine Corps upon graduation. I was very impressed by the Marine officer instructor, Major William Riley, a Korean War veteran, so I opted for the Marine Corps and never regretted it. My father was not a big fan of the Corps. He would have preferred to have me safe on a big ship and not crossing rice paddies under fire.

Upon completion of graduate school, I reported for active duty with the Marines in June 1968. All new Marine officers must attend Basic School, a 20-week course at Quantico, Virginia. With the war in Vietnam in full spate, the Corps put us through one thousand hours of classroom and field instruction with the sole purpose of preparing young officers to lead men in battle. We learned to fire every weapon organic to a Marine infantry battalion, from the .45 pistols to 81mm mortars. The training was intense, well designed, and, at times, dangerous. Our instructors were all combat veterans, officers and non-commissioned officers with decorations including many with the Purple Heart ribbon indicating the wearer had been wounded in combat.

During a demonstration of firing flamethrowers I forgot an important admonition in the military: never volunteer. I should have remembered that was how my father became a glider pilot. I agreed to fire a World War II vintage flamethrower that may have seen action in the Pacific. With my classmates in the First Platoon of Basic School Class I-69 watching intently, I strapped on the backpack weapon. A young corporal tutored me in the operation of the infernal machine, which was loaded with a napalm-like mixture of burning death. As we approached a cave, ostensibly occupied by the enemy, the corporal whispered in my ear, "Aim low, and let the flames roll into the cave. If the flames don't get 'em, they'll die from lack of oxygen." I had my fingers on the trigger when the corporal said he was turning on the valve to provide pressure to propel the flames into the cave.

The corporal turned on the valve to provide pressure to propel the flames into the cave. That was when the antique on my back malfunctioned. The pressure blew the handle out of the fuel tank, covering both of us with about 15 pounds of napalm.

The corporal quickly pulled the tank off my back as we ran to a nearby pond. We washed off the napalm on each other as fast as we could. As we emerged from the water, soaked but alive, the instructor looked at me and said, "I sure am glad you didn't light us up, lieutenant." I nodded agreement. It was another day in the Corps, "where every meal is a banquet and every day is a holiday."

One of our favorite instructors was Major Patrick Collins, a Recon Marine. The motto of the elite reconnaissance units, which undertook dangerous missions, often behind enemy lines, was "Swift, Silent, and Deadly." Their work usually found them swift, silent, and surrounded. They were the toughest of the tough, and "Recon Collins" was one of the best. In his signature lecture he stood up to his neck in the water of Chopawamsic Creek, a body of water common to several species of venomous reptiles, in the dark, teaching us on how to cross water silently.

Although we had little time for rest or recreation at Basic School, during the occasional weekend off, some of us headed for Washington DC and Matt Kane's Irish bar on R Street, which featured live Irish music and Guinness stout. One evening I was there with a group of classmates sporting the "high and tight" haircut emblematic of Marines. We were enjoying a pleasant evening of live Irish music and pints of Guinness stout when Major Collins walked in. We invited him over and he regaled us with stories from his service in Vietnam. Someone later told me the story about Collins leading Marines into forbidden Laos to ambush the Ho Chi Minh trail. The story may have been apocryphal but the way I heard it, the Marine Corps had the choice of court-martialing the major or decorating him. They chose the latter. At the end of the evening, as the pub was closing, Major Collins led us in a loud rendition of the Marine Corps hymn. To my surprise, most of the regulars stood and sang with us.

Early on I thought Basic School training would make a good photo story for the *Naval Institute Proceedings*, the premier publication for Naval and Marine Corps matters. I broached the idea with Basic School leaders who were enthusiastic. I wrote to the editors and they invited me to Annapolis for a chat, which went well. As a result, in addition to an M-14 rifle and all my gear, I carried photo gear into the bush. The March 1969 issue of the magazine ran 15 pages of my photos and text. By that time I was somewhere in the western Quang Nam Province of Vietnam, leading a platoon of Marines in combat.

During the rigorous training, instructors reminded us more than once that we had a good chance of being killed in Vietnam, a possibility reinforced by the nightly news on television. Having lived very compatibly with BJ for the past few years, it seemed only right that we get married before I went to war. BJ accepted my proposal and her father gave his approval. We arranged to be married in the Quantico base chapel as soon as the basic training ended. Fortunately, the Supreme Court had thrown out Virginia's miscegenation laws that forbade interracial marriages in 1967.

I walked past a statue commemorating Johnny Reb to get my marriage license at the Manassas, Virginia, courthouse.

The day before, we were in Washington DC for the wedding of a Marine classmate. I wore my dress blue uniform. Sam Angeloff, a *LIFE* magazine writer, and an old roommate of mine, and Bob from Seattle, hosted a dinner. Bob and his wife, Lynn, drove down from New York. After the dinner BJ and I headed for Quantico, only to have my little Fiat 850 sports car hit broadside by two teenagers in a stolen car running a red light, with police in hot pursuit. The car hit the side of my car and my head went into the side window. The gas tank ruptured but did not ignite. BJ was shaken up and her beehive hairdo was knocked off-center but otherwise she was all right. We were quickly taken to a hospital, where a doctor sewed up my head while a nurse cleaned the blood off my blues. It would have been much worse if I had been wearing my summer white uniform. Bob took us to a hotel and a few hours later we drove down to Quantico to get married.

BJ and I married on November 30, 1968. Bob Peterson was on hand as best man and wedding photographer of our small ceremony. It was a busy weekend at

Marine Corps' sword arch by my classmates at our wedding at the Quantico Marine Corps Base on 30 November 1968. I had just finished the Officers' Basic Training course and was under orders to Vietnam. (Photo by Bob Peterson)

the Quantico chapel. Weddings were held every 15 minutes. Because of the press of time with my impending departure to war, neither of our parents would be at the ceremony. Hal Buell, my old boss at the Associated Press, came down from New York and gave the bride away. A sword arch of Basic School classmates gave a martial touch to the occasion. It was a no frills wedding. I invested $10 for the sheet music of "The Hawaiian Wedding Song," which a pianist played as BJ walked down the aisle, and hosted a small reception at the officers' club, Waller Hall, an elegant old manor looking down on the Potomac River. A thoughtful wedding gift, one that only a Marine could appreciate, came from AP photographer Eddie Adams. It was a pristine set of Marine Corps utility uniform, of the celebrated "herring bone" style used in World War II and Korea. Eddie saved it from his service in the Corps in Korea and never wore it. The uniforms went out of service in 1957 with the proviso that they could be worn until they were worn out. I still have mine.

With Basic School was over, I became an officer of infantry, the "The Queen of Battle" and received my orders: Fleet Marine Force, Pacific. That meant Vietnam. For our honeymoon, BJ and I drove to Seattle in our battered Fiat, which had a

Best man Bob Peterson getting ready for our wedding in Quantico in November 1968. Bob was working as a *LIFE* magazine photographer in New York at the time. (Photo by Sam Angeloff)

new fuel tank and windows. We didn't have time to repair the huge dent on the driver's side. BJ went back to teaching in Seattle. I headed for Camp Pendleton, California, for one month of preparation for Vietnam.

The Marine Corps organized its soldiers heading to the war into groups of 165, that is, one planeload. Training at Camp Pendleton focused on two things: getting us into physical shape for the tropics and educating us about Viet Cong and their lethal tricks. We did a lot of hiking in the beautiful hills overseeing the Pacific Ocean north of San Diego. It is not quite so beautiful with a 65-pound pack on your back, an ill-fitting steel helmet on your head, and a heavy M-14 rifle in your hands. (Lighter, better, newer M-16s were waiting for us in Da Nang.)

The powers that be put me in "command" of one of these hodge-podge units of Marines of all enlisted ranks. Upon landing in Vietnam the Corps sent us to the units to which we were assigned. In my case, that was the 1st Marine Division. One of my senior non-commissioned officers was a veteran of both World War II and the Korean War who had stayed in the reserves and volunteered for Vietnam.

"Lieutenant," he told me, "I sure hope I don't get captured."

"Why is that?" I asked.

"Because I got captured in the Philippines in '42 and captured in North Korea in '50." With the exception of some downed Marine flyers over North Vietnam, very few Marines were captured in Vietnam. I am confident he survived Vietnam without being captured.

My first decision of my hodge-podge command was to hold a "junk on the bunk" inspection for illicit items such as alcohol, pornography, or weapons. I was surprised to see a set of bagpipes on one young Marine's rack. I asked why he was taking bagpipes to Vietnam.

"Sir," he answered, "my uncle carried these through World War II in a Scottish regiment. He taught me to play the pipes and assured me they put fear into the enemy."

"Can you carry them along with your gear on conditioning marches?"

"Yes sir," he said.

"Then you are my piper," I responded.

During breaks in the hike (walk 50 minutes, rest 10), my piper would walk up and down the line of recumbent Marines playing songs like "Cock of the North," "Scotland the Brave," or the "Skye Boat Song," all of the tunes of glory. He never played the Marine Corps Hymn because that would have required all hands to jump to their feet, put out their cigarettes, and stand at attention.

Less arduous than long hikes with full battle gear were our visits to the "Viet Cong village" at Camp Pendleton, a fairly realistic replica of a Vietnamese hamlet in enemy hands. They had caches of weapons, food, and most dangerous of all, booby

A Marine plays the bagpipes in the hills of Camp Pendleton, California, during a rest stop in conditioning training of Marines heading for Vietnam in early 1969. The Marine was taking his pipes to Vietnam. I later met the young Marine in a hospital in Da Nang. He was recovering from malaria but still had his pipes and was eager to get back to his unit.

traps. The division lost one leg a day to booby traps, some of them homemade, all of them deadly. The VC ville had all sorts, from grenades with pins pulled in C-ration cans and a trip wire, to unexploded bombs wired to be blown by remote control. A visit to the ville let us know what was waiting for us in the Republic of Vietnam.

***

At the end of January 1969, I went to war. After saying goodbye to my 164 Marines at the Da Nang Air Base, I headed for the headquarters of the 1st Marine Division. First formed in 1942, it was the oldest division in the Corps. Its shoulder patch carried the name of its first battle, Guadalcanal. They were called The Old Breed. There were two Marine divisions in Vietnam, the 1st and the 3rd. Each was "heavy" with about 20,000 men each. The 1st Division's mission was to protect Da Nang, South Vietnam's second largest city. Each division had three infantry regiments and one artillery regiment. Each regiment had three infantry battalions with about 1,000 men in each. Each battalion had four infantry companies and each company had four platoons. My old Marine instructor at the University of Washington, William Riley, now a lieutenant colonel, greeted me at the division headquarters outside Danang.

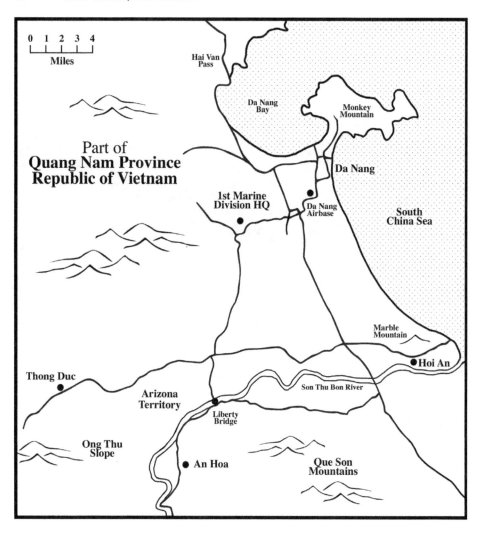

He was in the G-1 office, personnel. He asked where I would like to be assigned. Without thinking, I said, "Where the action is." "That will be the 5th Marines," the colonel said, "the most highly decorated regiment in the Marine Corps, and in constant contact with the enemy."

I was on the next convoy heading west to An Hoa, the regiment's headquarters which was located in Quang Nam Province, about 20 miles west of Da Nang. The An Hoa Combat Base was of considerable strategic importance. It was the closest allied base to the mountains astride the Vietnam–Laos border. The 2nd Division of the North Vietnam Army (NVA) was in the area with the mission of attacking and destroying the air base at Da Nang, among other things. It moved supplies and troops off the Ho Chi Minh trail in Laos into Vietnam and local communists forces of the Viet Cong (VC). The whole area was hostile to Marines and mines and booby traps were the main cause of Marine casualties.

We arrived without incident. En route to the heavily sandbagged command post of the 5th Marines we drove past an airstrip with a C-130 that had lost a wing in a rocket attack the night before. The sound of outgoing artillery, or "friendly fire" punctuated the day. Much better than "incoming" fire. One learned to tell the difference fast. At the Command Post I was ushered into the presence of Colonel James B. Ord Jr., the regimental commander. A large, gruff veteran of several wars, he sported a bushy moustache, which definitely contravened Marine Corps regulations. Officers can wear moustaches but they must be trimmed and not venture beyond or lower than the mouth. The colonel's did both. The colonel noticed my gaze and bellowed, "Welcome to Ord's Horde lieutenant. You *will* have an unauthorized moustache! What are they going to do? Shave your head and send you to Vietnam? You're here." My moustache started that day.

I was assigned to the 2nd Battalion of the regiment under the command of Lieutenant Colonel James H. Higgins. It is written 2/5 and pronounced "Two Five." Its motto, "Retreat Hell," dated from the battle of Belleau Wood in France in 1918, where the battalion was sent to shore up the line against attacking Germans heading for Paris. A retreating French officer advised the advancing Marines to pull back. The Marine commander reportedly said, "Retreat? Hell, we just got here." The Marines held the line, and a grateful French army bestowed a decoration in perpetuity on the 5th and 6th Marine Regiments. It was the green fourragère, a braided cord worn on the left side by everyone serving in the regiment. These two regiments were the only two American units so honored by the French in the war. Marines call the cords pogey ropes. I was issued mine along with my M-16 rife, .45 pistol, flak jacket, and other gear. I never got to wear my fourragère because I never got to wear my class A uniform while I was in the 5th Marines. It is still in my sea bag.

My first company commander was Captain Ronald Drez. He commanded Hotel Company of the second battalion of the 5th Marines, usually written H/2/5. He put me in command of the second platoon whose lieutenant had been medevac'd with malaria. A full-strength platoon had 46 men. Mine had 24 counting machine gunners and a Navy corpsman (medic). That was about normal for a company that had seen a lot of fighting.

Everyone had a "bush" name. My predecessor was "Batman." The platoon sergeant was "Robin." I became "Kiwi," a flightless bird. To make the work of enemy snipers more difficult officers never wore their insignias. Some carried M-16 rifles instead of .45 pistols. There was no saluting, no "sirs." We were just a bunch of Marines looking for trouble.

One of my men was in the brig in Da Nang for murder. The company had taken heavy casualties in Hue city during the 1968 Tet offensive and the alleged murder occurred during the house-to-house fighting that typified the brutal battle. The man was eventually found not guilty but never rejoined the company. Stanley Kubrick's film *Full Metal Jacket* tells the story of H/2/5 at Hue.

After two days of settling in, the company saddled up for Operation *Taylor Common*, a multi-battalion operation into the mountains west of us to disrupt NVA efforts to infiltrate from Laos. We choppered up to a small landing zone on a hilltop. Blown trees littered the zone preventing the bird from landing. We jumped into the debris and formed a 360-degree defensive perimeter. Helicopters brought in mini-bulldozers that cleared away the trees and leveled off the hill. Then came 105mm artillery suspended from large CH-53 helicopters. Soon we had a "fire base" with artillery that could be called in for miles all around us. This would be our home for a month.

A few NVA "trail watchers" ambushed us on my first patrol. They fled after firing a few bursts. One Marine was wounded. The Doc (all corpsmen are called Doc) said the man needed to be medevac'd by air. Within minutes a CH-46, the workhorse

Hotel Company officers preparing to participate in Operation *Taylor Common* in Vietnam in 1969. Back row from left, Lt. William Vonderhaar, Lt. John McKay, Gunnery Sergeant Charles Jackson, Captain Ron Drez, Lt. Barry Broman, and Lt. Homer "Bo" Brookshire. Front row from left, Lt. Jeff Steger, Lt. James Hartneady. Most of the officers were wounded in Vietnam; six hours after the photo was taken, Lt. Vonderhaar was wounded and lost both legs.

helicopter of Marines in Vietnam, was on station lowering a "jungle penetrator" through the jungle to the smoke grenade we popped. The man was secured inside the small cage-like apparatus and lifted up. This is when the chopper is most vulnerable to ground fire, and we knew the NVA were all around us. As it rose, the penetrator bumped into trees so we asked the pilot to climb quickly. He did so and the wounded man gave out a long, fearful, moan. At about three hundred feet he was winched safely up to the bird. Forty-five minutes later he was in the fully equipped Navy hospital at China Beach in Da Nang.

At home, BJ kept all the letters I sent from Vietnam. On February 11, 1969, I wrote: "Well I'm two for two now. I took another patrol out today and we ran into Charlie (the enemy, short from Viet Cong, Victor Charlie in Marine-speak.) We hit *him* this time and didn't take any casualties. Mine is the only platoon that has made contact … I pulled off my first leech today."

Action was sporadic but leeches and malarial mosquitos were everywhere. Bug juice got leeches off but "hard core" Marines burned them off with cigarettes. At night we would send out ambushes and listening posts to warn of NVA moving in our direction. One third of the men were awake at any time. Many Marine "grunts" would spend their 13-month tour in Vietnam getting no more than a few hours' sleep at a time. Our arsenal included the Claymore mine, a small device that contained seven hundred ball bearings that could be exploded by a hand detonator in the face of the enemy. This directional mine had to be pointed at the enemy. To be safe, we always kept our heads down when touching off a Claymore.

All but one of us, Cletus Foote, a Hidatsa Indian from North Dakota and known as "the Chief," handled the Claymore mines the same way. Instead of covering the mine to disguise it from the enemy sappers crawling toward our positions, he would put the mine in the middle of the trail, aiming at the enemy. He watched closely from a concealed position and waited. When an enemy hand appeared to turn the mine around, the Chief would hit the trigger and the would-be attacker was off to the happy hunting ground. One night the Chief set off a Claymore and in the morning we found the hand that touched the mine belonged to a rock ape.

As Operation *Taylor Common* ended, helicopters lifted off the artillery pieces first. We burned anything of use to the enemy such as ammo boxes that once held artillery rounds. The perimeter shrank, and choppers ferried the troops back to An Hoa. Hotel Company was the last off. When a big CH-53 helicopter came in for my platoon, the heat from the burning ammo boxes nearby prevented the bird taking on a full load. So I spent the night there with about a dozen Marines. We were on our own. The artillery had gone. We still had air support if we needed it. But calling in air, in the dark, in the mountains, at close proximity to the enemy, was hard to do. We had two machine guns and hand illumination "pop up." When in use, you had to keep one eye closed so as not to lose your night vision. We formed a tight 360-degree perimeter, put out Claymore mines and trip flares, and waited

On an operation in Quang Nam, Province, Republic of Vietnam, in 1969, wearing my "lucky" bush hat purchased when I was on assignment in Saigon in 1963. (Photo by Lance Corporal Dennis Mowbray)

for Charlie to hit us. Black Marines were more respectful. They called the enemy Mr. Charles. It was a long night, as rock apes and wild boars scavenged in garbage pits around us. The NVA left us alone, and at first light a helicopter lifted us off back to our base camp and the first hot meal and shower in a month.

At our base at An Hoa, on February 21 I wrote:

> Just a quick note to say that I am now the company executive officer (XO), second in command. We are going into the field. Something came up and we have 30 minutes to move .... Even though I am XO I am taking my platoon to the field because our junior lieutenant is brand new. [He was killed in action a few weeks later.]

Back in the rice paddies after a month in the mountains, Captain Drez led a company-size patrol into an area that was sympathetic to the Viet Cong where we could expect booby traps and ambushes. We had an amphibious tractor, Amtrak, with us to carry C-rations, water, and ammunition. On top was a 106mm recoilless rifle, a very effective weapon against armor or personnel with a range of one mile. We moved quietly through rice paddies with farmers in the distance working their fields. At the end of our patrol route we were on a piece of high ground, no enemy in sight. The captain called for the recoilless rifle team leader.

"See that hootch?" he said, pointing to a hut about half a mile away.

"Yes sir," replied the young corporal.

"Blow it away?" said the skipper.

"Yes SIR," said the Marine, "FIRE MISSION."

The crew of the weapon came alive and fired a spotting round from a .50 caliber gun attached to the long rifle in preparation for firing a high explosive round. The puff of the bullet landed right in front of the door of the hut.

"Fire," called the corporal and a three-pound, explosive round, was on its way. It went into the door of the thatched hut resulting in a huge explosion. Instantly, all the famers in sight started to run. The hut contained VC explosives. How did the skipper know? I assumed he was acting on intelligence obtained before we made our sweep. "No," he told me long after the event. "I suspected that hootch had a cache of arms and explosives and I was right." Sometimes, instincts and experience are enough.

On February 24 I wrote:

> We are back in the field again … Charlie has started an offensive. They hit our base at An Hoa and blew up ammo dumps … We had six men killed in the field when a "friendly" aircraft dropped a bomb on them. I saw my first man blown away yesterday. He stepped on a booby-trapped 105mm round. He never knew what hit him.

Whenever we lost a lieutenant to wounds or death. I quickly reverted to platoon commander until a replacement arrived. Among my duties was visiting wounded men from H Company in various hospitals in Da Nang hospitals to pay them. Those who were not seriously wounded were treated at the 1st Medical Battalion near Da Nang. The Marines sent the more seriously wounded to the larger US Navy hospital at China Beach in Da Nang for treatment and possible evacuation to Japan or the United States. Two of my Marines were in the air-conditioned malaria ward. I found them, paid them, and told them what was happening in the "bush." As I was leaving, a Marine called to me.

"Lieutenant Broman, is that you"?

"Are you with Hotel 2/5?" I asked.

"No sir, I'm your piper from Camp Pendleton." He was with another battalion. I sat with him for a while and asked if he still had his pipes.

"Yes sir," he said, "That's why I have to get back to my unit. The gunny is taking care of them and says the troops miss their piper." Unfortunately, I do not remember his name or unit. I hope he made it home safely with his pipes.

***

We found more action much closer to home. Across the Thu Bon River, not far from An Hoa base camp was the bloodiest war zone in Quang Nam Province. It was known simply as the "Arizona Territory," named for Operation *Arizona*, which had taken place there some years earlier. It was well named as this really was "Indian country." It was a major prime infiltration corridor for the NVA coming east out of the mountains and was so full of Viet Cong sympathizers. We suspected everyone there of being an enemy and were usually correct. Many main-force VC had been killed in the Tet offensive of 1968 and had been augmented by NVA coming down the Ho Chi Minh trail. This was a "free fire zone." Booby traps and mines were everywhere.

In an area pockmarked by bomb craters and steeped in killing, the normal rules of engagement did not apply in the Arizona. Anything that moved was fair game. Every night, artillery from An Hoa rained; what the Marines call "Harassing and Interdiction" (H&I) fire, into the Arizona in addition to the direct support being provided for Marines on the battlefield. When things got really hot, we called for Spooky—also known as Puff the Magic Dragon—a C-47 aircraft fitted with a death-dealing machine gun that fired 4,000 rounds per minute with incredible accuracy. To illuminate the battlefield, we called for Basketball, a C-130, a cargo plane that dropped huge flares turning night into day.

I saw both in action one night when we were hit by NVA trying to overrun our small perimeter. First, we called for Spooky. Our air liaison officer crawled to a forward fighting position, a bomb crater and popped his strobe light to let the aircraft know where we were. A rain of bullets from the plan chewed up the rice

H Company, 2nd Battalion, 5th Marines in the notorious "Arizona Territory" of western Quang Nam Province in search of North Vietnamese Army infiltrators from Laos. Machine gunner Lance Corporal Al Gautschi is on the right.

paddy around us. Then Basketball came on station and lit up the battlefield. Machine guns ripped into the NVA while on-call artillery shelled their rear. In the morning we checked the dead NVA, took their weapons, and moved on.

Captain Gary Brown took command of Hotel Company. Ron Drez's second tour in Vietnam was up. He went home, left the Marine Corps, and became a respected researcher and writer of military books. Brown was on his second tour and knew how to run a rifle company. That was good, because we were headed in the Arizona on our own to "find, fix, and destroy the enemy." We were the point of the spear in the defense of Da Nang, Vietnam's second largest city.

Surrounded at An Hoa by the enemy, we never knew whether the civilians we encountered were friend or foe. Often, a friend by day was a foe by night. To help us we had a Kit Carson Scout (KCS). He was a former Viet Cong who had changed sides. The Marine Corps had a program to employ these tough and savvy fellows to help locate weapons and food caches, spot booby traps, and assist with the field interrogation of prisoners.

Our gunnery sergeant (gunny) was a large American Samoan named Saima'Auga M. Napoleon (no relation to the Corsican corporal). Affable and experienced, he took the KCS under his wing. One day, we moved into a village and set up a defensive perimeter with the intention of spending the night. The troops dug in, with machine gunners assigned where to site their guns. Mortarmen set up their 60mm weapons in case they were needed. Marines, one squad at a time, went to the village well to take showers. Young village boys drew buckets of water from the well for Marines to take "Navy showers." We had two buckets: one to get wet and soap up; another to rinse. We paid the kids in C-ration candy or, sometimes, cigarettes.

When it was the turn of the company command post (CP) for showers, Captain Brown went down to the well with a few of our radio operators. I stayed with the gunny and the KCS to man the radios. When the skipper returned, he discovered that his watch was missing. Apparently, one of the kids had stolen it while the captain showered. He was quite upset; it was a gift from his wife. Our KCS, a wily little fellow about 30 years old and with very little English, understood the situation. He gestured to the gunny that he could get the watch back and said, "I fix."

The KCS rounded up all the little kids around, boys and girls. He was firm but friendly. They ranged from ages 5 to 10. They were apprehensive as were their mothers watching in a group 50 yards away. There were no men; this was a VC ville. The men would return when the Marines had gone. The KCS explained that he wanted the watch returned. When no watch appeared, he grabbed a little girl, the cutest in the bunch, and pulled out his .45 pistol. Now the skipper, gunny, and I shared the apprehension of the mothers who had begun to wail. It was an ugly moment. Before we could do anything, the KCS put the little weeping girl into the bunker and fired his weapon. All the children screamed in terror, along with their mothers. All the Marines were worried. The KCS returned to the huddled children brandishing his pistol. He said a few words and we watched as the captain's timepiece flew out of the crowd in a high arc and landed at the feet of the KCS. He picked it up, moved to the bunker, and pulled out the little girl, unharmed but probably with ringing in her ears. She ran home. The wailing ceased. Our KCS shyly approached Captain Brown and handed over the watch. Problem fixed.

Every hut had a bunker for protection against air and artillery attacks. The NVA and VC also used these bunkers. When the Marines passed through a village, every bunker had to be cleared. US soldiers began the process, first calling people out (*lai dai*) or asking them to surrender (*chieu hoi*). If no one emerged, US soldiers would throw a fragmentation grenade into the bunker. This was bad for two reasons. First, many civilians who were simply too afraid to come out were killed or maimed by grenades. Second, properly constructed bunkers had a barrier inside to protect half of the bunker against grenades. CS gas—a non-lethal, irritant, delivered in grenade form—proved more humane and effective because it would get everyone without exception out of the bunker. CS gas saved many lives.

We normally would stay in a village for a few days, sending out day and night patrols, seeking to contact the enemy. One day I noticed some village boys kicking around a battered soccer ball. One boy had trouble running. He seemed to have a huge growth on his stomach, maybe a tumor. I found the senior Navy corpsmen at the command post and asked him to have a look at the boy. With our KCS interpreting, the 10-year-old boy told us he had been hit in the stomach by shrapnel from a bomb or artillery shell some weeks before. His entrails spilled out and eventually hardened. He had received no medical treatment for the wound, and at the time his mother thought he would die. The doc had never seen anything like it. Normally, the boy would have died from loss of blood or infection. But he recovered well enough to play soccer.

The doc said the boy's stomach could rupture at any time; he needed emergency treatment. The boy's mother understood the seriousness of her son's condition and gave us permission to evacuate him for medical treatment. There was a West German Malteser hospital near An Hoa that cared for Vietnamese civilians. In early 1969 the hospital was attacked by the NVA. Several of the German staff were killed, others were captured.

We decided I should take the boy there. The following day one of our platoons got into a firefight resulting in some wounded Marines (and dead NVA). We called in a medevac chopper and I took the boy on board to get him to An Hoa. As the helicopter lifted off the ground the little boy panicked and ran to the open rear of the CH-46 to jump off. A wounded Marine reached up and grabbed the boy's leg. We were about two hundred feet in the air and the boy landed on his stomach on the exit ramp. I moved back and took hold of the terrified little fellow, fearing what I would see when I turned him over. His stomach had not ruptured. The wounded Marine had saved his life.

When the German doctor unbuttoned the boy's black shirt, he said, "This boy should be dead. We must operate immediately." He took a photo of the dried intestines, saying, "I have never seen anything like this." He operated and the boy recovered. I visited the boy several times, each time taking gifts from Marines in An Hoa. I asked the Germans to let me know when the boy was ready to return to his village. When the day came, I went to the battalion S-3 (Operations) shop to see how I could get the boy back to his family. After some checking, the officer said, "Sorry lieutenant, that village was blown away last week. There is nothing left for him to go home to." I took the little guy back to the Germans, who said they would place him in an orphanage in Da Nang.

We celebrated Easter Day 1969 in the Arizona. The battalion chaplain, a Navy officer, flew in by helicopter to hold services. Everyone wanted to attend, so Gunny Napoleon and I each manned an M-60 machine for security during the service, which was held in the open on a piece of high ground. Neither the war nor the enemy interrupted us.

Parcels from home were always welcome, but for those fighting in the Arizona they were especially treasured and needed. I am not talking about cookies and fruitcake. I am talking about serious gifts, like Kool-Aid, the powder that has fruit flavors when mixed with water. I was never a fan of Kool-Aid, until I got to the Arizona Territory. When water re-supplies were late, we often drank river water or, in extreme situations, water from bomb craters. We always added water purification tablets, but the bad smell never went away. Hence, the widespread popularity of Kool-Aid.

Socks were highly valued. We usually traveled with at least two pairs and after a day crossing wet rice paddies or streams, it was important to put on a dry pair to prevent immersion foot, a condition in which rotting skin peels off your feet making it impossible to walk without great pain. It was always nice to have an extra pair, or two. BJ was very good at keeping me supplied with such necessities. She also would send me plastic baby bottles, filled with Scotch whiskey. They were very welcome in the Arizona.

While on operations in the Arizona, whenever an officer or senior enlisted man travelled to Da Nang, a 15-minute helicopter ride away, he would try to stop by the large Marine Corps PX at "Freedom Hill" near our division's headquarters. He would be expected to buy a bottle of Crown Royal whiskey. I don't know why this brand was the chosen beverage, it seemed to be a Hotel Company tradition. The bottle emerged towards the end of the afternoon operational meetings the skipper held with his platoon commanders and senior NCOs, the gunny, and platoon sergeants. The meetings covered issues like night ambushes, listening posts, and operational plans for the next day, etc. After the business discussion ended, the donor would break out the whiskey, take the first drink, and pass it around. The bottle made two circuits among the parched Marines and always ended with the man who brought it. He had the last drink.

The troops under the rank of staff sergeant were not allowed to buy alcohol, regardless of their age. But on a few rare occasions beer was flown into the Arizona in external loads hanging from the helicopters in cargo nets. It was always Carling Black Label, a forgettable brand, and it was always about 80 degrees Fahrenheit. But it was beer, it was wet, and it was appreciated.

I ate rather well when I was in the Arizona. In the rear, I traded for South Korean rations from a friendly Republic of Korea (ROK) Marine captain, who would swap tasty and spicy Korean rations for captured AK-47 guns. Marines could not take them home as souvenirs but Koreans could. Gunny Napoleon and I loved them. So did our ex-VC, Kit Carson Scout as well as a few other members of the command post who needed something besides McIlhenny's Tabasco sauce to pep up a meal.

While patrolling in the Arizona one day, I noticed a CH-46 helicopter approaching. It was trailing a long Simmons Rig ladder. On the ladder were eight Marines about 200 feet in the air moving about 90 miles an hour, heading east. They were Recon Marines returning from the mountains after a reconnaissance mission. I grabbed my Nikon F and snapped a few photos as they flew overhead going home.

Recon Marines hang from a CH-46 helicopter as they fly over Hotel Company on an operation in the Arizona Territory.

A few weeks later I was in Da Nang on company business and had the black-and-white film processed. The pictures looked good, so I clipped a negative and sent it to Hal Buell, deputy chief of AP Photos in New York. Weeks passed, and I received a thick envelope in the mail. It contained several clippings from American newspapers, including *The New York Times*. Each clipping had my photo accompanying reporting from Vietnam from that day. The *St. Louis Post Dispatch* ran the picture eight columns wide on the front page. With the clippings, Hal sent me a note thanking me for the photo and included a check for $15, the standard rate, apparently, for a stringer in Vietnam. He also said he owed me a dinner, which I collected some years later.

Our miserable time in the Arizona with all the booby traps was rewarded in early May, when our battalion (2/5) along with the 1st Battalion of the 5th Marines (1/5) caught an NVA regiment in the open heading for Da Nang. With one battalion blocking and another assaulting, the North Vietnamese were trapped. Marines made maximum use of supporting arms, calling in air strikes of bombs and napalm while the 11th Marines in An Hoa pounded the hapless regiment with artillery. Hundreds died, more were wounded. For days, NVA bodies floated down the Thu Bon River to Hoi An. Both battalions received the Meritorious Unit Citation for this action. By coincidence, when *The New York Times* reported the battle in the May 9, 1969 issue, the photo that ran with the story was my snap of the Recon Marines crossing the Arizona Territory some weeks earlier.

When Hotel Company was not in the "bush" we were usually in An Hoa, our regimental base camp. There was no town, and there were no Vietnamese. An Hoa housed Marines and artillery. It had an airstrip, and a lot of dust until it rained; then there was a lot of mud. NVA regularly tried to infiltrate, so we had lots of bunkers and slit trenches. However, to Marines who had been sleeping in rice paddies, sometimes with ponchos rigged to keep the rain off, An Hoa was heaven. A tin roof sheltered the cots and we had hot meals and hot showers. Our uniforms were washed and we had free haircuts. Most of all, we weren't patrolling in mine fields, or dodging booby traps.

In the spring of 1969, Captain Brown was replaced by Captain William Fite III who was on his second tour in Vietnam. He had been an advisor with South Vietnamese Marines and knew his way around a battlefield.

Every soldier, Marine, and swabbie in Vietnam, regardless of rank was given a one week R&R (rest and recreation) somewhere in Asia or Hawaii, all paid for by a grateful government. One day, a Marine who had been to Kuala Lumpur, Malaysia, on R&R, where he met a local girl, and wanted to marry her, came to see me. He wanted to extend his tour in Vietnam by six months, which would qualify him for a 30-day leave anywhere in the world. During his leave he planned to fly to Kuala Lumpur and marry the girl. He denied that she was a prostitute and said that he had met her through her brother, a taxi driver. Seeing potential problems ahead for the young Marine, I sought more information about the girl. I asked for more details about her and then asked the gunny to let me know who was next going to Malaysia on R&R. I gave the Marine the girl's name and how to find her, and asked him to see if he could get a photo of her. The Marine returned with a sheaf of Polaroid images of the girl, an attractive Indian-Malay woman, naked in provocative poses. I selected one and called in the would-be husband. I showed him one of the photos. All he said was, "Guess I won't be extending my tour," and left. He survived the war and returned home on schedule, still single.

I was told that one squad in the company expected all its Marines to choose Bangkok as their R&R venue. At some time in the past a Marine from the company met a bar girl, I will call her Daeng. They became close friends and he recommended her to other Marines, thereby starting the tradition. Daeng must have been an exceptional young lady. She became a friend as well as a lover. Daeng knew the name of the next squad member headed for Bangkok. She cleared her schedule for Hotel Company arrivals. Daeng received and sent presents back. Sometimes, Marines she knew were killed in action or medevac'd home. Daeng was never informed. For her, the war was far away and her new friends never spoke of it. They wanted her to carry the thought that none of her Marines were hurt. She was the squad mascot and huggle bunny. It is little wonder that Thai women are so widely cherished.

Hotel Company had a number of foreign-born Marines who had volunteered to serve their new country. One, machine gunner, Lance Corporal Ernst "Woodie" Woodruff from Germany, was one of the toughest Marines I ever met. One night Woodie and his squad staked out a well that we suspected the NVA was using. At first light short bursts of machine-gun fire woke us up. Woodie radioed that they had surprised some NVA filling water bottles at the well. Woodie killed three of them with the first burst of his machine gun. When the squad returned into our perimeter, I saw Woodie with a big grin on his face, toting his M-60 machine gun over his shoulders, sporting a peace symbol on his helmet.

"Woodie," I asked, "How can you kill three men before breakfast and come back into our lines with a peace symbol on your helmet?"

"Is easy, Lieutenant" he replied. "I am hypocrite."

After another firefight I took a photo of Woodie holding the remains of his Zippo lighter, that sitting in his pocket had stopped an enemy bullet.

I felt a personal loss at the death of another young foreign-born Marine—Irish Lance Corporal Peter Nee. Born in the wind-swept hills of Connemara, he immigrated to Boston at the age of 17. He wanted to be an American and enlisted in the Marine Corps to prove it. On March 31, 1969 he was killed by a booby trap in the Arizona. I remember Peter for his wit, his charm, and his gentle Irish brogue. I wrote the condolence to Peter's next-of-kin, his sister, Mary, in Boston. When I went through his effects prior to sending them to Mary I found he was also a poet. I found one of his poems. Here is how one of his poems ended.

How much have I contributed to life? Nothing.
Why must a man travel onward without knowing where he is going?
Why all of a sudden does he realize that the things that he valued in life are valueless?
The things he believed in he finds he never really believed in at all.
Why does he find this out when it is too late?
The sun slowly descends behind the mountain; the valley is quiet.
Crouched behind a fallen tree a young man awaits eternity.

It is not wise to form close relationships in combat because death is always nearby. This is easier said than done, especially for the young men who form lifelong friends even when that life might not be very long. It is also true of officers who must give orders that will send men to their deaths. I noticed the distance maintained with me by several of my company commanders. At any moment they might be called to send me on a hazardous mission, better not to have any sentiment that could cloud the necessity of a fatal decision. This is difficult, but it must be done at every echelon of command.

In April we were in heavy contact in the Arizona. Hotel Company ran into NVA regulars in a village fighting from well-concealed bunkers. I was with Fite in the command post while bullets impacted around us. A lieutenant approached us doing the low crawl as the whine of AK-47 rounds zipped by. I wished I could have joined the officer on the ground but Fite, a seasoned and heavily decorated Marine, coolly ignored the fire, even as a round went between us and cut down a banana stalk.

On April 15, I wrote to BJ:

> Sorry I haven't written for so long. Things have been quite hectic. I went to the bush five days ago. The day before yesterday one of our lieutenants, an Annapolis man, was shot in the face while assaulting a bunker. I took over his platoon. We have been in heavy contact and they're all around us ... We didn't have water or chow for two days and the temperature was over 100 degrees. We're OK now, a chopper came in last night ... A little Vietnamese boy was hit when Marines threw a fragmentation grenade into a bunker he was in. He died in the night ... Looks like I will be out here until we get another lieutenant.

The lieutenant who was hit was John McKay. His platoon was attacking NVA bunkers when John was hit at point-blank range. Captain Fite sent me forward to take over John's platoon. Two Marines brought McKay back with one eye missing and still conscious. At the same moment, a helicopter landed nearby to drop off ammo and water and take out wounded. Gunny Napoleon, a hefty Samoan, picked up the lieutenant and ran to the chopper. McKay survived and stayed on active duty wearing a black patch over one eye. He retired from the Marine Corps as a full colonel.

Not far away during the same action, another foreign-born machine gunner, a Jamaican named Elton Armstrong and his assistant gunner, PFC Steve Russell from Alabama, were pinned down by fire from NVA bunkers. Armstrong attacked the bunkers firing his machine gun from his hip and outrunning grenades thrown at him without dropping his gun. The surviving MVA surrendered and Armstrong received the Silver Star medal for his actions. Later, I asked Armstrong what impelled him to assault the bunkers. "I heard an SKS, lieutenant," he said "And I wanted it." An SKS is a semi-automatic rifle and could be taken home as a souvenir. The more common AK-47 is an automatic weapon and could not be taken home. After the war Armstrong became an American citizen and today lives in a Veterans Administration hospital in Pennsylvania. His old buddy Russell visits.

In a separate action in the Arizona I was walking near Captain Fite when a booby trap exploded up front. A Marine had tripped it walking through a tree line. The call went out, "Corpsman up!" It was time for our Navy medics to go to work. The Marine had lost both legs and was bleeding out. He needed a medical evacuation to a hospital about 20 minutes away by helicopter. There are four levels of priority for medevacs: Emergency, Priority, Routine, and Permanent Routine. The last was for taking out Marines who were already dead. Although this ranked as an emergency the 1st Marine Division, stretched thin that day, had no helicopters available. The skipper, normally a calm, unemotional, leader, got on the radio himself demanding a medevac, to no avail. Just then, the sound of an Army gunship chopper was heard. The pilot came up on our emergency radio frequency. "You guys need a bird?" he asked. "I can take one man. Pop smoke!" A smoke grenade was thrown into the field that would be our landing zone. "I see green," the pilot radioed. "Coming in." A gunship is not designed for passengers, but somehow the corpsmen staunched the blood and got the wounded man on board. The young Army warrant officer flew away, saving the Marine's life.

All corpsmen, called medics in the Army, belonged to the United States Navy. They happily wore Marine camouflage uniforms and were (usually) unarmed. They were admired and respected by Marines, especially those who saw them in action. Corpsmen were favorite targets of the NVA who liked to shoot them when they went to the aid of wounded Marines. My favorite bumper sticker reads: "The best thing about the Corps is the Corpsman." Marine grunts love corpsmen. The rest of the Navy are "squids."

On April 26, I wrote BJ:

> This afternoon I returned to An Hoa from Da Nang by convoy to receive some very unhappy news. Last night the company got hit in the Arizona … The skipper (Captain Fite) had shrapnel wounds to the chest and legs and was an emergency evac. One man died, 20 others were wounded … Captain Fite was the best man I have met out here. He stayed in Vietnam over 26 months straight. He really liked the Vietnamese and he didn't like the way we were running the war … We agreed on just about everything.

Fite survived his wounds. I last saw him at a twilight parade at Marine Corps Barracks, Washington DC where he was posted in 1972. He retired as a full colonel.

On May 11, all hell broke loose in An Hoa when an NVA sapper team tried to sneak into the artillery battalion of the 11th Marines and destroy the heavy guns that made lives difficult and often short for our enemy. Hotel Company was responsible for a section of the perimeter and as company XO I was in charge. We had bunkers with machine guns behind well-constructed barbed wire in depth. Moreover, we were told that in front of our position was an old French army minefield dating from the early 1950s that had never been cleared. Our lines were not attacked but there was a hell of a fight not far away.

In the morning, all defense sector commanders, including me, were convoked to the scene of the action. A dozen NVA sappers armed with satchel charges of high explosives tried to get through the even more sophisticated wire outside the artillery positions. Twelve NVA died in the wire. The sole survivor was a young fellow who was taken prisoner unharmed. He seemed to be in good humor as he gave a demonstration of how they moved through the wire. Wearing nothing but his underpants and carrying only a pair of wire cutters, the young sapper slowly crawled and cut his way through the tangle foot and concertina wire. It looked as easy as crap going through a goose. I returned to our positions to make some improvements to our defenses.

***

Life in 2/5 was not all blood, guts, and incoming rockets. One day LTC Higgins, our commanding officer, decided we should have a mess night. This was a formal dinner for officers and their guests. He saw no need to let the war interfere with a hoary Marine Corps tradition, even if most of the battalion's officers were fighting nearby. Mess nights follow a strict sequence of events, but the seriousness of the occasion is tempered by the heavy flow of wine that accompanies the traditional meal of roast beef. Numerous toasts to the Marines who came before punctuated the evening. My first, and only, mess night experience was at Basic School in Quantico, just before graduation. We wore dress blue uniforms, invited a three-star general as our senior guest, and enjoyed a fine meal, accompanied by several wines and followed by numerous toasts with port wine. There was not much frivolity on that occasion.

In An Hoa it was somewhat different, although the colonel tried to follow tradition as closely as he could. The battalion supply officer scoured Da Nang for the best shrimp for the before-dinner cocktail, and beef for the main course. He purchased fine red and white wines as well as the mandatory port. That's about as much tradition as we could muster. No one wore their dress uniforms. My blues were back home along with my whites, which would never be worn. We were in our best camouflage utility uniforms with buckskin-looking combat boots. No spit shines in An Hoa. We had no music, except for outgoing artillery from the nearby artillery batteries, which was always music to our ears.

Finding suitable guests for the occasion proved challenging given our isolation and how surrounded we were by the enemy. I suggested inviting German doctors and nurses from the nearby Malteser hospital. "Make it so," the colonel ordered.

The German doctor I visited remembered me from bringing in the little boy with a stomach wound. He and his nurses would be delighted to join our soirée. None had ever been inside our heavily fortified base and looked forward to enjoying a good American meal. In many respects these angels of mercy to the local Vietnamese civilians were more isolated than we were.

The event took place in the battalion mess hall, a basic structure with screens in lieu of windows and a thin sheet of galvanized tin for a roof. The colonel needed a venue for before-dinner drinks, and the staff non-commissioned officers' "club" volunteered their humble "club," a barracks "hootch," made of plywood, tin, and screen that was common to all Marine structures in Vietnam. This small room featured a wall of pinup art confiscated from the original owners.

I delivered the four German guests, two physicians and two blonde and very pretty nurses. A special bar was set up and drinks were served to the assembled officers of the 2nd Battalion. With Hotel Company in the field I represented the company. The German doctors made a beeline for the wall of art. The colonel who was making his first visit to the Staff NCO Club clearly regretted not having inspected it in advance. The two nurses demurely avoided the wall of pinups and enjoyed their drinks with young Marine officers, who were delighted to meet the ladies.

One of the evening's highlights occurred when two naked Marines, wearing old flip-flops, walked by from the showers with towels draped around their necks.

Morning in the Arizona Territory of Quang Nam Province. At left, sitting on his rubber air mattress is Lt. Jeff Steger, an engineer attached to Hotel Company. I am sleeping "rough" in the rice paddy.

The nurses were standing in the doorway as the Marines approached. Seeing the women they hastily wrapped their towels around their waists and ran away as fast as they could. One nurse put their embarrassed hosts at ease. "Not a problem. We are nurses, but it has been a long time since we saw naked white men," she said with a wistful smile.

The meal was a tour de force of what a resourceful Marine supply officer can do under difficult circumstances to maintain a tradition of the Corps. Enlisted mess men, who had never seen alcohol in the mess hall before, served an excellent meal. The colonel also provided a case of Champagne chilled on ice in a huge aluminum bowl. At the end of the evening, after the toasts and port, after our guests had been given an armed escort back to their hospital, the colonel sat around with his officers and drank the last of the Champagne. It was a rare moment for the colonel to socialize and relax with officers who he would not normally see in combat situations or during a hospital visit. The evening had been such a success that when two very drunk lieutenants poured the icy water that had cooled the Champagne over the equally squiffed colonel, there was no cry of alarm or rebuke. The colonel took the illegal and audacious deed as a gesture of respect and affection, as it was intended. Much like football players pouring cold Gatorade over their coach at the end of a victorious game.

***

During my seven months with Hotel Company we made numerous trips into the Arizona as had Marines before us. In retrospect, it seems like a huge waste of time and, more importantly, for Marines. We knew where the NVA were coming from, Laos not far away. We should have gone in, cut the Ho Chi Minh trail and changed the outcome of the war. The NVA had already violated the neutrality of Laos. There was no good reason not to go in. President Johnson thought otherwise. On a very hot day in the spring of 1969, Hotel Company, about 140 strong, was sent back into to the Arizona on a company-size patrol. We were spread out, moving slowly and looking for trouble. In the words of the poet Robert W. Service, we were "dog dirty and loaded for bear." The scene reminded me of a graffito—a modified portion of the 23rd Psalm—that I saw on the back of a Marine's flak jacket. "Yea though I walk through the valley of the shadow of death I will fear no evil, for I am the meanest motherfucker in the valley."

The Chief, Cletus Foote, was walking point. Being the first man is always a dangerous assignment. I followed behind him with a fire team of Marines. We walked quietly and carefully across abandoned rice paddies, around bomb craters and through bamboo tree lines. Despite the quiet, we knew the NVA were close. Every man looked for booby traps. Suddenly, the Chief raised his hand. The company stopped. I moved up to the Chief.

"We are being followed," he said quietly.

"Chief," I said, "we are all spread out and you, the point man, tell me we are being *FOLLOWED?*"

"One man," he added, "with a pack and rifle."

I waited for the company commander, Captain Fite, to catch up to us and reported the Chief's intelligence. The skipper told the sniper attached to the company to drop out at the next tree line and look for someone following the company. The company moved on. A few minutes later a shot rang out. The sniper had fired. The drag element checked it out. They found one NVA with a rifle and a pack, dead from a gunshot wound to the chest. Score one for the sniper who hit his target at 1,100 meters. And score an assist for the Chief.

In early May when I was in An Hoa, the battalion operations officer, a major, summoned me. He explained that Golf Company had been in a heavy firefight and Hotel Company was rushing to their assistance in the Arizona. An airborne resupply of food, water, and ammo was scheduled for Hotel Company but since it was on the move someone had to be on the ground to receive the resupply. That someone turned out to be me along with anyone else from H Company still in the rear who could assist. We had a few men with two Purple Hearts; they all volunteered to go. In Vietnam if you received three Purple Hearts (three wounds) you went home. Your tour was over. Our policy was to keep men with two wounds in the rear assigned to duties like company driver, mail clerk, etc. We also had men who had just returned to duty from the hospital or R&R. In all, I had about 10 men for the mission. We loaded up with a pair of machine guns, M-79 grenade launchers, and M-16 rifles. A chopper took us across the Vu Gia River to a lonely little piece of high ground where the resupply would arrive soon. The company was en route. I hoped very much that they would reach us by dusk.

We quickly formed a tight perimeter with room for the supplies in the center. As the men dug in I prepared on-call artillery missions around us for the guns in An Hoa. The choppers came in on time with external nets filled with supplies. They dropped their loads in the perimeter and left us alone with plenty to eat and drink. We broke out ammo for the machine guns. As the light dimmed Hotel Company arrived, bone-tired after their forced march. They dug in and broke out C-rations food, water, and ammunition for their guns and M-60 mortars. I expected we would be hit and I was not disappointed.

We set up listening posts but did not send out any ambush teams. Around four in the morning a listening post reported nearby movement. We called in the listening post and put the company on full alert; everyone was up and ready. The NVA hit us in small groups trying to penetrate our makeshift defenses in the broken terrain of bomb craters and heavy undergrowth surrounding our little piece of high ground. We shot off illumination rounds from our mortars and hand-held "pop up" flares. We fired small arms at the exposed enemy. The fight did not last long and we suffered no casualties. As the sun came up we found more than a dozen dead NVA all around us. We also found blood trails where the NVA had carried their wounded away. One of the dead had been hit in the belly and as he crawled away he left a trail of intestines.

PFC Steve Russell said he heard movement inside our lines. We checked it out. A Marine whispered he heard movement in a bomb crater. With my .45 pistol in hand I moved toward the crater and called out *"Chieu hoi"* or "surrender." No answer. There was someone in the crater and it was not a Marine. I shouted, *"Lai dai, chieu hoi,"* which meant "come here, give up." An NVA, armed with an AK-47 he clearly intended to use, emerged from the crater. I opened fire. So did Steve, firing from the hip. The NVA went down. When we turned the body over I saw he had a Chicom grenade in his hand. His wallet contained a photo of himself in a NVA captain's uniform festooned with medals. Another photo showed him with his wife and two small children. He also had a diary that we sent back to the S-2 (Intelligence) officer along with his wallet. I kept one of his dog tags. Later that morning we saddled up and moved out leaving the dead NVA lined up for their comrades, who were watching us, to recover later.

In 2007, I was in Hanoi for a few days while working on a magazine story. I brought dog tags from the dead captain with me as well as my written statement describing the circumstances of the officer's death in Quang Nam Province in 1969. I gave them both to a friend in the American Embassy to pass on to the Vietnamese, who have an office dealing with cases of men missing in action from the war. I knew that they had recovered the body but there was no NVA alive to say how he died. I figure I owed the captain that much and still wish he had surrendered.

I reported the action to BJ in a letter on May 18:

> I fired a full clip from my .45 into the NVA. We finished him off with a machine gun burst. It was my first kill … That's the way it is here, the quick live and the slow die … Good news. Hotel Company is coming out of the bush after over 80 days in the Arizona. The battalion has 156 men the hospital … We are known as "Hospital Hotel." Golf Company is called "Graveyard Golf."

Three days earlier, I wrote:

> Today has been unpleasant around old An Hoa. First of all, it is 103 degrees. The battalion has two companies about three kilometers away, both in heavy contact with the enemy … We had another KIA (killed in action) today. Lost both legs to a booby trap and died on the operating table. That makes eight letters of condolence that I wrote this week.

During my time as XO of Hotel Company, I wrote 34 letters of condolence to the next-of-kin of Marines killed in action, always in the name of the company commanders who were still in the field.

***

The last gunnery sergeant I served with was also the best. Anthony "Tony" Marengo, was an Italian-American from Brooklyn. He believed that if the country was at war and you were in the Corps you belonged in the war. A bachelor, he kept extending his tours instead of going home. One night I asked if he had ever been in the Arizona. He had, first in 1966 when there was only one battalion, 2/5, at An Hoa. Tony told me the story of his most memorable, and horrific, venture into that hostile area. It was in early June 1967. Tony, a staff sergeant, was assigned to Fox Company, 2/5, serving as a platoon commander. The Corps always seemed to be suffering from a shortage of infantry officers because the Marines invariably served in the hottest of the combat zones. The skipper was Captain James Graham, a savvy and much respected officer on his first combat tour.

Fox Company was on Operation *Union* attached to the 1st Battalion, 5th Marines (1/5). It was outside the range of An Hoa's artillery when it walked into an NVA ambush. Tony's platoon, fighting separately from the command element, was reduced to seven effective Marines. He spoke on the radio to Captain Graham, who was wounded. The skipper had ordered the company to fall back while he stayed with the wounded and one corpsman, "Doc" Donovan. It was the doc's birthday. Surrounded by the NVA and out of ammunition, the captain's last words to Tony on the radio were: "Tony, they look good. They are firing and moving in." Tony was with the Marines who found the bodies of Captain Graham and the men he had stayed with. NVA had executed them with pistol shots to the head. Before he was killed, Captain Graham and his command group had assaulted and overrun two enemy machine gun emplacements.

Captain Graham received the Medal of Honor for his valor in the action that day. The command nominated Tony for the Navy Cross, the second highest decoration a Marine can receive, but it was downgraded to Bronze Star, maybe because he had just received a Silver Star—the third highest decoration—for a different act of heroism. He also received a battlefield promotion to gunnery sergeant, a rare event. In October 1967, while still serving in Vietnam, Tony was ordered to Marine Corps Headquarters in Washington DC. Captain Graham's widow had asked that Tony be at the presentation of the Medal of Honor to her by President Nixon at the White House. Then he returned to the war. By the end of the war, Tony had served in Vietnam almost five years, and in addition to his Silver and Bronze Star medals, received three Purple Heart Medals for three wounds.

About the same time that Gunny Marengo joined Hotel Company in the spring of 1969, we also had a new company commander, Captain Robert "Bob" Poolaw. Captain Fite had been badly wounded in the Arizona and Poolaw took over command. Bob had been wounded while commanding Golf Company, but returned to duty prematurely to take over Hotel. He was ex-enlisted, softly-spoken, and very tough. Poolaw, a proud descendent of a long line of Kiowa warriors, was a credit to his people and the Corps.

On one of my last operations with the company, we were sent south of An Hoa in response to reports that the NVA were infiltrating the area around Hill 25, which was in the hands of South Vietnamese Regional Forces (RF), "Ruff Puffs" to Marines. These were poorly trained and armed militia who operated only in the province where they lived. Warrant Officer Le Bon, an old fellow who had served in the French Army before 1954, commanded this small group. He spoke little English, so I used my schoolboy French and we got along fine. He and his troops were very happy to see us. They expected an NVA attack from the nearby mountains and stood little chance of stopping them alone.

Hotel Company set up quickly in the RF hill top positions and dug in. We placed our machine guns in areas with good fields of fire and set up our own artillery, 60mm mortars that used illumination rounds to light up the battlefield in addition to high explosive rounds. We also had a new weapon: CS gas. CS gas was not actually a gas; rather it was a micro-pulverized powder that made you want to get away from it! We carried CS grenades routinely, mainly to clear bunkers. A fragmentation grenade might not kill everyone in a properly constructed bunker but

With Captain Bob Poolaw, center, and Gunnery Sergeant Anthony "Tony" Marengo, right, in the field. Both of them were wounded in action, Tony three times.

no one could stay in a bunker when a CS grenade popped in. They were non-lethal but much very persuasive.

The new weapon came on an M-8 backpack containing 48 CS grenades and employed in the defense to break up an enemy attack. Like a Claymore mine, it was fired by hand. None of us had used it before and it had one major constraint. We had to always make sure the wind was blowing in the right direction. Marines carried gas masks; or rather they carried gas mask pouches. Since the NVA did not employ gas weapons, most grunts dumped the masks and used the pouch to carry extra chow or socks. Since we had the weapon, were in a defensive position, and did not know the enemy's strength, Captain Poolaw had the M-8 set up in a position where it could be used if the NVA came down the slope in front of us, the natural axis of advance. We set out listening posts after dark, shared our chow with the Ruff Puffs, and waited. Another edge for us was our Starlight night vision scope. This handy $6,000 gadget let us see in the dark.

Before first light we picked up movement on the slope through the Starlight scope and called in our listening posts. The NVA were quietly moving toward us. We held our fire. The skipper thought this might be a good time to test the M-8 since the wind was in our favor. We fired an illumination mortar round, which lit up the NVA, and then fired the M-8. It worked like a charm. The grenades shot out in a high arc, burst, and lay a small cloud of CS that rolled into the ranks of the oncoming NVA. Then we opened fire with small arms, including short bursts from the machine guns.

I do not recall any incoming fire from the NVA but some may have used their weapons. I do recall the NVA stopping their advance and retreating as fast as the survivors could into the jungle on the hillside. We suffered no casualties. At first light the RFs went out to count the dead and recover weapons. They brought in 17 AK-47 rifles and quite a lot of other gear. We gave it all to the regional forces, as they could claim a $75 bounty for each weapon they captured. This had been my first and only opportunity to fight alongside South Vietnamese troops and it was a good experience. I think they would say the same about us.

Marine infantry officers in Vietnam were usually given "split" tours meaning they would serve half of their 13-month tours (vice 12 for the army) in a combat role and half in a staff position. That way every officer had an opportunity to be shot. It seemed fair to me. It was always better to spend the first half on the line and the second half in the rear. Those in the bush often considered people in the rear as REMFs, rear echelon motherfuckers. Grunts who had served in the line were exempted.

Of particular disdain were US Air Force personnel assigned to the huge Da Nang Air Base, which had amenities Marines in the bush could only dream of. They had beds, hot meals, a driving range for golfers, pizzas, massage parlors, and, for officers, the DOOM club, the Da Nang Officers' Open Mess, a vast improvement over the pathetic little "club" the Marines had four miles away. I was told, and hope it is not true, that the Air Force commander of the base asked that walking wounded heading for the Navy hospital at China Beach south of Da Nang, not hitch-hike across the air base as it upset the airmen.

***

For the second half of my tour I was assigned to G-5 (Civil Affairs) at the headquarters of the 1st Marine Division (Reinforced) outside Da Nang. My bush time was over. But first I was going on R&R. I took my R&R in Hawaii, where BJ met me in Honolulu. Married GIs preferred to take their R&R in Hawaii for two reasons. First, Hawaiians treated soldiers serving in Vietnam like royalty and hotels and restaurants offered special rates. Second, the state was largely devoid of the anti-war sentiment that affected other parts of the country.

In one sad note, however, BJ told me that while she was waiting for my flight, a handful of women waiting at the R&R center were called aside. They were informed that their husbands/boyfriends would not be joining them. They had either been killed in action or wounded before getting on the plane to Hawaii. This was a regular occurrence and military chaplains were standing by. It was probably the worst duty assignment of their careers.

After a day on Waikiki beach, we went to the Big Island, BJ's home. She is from the Pepeekeo Sugar Plantation, not from Hilo on the wet and green windward side of the island. The area was beautiful and unspoiled. Her parents owned a small house near Pepeekeo Point. Her father, who emigrated from the Philippines in 1928 to cut cane, had worked his way up to foreman. Her mother was born in Hawaii to Japanese parents. Her grandfather was the black sheep of a samurai family, and the family welcomed his departure to the islands. During World War II he hoped the Imperial Japanese Army would arrive to add Hawaii to their empire. To his great chagrin, two of his sons joined the famed 442nd Regimental Combat Team (Go For Broke) of the US Army. They served with distinction in Europe. Everyone in the family agreed that it was good that BJ's grandfather was not around in 1969 to meet Marine Lieutenant Broman.

It was great to see BJ in Hawaii and meet her family. The hard part of my Vietnam tour was over. I was out of the bush and had returned to Vietnam and a new job, one that I had requested. The G-5 (Civil Affairs) shop at the headquarters of the 1st Marine Division near Da Nang. This was an assignment I had requested. Specifically, I was the division Personal Response officer. The division had more than 20,000 men with the mission to find, fix, and destroy the enemy. One man assigned to persuade Marines they should get along with our South Vietnamese allies. That one man was me. My mission was a tough sell to Marines, who invariably operated in terrain controlled by and sympathetic to the enemy. The division was losing one leg a day from booby traps, many of them planted by civilians. I spoke to units throughout the division scattered around Quang Nam Province citing examples of how Vietnamese had come forward with information on the enemy, warning of booby traps, etc. as a response to Marine kindness and assistance. Still, it was a hard sell.

I wore a number of hats. I organized a "culture tour" of Da Nang for Marines in the rear. This was especially popular as Da Nang city was off limits to Marines. The tour included visits to the Catholic cathedral, a Buddhist temple in a cave at Marble Mountain near the US Navy hospital at China Beach, and the French-era Museum, which housed perhaps the world's best collection of pre-Vietnamese Cham art. The Hindu and later Islamic Cham dominated central and southern Vietnam for a thousand years, centered in the Da Nang area before the Vietnamese moved south and conquered the Cham. The last stop was the Da Nang orphanage where Marines could interact with small children. Marines love little kids. This was always the highpoint of the tour.

My grad school background in anthropology helped me in my role as the division's ethnic minority officer. The job put me in direct contact with the Katu hill tribe, a primitive group known for being the last tribal group on the mainland of Southeast Asia that practiced human sacrifice. The only Katu village in friendly hands was located next to the US Army's Special Forces camp at Thuong Duc, in the mountains west of An Hoa and surrounded by the enemy. I would fly into the village courtesy of the Special Forces, who had a 15-man A-Team in the camp, along with several hundred tribesmen working for the Special Forces. An Australian woman missionary, Nancy Costello, who was translating the bible into Katu, helped me communicate with the tribe. She kindly helped me set up a small business for the Katu to sell handicrafts, which I transported to Da Nang. Our biggest seller was the crossbows, the traditional weapon of the Katu who were the last tribe on the mainland of Southeast Asia to practice human sacrifice. I made sure the bamboo arrows for the crossbows did not contain the poison that the Katu used when hunting.

I quickly made friends with First Lieutenant Jim "Jonesy" Jones from Buffalo, New York, who spent his bush tour as an artilleryman. Jonesy spoke fluent Vietnamese and loved working for G-5. He supervised our agriculture programs, which included introducing IR-8 "miracle" rice from the Philippines, which greatly increased a farmer's crop. We also introduced tilapia fish to provide inexpensive protein. Jonesy also introduced large American Hampshire boars to the Vietnamese to breed with local sows and improve the quality of swine in the province. This job earned Jonesy the in-house title of 1st Marine Division Pig Officer. He named one General Cushman and the other General Walt after the two most senior officers in the Marine Corps. The boars would be lent to farmers to breed with small Vietnamese pigs. Jonesy would get the pick of the litter and move the boar to his next assignation. The project was working smoothly until the day we received a call from the Civil Affairs officer of the 5th Marines in An Hoa reporting that General Walt was killed earlier that morning "in a firefight at the village where he was performing his duties."

The boar's death was a setback to the program but it got worse. The division commander heard a rumor that General Walt had been killed near An Hoa and convoked our colonel. First, the general did not know that the Assistant Commandant of the Marine Corps Lewis Walt was in country. Second, he did not know that G-5 had a pig from Iowa named General Walt that was killed in action. Jones was summoned by the colonel to explain the confusion. The program and Lieutenant Jones survived, but our swine were no longer named after senior Marine Corps officers.

One of the few perks of being a civil affairs lieutenant was the opportunity to attend a one-week training course offered by the Army in Saigon. The course was designed for US military advisors and outlined the many civil programs implemented by the US and Vietnamese governments and operated throughout the country. Most of the serious fighting in South Vietnam took place in the northern provinces known as Eye Corps where the Marines were stationed. There were far fewer pacified areas under the control of the South Vietnamese government. The Marines were given a quota for one officer in each monthly running of the course.

Other than the embassy guards, few Marines ever saw Saigon. A week in Saigon was like an R&R to Marines. When my turn came I enjoyed every minute of being back in Saigon. I called on my old AP friends Horst Faas and Peter Arnett who very kindly showed me their favorite restaurants when they were not covering the war for the AP. Unlike the quiet city I remembered from 1963, when there were no American combat troops in the country, Saigon in 1969 looked like an American army town. It was full of bars, and massage parlors with names like Artistic Hand and Magic Fingers. I found a shop selling souvenirs on Tu Do Street in the heart of old Saigon. Among other specialty items, it sold Zippo lighters with personal inscriptions. The young Vietnamese manager showed me a notebook with suggested ideas. I wrote down a few:

- "We are the unwilling, led by the incompetent, to do the unnecessary, for the ungrateful" (probably from an army draftee).
- "Born to love, taught to kill, bound to die" (philosophy).
- "While you live, live in clover, because when you're dead, you're dead forever" (pragmatic).
- "To really live you must nearly die" (more philosophy).
- "For those who have fought for it, life has a flavor the protected will never know" (attributed to a Navy chaplain).
- "Heart breaker, life taker" (self perception of most Marine riflemen).

I thanked the young man and gave him two quotes from Eye Corps, which I added to his notebook:

- "When I kill, all I feel is recoil" (from a sniper's flak jacket).
- "Killing is my business, and business is good" (from a Marine's helmet).

A sharp young lieutenant G-5 who had studied at Oxford University in England and finished a bush tour in the infantry was selected to take the Saigon training course. I will call him Will. I briefed him on the delights of Saigon, from the cafés and shopping tips to the bar that catered to the Marine Security Guards from the embassy. A week went by with no sign of Will. The colonel called me in. "Where's your buddy," he enquired. I opined that officers had probably bumped Will from his flight with higher travel priority. Or maybe he was sick. "Let's give him another day," I suggested. The colonel said "Only one."

Will called later that day from the Da Nang Air Base about 10 miles away. He wanted me to pick him up in my jeep.

"Just hitchhike," I told him. "You won't have any problem getting a lift."

"Normally you're right," he said "but I am wearing the uniform of an Air Force enlisted man."

"Stay where you are," I said, "I'm on my way."

On the ride to division headquarters about five miles from the air base, Will explained his situation. He said he went to the bar I suggested on his first night in Saigon. He had paired off with two ladies instead of one. "I always wanted a tag-team," he explained. "I didn't program funds for two girls so I sold my Marine camouflage uniforms, which are in demand on the black market. They gave me the air force fatigues so I had something to wear. I'm late because the girls freebied me the last night after my money ran out and I went UA" (unauthorized absence.) He added, "What are they going to do, shave my head and send me to Vietnam?"

Will thanked me for the lift, changed into a Marine uniform and went back to work. The next day he stomped into my office with a worried look on his face and in an accusatory in his voice demanded:

"Who did you tell?"

"No one," I replied, honestly. "Why do you ask?"

"I've just been ordered to see the division commander. He must have heard about what I did in Saigon."

"Relax," I said. "Major generals do not chew out lieutenants. That's what captains, majors, and colonels are for." Will calmed down and went to see the general.

Two hours later he was back with a grin on his face. The general, he said, knew nothing of his adventures in Saigon, his wearing an Air Force uniform, or being UA.

"Why did he call you in?" I asked.

"He said he had been reviewing record books and asked me to be his aide-de-camp," Will replied. I said, "No thanks, sir."

Marine lieutenants don't usually say no to generals. I asked, "How did the general take the news?"

"Not well. I explained that I was a reserve officer and would get out of the Corps when my three years were up. I said the job should go to a regular officer to get the experience. The general said he still wanted me. I told him I have a phobia about flying and that generals spend hours in choppers every day and really didn't want the job."

"Are you off the hook?" I asked.

"No. He thanked me for my candor but said his mind is made up." Will smiled, "So I played my ace. I told him three days ago I was UA in Saigon, shacked up with two hookers, and sold my uniforms to pay the girls."

I shook my head. "Jesus, Will, you're in deep shit now. What did the general say?"

"He said, 'now I *know* I want you for my aide.'" And so Will became a general's aide. He survived the helicopter rides and became an author and successful screenwriter in Hollywood.

***

One of the more interesting G-5 projects was providing repairs to the ancient "Japanese bridge" in Hoi An, a coastal town about 10 miles south of Da Nang with a rich history as a center of commerce dating from the 15th century. In the 16th century, Japanese traders built a beautiful covered bridge, the most famous bridge in South Vietnam. By 1969, the bridge was on the verge of collapse. G-5 was asked to help and brought US Navy Construction Battalion (Seabees) in to do the work shoring up the old bridge. They used 12-inch × 12-inch wooden beams purchased, I was told, in Vladivostok, USSR. UNESCO made Hoi An a World Heritage site in 1999 and today it is a major tourist attraction. The bridge, held up by Russian timber, looks good, thanks to US Marines and Navy Seabees.

Life at night at 1st Marine Division headquarters was dull after the excitement of the "bush." We were on the eastern slope of Hill 327, about four miles west of Da Nang. There was an officers' club but it was grim, consisting of a tin-roof "hootch" like the officers' quarters adjacent. There was no air conditioning, no food, and no females as there was no bathroom for women. On the positive side, drinks were 20 cents each. For entertainment there was a ping-pong table. One night I made $240 hustling a lieutenant from Ole Miss who thought he was a whiz at ping-pong. It turned out he wasn't. I told the lieutenants on hand that if I was paid in a day, all drinks were on me. The Mississippian paid up and I hosted all hands all evening for less than $30.

The place to be for a pleasant evening was the Air Force officers' club on the Da Nang Air Base, the Da Nang Officers' Open Mess, known was the DOOM Club. Although Da Nang was off limits to most Marines, we at G-5 had passes that allowed us in. The DOOM Club gave a clue how Air Force officers lived in Vietnam. These were the guys we were protecting and the prime target of the 2nd NVA Division. And they were sometimes protecting us with close air support. The club offered surf and turf (lobster and steak) dinners with a selection of wines in an air-conditioned building. The wait staff were attractive young Vietnamese ladies wearing traditional *ao dai* dresses of white silk pants with turquoise tunics. Every evening there was a film.

Attached to G-5 was a US Army psychological warfare detachment under the command of Captain Tom Kollins, a squared away fellow. One evening, Tom invited me for a film and dinner at the DOOM Club. We drove to the air base through quiet and friendly villages. We found a table at the club and were enjoying a pre-dinner martini when an Air Force major in a flight suit asked if he could join us. We said, of course. The major noticed my camouflage uniform and asked if I was Marine.

"Yes, sir," I said.

"Have you been in combat?" he added.

"Yes sir, seven months. Now I am a Civil Affairs officer at 1st Marine Division Headquarters down the road."

"I have flown close air support missions for the Marines in my (F-4) Phantom, but never met one. What are the villages like out there?"

"Pretty much like the villages outside the base but without the booby traps and Viet Cong."

"I've never been outside the base," the major said.

"How long have you been in country?" I asked.

"Eight months." I invited the major for a post-dinner drink at the Marine officers' club but he declined.

"No thanks lieutenant," he said. "When I'm not in the air, I plan on spending my tour on base."

In 1969, Da Nang's Air Base was the busiest airport in the world, edging out Chicago O'Hare. Its fighters not only supported infantry troops in action, they flew missions flew in harm's way over North Vietnam and Laos. I figured the major had the right to stay as safe as he could for as long as he could.

As my tour in Vietnam drew to an end, I received transfer orders to the 2nd Marine Division in Camp Lejeune, North Carolina. My colonel congratulated me and was taken aback when I said I would not be going.

"What do you mean you're not going?" the colonel demanded. "Orders aren't optional, lieutenant!"

"I was thinking of extending my tour in Vietnam, sir," I responded.

"Oh," said the colonel. "That's different."

The Marines were always looking for people who would extend their tours in Vietnam because by the time someone had learned his job it was almost time to go. I knew that BJ would not be overjoyed by my extending but what neither she nor the colonel knew was that I had been offered a job as a liaison officer in Thailand for the military's R&R program. More than half of my extension would be in Bangkok and BJ could join me. Each R&R city has a liaison officer from the Military Assistance Command, Vietnam (MACV), which funded the R&R program. Its liaison officers were there to make sure the MACV money was well spent. The Marine Corps provided officers to two of the dozen or so sites: Bangkok and Taipei. Honolulu was the only site not in Asia.

To qualify for this plum assignment, an officer had to have served in combat and be on a six-month extension. My Thai-language training from graduate school swung the job in my direction. A senior Marine officer, who had served as an advisor in Thailand, told me about the assignment and said he thought I should go to Thailand. So did I. He made it happen. BJ concurred.

My G-5 supervisor, still unhappy over the night when Lieutenant Jones and I borrowed his jeep for an evening in Da Nang, gave me a choice. I could take the job in Bangkok or receive a Navy Commendation Medal, not both. I did not need the medal and I badly wanted to get back to Bangkok. Jonesy was philosophical when he received a letter of reprimand for his midnight requisition of the colonel's jeep. "A letter of reprimand is better than no mail at all."

***

Bangkok was much changed since I left it six years before. By 1969 the United States had 40,000 US troops—mostly Air Force—serving in Thailand. They flew combat missions in and around Vietnam from bases my father helped construct a few years earlier. I checked into the somewhat seedy but very popular Nana Hotel, where I paid $165 per month for a two-room suite. US Army personnel ran the R&R center in Thailand. The boss—a major, nice guy, ex-enlisted, and a Special Forces officer—had just lost a son killed in action in Vietnam. He was still in mourning and would seek out soldiers from his son's outfit to see if they knew him. An airborne captain, a bit of a wild man, served as his deputy. Half a dozen senior sergeants rounded out the unit. Most of them had Thai wives. At parties I spent much of my time interpreting for couples who spoke little of each other's language.

Of all the R&R sites, I am convinced that GIs got the best bang for a buck in Thailand. The average trooper on R&R in Tokyo, for example, spent $710. The average in Thailand was $290. Tommy's Tours can take much of the credit for the low cost of R7R in Bangkok. Tommy was Tommy Clift, an Anglo-Burman who had fought in World War II as an RAF Spitfire fighter pilot. After Burma's independence Tommy became commander of the Burmese air force. When the Burmese military seized power in a 1963 coup, Tommy fled to Thailand and set up his company. He worked closely with the Royal Thai Air Force generals and in agreement with the US military command in Thailand. It was a pleasure working with him.

Tommy brought more than 50 hotels into a consortium that, in addition to having a liberal guest policy, offered air-conditioned rooms, swimming pools and 24-hour restaurants for $5 a day. Tommy's hotels also had the benefit of having their kitchens and pools inspected by US medical personnel for sanitation.

Tommy's Tours had a monopoly on hotels offering R&R packages to troops but no one was forced to stay in one of the consortium hotels. The US military had certified four other hotels as suitable. Moreover, anyone of any rank was not limited to R&R hotels. They could stay at any hotel in Bangkok but rarely chose high-end hotels that could not compete with the price and amenities of R&R hotels. In addition to the good hotel rates, cabbies in Bangkok often drove their passengers for free; relying instead on commissions from tailors, bars, and massage parlors to make up for lost fares.

On any given day in 1970 there were more than one thousand US troops on R&R in Bangkok. US army personnel assigned to the R&R center in Bangkok greeted soldiers arriving for R&R at Don Muang airport. The soldiers picked a hotel and received briefings on do's and don'ts in Bangkok en route to town in buses. A liaison officer greeted full colonels and above and provide a private briefing while escorting the officer to his or her hotel of choice.

The bulk of my problems came from senior officers. I remember one army colonel in particular. During the briefing on the ride into Bangkok, I suggested a few upscale hotels he might enjoy. "Not necessary, lieutenant," he said. "I would like to go to the 999 Hotel." He gave me an address. It so happened that I had heard of the 999. It was a shabby "short time" hotel/brothel, not far from the Bangkok Officers' Open Mess (BOOM Club). I tactfully tried to point out that the hotel was not really suitable for senior officers. All he said was, "It comes highly recommended." He did not say by whom. I took him there and helped him check in. The desk clerk was a surly lout with little English. I got him the best room and gave him the time and date when I would pick him up six days hence. I gave him my card and wished him a happy R&R.

At the appointed time, I arrived at the 999, but the colonel was not waiting for me. The same desk clerk said with a smirk that the colonel was still in his room "with two lady." I knocked on his door. No answer.

"I know you're in there, colonel. Time to go back to Saigon." No answer.

"Don't make me call the MPs, colonel." Then he spoke.

"I'm not going back. I am taking leave. Shove off lieutenant."

When I answered, it was in Thai. Speaking to the girls, I said "If he is not out in five minutes, you will both go to jail for 30 days. Prostitution is illegal in Thailand and I can have Thai police here in ten minutes."

I heard the girls talking to each other in loud voices. Then talking to the colonel, who appeared, packed, in five minutes. He paid his bill and we rode to the airport in silence. When I wished him a good trip back to Vietnam, his parting words were, "Fuck you, Marine."

One night, Thai police found two GIs lost in Chinatown, far from the bright lights of Petchaburi Road, where most of the bars and nightclubs that catered to R&R troops were located. A friendly Thai policeman called the R&R center, which dispatched a car to pick them up and relocate them. To prevent a repetition, the incoming brief was changed, warning the troops to avoid Chinatown. The next week, Thai police found a dozen GIs lost in Chinatown. The briefing was changed again, omitting any mention of Chinatown, and we never lost a soldier in Chinatown again.

The R&R program was for American servicemen assigned to Vietnam. But sometimes, senior South Korean Army (ROK) officers were allowed to fly to Bangkok from Cam Ranh Bay where the ROKs had an infantry division stationed. Whenever there was an inbound ROK VIP on the way, I received a message from Saigon. I then called Captain Kim at the Korean embassy in Bangkok. He took it from there. Only once did I have a problem. A Korean general, colonel, and captain came to town and Captain Kim picked them up. After they arrived at Don Muang for their return trip, the American civilian airline manager responsible for the charter flight called me to sort out a dilemma. "I hate to bother you, lieutenant," he said, "but the ROKs have sent over seven hundred pounds of luggage for their flight, which leaves in a few hours. They are authorized only one hundred. What should I do?" I said I would get back to him.

I called Captain Kim and explained the situation and emphasized that each person was only authorized 45 pounds of checked luggage each. He thanked me for the call and said he would take care of it. The next call was from a senior American army officer, who had received a call from the Koreans, ordering me to put all of the baggage on the plane. I said no. That's when the colonel learned that not only was I not an army officer, but I didn't work for the military in Thailand. I was a Marine working for MACV in Saigon. The colonel hung up, and minutes later I was called into the office of the major who ran the R&R office. He *was* army and he *did* work for the Thailand command. Sweat was pouring down his face as he begged me to call the airline man at Don Muang and get the baggage on board. I said I would make the call.

I explained to the American civilian that the local command wanted the baggage loaded but that I didn't work for them. Moreover, although I didn't know what the ROKs were shipping I did know that they weren't authorized that much weight. The American told me not to worry; the decision was his. He made the call. The overweight came off the plane. I told him if he got any flak from the army to blame me. In the end, the Koreans flew back to Vietnam; their baggage didn't. The next day the Koreans sent their own plane from Vietnam for the baggage. We never heard another word about the incident.

The BOOM Club, the Bangkok officers' club, was a good place to start an evening on the town. Drinks cost 25 cents. One night while I was entertaining two Royal Thai Marine Corps officers, who were classmates of mine from Quantico, prior to heading out for Thai food, an American colonel walked by. Hearing me speak Thai, the colonel stopped and introduced himself. Daniel Lord Baldwin III, senior advisor to the Royal Thai Army's First Infantry Division, asked if he could join us for a drink. Multiple rows of ribbons, including at least five Purple Heart medals, hung on the colonel's uniform. Often, an officer's ribbons can tell you more than his record can.

Colonel Dan bought a round of drinks and wanted to know what a Marine lieutenant, speaking Thai, was doing in Bangkok. He had commanded Special Forces around the Marine base at Khe Sanh, claimed to have a certain affection for the Corps, and gave me his card. Thus began an unconventional friendship that never would have happened if we had been in the same service. It transpired that Dan was more interested in my Thai language abilities than my being a jarhead grunt. He entertained senior Thai officers a lot, and thought I could be an asset. When he heard that BJ was coming to Bangkok he was appalled that I would consider putting her in the Nana Hotel and insisted that we move into his sumptuous four-bedroom house on Soi Rajakru. His wife had opted to stay in the States so he had the big house to himself. I accepted.

Dan had been wounded numerous times in Korea and Vietnam. One day we went to see the film *MASH* about a US Army field hospital in the Korean War. During the film I noticed that Dan was shaking rather violently. I thought it might be a malaria attack and asked him if he wanted to leave. "No," he whispered. "An Army doctor saved my arm in Korea in a tent that looked just like the one on the screen." He was tough on his officers, some of whom he found wanting. Over breakfast one day he read me several lines from draft fitness reports he was preparing. One was:

"This officer fails to live up to the low standards he has set for himself."

"With constant supervision, this officer does a mediocre job" was another.

These are career-ending words and a hint of what a tough son of a bitch the colonel could be. I offered him a line a British Royal Marine officer had written in a fitness report:

"This officer deprives a village somewhere of its idiot." Dan laughed, and said he would use it for a major he had in mind.

As soon as the school year ended in Seattle, BJ who was teaching at Bothell High School, boarded a plane to Bangkok, her first foreign travel. Installed at Dan's mansion, she loved the experience. Everywhere we went people assumed she was Thai, and were bewildered when I answered questions posed to her in Thai, usually from cab drivers. One night I gave BJ a night tour of Bangkok, starting with the infamous Mosquito Bar, the closest bar available to arriving seamen. We enjoyed dinner at an outdoor Thai restaurant where the female singer serenaded BJ at our table thinking she was Thai. She sang her hit song "Love Letter from a Rented Wife." She was disappointed to learn that BJ was from Hawaii and didn't understand the words of the sad song about an American airman going home without his Thai girlfriend. The singer informed the audience that BJ wasn't Thai but was a Hawaiian. This brought a round of applause for BJ. Two Thai army officers at the next table sent over a half bottle of Thai whiskey. We ended the evening at the coffee shop of the Nana Hotel where I lived before BJ came to town. The roly-poly mama-san came up to the table:

"Lieutenant, long time no see," said the mama-san with a smile.

"Who is this woman?" BJ asked. I explained she ran the place.

"Mama-san, this is my wife," I said, introducing BJ. She smiled at BJ and said:

"Lieutenant, you bullshit me too much." We probably should have skipped the Nana.

When I flew back to Da Nang at the end of my 105-day temporary duty, BJ stayed in Bangkok for a few days, planning to return to Seattle via Japan. I hoped that we could meet in Japan and visit the Osaka World Fair. I rated an R&R for my six-month extension, and broached the subject with the major who was my immediate supervisor at G-5. An unhappy fellow, about to be retired from the Marine Corps having been passed over for promotion, he seemed to dislike people who enjoyed their Vietnam tours, like Jim Jones and I did.

"Major, I would like to put in for an R&R to meet my wife in Tokyo next week," I said.

"You just got back from three months of R&R," he exclaimed. "Forget about Japan!" I asked if I could see the colonel.

"Help yourself," he said, "but forget about taking an R&R."

I went into the colonel's office and handed him the Thai rings, bracelets, and other items he had asked me to buy for his wife and daughters. He thanked me and paid for them. Things were quiet in Da Nang. The First Marine Division was preparing to go home, part of President Nixon's "Vietnamization" of the war. I told the colonel that BJ would be in Tokyo in a week and that if I could get an R&R I would like to meet her there. He said that if I could get a seat for Tokyo I had his blessing. I then called MACV, J-13, in Saigon, the unit that ran the R&R program, and asked to speak to my old boss, an Air Force lieutenant colonel. In two minutes I was booked on a plane from Da Nang to Tokyo.

I arrived late at night in Tokyo to find an army captain standing at the ramp holding up a sign saying BROMAN. I saluted and identified myself. The first thing the captain said was, "Who are you? I am the MACV liaison officer here and I normally don't meet flights with officers under the rank of full colonel. This morning I received a message from J-13 telling me to meet your flight, and to tell you that your wife is waiting for you at the Sanno Hotel." I apologized for putting the captain out, and told him that a week before I was his counterpart in Bangkok. "Say no more," he said. "My boss in Saigon said to give you VIP service." Then he dropped me at the Sanno, the American officers' hotel in downtown Tokyo. BJ and I had a very happy visit to Tokyo, Kyoto, and Osaka. It was her first chance to see her maternal grandparents' homeland and to practice Japanese. When I returned to Vietnam I learned that people were being sent home short-of-tour due to the division's drawdown. So I went home early to my new assignment, Camp Pendleton, California.

***

With less than a year to go on my hitch in the Corps, I found myself back on the West Coast and assigned as Camp Pendleton Press Officer in southern California. I didn't request the job but enjoyed working with the press again, even if I wasn't one of them. I worked for a very squared-away female Marine lieutenant colonel, but my favorite person in the office was a Warrant Officer-4, a rank known as gunner. Gunner Omdahl, a big Swedish-American fellow, sported an outrageous and completely illegal mustache. As a commissioned officer I outranked the gunner, but only technically. He drew a major's pay and turned down a commission. Omdahl had spent decades in press affairs and was a complete pro. One day, we were having a wet lunch in the officers' club when a two-star general walked in. He saw us sitting at the bar and yelled "Omdahl!" The gunner jumped up and stood at attention. The general walked over, inspecting the wild growth under the gunner's nose. I was sure the gunner was going to get chewed out for his non-regulation moustache. "Looking good, gunner," the general said and walked away. The gunner resumed his seat on the barstool and explained, "We served together in the Pacific when he was a lieutenant." I think it was on Guadalcanal.

I led a pleasant and uneventful life at Camp Pendleton until the day the Corps promoted me to captain. The 1st Marine Division had returned from Vietnam and the division commander wanted his infantry company commanders to be captains. This thrust me back in the 1st MarDiv again but this time no one was shooting at me. The highlight of my time as commanding officer of H Company, 2nd Battalion, 7th Marines, was winning the regimental tactical test, especially satisfying as I was the only reserve officer commanding a rifle company. The rest were career Marines.

The test, a 24-hour simulation of the company in combat, had Marine "aggressors" playing the role of the enemy. In peacetime this was an important annual event that gave company commanders bragging rights and also helped with career advancement. This was the first time since the division went to Vietnam in 1965 that the regiment had run a tactical test. I was the only reserve officer in the regiment. I spent an intense day and night of patrolling, attacking, and maneuvering using simulated artillery and air assets in the attack. A senior officer, monitoring my every step, kept throwing obstacles in my path. Since there was no live ammunition involved, it was great fun.

I credit much of the success of my company to the savvy and experienced senior non-commissioned officers of the company, career men with years of combat behind them. My executive officer, First Lieutenant Don Coleman, had been wounded in Vietnam and I suspect would have had a successful career in the Corps if he had stayed. But he was a theater-design major in college and waited for the day he could return to the theater. One day, he asked if he could address the company briefly during morning formation. With the company standing at parade rest, Coleman said, "Men, I want to let you know that my wife will be appearing in the film *Angels Hard as They Come* at the Camp Pendleton drive-in theater this week. And she's topless." The company went en masse to the R-rated biker film in which Mrs. Coleman exposed her ample bosom emblazoned with the words "Property of Hell's Angels."

First Lieutenant Sam Garland, a Virginian who enlisted in the Corps right out of high school and earned his commission in Vietnam, replaced Coleman as my executive officer. One day during a tactical exercise in the beautiful hills of Camp Pendleton, the point man halted the company with the words "Rattlesnake at 2 o'clock." I looked off to the right and saw a big rattler coiled up on a flat rock. We did not carry live ammunition so I walked gingerly up to the six-foot reptile and pointed my M-16 rifle at its head at a distance of about six inches and fired. The wadding in the blank round took off the snake's head. "Dinner," I told Sam when he walked up. "Can I have the skin, skipper, to make a belt?" he asked. Sam got his belt and BJ made an excellent teriyaki rattlesnake that night, grilled on her hibachi. I didn't kill any more wildlife at Camp Pendleton.

As my time in the Marines neared an end, I recalled the words of the CIA recruiter I talked to while in grad school three years before who said, "If you live, give me a call six months before you leave the Corps." I called the number in Portland not expecting it would lead to anything. The recruiter answered the phone, I told him I had survived Vietnam, was stationed at Camp Pendleton, and looking for work. He said, "Hold on, let me get your file." Thirty seconds later he said, "Meet me in the lobby of the Coronado Hotel in San Diego next Thursday. Wear your uniform."

The meeting went well. The recruiter pronounced me qualified to be either an analyst in the Directorate of Intelligence or an operations officer in the Clandestine Service. I told him I was only interested only in operations, and asked what pay I could expect. He said that with my AP and Marine experience along with my MA, I could start as a GS-10 with an automatic promotion of GS-11 in a year, if I lasted that long. As a captain I already made GS-10 pay. He told me they might try to get me to sign up for lower pay but that I should be firm. He was right; some my classmates came in one or two grades lower. Farewell Marines; hello CIA. My next stop was Langley, Virginia.

For the record, I believed, and still do, that the Vietnam War was a just war but poorly fought. We should not go to war unless we are prepared to win it. Winning never seemed to have been on the minds of the politicians who sent us to Vietnam. We never lost a battle. In fact, we didn't lose the war. We went home. The last American combat troops left Vietnam in 1972. We cut off military support for our South Vietnamese allies in 1975 and the North Vietnamese took power. The same thing happened with our Cambodian allies next door. They fought almost to the last round. When the Khmer Rouge started their reign of terror in 1975 there were two bombs left in the Cambodian Air Force arsenal. Things would have been very different if we had cut the Ho Chi Minh Trail.

I have been back to Vietnam numerous times since the war, including extensive travel in northern Vietnam. I have never had any problem in the north when men there learned I had fought against them. However, in the south, when old South Vietnamese veterans learned I had served in the war, they inevitably asked, bitterly, "Why you leave us?" I had no good answer.

During the war in Cambodia, Alan Dawson of UPI gave me a much-copied audiocassette tape made by three drunken US Air Force officers serving in Vietnam. The tape is known as *What the Captain Meant to Say*. It purports to be an interview with a fighter-bomber pilot in the presence of an Air Force Public Information Officer (PIO) who corrects each answer from the pilot with the words, "what the captain meant to say." For example, the "journalist" asks, "Captain did you ever go after the bridges in the jungles of North Vietnam?" "You bet your ass I did," said the pilot. "I must have dropped 50 tons of bombs on those swinging bamboo mothers and never hit one of them." The PIO explains, "What the captain meant to say is that we find it very effective to crater the approaches to the bridges."

At the end of the interview, the journalist thanks the pilot and asks, "Could you sum up the war in a few words?"

"You bet your ass I could," says the pilot. "It's a fucked up war."

The PIO says, "What the captain meant to say is, it's a fucked up war."

And so it was.

CHAPTER 4

Spy

My father, who was lukewarm about my being a photojournalist and barely tolerated my joining the Marine Corps, positively loved my going into the Central Intelligence Agency. My only concern was his ability to keep it a secret. If all went well, I would be under cover my entire career.

It proved a propitious time for someone with my experience to work for the Agency. In 1971 with the Cold War in full spate, shooting wars under way in Vietnam, Cambodia, and Laos and Thailand threatened by communists, I hoped to go back to Southeast Asia.

Although I received my security clearance in June 1971, BJ's background check took longer because her father was born in the Philippines. The Career Training (CT) program had two classes per year: one in July and one in January. Missing the July class meant joining the January class. After three busy years in the Marine Corps, I welcomed the break and we decided to explore Europe. However, a short 10 days after I left the Marines, BJ's clearance had come through. Europe would have to wait. We drove across the country in four days and on June 15, 1971 I began my career in the Agency.

At that time, the Agency had about 20,000 employees organized in four directorates: Operations, Intelligence, Administration, and Science & Technology. The sharp end of the spear of the Agency is the Directorate of Operations (DO), home of the Clandestine Service (CS), a small percentage of the Agency's population charged with conducting espionage and sometimes covert military action authorized by the president. CS case officers are not spies; they recruit and "run" agents for the Directorate of Intelligence (DI) who are the actual spies. The raw intelligence provided by the CS is analyzed in the DI along with an enormous amount of "open" source information. They produce "finished" intelligence, which is then provided to the Agency's "customers" headed by the president of the United States.

The Agency organized the DO geographically, into area divisions. My goal was being accepted into the Far East Division (now East Asia Division). The largest of the area divisions, it had three main interest areas: China, Japan, and Southeast

Asia. I was interested only in the latter. Rather like a fraternity, you had to be asked to join.

On day one, I met my classmates. We numbered about 30, mostly male, mostly white. Most of us had been in the military, which was not surprising since the United States still had the draft. A few had advanced degrees and most had experience overseas. One fellow only wanted to serve in India; his wish was granted. At our first break, we found out our starting civil service ranks which ran the gamut from GS-7, the equivalent of second lieutenant, to GS-10, the equivalent of captain. The agency determined incoming civil service grades based on experience, languages, military service, and educational degrees.

Other classmates with similar qualifications came in at lower grades. I followed my recruiter guidance to accept only a GS-10 and got it. Others either had not received this advice or didn't follow it. We all joined the company credit union and I was surprised to see that a number of my classmates immediately applied for loans.

The agency assigned us each an "advisor," someone we could contact if we had questions or problems. My advisor, an experienced operations officer, had a background in Asian affairs. At our first meeting I noticed all of the memorabilia that decorated his office. One item that drew my attention looked like a large white plaster cast of a human molar, measuring about twelve inches on a side. When I asked what it was, he took if off the wall and placed in on a table. "In my youth," he said, "I was an analyst working on Vietnam during the French war. In 1954 the Viet Minh at Dien Bien Phu surrounded French forces and the French asked President Eisenhower to provide massive air support. This is a model of the Dien Bien Phu valley that I used as a visual aide when I briefed the president on the situation there. The Viets had the high ground with artillery and the French, exposed on the low grounds in the valley, were getting chewed up."

"What happened?" I asked.

"Ike looked at the model as I briefed him. At the end, the president said, 'They're fucked.' The French did not get the support they requested," he said. American CIA pilots flew clandestine missions to support to the French at Dien Bien Phu but it was too little, too late.

After a week of orientation, the Agency assigned each of us to an area desk for three months as an interim assignment with both the Directorate of Operations (DO) and the Directorate of Intelligence (DI), The idea was to give incoming officers exposure to both the operational and analytical sides of the Agency. I did my first three months on the Cambodia desk of the DO, where I quickly became involved in the running of a small CIA field station in the middle of a brutal war. The Agency put me on the Cambodia desk of the Office of Current Intelligence (OCI) in the DI for my second three-month training stint. This introduced me to not only how field intelligence was gathered and disseminated, but also how analysts took this information and—weighing it with multiple covert and overt sources—produced an analysis of a situation for policy makers.

In a stroke of good fortune, I worked for Serge Taube on the Cambodia desk. Known as the "The Grey Fox," Serge became my mentor. Descended from Volga Germans, who were recruited in the 18th century by Catherine the Great (a Prussian princess) to move to Russia, Serge spoke native Russian and French. The Cambodia desk fell under Vietnam Operations (VNO), run by Dan Arnold, one of the "mandarins" of the DO. As a young enlisted Marine, Dan was wounded in the Pacific in World War II. Now he was the equivalent of a three-star general in the Corps.

One day, I needed to make a "secure" call to the FBI. Since Dan's office had one of the few secure phones in the division, I arranged to use the phone while Dan was at lunch. During the phone call, as I looked out the window at the trees surrounding the headquarters building, I sensed a presence in the room. Slowly, I turned to find Dan himself standing about one foot behind me. "Have a seat," I said, "I'll be with you in a minute." Showing no emotion, Dan sat at his desk as I finished my call. He then welcomed me to the division. Although we had not met, he knew I had just joined from the Marine Corps and asked me about my service in Vietnam. A few years later I served under Dan in the field. He became another important mentor and a friendship developed that transcended our time in government service.

At the end of my two interim assignments I was offered jobs by both the DO and the DI. I enjoyed my time on the Cambodia desk of the Office of Current Intelligence (sometimes called Of Continuing Interest) in the DI and even had a short piece appear in the President's Daily Brief (PDB), the top secret and most prestigious daily publication in Washington. However, I wanted a career abroad with the DO. This required doing well in a six-month operational training course that was next on my agenda. That would take place at the large and rather elegant training facility in Virginia known as the Farm. It had an airfield and state-of-the-art facilities. Instruction focused on everything: teaching espionage, weapons familiarization, and parachute jumping. It was the best training I ever received.

My classmates were an assortment of ex-military, academics, area specialists, and adventurers. They all had interesting stories. One, a Cuban-American had debated Fidel Castro in the 1950s while earning a PhD in political science in Havana. Captured at the Bay of Pigs fiasco in 1961 (thank Jack and Bobby Kennedy for that), he was ransomed by the United States government and went on to serve in the Special Forces in Vietnam before joining the Agency. We had a young woman who had been an Agency secretary in a foreign country where she was arrested by the host government. She had handled herself so well the Agency offered her a chance to become an operations officer. Another classmate had been a contract paramilitary officer working with the Bolivian Army patrol that captured Che Guevara in 1967. My best friend at the Farm, Johnny, had also been a paramilitary officer who had performed well in Laos. He was converted to staff officer and sent to the Farm. We planned to serve together in Asia but he was killed in action on his second deployment to Laos in 1972. He was the first of my friends to earn a star on the Wall of Remembrance in the lobby of CIA's headquarters building for officers who have died in the line of duty. By 2017 there were 127 stars on the wall. A number of them were friends of mine.

The Basic Ops Course focused on "tradecraft" or, put another way, how to commit espionage and get away with it. Espionage, or spying, is sometimes called the second oldest profession (prostitution being the first) and is sometimes considered no more honorable than the first. Case officers obtain intelligence that cannot be obtained through overt means. A wise old case officer said the mission was simple: "We are in the business of making dreams come true. Everyone has a dream. Maybe starting a new life in America or putting children through university. Some people want money to buy a dacha in a birch forest outside Moscow. We can make those dreams come true, but they have to work their passage."

Being a CIA case officer is not a job for the timid. It sometimes requires you to put your life on the line, but more often involves putting the life of your agents on the line. Most often, when spies are caught, they are executed. Both case officers and the agents they "run" lead dangerous lives. I sleep better at night knowing that none of the dozens of agents I recruited or handled were ever caught. Moreover, I was never identified committing espionage. The ensuing "flap" can damage US relations with that country. Part of the reason I was never caught was the training at the Farm.

We spent a lot of our time at the Farm role-playing in a scenario where we learned how to perform acts of espionage on the streets of America. One day, one of my classmates was preparing to meet an "agent" in a hotel room to photograph sensitive documents. One of our better instructors, a salty old Asia hand, who kept his trainees on their toes, played the agent. I will call him "Ben." He had a fondness for alcohol. Not only did he show up for the meeting drunk, but also had a young woman of dubious character in tow. This was against the rules, but Ben was of an older generation and was known to sometimes bend the rules.

The scene began with Ben asking his "case officer" if the room had been paid for in advance. The young trainee was aghast that Ben would be so unprofessional as to bring a prostitute with him. Ben assured him that they could conduct business in 20 minutes. The case officer could then be on his way, and that then Ben and his companion would stay in the room for a while. When the case officer told Ben he could not bring the woman into the room, Ben exploded. "You CIA pukes piss me off. Here are the documents, photograph them, and get out of here." The young lady, unhappy to be kept waiting in the hallway, yelled, "CIA! What the fuck is going on here?" While Ben tried to calm her down, the case officer packed up his camera gear and vacated the hotel very upset and ready to blow the whistle on Ben.

It later transpired that Ben was not drunk, nor was the girl a "working girl." She was, in fact, the daughter of another instructor who had been brought along by Ben to role-play or, as he put it, "to throw a little shit in the game." My classmate did the right thing and got out of there. A successful case officer must be flexible.

One evening we had an exercise on how to handle a "walk in." This is someone who wants to provide intelligence in the hope they can then defect to the United States. Officers in the Soviet KGB (civilian intelligence service) or GRU (Soviet military intelligence) were at the top of the list of people we wanted. The ideal "walk in" would be an officer willing to go home and "work in place" before being granted asylum. We waited in our roles, about to play the role of a duty officer. They should expect a walk in to approach their facility. At the appointed hour, I heard knocking on doors along the corridor. The walk ins had arrived. I answered my door and found a senior instructor of eastern European origin with many years of dealing with "Ivan," our Soviet target.

I welcomed him and began to go through established procedures. He identified himself as a Soviet military intelligence (GRU) officer but beyond that refused to cooperate. He became hostile when I tried to pin him down with questions. With the conversation not going so well, I offered him a drink, which he quickly accepted. "Ivan" began drinking my vodka but still refused to open up. We talked about his job, his family, how his career was going, and as we talked he continued to put a large dent in my vodka bottle. I began to hear doors opening as my colleagues finished their exercises, said good night to their walk ins, and headed out to write up cables reporting the events. My guy just kept drinking. Hours ticked by. My peers were returning to their rooms and going to sleep. In four hours I had achieved very little. My new friend had not left and was beginning to unload all his problems on me. He had problems at home and problems at work.

In the early hours of the morning, the vodka bottle empty, he exclaimed, "Now I trust you." He explained why he had approached the Americans and what he needed. That began a new round of negotiations, which took a few more hours. Eventually, he produced some documents to prove his bona fides and agreed to meet again after I reported his approach. He went home to bed. I went to work writing up the events of the evening. The next day, the instructor approached me and profusely apologized for the lengthy interaction the night before. "I know the exercise should have taken only a few hours but I was having too much fun. I want you to know how these things really work. I liked the way you handled me, so I cooperated. I hope you learned something from this exercise. Walk-ins often become our best agents. And thank you for the vodka."

The Farm also brought in guest speakers. One had been chief of station in a "denied area," a country of the Soviet-led Warsaw Pact. These stations often had the best and brightest of the men and women of the Clandestine Service. They are the ones who recruit and handle some of the best agents working to assist the

United States in the Cold War. Their courage and coolness in life-and-death situations is inspiring. Our visitor described the very short "brush pass" he made with an agent during a critical moment in the Cold War. The officer had to make the brief meeting knowing he was under surveillance. If caught, he would immediately be sent home. It would be much worse for the agent who would face torture before execution. The meeting was meticulously planned and the pass timed to the second. The case officer would spend hours walking, shopping, having lunch, in preparation for turning on a corner near an alley. He only had a few seconds before surveillance caught up with him. The agent was standing at the entrance of the alley. He would receive a package of microfilm from the agent and pass him new requirements. When our officer put his hand out to receive the agent's microfilm, he felt his hand being grabbed. He feared that the operation was over. He was caught. The United States had lost a brave asset. However, when the case officer looked at the man who was still holding his hand he saw it was the agent. "Thank you for coming," the agent said, "I know it was not easy." After passing along important information, the agent turned and ran down the alley. Seconds later, our officer was back on the street undetected.

As I mentioned, joining the Clandestine Service is much like joining a fraternity or sorority. At the end of each running of the Basic Ops Course, each area division sent its chief and one or two associates to encourage the selected to join their division, much like fraternity "rush" week. As part of the ritual, each division chief gave a talk about the benefits of joining their division and then spent the evening chatting with students at the Farm's officer club where the real action took place. When the Chief of Africa Division came to speak, I wanted to talk to him because he had been chief of station in Laos. I approached him at the bar and he bought me a drink. I asked a few questions about Laos. He answered, but then said, "I know you're going to the Far East Division [later East Asia Division]. Bugger off and let me do some headhunting for Africa." I moved off, happy in the knowledge that I was going where I wanted to go. It didn't hurt that I graduated top of my class.

Back in Langley, I was assigned to a desk to prepare for my first assignment. Since I already spoke the language I didn't need training. Then Serge Taube, still chief of the Cambodian desk and about to leave for a posting as deputy chief of station, Phnom Penh, told me that an important post was opening up in Phnom Penh. He asked me to take the job. I told him I was already under orders to Bangkok. "I know that," he said, "and I can fix it." I wasn't sure anything needed fixing but Serge put me straight. "That station is big and you could be lost in the shuffle," he said. "Phnom Penh is small and Cambodia is at war. You will make your career in Cambodia where every man is handpicked. I pick you." When I explained the offer to BJ, she said OK even though accepting the Cambodia assignment meant another separated tour. For BJ, ever the trooper, the upside this time was that she would be "safe-havened" in Bangkok, an hour by air from Phnom Penh, and that I would visit every month.

The Agency changed my orders and assigned me to Phnom Penh. Since the posting required me to speak French, Serge got me enrolled in a 20-week intensive course in the French language. During this excellent but stressful training, a small group—no more than five in a class—studied six hours of French instruction every day. We spoke no English. Teachers changed every four weeks.

At one point my class had shrunk to just two of us, me and a senior Foreign Service officer assigned to Africa, trying to conjugate subjunctive French verbs. I couldn't tell him that I worked for the Agency. We became friends, and eventually he said, "I can get your orders changed. You shouldn't go to Cambodia. Let me do some work." I thanked him but pointed out that I was an Indochina hand and wanted the assignment. A few years later, he bumped into one of my State Department friends in Geneva. Knowing my friend had been posted to Cambodia, the Africa officer mentioned my name and said I was one of his best friends in the Agency. "The Agency!" cried the Africa hand, "Son of a bitch!" My friend smiled. "Need to know," he said, and the subject was dropped.

Every Friday afternoon while I was in language training, I would stop by Agency headquarters to catch up on events in Cambodia and take care of administrative matters. One day, I was running on the track in the basement of the building with a former Marine Corps buddy of mine. In the locker room after our run I was telling my friend of the excellence of the French program and how officers were motivated to do well by not being promoted until they had achieved proficiency in at least one foreign language.

An elderly, heavy-set man overheard my comments and interceded. "My wife teaches French in the Agency's language school," he said, "and our school is far better." I didn't argue with the officer but pointed out that there was little pressure to excel at our school. The old fellow was not pleased.

"Bullshit!" he exclaimed, "Do you know who I am? I'm a DO division chief."

"No offense," I offered. "Do you know who I am?" I asked.

"No" he said.

"That's good," I answered. He laughed and walked away.

Serge went off to Cambodia while I labored in language training but he came home for a family emergency. We invited him to dinner. BJ outdid herself preparing an elegant French meal that Serge relished. He warned me that Cambodia was going to be extremely challenging but also promised to guide me through my first year. He hinted that when the military situation permitted, BJ could fly into Cambodia for brief visits on one of our aircraft. Then he said something strange and prophetic. "When you get to Phnom Penh you are going to meet an embassy officer named Tim," Serge said. "He is going to become one of your best friends." I had never heard of Tim and it seemed a weird thing for Serge to say. But he was right.

***

Protocol required that I write to my new post. The administrative officer made all the arrangements to welcome and house new arrivals. While I was drafting my letter, an old Indochina hand, Stan, looked over my shoulder. "Where are you staying in Phnom Penh?" he asked.

"Le Phnom," I answered, "That's where they usually put incoming personnel." This was the old Le Royal, Phnom Penh's finest hotel.

"Let me make a suggestion," Stan said. "Show them you know your way around. Forget the Phnom, it's a dump. Ask for Hotel de la Poste. It is an old colonial place opposite the post office near the river. And it is right next door to La Taverne, the best bistro in town."

"Sounds good to me," I said, thanking Stan.

"And," he added, "I suggest you ask for room number nine; it's the best." I took his advice. In due course the administrative officer answered my letter. Someone would meet my flight. I was booked in room nine of Hotel de la Poste.

My Air Cambodge Caravelle aircraft (Motto: Lose your clothes, fly Air Cambodge) touched down in Phnom Penh on a blisteringly hot May 1, 1973, 10 years to the day after I had first landed in Cambodia as a 19-year-old Associated Press photographer covering the president of China's visit to Cambodia. I saw an American-looking young man in a Palm Beach suit standing on the tarmac, but I walked right by him when it appeared he was looking for someone else. However, there was no one waiting for me in the arrival hall. The fellow approached me and asked if I spoke English. I said I did. He asked if I saw a black male passenger on the plane. I said I hadn't. Then he asked, "Is your name Broman?" I said yes. "Son of a bitch," he exclaimed and then laughed. He identified himself as the officer I would be replacing, and welcomed me to Cambodia. It seems the office wag had told him that Broman was black for reasons I never understood. It may have been to do with the officer's southern pedigree, whose ancestors had fought with distinction for the Confederacy in the War Between the States.

He drove me to Hotel de la Poste, noting that no one he knew had ever stayed there. I told him I had been in Phnom Penh before and wanted to try it. Room number nine turned out to be a little seedy with a bed that sagged in the middle but it was large and quite pleasant. A few weeks later I received a note from Stan asking how I liked Phnom Penh and if the bed he had broken on his last visit had been repaired.

I spent my first evening in Phnom Penh at a hail and farewell for my predecessor, whose southern drawl hid the fact that he was Yankee educated with degrees from Harvard, Yale, and Princeton. The quiet affair comprised mostly junior officers and introduced me to the men and women I would be working with for the next two years. At the end of the evening, Tim, the officer Serge had told me about, offered me a ride back to my hotel. On the way, he suggested we stop by his villa for a nightcap, and I accepted with pleasure. Tim, a military brat like me, broke out a bottle of Irish whiskey, which we drank neat on his verandah accompanied by the sounds of outgoing artillery in the background.

Tim, an MIT graduate and a fluent Cambodian-language speaker, had studied at the University of Grenoble and also spoke excellent French, the official language of the Cambodian government. Tim had also served in Saigon during the Tet offensive of 1968. We talked through the night and he gave me an excellent briefing of Cambodia at war, a subject he knew better than almost anyone else. Like me, Tim was a service brat. He had lived in Taiwan as an Army dependent while I had been in England and Thailand as an Air Force dependent. We finished the bottle of Irish whiskey and the next thing we knew the sun was coming up and the whiskey bottle was empty. We had coffee, shaved and went to work. It was a nice welcome to Cambodia. I thought to myself that Serge Taube was a smart fellow.

When I arrived in Phnom Penh in 1973, the country had been at war for three years. On March 18, 1970, military and civilian leaders deposed Prince Norodom Sihanouk while he was out of the country. The Cambodian parliament unanimously supported the putsch because Sihanouk had allowed the North Vietnamese to transit neutral Cambodia to attack South Vietnam. Sihanouk also permitted the North Vietnamese to use the port of Sihanoukville to ship war material through Cambodia.

The coup d'état put General Lon Nol, a long-time Sihanouk loyalist and marginally effective military leader, in charge of the country. Sihanouk was on his way to China from the Soviet Union when he received the bad news that he had been overthrown. The arch-royalist and longtime foe of the Cambodian communists did a quick about-face and gave his full support to the Khmer Rouge. In his book (written with considerable assistance from Australian communist Wilfred Burchett) *My War with the CIA*, Sihanouk falsely blamed the Agency for the coup.

Lon Nol quickly decided to invite American and South Vietnamese forces into Cambodia to fight the thousands of North Vietnamese soldiers already there. This led to a limited incursion that for a time disrupted the flow of men and materiel into South Vietnam. However, President Richard Nixon was under pressure to get out of Indo-China, and the opportunity to inflict serious damage on the North Vietnamese was lost.

The United States did not deploy American troops to Cambodia. We had no military advisors working with the poorly led, trained, and equipped Cambodian armed forces. The number of American officials allowed in Cambodia was capped at two hundred. This included all embassy personnel, CIA officers, USAID workers, and military assistance deliverymen, and embassy Marine guards. We had a daily head count. If officials from Washington, for example, pushed the number over two hundred, someone had to leave the country.

***

I settled in to work quickly, handling my stable of assets and working directly for the chief of station (COS). He was a genteel Southern aristocrat whom I will call Laird. Laird was rarely seen outside the office. For one thing, he was not well. For another, he was a very private man. Every Sunday he ate alone at the Hotel Phnom restaurant by the pool where he could have been mistaken for a Frenchman with his urbane manner and excellent French. The only time I ever saw him express emotion was with his bulldog, Hannibal.

Laird, nevertheless, enjoyed a good relationship with the embassy and spent much of his time meeting with senior Cambodian officials, both civil and military. The Cambodian military suffered from poor leadership and lack of resources. One of his contacts was so senior that Laird asked Langley if he should report the relationship to the ambassador. Apparently, the Agency broached the matter directly with Henry Kissinger who was serving as both Secretary of State and National Security Advisor. Laird told me that Kissinger, wearing his National Security hat, said not to tell the ambassador.

In addition to acting in a liaison role with the Cambodian government, Laird handled two senior military officers who wanted to lead a coup d'état against the

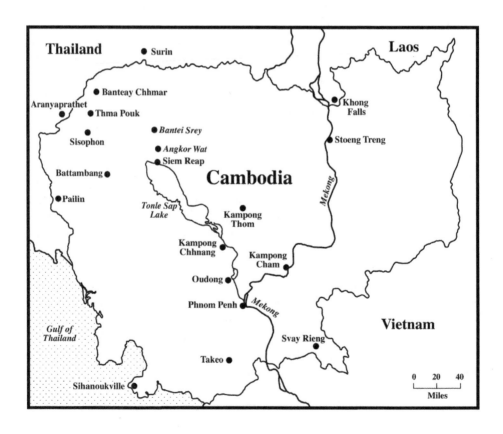

ineffectual and corrupt Lon Nol regime. Washington didn't want any changes at the top, and both officers were signed up as reporting assets.

Serge Taube, the Deputy Chief of Station, handled liaison with the Cambodian military intelligence and police services. He also kept an eye on me and encouraged me to be active on the diplomatic circuit as well as around town, including fraternizing with both branches of the Cambodian royal family, the Norodoms and Sisowaths. After being ousted in 1970, Prince Norodom Sihanouk sided with the Khmer Rouge and their Chinese backers. Many of his supporters and family remained in Phnom Penh. Prince Sirik Matak, an able and honest man who helped mount the coup against Sihanouk, led the Sisowath branch of the royal family. With plenty of intrigue afoot in Phnom Penh, not to mention a shooting war, a young spook had a lot to cut his teeth on.

Serge wanted me to develop a wide net of contacts with a view towards recruiting some of them—"targets"—as unilateral reporting sources. In other words, spies. He told me that 10 percent of case officers recruited 90 percent of our best clandestine sources. He groomed me to be one of these "headhunters."

Phnom Penh station was not typical. We didn't have to worry about working against traditional "hard targets," Soviets, Chinese, narcotics traffickers, and such. We focused solely on the war. All officers had to speak French or Khmer. Most of us were "declared" to the host government and worked together with Cambodian officials to gather intelligence about the Khmer Rouge and ideally to recruit assets inside the Khmer Rouge. Two officers were not declared. They handled penetrations of the Cambodian government and other sensitive matters. The best asset I "handled" was a bright, well-connected fellow who was the station's leading producer of intelligence.

Laird was a South Carolinian, a descendant of a British deputy governor of the colony while another ancestor served as a general with the rebels during the American Revolution. A life-long bachelor who had studied in Paris and spoke fluent French, Laird was soft-spoken but tough. I worked directly for him, and my reporting went through him before being transmitted to Langley. He handled some very senior assets, while Serge Taube handled liaison contacts in the Cambodian military and police.

Laird believed we should "give them their intelligence with their coffee." This meant that our reporting on the internal target was perishable and therefore needed to be disseminated as quickly as possible. If it was 8AM in Langley, it was 8PM in Phnom Penh. I met most of my agents at night before the 10 o'clock curfew. If I met an asset at eight, I wrote my reports fast and took them to Laird for approval. Then back to the office for transmission to Langley. Sometimes, the span of time between meeting an agent and sending the report to Headquarters took less than 90 minutes. The analysts got their intelligence with their coffee.

It was apparent that Laird was in poor health. In fact, he was denied medical clearance for his Cambodian assignment until the director of central intelligence personally intervened and approved the assignment. Laird had a dour countenance and was all business. But one night he thanked me for coming with a report just before curfew. He read the report quickly, signed off and handed it back with the words "Take the rest of the day off." It was only then I knew he had a sense of humor.

For most of my tour in Cambodia, the ambassador was John Gunther Dean, a career Foreign Service Officer with a distinguished record. He led the embassy through difficult times with courage and, at the end, with chagrin. I had little direct contact with him but found him supportive and congenial. Once we were partnered in a tennis match at the Australian ambassador's court. I was serving; Dean was at the net. My service hit the ambassador directly on the back of his head. Dean turned and in a calm voice said, "Not a good career move Broman." Everyone in earshot laughed.

Despite the difficulties of daily life, largely no electricity and frequent incoming rockets, Phnom Penh had its charms. It had the air of a colonial French city complete with spacious villas, a few excellent French and Chinese restaurants, and fresh French bread. I lived in an art deco villa, known as the "escargot house" because it was built on the round with no corners, in a fashionable neighborhood. I spent most of my time there on the large verandah with dozens of potted plants, including one marijuana plant that had been a house-warming gift from a Cambodian friend. The same friend also gave me the recipe for a favorite national soup that called for chicken, tomatoes, and pineapples, garnished with chopped marijuana which cost about fifty cents a kilo in the market.

Happily, I inherited one of the finest chefs in the city from a departing officer. Of French-Vietnamese ancestry, Jeannot Martin had served as a pastry chef in the French Army. Somehow, he managed to house his Vietnamese wife and about 8 of their 19 children in the servant quarters. His two eldest daughters, Nga and Loan, worked as maids. When carrying food or drinks up the spiral staircase, they did it on the run to avoid a large and ugly tokay gecko that lived behind the wood paneling. The gecko, which looked very much like a gila monster, frequently poked his head out looking for something to eat. He never attacked the girls but kept the mosquito population down. Cambodians considered it lucky to have a gecko and although the house was struck four times by shrapnel from incoming rocket fire, no one was ever hit.

One evening, I ventured into the kitchen to check on preparations for a dinner party to find three French women there whom I did not know. One quickly explained that she saw Jeannot shopping for dinner in the central market and when she learned that dessert was going to be the classic, towering *croquembouche*, she asked if she could come along to watch it being made. She brought two friends. The only problem in learning how to cook from Jeannot was that he never measured. But the food was always spectacular and desserts were his specialty.

On the verandah of my villa in Phnom Penh, Cambodia, with the two daughters of my French-Vietnamese cook Jeannot Martin. Loan, left, and Nga worked as maids. I am holding a vintage M-3 "grease gun," a gift from embassy political officer Bill Harbin upon his departure from Cambodia.

I entertained mainly to repay my social obligations and to show off Jeannot's cuisine. He gave me a white tablecloth for Christmas, saying good French food deserved it. Tim hosted dinners more frequently than I did. He had a wide assortment of friends, mostly diplomats and influential Cambodian officials. He often served excellent Cambodian food and his evenings always featured dancing after dinner. I counted myself lucky to be a frequent guest. The parties rarely went late, as many guests had to be home before curfew. Frequent electrical outages made air conditioning unreliable so Tim often served dinner on the verandah outdoors. One evening a visitor from Washington was the guest of honor, and at the sound of heavy artillery he threw himself on the floor in a panic. No one else moved. Tim leaned over. "Outgoing," he announced. "Friendly fire." There was a Cambodian artillery battalion nearby, at work. Embarrassed, the visitor took his seat and tried to resume eating. A few minutes later, everyone hit the deck, as an incoming 107mm rocket approached. The guest remained seated until Tim yelled, "Get down! Incoming." It didn't take long to learn the difference between "friendly" and "unfriendly" fire.

The French naval attaché lived next door to me. Like many of the French in Phnom Penh, he associated mostly with other French people. He owned a large and vicious Alsatian dog. One morning, as I was leaving for work in my armored Pinto car, the dog got out and began mauling a small Cambodian child. I grabbed the M-16 rifle from my not-very-efficient day guard and tried to get a shot at the dog without hitting the kid. The attaché's cook, hearing the child screaming, came out and dragged the dog away. The little boy ran off bleeding, and I told the cook if I ever saw the dog outside again I would shoot it. I gave the gun back to the guard, one of three who "protected" me in three shifts. All I expected of them was to let me know we were under attack before they ran.

A few weeks later, I was driving home for lunch when I saw a group of Khmer soldiers gathered around in front of my house. Most were guards of the city's mayor who lived across the street. I stopped the car and Nga, my maid, ran over. The attaché's dog had gotten out and was killed by a passing car. "What are the soldiers doing?" I asked. "Butchering the dog," she said. Cambodians are not known for eating dog but fresh meat was expensive and out of reach for most Cambodian soldiers. The dog had never missed a meal and probably weighed 40 pounds. The soldiers were expertly cutting up the dog in my front yard and sharing it with my guards, who already had a wok heating up. I watched as bits of the hound was sautéed in oil and peppers. I was offered a taste; it was delicious. The dog's head was resting nearby. I had it returned to the owner in a hatbox. A few weeks later I was at the Cercle Sportif for a tennis match and saw a group of French officers at the bar; one of them was my neighbor. He pointed at me and I heard him say in French: "That's him! He's the guy who ate my dog." I nodded with a thin smile and was never troubled by my neighbor's dogs again.

In 1974, Laird was replaced by Dave, a tough, gruff, pipe-smoking pacer who had served in the British Army's Gordon Highlanders in World War II. Dave served the Agency with distinction in the Congo in the early 1960s and was very familiar with running intelligence operations in a poor country at war. There was bad blood between Laird and Dave dating from the 1950s. Laird declined to put Dave up in his palatial residence and instead booked him into a hotel that often lacked electricity. Laird also refused to turn over his two senior agents to Dave and instead turned them over to me, his most junior officer.

Dave's leadership style differed significantly from Laird's. He did not expect me to make late-night visits to the chief's residence with intelligence reports. They could wait until working hours the next day. Unlike Laird, a Paris-educated Francophile, Dave was very pro-British and had served in London Station. With my prep school English education and combat experience, Dave and I got along fine. One night, over Cognac at his villa, the phone rang and Dave answered. A few minutes later he returned and said there had been an incident at one of our upcountry sites. The town was taking mortar fire and our officer was requesting to be pulled out. "What did you tell him?" I asked. "Hold until dawn," he replied. Then he chuckled, poured himself another snifter of Remy Martin, added, "The man is a good officer but drinks too much. The city is not under ground attack. In the morning he will be sober and alive. Know your men," he counseled.

Dealing with Langley was usually a no-nonsense business. I only recall one instance when humor was injected into an otherwise deadly serious routine. Agents are known in communications and even verbally by their cryptonyms to prevent the use of their true names. These code names are assigned by Headquarters. Two of my assets were senior military officers. One had a cryptonym close to the word VALIANT. The other's was something like DOMINATOR. This bothered another station officer who had a military agent with a cryptonym like SLIPSHOD. He remonstrated to the chief of station who agreed, his agent needed a better code name. Headquarters agreed. The asset's cryptonym was changed to something close to PATHFINDER along with a comment that Langley hoped this would lead to better results on the battlefield and in his reporting.

***

Most CIA case officers avoid the press like the plague, and with good reason. The spy business makes for good copy, and journalists are always looking for a story. But having worked as a journalist myself, I liked hanging around foreign correspondents. The professions are not that far apart. We all are looking for sources and for information.

It is CIA policy not to recruit journalists working for American media. But most of the rest are generally fair game, and some, such as Soviet TASS correspondents (most of them spooks anyway), are legitimate targets. Over the years I recruited a number of foreign journalists, but that was after my years in Cambodia. While we don't recruit American journalists, we are allowed to listen to them when they want to volunteer important information such as an imminent bombing by terrorists.

In the decade since I worked briefly for the AP in Cambodia, the foreign media coverage had grown substantially. In 1963 the AP had one lone reporter in Phnom Penh, a stringer named Seng Meakley in Phnom. A nice fellow who helped me during my photo assignment in Cambodia, he was known as "Meakley who files weekly." Cambodia was very much off the front burner for news. By 1973, dozens of journalists, photographers, and cameramen—a cast of characters from around the world—had arrived to cover the war.

The journalists included some top-notch writers, such as William Shawcross from the *London Sunday Times*, who later wrote a scathing account of American perfidy in Cambodia in his excellent book *Sideshow*. Some foreign correspondents were self-serving with an agenda: get the United States out of the war. They wanted to make a name for themselves seeking to win a Pulitzer Prize as a number of newsmen had already done in Vietnam. As a general rule, the more important the publication, the less time its correspondent spent visiting the front lines of the war.

The major wire services—the Associated Press (AP), United Press International (UPI), Reuters, and Agence France Presse (AFP)—had offices in Phnom Penh. I was in regular contact with the men of the AP, my alma mater, led by bureau chief, Matt Franjola. Matt had kicked around Southeast Asia for years working in Thailand and Laos before becoming a UPI journalist in Vietnam, where he picked up a reputation for reporting from the front lines and speaking Vietnamese. He moved up to AP, came to Cambodia, and learned Cambodian at a time when most journalists relied on French to deal with Cambodian officials. Also on the AP team during my time there were Denis Gray, Dick Blystone, and Cambodian reporter Chhay Born Lay, and a merry band of Cambodian photographers who covered the day-to-day fighting that surrounded Phnom Penh. Lay was the last journalist out when the city fell in 1975. Alan Dawson, a Canadian who had served in Vietnam in the US Army, represented UPI. The AFP chief was the affable Count Charles Antoine Marie de Nerciat, known as Count Charlie. He looked every bit the aristocrat he was and could easily be mistaken for British. His mother was English; he was a graduate of Cambridge University, and was totally bilingual.

Among the most fearless and experienced journalists was Australian Neil Davis. Neil had been covering both Vietnam and Cambodia for years. A cameraman who spent most of his time on the front lines with Vietnamese and Cambodian troops rather than with US soldiers, Neil recorded some of the most compelling footage and disturbing stories from both wars. In one instance, he covered the effort to relieve the surrounded town of Kompong Seila on Highway 4, west of Phnom Penh. The Cambodian army unit there had been surrounded for months, barely surviving by sending out hunting parties to kill the enemy for guns and ammunition and also for food. After their relief, the cannibals of Kompong Seila were given a wide berth by other Forces Armée Nationale Khmères (FANK) units. Neil interviewed the cook who had literally served his fellow men. Apparently, the lungs were considered a delicacy.

Sadly, dissident Thai army troops killed Neil in Thailand in 1985 when he covered a failed coup d'état. In a sad and ironic passing, he filmed his own death; his dropped camera kept running on its side, recording his death from a machine gun bullet. Neil had already cheated death many times before on battlefields but on a street of Bangkok, death won.

The last time I was under fire was with Horst Faas in 1974 in Cambodia. Horst was on assignment to photograph the war as things were quiet in Vietnam, his normal beat. Horst had survived hundreds of firefights. The year before he had been wounded covering the 1973 war between Israel and Egypt, and had sworn off combat coverage. But here he was in Phnom Penh, asking me where the action was. "Pick a front," I said. "Phnom Penh is surrounded. You can drive down any road from the city and be in a firefight in an hour." He chose Highway Four, leading west from Phnom Penh to the port of Kompong Som. I organized a trip down the highway

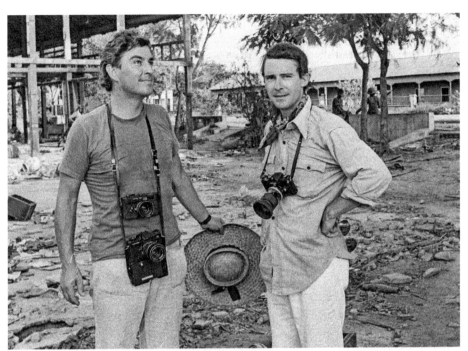

With Associated Press photographer Horst Faas during a lull in fighting on Highway 4 in Cambodia west of Phnom Penh. The first time I was shot at in a combat zone I was with Horst in Vietnam in 1963. The last time was also with Horst, the day this photo was taken in 1974.

and invited the doyen of Phnom Penh war photographers, American Al Rockoff, to come along. Al knew the battlefields of Cambodia better than anyone and carried the scars to prove it. Also along on our field trip was a young American journalist, Claudia Ross, from the *Bangkok Post*. She was in a combat zone for the first time.

Horst rented a car and driver who was a little chary about risking his car on Highway 4. After a brief re-negotiation concerning money, we headed west, out of the city, past Pochentong Airport, and toward the front. The "front" was sometimes difficult to find in the Cambodian war. Front lines tended to shift constantly. There were often gaps in the government's lines through which the Khmer Rouge could easily enter. Ambushes along the main lines of communication were frequent, which helped account for the fact that more journalists were killed in Cambodia than in the much larger and longer-lasting Vietnam War next door.

Al said a Cambodian Army brigade was holding the road ahead, trying to clear it of Khmer Rouge, Cambodian communist forces. We soon found the FANK command post in a dusty, mostly deserted town. Nearby, a 81mm mortar team was firing at enemy positions about a half a kilometer west. I introduced myself to the brigade commander, an affable French-speaking fellow who invited us to look around but not move too far forward. "*La situation est un peu fluide*," he said, suggesting that things were getting warm. We walked over to the mortars and took a few photos. As we walked back to the highway an incoming barrage of Khmer Rouge 82mm mortars landed amid the FANK mortar men, killing a few and wounding most of the rest. Horst took a few snaps and said, "Time to go home." We bade farewell to the brigade commander and returned to Phnom Penh with fresh photos of the war. Horst, as always, was cool under fire. Claudia acquitted herself well. Al had moved forward with the infantry and stayed at the battle. A day later Horst was back in Saigon. Claudia survived her war experience and returned to Bangkok to file her story. Sadly, she was murdered in Bangkok a few months later. The crime was never solved.

Al Rockoff went in harm's way more often than any other foreign newsman in Cambodia. He had served as an army photographer in Vietnam and was no stranger to combat photography, an art within an art. A freelancer with no steady stream of income, he lived by selling pictures. To get the pictures he often risked his life, sometimes for $1.50 per day, the rate the AP paid their Cambodian stringers. Constantly in the thick of battle, he experienced a grim war from the Cambodian perspective. FANK had no medical evacuation helicopters available to move the wounded quickly to get medical attention. Wounded soldiers often bled to death before they could be trucked to Phnom Penh or the nearest regional town it was where questionable medical treatment awaited them.

Once, during a firefight, Al shot a series of photos of a FANK soldier standing with a rifle about to shoot. The strip of negatives shows a frame with the soldier standing. The next frame shows the soldier still standing but without a head. The rocket-propelled grenade that took off the soldier's head also sent a small piece of shrapnel straight into the lens of Al's camera, which probably saved his life. Another small piece of shrapnel hit him in the thumb. I recall that Al was wounded at least nine times during the Cambodian war, but that may have included his Vietnam wounds.

During an action on Highway 4, a bullet penetrated and exited both of Al's legs. Fortunately, he received quick medical attention and was put into the cab of a 2½-ton truck heading back to Phnom Penh on an ammunition resupply mission. In shock, in pain, and oozing blood from both legs, Al lay curled in the passenger side of the cab on the floor as the young FANK soldier drove into town. At the main intersection of Monivong Boulevard, the driver told Al that he was turning right to get to the ammo dump. He suggested that Al get out and take a pedicab to the nearby Calmette Hospital. Al did as he was told, crawled out of the truck, thanked the driver, and hailed a passing three-wheeled bicycle taxi. Al dragged himself onto the seat, negotiated the price, and told the *cyclo* driver, "Calmette, and step on it." During the ride to the hospital Al passed German photographer Dieter Ludwig who recognized his photojournalist colleague. "Hey Al," said Dieter, who was unaware of Al's condition, "been shot lately?"

Al had an even closer call the day he was in Kompong Chhnang, a provincial town northwest of Phnom Penh, photographing a battle. A piece of shrapnel hit him in the chest, penetrating his heart. Luckily, there was an Agency officer there and he radioed the station in Phnom Penh about Al's situation. Even luckier was the presence of a Swedish Red Cross surgical team. The doctor in charge concluded that Al was near death. He needed an emergency medevac. The ambassador requested the COS, Dave, to authorize the agency's airline Air America, sometimes called "The most shot at airline in the world" to rescue Al. Dave approved Air America to fly into Cambodia from Vietnam to evacuate Al to the American military hospital in Saigon. An Air America crew quickly volunteered for the hazardous mission and they launched from Than Son Nhut Air Base.

By the time the plane made it to Kompong Chhnang, it was dark. The airstrip was a two-lane, paved road, with no lights. The aircraft set down between the headlights of two jeeps a few hundred feet apart. The medical team loaded Al in the plane, and a Swedish nurse kept him alive by pumping his heart by hand until they made it to Saigon. Al underwent immediate surgery. Once he was stabilized, he was flown to the better-equipped US military hospital at Clark Air Force Base in the Philippines.

Al woke up in the intensive care ward at Clark and learned what had happened to him. He also learned that he would have to repay the US government for his medical treatment (the Air America ride was free), $129 per day. Hearing this, Al discharged himself from the ICU and made his way to Manila by bus with a collapsed lung and a chest tube draining fluids from a hole in his side. He borrowed money from the AP bureau and flew back to Phnom Penh. I attended his welcome-home party at the Phnom Hotel, where a group of friends had gathered. An Australian lady presented Al with a platter of marijuana brownies she had baked in his honor. Though in pain, assuaged somewhat by the ganja, Al recounted his story in a rasping voice powered by his good lung. He ended the story, "I bought the farm, but the check bounced."

For all his bravery under fire and experience as a combat photographer, Al had an air of innocence. Shy, softly-spoken, and quiet he wore his hair long, parted in the middle and tied in a ponytail. He usually wore military fatigues, souvenirs from his service in Vietnam. Al loved cannabis, a herb Cambodians cook with and that was available at any market for about 50 cents per kilogram.

Ambassador Dean, who had authorized the Air America flight into Cambodia that saved Al, took a liking to the quiet American, and once invited him to a diplomatic reception. New to the diplomatic circuit Al accepted the invitation and wore his best set of US Army pressed jungle fatigues. The story went around the next day that at the party Al walked up to the ambassador, thanked him for the invitation, and held up a marijuana "joint." "Want a hit?" asked the polite Al. The equally polite and unflappable diplomat is reported to have replied, "No thanks Al, I'm trying to quit." I don't know if the story is true but I hope so.

Al survived Cambodia. He refused to leave the city when Marine helicopters arrived to evacuate Americans and others on Operation *Eagle Pull*. He was one of the few newsmen who were on hand when the Khmer Rouge walked into Phnom Penh on April 17, 1975. Actor John Malkovich portrayed Al in the film *The Killing Fields*. Al became one of the war's walking wounded. For years he lived, off and on, in Cambodia making a meager living. The last time I saw him was in 2009 when he appeared at the launch of a book I had written on Cambodia. He bought a copy, asked me to autograph it, and left.

Dave welcomed my requests to occasionally check out battlefields near Phnom Penh. The Khmer Rouge surrounded the troops and travel down any highway quickly led to the front lines. As the noose tightened around Phonon Penh, I ventured out more often. I usually went to the front with Matt Franjola, a veteran combat correspondent who had covered the war in Vietnam. Although Franj, as he was known, never served in the military he had seen more action in Vietnam and Laos than most military officers I know. Franj joined the Peace Corps out of Cortland State University, New York, where he majored in physical education and became

With men of the 28th Brigade of the Republic of Cambodia Army at the successful conclusion of the battle of Veal Sbau, a village not far from Phnom Penh in 1973.

an all-American lacrosse player. Trained in the Thai language in Hilo, Hawaii, Franj was "de-selected" from the Peace Corps for being, in his words, a "free thinker." Undeterred, he set off for Bangkok where he became a teacher. He moved to Laos and Vietnam, where he gravitated into journalism.

Dressed in a bush jacket and sporting a big-game hunter's field hat, Franj was larger-than-life as he zipped around battlefields in his jeep, an acquisition of obscure origins. Tall, good-looking, and infected with a sense of mission and a sense of humor, it was inevitable that he became known as Captain America. A bachelor and a lady's man, he could pitch woo in Thai, Lao, Vietnamese, or Cambodian. And English, if pressed. He disdained French, the language of the Cambodian government, as a colonial language, and always conducted interviews at the front in Khmer.

Phnom Penh was surrounded by the Khmer Rouge during the two years I was posted there. A short drive down any of the roads radiating from the city was pretty much guaranteed to lead to combat. One day Franj invited me to visit the front on Highway 3, the main route to Kampot on the Gulf of Thailand. Franj hadn't been there in a while and wanted to check it out. Although it seemed pretty quiet we noticed that traffic steadily lessened until there was no traffic at all. This is never a good sign. We stopped at a FANK position along the road and asked a soldier how far away the Khmer Rouge positions were. He pointed to a tree line of sugar palms. "They are in those trees," he said with a grin. It was lucky we stopped. The Khmer Rouge rarely took prisoners. We located the Cambodian battalion commander in a destroyed house. He had never seen either a foreign journalist before, or a diplomat. The colonel, nevertheless, gave us a situation report answering my questions in French and Franj's in Cambodian.

Mission accomplished, we headed home. As we moved north, we passed a FANK soldier limping along the road. We stopped and Matt offered the wounded soldier a lift. He gratefully accepted and gingerly climbed into the jeep's back seat. He told us he had been hit in the foot by shrapnel and didn't really require evacuation, but his wife had been more seriously hit a few days before and he was going to Phnom Penh to see if she was still alive. While we drove, Franj did an interview with the soldier. A Cambodian born in South Vietnam—a group referred to as "Khmer Krom"—he had been fighting since he was 14 years old. Like many Khmer Krom who had fought first for the French and then the Americans, he had been a rifleman with the US Army's Special Forces in Vietnam before joining a Khmer Krom unit in the Cambodian army in 1970. He had no idea what he would do if peace broke out. He said he liked working for the Americans and he also liked being part of an elite Khmer Krom unit. His only concern was for his wife. We dropped him at the military hospital, wished him good luck, and headed for the Phnom to write the story.

Franj wasn't a wordsmith like Peter Arnett, Dick Blystone, or Denis Gray but he got his facts right and got the story out, usually before the opposition. Dick Blystone

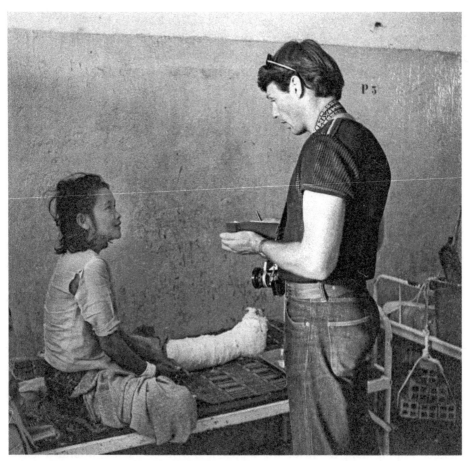

Associated Press bureau chief Matt Franjola interviews a wounded Cambodian girl in the military hospital in Phnom Penh in Cambodian. He also spoke Thai, Lao, and Vietnamese.

was a real pro and a mentor to the younger Franjola. I remember the lead of a story by Dick following a visit to a military hospital. He began his story something like this. "Room number five has four men and three legs." Few journalists went in harm's way as often as Franj did and fewer conducted their interviews in Cambodian or Vietnamese. The consummate wire-service writer, he had no agenda. He reported the news and he led from the front.

On a slow news day in 1974, Franj invited me to ride shotgun, figuratively, for a visit to Oudong, an ancient royal capital located about 25 miles northwest of Phnom Penh off Highway 5. Cambodian kings had ruled from Oudong for more than two centuries before abandoning it in 1866 in favor of Phnom Penh. The Khmer Rouge who captured Oudong briefly in 1974 inflicted heavy damage on the historic town. Franj mainly wanted to see what remained of the ancient city and also find out what had happened to important antiquities that had been crated for movement to safety by the United Nations before the town fell. We drove along the Tonle Sap River, which links the Mekong River with the great lake of Cambodia. The Cham people—Muslims descended from the Champa kingdom that once controlled much of southern Vietnam—populated many of the villages along the river. In 1177 the Cham briefly conquered the great kingdom of Angkor. Brigadier General Les Kosem, one of Cambodia's few "fighting generals," led the 5th Brigade of the Cambodian Army, a Cham unit noted for its tenacity. After they seized power in 1975 the Khmer Rouge killed most of the remaining Cham in Cambodia.

En route to Oudong, we passed many mosques destroyed in recent fighting with the Khmer Rouge. Troops of the 5th Brigade—all teenagers—guarded some of the ruins. Not far from Oudong we found the remains of a Peugeot 404 that had been hit by a rocket or mortar. Shrapnel had pockmarked its side. We stopped and photographed each other leaning out the driver's window, a grim souvenir of the trip.

Oudong was in ruins. Small children picked through the debris looking for something to salvage, usually in vain. At one intersection we found the burned-out shell of an American-made half-track armored vehicle, a relic of World War II vintage. An eyewitness told us a young FANK lieutenant manned the machine gun in the half-track until he ran out of ammunition and was killed. We found

In a damaged Peugeot 404 automobile that was hit by artillery shrapnel in the fighting for the town of Oudong, a former capital of Cambodia west of Phnom Penh, 1974. (Photo by Matt Franjola)

his bones surrounded by hundreds of rounds of expended machine gun brass. We never discovered what happened to the post-Angkorian treasures that disappeared when the Khmer Rouge took the town.

One day in 1974, a rocket hit my house. I was not at home at the time and none of my staff suffered any injuries. I called Franj and asked him if he wanted any shrapnel to decorate his office. He declined but invited me to join him for dinner at the Hotel Phnom where he had a suite that served as both his office and living quarters. The office was downstairs; Franj's apartment was upstairs. When I arrived around 6PM, Franj was writing his nightly wrap-up for the AP. The office radio tuned to a Khmer Rouge propaganda station broadcasted "news" in broken English. While waiting for Franj to finish, I had a chance to look at a large battle map posted on the wall. AP staffers and stringers covering the battlefields updated the map daily, keeping close track of enemy and friendly positions. I heard the announcer say, "Today the freedom-loving fighters of the Cambodian Communist Party, under the guidance of our father, Prince Norodom Sihanouk, came close to killing the running dog lackey Barry Broman whose house was hit by one of our

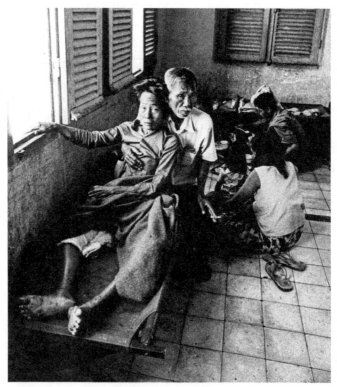

A Cambodian civilian holds up his wounded wife so she can see out the window in a Phnom Penh hospital in 1973. Because of crowding, her cot was in the corridor of the hospital.

missiles. We may have missed Broman today but we know where he lives and we will not miss the next time."

Franj kept typing, obviously not listening to the broadcast. "Franj," I shouted, "Did you hear that? The Khmer Rouge are gunning for me." My mind raced. Franj kept typing but said, "Could you hold it down for a few minutes while I finish the night?" I stayed silent, but wondered how and when the Khmer Rouge would strike next. We knew they had agents in town. Earlier, the Khmer Rouge tried unsuccessfully to assassinate a senior embassy officer who was saved by his armored sedan. His outriders were not so lucky.

Just then Franj's friend Doug Sapper, an American adventurer, walked in. Franj knew Doug from Vietnam. Typical of the kind of people attracted to Phnom Penh by the adrenalin rush of war, Doug fitted right in with the danger and controlled chaos that was Cambodia. He was working as security chief for one of many one-airplane airlines that flew goods and passengers around the country because the roads were not safe. These airlines mostly operated elderly C-47 "Gooney Bird" aircraft. The pilots of this motley assortment of aircraft were proud members of the Pig Pilots of Phnom Penh Association. They took their name from an incident in which an untethered load of swine aboard one of the aircraft shifted on takeoff from Battambang, resulting in the death of all on board and the end of one of the last two remaining Boeing 307s.

"Doug," I said in a subdued voice, "The Khmer Rouge are trying to kill me." Doug replied, "They're trying to kill everybody. That's why they keep shelling the city." I told him about the radio broadcast. He scoffed, "That doesn't mean anything. Ninety percent of their reporting is bullshit. Why would the communists want to kill you? They had their chance in Vietnam."

Franj finished his story and agreed with Doug that I was imagining things. We headed off for dinner at the nearby La Taverne restaurant, a down-at-the-heels bistro in a charming old colonial building across from the Central Post Office. Often a blind Cambodian was busking for coins playing the zither outside. His favorite song was "Cherry Pink and Apple Blossom White." It was couscous night. Looking over my shoulder, I suggested we eat inside. Sidewalk tables offered an inviting a target for a passing motorcyclist armed with a hand grenade. We found a nice table deep inside and I installed myself in a chair facing the front door.

Sipping warm wine, I tried to relax. Neither Franj nor Doug seemed the least bit interested in my imminent demise. Franj described fresh fighting on Highway 4, which threated to cut off Phnom Penh from the port at Kompong Som. Sapper wanted to talk about the dozens of incoming rockets that almost put him out of a job earlier in the day. Then Doug turned toward me. He lowered his head and his voice. "Today the freedom-loving fighters of the Cambodian Communist Party, under the guidance of our father...." He repeated. I stopped him. "Son of a bitch," I said, or something similar. I recognized the words, and the voice.

Franj and Doug broke into peals of laughter. Franj said, "I couldn't let it go on any longer. You might have had a heart attack if a car backfired." I had truly been had. Doug had been sitting in the bushes outside Franj's office, with a hand mike wired to the radio to make his "broadcast." It was brilliant. In my state of happiness at the removal of the death threat I sprang for the dinner. The spoof was Franj's brainchild. In the midst of a war and ably assisted by the puckish Doug, he found time to pull off a prank. Alas, they are both gone now, and I never got even.

In his seminal book *The Cambodian Wars: Clashing Armies and CIA Covert Operations*, Kenneth Conboy described a new effort that began during my tour in Cambodia. "Still in need of a solution to provide Washington with intelligence from the Cambodian countryside, and yet still facing a strict manpower ceiling," he wrote, "the CIA in early March 1973 agreed to the risky proposition of stationing just a handful of US intelligence officers in the provinces." Laird told me that the idea for his program came from Kissinger. The Agency concurred and put Laird in charge but he was not very enthusiastic. Having seen similar efforts fail in Vietnam, he insisted that all officers not only be able to speak French, but also have experience in producing foreign intelligence. He wanted men with military experience but not men who would serve as advisors to their Cambodian military counterparts. Those selected had to walk a fine line and were clearly ordered to avoid combat. I knew and liked a number of these officers, who on the whole responded to a crash requirement by the Agency with courage and professionalism.

Our upcountry officers usually didn't have charming old colonial-era restaurants in their rustic towns in the countryside surrounded by the Khmer Rouge. One of our hard-charging upcountry officers was serving in a hot battle zone north of the Great Lake, working with a dynamic young Cambodian military commander. One day, Dave learned that the officer was being awarded a Cambodian medal for valor. It turned out that the officer had accompanied the general on an operation and in a firefight killed a Khmer Rouge soldier who was trying to kill the FANK general. Our man had violated the strict order to avoid combat. "What will you do?" I asked the avuncular Dave. He lit his pipe, paced a while, and replied "I should send him home, but I won't. He is a good officer doing a good job. But he can't have the medal."

We had two Cambodian-speaking upcountry officers known affectionately as the Bear and the Snake. The Bear was Dave Spillane, a former football lineman, with a black belt in Judo and a degree from the University of Pennsylvania. Dave spoke fluent Vietnamese, Cambodian, and Thai. Before joining the CIA, he had been a Vietnamese linguist in the army. Snake was Al Bindie, a very savvy officer from the coal country of Pennsylvania. He was also a linguist. Besides Cambodian, he spoke Thai, Lao, Hmong, and Tagalog. Together they made a great team, especially with the FANK 13th Brigade in Kompong Speu, west of Phnom Penh.

The Bear studied Thai with DEA officer Peter "PT" Tomaino. They shared a dangerous moment in Cambodia. One morning Air America, the CIA's airline, dropped the Bear off with a FANK unit at Takeo near the Vietnamese border where we did not have an officer assigned. The Bear was to talk to the local commander, and get a feel for the situation and be picked up by Air America in the afternoon. Air America used a two-lane paved road as an airstrip. The Bear arrived all right and got his report. But when the plane came in to pick him up, the Khmer Rouge, who surrounded the town, started mortaring the road. The plane landed and slowed down to pick up the Bear who, wearing a flak jacket, carrying a single side band radio, and a Swedish K machine gun, ran to board the moving aircraft under fire. Tomaino, one of the passengers on the plane, had hopped on the flight in Saigon thinking he was going non-stop to Phnom Penh. Pete was at the door as the Bear approached and helped pull him on board. As the plane took off, Pete looked at the Bear and said "Fancy meeting you here." The plane made it safely to Phnom Penh and the two became close friends.

***

It was difficult to enjoy life in a country that was bleeding and soon to die. But many of us did. No one knew how to make the best of an ugly situation better than Frederick Kroll, the director of ESSO in Cambodia. A Yale graduate and former Marine Corps reconnaissance officer, Fred was the leading American businessman in Cambodia. His previous ESSO postings included Vietnam and Laos, where he provided the product to keep Air America flying and ground vehicles running. He carried on this essential service in Cambodia. Born in Haiti where his father worked as an engineer, Fred had grown up speaking French and creole and thrived in the danger of Phnom Penh at war.

Fred lived in a large colonial-style mansion in the high-class French quarter of the city, not far from the Catholic cathedral and the Hotel Phnom. He hosted dinners at home but was best known for his Sunday lunches served on his houseboat moored on the Bassac River on the outskirts of town. He shared the cost of the boat with Pierre Elissabede, a French-American USAID official. Every Sunday, weather and security situation permitting, Fred hosted lunch on the houseboat, after which he broke out the water skis. Fred, an expert skier, would jump off the boat with a cigarette in his mouth, take a few laps on one ski, and return with the cigarette lit and intact. Those who enjoyed skiing had to take special care when going under the bridge for Highway 1. Guards were known to drop hand grenades into the water to keep Khmer Rouge frogmen from attacking the bridge. Incoming rockets were also a continual worry, but the boat remained untouched throughout the war.

Fred's guests ranged from Cambodian royals, diplomats, and expatriate businessmen to pilots, aviation ground crews, and journalists. Fred invariably served a spicy Cambodian curry, and Pierre provided Chateau Pavie wine from his family's cave in St. Emilion. It bordered on criminal to drink this elegant wine, served at a temperature of about 85 degrees and paired with curry. However, Pierre never batted an eye. "Can't leave it for the Khmer Rouge," he would say. We all helped by drinking with gusto. I would secretly slip a little ice into my wine, a terrible gaffe.

One day Fred invited me to Sunday dinner after lunch on the houseboat. An Air America pilot had brought him two large, live lobsters from Nha Trang in Vietnam, so he said there would only be two of us at dinner. I was to bring the wine. As it turned out, the lunch houseboat party got somewhat rowdy. Fred ended up also inviting around 10 somewhat inebriated aviators and their girlfriends for dinner. He pointed out very clearly that he and I would be having lobster with wine; everyone else would eat Cambodian noodles with beer. The dining table accommodated 12. Fred sat at one end with his lobster and a bottle of chilled white wine; he put me at the other end with my crustacean and wine. In between us sat the other guests, enjoying their noodles and getting ever more drunk. The unusual dinner proceeded amicably enough until one young lady, taking umbrage at a remark made by another lady·opposite her, threw a handful of noodles thrown across the table. This immediately led to a food fight. I toasted Fred from my end of the table as a pile of noodles landed on my head. Fred returned the toast. Just another Phnom Penh dinner party. I wore the noodles home.

The French kept pretty much to themselves in Phnom Penh despite their colonial history in Cambodia. A few could be seen at the Cercle Sportif sports club including a number of charming old colonials who wanted to spend their last years in the warmth of Cambodia where the cost of living was low. A few of the wealthier businessmen had houseboats on the Bassac for weekend recreation. The better restaurants and bars were run by French, often Corsican, businessmen.

It was an open secret that large French rubber plantations were still in operation, although they were located in areas under control of the NVA or Khmer Rouge. Before Sihanouk was overthrown in 1970, the NVA 5th, 7th, and 9th Infantry divisions were based in Cambodia, some in or near rubber plantations. Sihanouk himself was paid handsomely to turn a blind eye to the blatant violation of Cambodia's "neutrality." Worse, Sihanouk allowed the NVA to bring heavy military equipment into the port of Sihanoukville. The prince's second instance of treason came when he was overthrown by his own parliament and army in 1970 only to immediately join the Khmer Rouge.

French rubber merchants in Phnom Penh would fly in small aircraft to their plantations to do business with the Khmer Rouge and quietly moved their raw rubber down the Mekong River, through Phnom Penh, to overseas markets, paying off the Khmer Rouge and probably Cambodian Republic officials as well to ease the passage. The giveaway to this trafficking with the Khmer Rouge was the sharp smell of acetic acid that was used to harden rubber latex into rubber sheets. The odor permeated the air of Phnom Penh, usually after dark, as the rubber transited the town.

Some of the stalwart clients of Madame Choum's opium den in Phnom Penh were French aficionados of "chasing the dragon," as opium smoking was known. The popular but discreet establishment also catered to a few dissolute diplomats. I knew one ambassador given to smoking as much as 40 pipes in an evening. It did nothing to curb his gambling habit. Some of the younger foreign correspondents found Madame Choum's calming after a busy day reporting on the war.

The senior West German diplomat in Phnom Penh, Baron Walter von Marschall, hosted far more serious evenings. An aristocrat from Freiburg, the baron held wine-tasting soirées. Normally, he invited seven male guests to taste eight white Baden wines—perfectly chilled—from his home region. The baron did not serve food at these quiet rather formal events. Rather, he provided cheese between tasting to cleanse the palate. Eight wines would be tasted, all of them chilled white Baden wines from the Baron's home region. The baron spoke about each wine in turn, starting with the dry and ending with the sweet. The wines were young and quite pleasant. His cellar contained hundreds of bottles and invitations to his events were much coveted. The baron included me in several of his wine tastings after he discovered I could be counted on to procure the cheese on my monthly trips to Bangkok to see BJ.

I saw a woman at the baron's wine tastings only once. One of the group's regulars, a Dutch aristocrat, asked the baron if he could bring a lady he was wooing. The baron relented. The woman, an attractive middle-aged lady, who worked as a secretary at the American Embassy, exuded a naivety as charming as her pronounced Tennessee drawl. I'll call her Fanny. Adhering to protocol, the baron seated Fanny at his right. The evening proceeded smoothly. After six or seven bottles had been consumed, the baron poured a sweet dessert wine. "My goodness," Fanny exclaimed, "I love this wine." The baron beamed his appreciation. "It's good enough to make me a wino," said Fanny.

The bemused baron turned to me, the only other American at the table. "Barry," he asked, "what is a wino?" To my unending regret, I replied, "Baron, this is an American slang expression. When someone is a true expert of wine, he or she is said to be a 'wino.'" The baron smiled and said, "So now I can tell people that I am the great wino of Baden." I don't know what made me do it. I blame the wine.

Toward the end of the baron's tour, I hosted a small farewell dinner for him. Although I usually had informal al fresco dinners on the upstairs verandah, I wanted to do something more formal in our dining room for him. I could not, however, count on having city electricity and did not want to run my noisy generator. My cook, Jeannot, proposed a solution. One bottle of Remy-Martin cognac, placed in the right hands at the power company would suffice for full power for the duration of the meal. Although skeptical, I handed over the bottle and, sure enough, at the stroke of seven o'clock the power came on. At ten o'clock it went off. The evening was a big success thanks to Jeannot who, knowing he was cooking for an ambassador, outdid himself in the kitchen.

Because of the war, the diplomatic corps often downplayed or even omitted many of its normal ceremonial events, such as national days and celebratory anniversaries. The Marine Corps Ball—an annual favorite hosted by the Marine guards at US embassies around the world—celebrates the birthday of the Marine Corps on November 10. These balls can be very grand with multi-course dinners, show casing traditions and punctuated by speeches. In 1974 the powers-that-be decided the birthday celebrations would be limited to a small poolside cocktail party at the Marine House in Phnom Penh. Most embassy and station personnel attended. Ambassador John Gunter Dean looked splendid in his tuxedo. It remained a quiet affair until a young Marine, his judgment possibly clouded by a few drinks too many, approached the ambassador, snapped to attention, saluted, wished him a happy birthday, and pushed him into the pool. The party instantly became silent with all eyes on Ambassador Dean slowly doing the breaststroke across the pool. Dripping wet, the ambassador approached the gunnery sergeant, the senior Marine of the Marine Security Detachment. The gunny could probably see his career in shambles despite numerous combat tours in Vietnam. "Happy birthday, gunny," the ambassador said, and pushed him into pool. The gunny's career didn't suffer from the incident; I can't say the same for the young Marine's.

The British embassy hosted a large New Year's Eve party in 1974. In fine English tradition, the embassy stipulated a "drag" dress code. In keeping with the spirit of the party, Tim and I wore sarongs. One young couple came as Stan Laurel and Oliver Hardy in tuxedos, the lady wearing a mustache. The Australian military attaché, Colonel D'Arcy, won the competition. A rotund World War II veteran, he wore a beautiful white wedding gown, which went well with his white brush moustache. That night, as if to highlight the contradictions inherent in our life in a country at war, the Khmer Rouge launched their final offensive against Phnom Penh. Rockets rained on the city. A ground attack across the Tonle Sap River burned the suburb opposite the Grand Palace. One by one, single side band radios carried by many military officers began to go off. The party was over. A few of us including Colonel D'Arcy headed for the river. We watched the village burn a few hundred meters away as sporadic incoming fire came into the city. I pointed out to the colonel that a photo of his corpse in a wedding dress could be on the front page of every Aussie newspaper. Taking the hint, the colonel immediately left to change into more suitable attire.

One night when BJ was visiting from Bangkok, a West German diplomat invited us to dinner and a film. The small party ate first and then gathered in the garden to watch the movie outdoors. Suddenly, the entire neighborhood erupted in the noise of "outgoing" gunfire and the beating of pots and pans. All the noise of the explosion and clanging caused no damage except to disrupt the film viewing. We later discovered that the West German diplomat's party coincided with a lunar eclipse, a small event to many of us but a big deal in Cambodia. According to Khmer mythology, a lunar eclipse occurs when a giant frog eats the moon.

Cambodians make a lot of noise to frighten the frog. The fact that thousands of Cambodians in the city were armed and dangerous added to the noise arrayed against the frog. Eventually, the moon was saved and the shooting stopped. Later, I was informed that stray bullets aimed at the frog had killed 12 people during the one-sided firefight.

***

Fred Kroll and Sino-Cambodian businessman Bing Pin Lim, known fondly as Skinny Pin, founded the only private club I knew of in Phnom Penh. It was the Chamber of Commerce of Kampuchea, popularly known as the COCK Club. Its members included local businessmen and a few diplomats. Located in a small villa behind the Phnom Hotel, the club featured one sport, darts. It could have been called The Dart Club, but that lacked class. Some of the members were serious darters, armed with high quality darts imported from Bangkok. Every Saturday the COCK Club offered a lunch followed by a darts tournament to determine the club's champion chosen for the week.

The city lacked high-class bars and had no pubs at all. So the COCK Club filled a need and provided a place to relax. The curfew forced most places to close early, but since most of its members had curfew passes and since the checkpoints around the club never changed, it wasn't too hard for people without passes to navigate late at night. The only time I recall anyone trying to "crash" the club was the evening when two Soviet diplomats walked in thinking it was a new bar. Informed that it was a private club and seeing Americans playing darts, they beat a hasty retreat, never to return.

The club was only busy on Saturdays, when it provided food. Anyone could bring a guest and I don't recall any rules at all. One memorable day a visiting celebrity dropped into the club. Cambodia was rarely visited by anyone unconnected with the war. So, we were pleased to welcome David Cornwell, an Englishman better known by his pen name John le Carré (French for John the Square). The guest of a Western diplomat he had known during his days serving in Her Majesty's Secret Intelligence Service, better known as MI6, David was in town researching his novel *The Honourable Schoolboy.*

As a rule, I don't read novels of the espionage genre. Many are phony and incorrect. I make an exception for David's books, especially his early works that featured the pluperfect British intelligence character George Smiley who hunts a Soviet mole inside MI6. David patterned the search for the mole after the real hunt for the "Cambridge five," Soviet spies in MI6 from the 1930s, led by Harold Adrian Russell "Kim" Philby, a very senior officer whose treachery caused the deaths of hundreds of British agents. He defected to the USSR in 1963. For me, David's writing transcended mere fiction. It was tightly woven literature of the sort I equate

Tim with me at the clubhouse of the Chamber of Commerce of Kampuchea, the COCK Club, in Phnom Penh in 1974. Tim is holding the dart "ladder" showing that I was the top darts player, a position I held very briefly. This is where I played darts with John le Carré.

with the work of British maritime fiction master Patrick O'Brian and his creation, Captain "Lucky Jack" Aubrey.

In gathering "atmosphere" for his coming book, David saw the COCK Club as a good place to start. A leading American journalist upon whom David based his lead character was helping David in the project. The quiet, polite fellow I assumed he would be, David also turned out to be a very good storyteller and a bit of a master of foreign accents. An Oxford man and former schoolmaster at Eton, Cornwell had served as a German-language interrogator during his military service, followed by time in Britain's internal security agency, MI5, before switching to the external service. He didn't talk about his government service and none of us asked. The British did not have anyone from MI6 in Phnom Penh for most of the time I was there. David was active around town and even experienced a little hostile fire from the Khmer Rouge, which always makes good copy. I wonder if he knew that two of the people who squired him around town worked for opposing sides. One was a CIA agent and the other was a suspected Soviet agent. Both these people died violent deaths but not in Cambodia. Fiction imitates life.

The highlight of the afternoon for me was engaging David in a game of 301 darts, the standard game. Modesty forbids me from saying who won, but I suspect that darts were rather déclassé for the diffident Brit, who clearly had not been practicing as much as I had.

***

Because of the danger in Phnom Penh, wives either stayed home in the States or were "safe-havened" in places closer to Cambodia. The regulations gave officers two days a month for "family visitation travel." That meant I could visit BJ in Bangkok for a four-day weekend every month. BJ found a pleasant one-bedroom apartment near the US embassy and settled in quickly. American University Associations (AUA), a US government-funded educational institution that supported a library and an English language school in Thailand, hired her immediately.

I usually took the 50-minute flight to Bangkok from Phnom Penh via Air Cambodge's only Caravelle jet. The airline gave passengers miniature bottles of Johnny Walker (Red) Scotch as they disembarked, a very civilized gesture I thought. Sometimes I would jump on a CIA charter aircraft making a "Bangkok run." Every visit included dinner at our favorite French restaurant, Le Metropolitan, located near BJ's apartment on Ploenchit Road. Its owner, Pierre Segui, had been a Spitfire fighter pilot for the Free French during World War II. He had restaurants in both Saigon and Phnom Penh during the French colonial days in the 1950s. With war consuming Vietnam and Cambodia he moved to Bangkok. A colorful and entertaining gentleman, Pierre could have stepped out of a Graham Greene novel. Our dinners at Le Metropolitan began with me giving Pierre a situation report on the war and an update on his French friends, who were running lesser restaurants in Phnom Penh. He was especially attentive to BJ who frequented his place with friends. He always made sure to find her a cab for the short ride home. He achieved additional fame for his excellent performance as a nightclub owner in Saigon in the American film *The Deer Hunter*. A natural for the role of owner of the nightclub where men played Russian roulette for high stakes he seemed to be playing himself, a man of action and of some intrigue.

Once, Tim accompanied me on a Bangkok trip to have his wisdom teeth pulled. However, rather than take the short flight from Phnom Penh to Bangkok, we decided to have a little adventure with Fred Kroll who, together with his charming Thai wife, Dao, planned to drive from Battambang, a major town in western Cambodia to Thailand. This was not very dangerous at the time since the government still controlled the highways in western Cambodia but no officials had ever done it. We flew to Battambang town and hired a car to take us to the Thai border at Aranyaprathet. We spent a night there with a Cambodian timber merchant who invited us on a deer hunt on the Cambodian side of the border. He was a comical character who someone had introduced to Fred as a good hunting partner. It turned out that he was a terrible hunter but a genial host. We ended up empty-handed, drinking Cognac with our host late into the night.

The next day, we took a car from the border to Bangkok, an easy four-hour drive over good roads. As we drove down Sukhumvit Road to BJ's apartment, I spotted BJ on the street. I rolled the window and waved to attract her attention. Not recognizing the obnoxious person hailing at her, BJ ignored me. Finally, she looked our way and saw me with Tim and waved back. The trip ended on a bad note for Tim, who not only had wisdom teeth extracted but had also picked up dengue fever on the trip. He spent some days in the dark in BJ's living room sleeping on the large teak coffee table that passed for a guest bed (with mattress) when needed.

In early 1975, after four days with BJ in Bangkok, I boarded an elderly Continental Air Service twin propeller C-46 aircraft headed back to Phnom Penh. The only other passengers were 40 Cambodian soldiers returning from training in Thailand. We bounced along for more than an hour. Just as we began our descent about 25 miles from Phnom Penh's Pochentong Airport, the port engine caught fire. After a very uneasy few minutes, the fire was extinguished but the engine stopped running. I told the crew chief that we should have no trouble coasting into Pochentong on one engine. "That's not the problem," he said. "We are not going to Pochentong, we're going back to Bangkok. We can land on one engine but we can't take off with one and we can't fix the plane in Cambodia."

The damaged plane headed west for Thailand over Khmer Rouge-held terrain and the Cardamom Mountains, losing altitude all the way. With everyone on edge, the Cambodian soldiers looked to me for reassurance, which I gave them. "*Pas de problem. Encore un nuit a Bangkok,*" ("No problem, one more night in Bangkok") I said, trying to act more confident than I felt. I kept re-reading the same page of my book but actually focused more on the ground that was getting closer by the minute. Instead of flying over the Cardamom Mountains, we flew through them, or more accurately, through mountain passes. At some length, we made it to what I determined to be the Thai–Cambodian border and flew increasingly lower over rice paddies. This made me feel somewhat better. The pilot had lots of space to put the plane down and there would be no Khmer Rouge to greet us. We dropped lower and lower. Farmers plowing fields with their water buffaloes looked up to see the now single-engine aircraft limping west.

The Thai government forbade flying over Bangkok. A normal flight path would be to approach Don Muang Airfield from the north. We did not have that option. As near as I could tell, the pilot was making directly for the airstrip, and not in the flight pattern, as we lost altitude. We passed a network of canals and more and more villages as we approached the metropolitan Bangkok region. Finally, Don Muang was in sight. The civil side of the airport was separated from the military side by the Royal Thai Air Force golf course in the middle. As we came down low over the trees I could see golfers scattering below us. With little margin for error, the skipper put us down on a runway that had been cleared for us. Crash wagons were standing by but were not needed. That pilot deserved the Distinguished Landing Cross. As we deplaned I thanked the skipper for doing a good job. A long-serving pilot who made the trip often, he responded, "I was looking for a dry rice paddy to set down on for 50 miles but there weren't any."

I located my luggage and took a taxi into town to BJ's apartment. I rang the bell and she opened the door. "Good to see you," she said before I could recount my adventure. "The office just called and said your plane had crashed." So I got two extra days in Bangkok while the engine was replaced. When we did leave, I noticed there were fewer Cambodian soldiers on board than there been before. We flew to Phnom Penh without incident. Walking away from the aircraft, however, an incoming Khmer Rouge rocket blew one wing off our trusty C-46. It never flew again.

***

Tucked in the hills near the Thai border and famed for its ruby and sapphire mines, the small remote town of Pailin was notorious for its high incidence of malaria. As far as I know, no official American had been there, certainly not during the war. The Khmer Rouge controlled most of the area around the town which had a small FANK garrison. Late in the war, Ambassador Dean decided someone should pay a visit and see if revenue from gem sales could augment the Khmer Republic's budget. He asked Tim and me to go. We packed our bug juice and asked Air America to drop us off. The Agency airline had never taken anyone to Pailin but the town had a small airfield and the pilot said he would try to get us in while making a milk run to Battambang which was not far away.

From the air we could see the extensive open-pit blue sapphire mines that abutted the coffee plantation owned by a Frenchman we knew, Christian Dupré. Christian was an agronomist and the son of a senior French colonial officer. He rarely visited Phnom Penh. He left the socializing to his Cambodian wife, Kim, a vivacious English-educated aristocrat who didn't dare expose her young sons to the malarial hills of Pailin and lived in Phnom Penh. Our pilot spotted the grass airstrip near the coffee plantation and after a low pass set us down neatly. The governor of the province, a young FANK colonel, who had been alerted to our travel, greeted us with a small welcome committee of armed guards.

The governor took us back to his office where he provided refreshments and a briefing on the military and economic situation in Pailin. The Khmer Rouge threatened all communications. His people only traveled overland to Battambang, the largest city in the region, in heavily protected convoys. The economy depended primarily on gemstones, most which were smuggled into nearby Thailand. The governor put us in Prince Sihanouk's old villa, which was basic but quite pleasant. The wives of the garrison troops used the swimming pool to wash their clothes. We noticed immediately that people shuffled along the unpaved roads with heads looking down, hoping to spot a sapphire. The week before we arrived a soldier had found a large stone near the entrance to the governor's headquarters.

The governor also organized a tour of the sapphire mines, a series of many shallow open pits operated with minimal equipment and unhindered by any rules or noticeable organization. The governor assigned two of his bodyguards to keep close as I took pictures, and Tim chatted in Cambodian with some of the miners, many of whom were women, and all of whom were friendly. They obviously did not get many Western visitors.

We also stopped at the leading Buddhist monastery in Pailin, where the abbot provided more information to Tim in Khmer. Hearing that I spoke Thai, the old monk said, "You must meet my German," and disappeared. He returned with a Westerner wearing the saffron robes of a Buddhist monk. The middle-aged West German had been living for some years in a monastery in Thailand and spoke Thai better than he did English. A very pleasant, if rather eccentric, fellow, he explained that he was on a pilgrimage to Angkor Wat. I pointed out that the Khmer Rouge occupied Angkor and they would certainly suspect him of being a spy. I added that the Cambodian communists did not take prisoners and would likely kill him. He responded, "I have lived many lives." I failed to dissuade him but I did get his name to pass on to German diplomats in Phnom Penh in case he was ever reported missing. I never heard of him again.

Aside from the endless battle against malarial mosquitos, and the avid search for gemstones, not much happened in Pailin. We rolled down our long sleeves, applied bug spray and set up our mosquito nets. After an early dinner with the governor and his staff we went to bed.

We had planned to be picked up by Air America and returned to Phnom Penh the next day. When the plane didn't arrive, I decided to join a convoy that was forming up for the run to Battambang. The plan was to send a plane for Tim. Just as the convoy was about to depart, a Cambodian Air Force helicopter landed. The chopper had come to get Tim who was expected in Battambang to meet with the governor there. I hopped on the bird with Tim and was saved a 10-hour drive through dust on a bad road. In Battambang I learned that the Air America flight had been cancelled by mistake. Our man in Battambang apologized. No harm done, we viewed the trip as a success and even had a few unset sapphires suitable for cufflinks.

Years later, Tim and I returned to the Pailin area but on the Thai side of the border. At the time invading Vietnamese forces were routing the Khmer Rouge. We ran into a Khmer Rouge patrol on the road to Pailin. But that is another story.

***

In March 1975, the Foreign Affairs Committee of the US American House of Representatives voted 18–15 against providing further military aid to Cambodia. The Senate Democrats voted 38–5 to cut aid. Once Congress voted down funds for Cambodia, against strong opposition from the White House, we knew our days were numbered. Phnom Penh had been virtually surrounded for a year. The Khmer Rouge began their final offensive on New Year's Day 1975 and the noose tightened. Feeding the city required an airlift that brought tons of rice into Phnom Penh under enemy mortar and rocket fire. It took about two minutes to offload 15 tons of rice, and it was a miracle that no aircraft or crews were lost.

At times the Khmer Rouge front lines were only one kilometer from Pochentong Airport. The Cambodians had no passport or Customs controls. An embassy van drove onto the tarmac to greet arriving US aircraft. Security personnel gave passengers flak jackets and helmets as they ushered them into vehicles for the run into town. Departing travelers boarded quickly, and the aircraft, which never shut down, made as rapid a departure as possible. Khmer Air Force vintage T-28 piston aircraft would take off under fire with a load of bombs, climb for altitude, bank left, dive on enemy positions, and drop their load and land. Each sortie took 90 seconds. One aircraft could make eight sorties in a day.

Those were difficult days. Refugees poured into the city. The number of ships lost running a gauntlet of enemy fire up the Mekong River continued to mount. Some embassies closed shop entirely and evacuated all personnel. Others, including the American, quietly drew down their staffs, as "non-essential" embassy officers were withdrawn. Many wealthy Cambodians left the country, leaving their homes and possessions behind. The Americans dusted off their evacuation plan for Cambodia: Operation *Eagle Pull* called for US Marines to fly into Phnom Penh in helicopters to pull out remaining Americans, allies, and senior Cambodian officials and their families.

As embassy personnel drew down, we helped some of our agents leave. One asset of mine who had a business was worried that he would be left behind despite my promises that he would leave before me. I got him out to Saigon but he was unable to take his account books with him. I went to his office, introduced myself as a friend of the owner, and asked for the books. When told that the boss was out and that I could not have the books, I laid a $100 bill on the table. The books miraculously appeared. My friend was eventually reunited with his family—and his account ledgers—in Thailand.

Another agent declined my offer to help him leave but did arrange for his family to leave Cambodia. He asked me to give all the money we owed him to his wife. I got the money to her and, eventually, they were reunited in Thailand.

Another agent, a senior official, also declined my offer to get him out. "If you lose a war," he told me at our last meeting, "you must pay the price." He then drew a pistol from his pocket. It was a tense moment. "This is for you," he said, handing me his sidearm. "I will be dead in a week and I don't want the Khmer Rouge to have my gun. Better you have it to remember me and Cambodia." A week later he was dead. I still have the weapon.

My last trip to the field with AP chief Matt Franjola took place in March as the days of the Khmer Republic neared their end. We visited the Parachute Battalion of the Khmer Army holding the line on Highway Five just north of Phnom Penh on the Northern Dike. The Tonle Sap River flowed on their right. The Khmer Rouge were attacking from the north while simultaneously trying to infiltrate around their western flank. We made our way to the battalion command post, which was under fire, and met with the battalion commander, a captain. He gave us a grim briefing on the situation. The battalion, normally 512 men, was down to 52. All officers senior to him were dead or wounded. He knew the end was near; he had been told there would be no resupply of ammunition. He had stopped haircuts for his men and ordered them to destroy their uniforms and attempt to return to their villages when the end came. There would be no surrender. The Khmer Rouge did not take prisoners.

The captain spoke to us calmly and matter-of-factly. His staff and radio operators, some of whom were sound asleep despite the incoming mortars and direct fire, surrounded him. "They are tired," he said. "We have been under attack for 96 hours." I asked what he would do at the end. "I will take my wife and my two children and pull the pins on two hand grenades. We will not be taken alive." Nearby, we met a Frenchman, Dominique Borella, who was fighting alongside the Cambodian paratroopers. Blond and middle-aged, he said he was a volunteer fighting for Cambodia. He asked not to be identified or have his picture taken. He wore the parachute camouflage utilities of the Khmer parachutists and a red beret. He said he knew the end was near but he could not leave his buddies. The Khmer Rouge later captured him and dumped him in the French embassy. Years later, I heard a sniper killed him in Beirut.

As the country was crumbling, Dave told me he was worried about one of his upcountry officers. "The man is too close to the Cambodians," he said. "I am afraid he will refuse to leave when we bug out and will die with his FANK friends."

"What are you going to do?" I asked.

"I will bring him to Phnom Penh on a routine matter and will send another officer down to close up shop." When the officer arrived in Phnom Penh, he had his attractive female Cambodian ops assistant (and mistress) with him. Dave put them on the next plane to Bangkok where the officer had a little explaining to do with his American wife who greeted the plane.

***

As we closed down our upcountry sites, one radio operator, a young Cambodian woman, said she did not want to leave and would stay at her radio and continue to report as long as she could. The station chief agreed to allow her to do this with the understanding that when the situation deteriorated she would destroy her single side band radio and escape. She continued her reporting as the country fell, and even after the departure of the Americans. She ignored all pleas to leave her radio. She was still on the air when a Khmer-speaking case officer in Bangkok begged her to save herself while there was still time. "I cannot leave," she said. "This is my job. I will stay as long as I can. They are now in the city." The case officer shouted, "Get out!" In her last transmission she reported, "They are in the building," After a pause, she added, "They are in the room. Good bye."

Al Bindie was in Kompong Speu, with General Norodom Chantaraingsy's 13th Brigade, on Highway 4. The general, a cousin of King Sihanouk, was one of the country's best fighters. He saw the end coming but refused to surrender or abandon his men. Instead, he led his brigade into the rugged Elephant Mountains of western Cambodia to continue the fight as guerrillas. Bindie was on the radio with Chantaraingsy's top man, Special Colonel Thach Ung. He stayed in Kompong Speu with a rear guard to give the general time to get away. Thach Ung asked Bindie for an ammunition resupply so his men could fight their way out and join the general. There was no ammo left; Al told the colonel he could not help. The war was over. The colonel, knowing he would soon be dead, said, "You are worse than the French." Two days later, Al received a radio call from Kompong Speu. It was Al's houseboy. The Khmer Rouge had taken the town. Al asked what happened to the colonel. "He and his officers will be beheaded at noon," the houseboy said. General Chantaraingsy fought on alone in the jungle for about two years until he was killed and the remnants of his brigade was wiped out.

The Americans pulled the plug on Cambodia on April 12, 1975 with Operation *Eagle Pull*, the evacuation of all-American personnel and allies by US Marine Corps helicopters launching from US Navy ships in the Gulf of Thailand. I left a few days earlier on the last fixed-wing American aircraft with some station personnel and some documents that we did not want to burn. The morning of the evacuation Ambassador John Gunter Dean invited senior Cambodian officials and their families to join the evacuation. After an emergency cabinet meeting the Cambodians declined the offer. Only a few senior Khmer officials and families left on helicopters. When the Khmer Rouge walked into Phnom Penh five days later, most of those people were killed either immediately or eventually. One of those who declined the American invitation was Prince Sisowath Sirik Matak, a leader of the coup against Sihanouk in 1970 and one of Cambodia's bravest and most able leaders. He wrote a letter to Ambassador Dean, which I quote here:

> I thank you very sincerely for your letter and for your offer to transport me towards freedom. I cannot, alas, leave in such a cowardly fashion. As for you and in particular for your great country, I never believed for a moment that you would have this sentiment of abandoning a people, which has chosen liberty. You have refused us your protection and we can do nothing

about it. You leave us and it is my wish that you and your country will find happiness under the sky. But mark it well that, if I shall die here on the spot and in my country that I love, it is too bad because we are all born and must die one day. I have only committed the mistake of believing in you, the Americans. Please accept, Excellency, my dear friend, faithful and friendly sentiments. Prince Sirik Matak.

The evacuation itself went smoothly. The choppers came into a landing zone not far from the embassy. Embassy personnel and all American citizens who wished to leave as well as allied civilians were lifted off without incident. Because Cambodian officials declined the invitation to leave, the helicopters had hundreds of empty seats. It was a sad day for Cambodia and for the United States. To one army officer, military attaché Major Alan Armstrong, who had served twice in Cambodia and lost many of his Cambodian army friends, it was doubly distressing. He was leaving and they were not. He was especially touched, and shamed, by the Cambodian policeman who saluted the American motorcade as it headed for the helicopters. Deputy Chief of Mission Robert Keeley, overshadowed by his more flamboyant, and sometimes pugnacious boss, Ambassador Dean, was a rock of stability and cool demeanor in the stressful last days in Phnom Penh. Another star performer among the embassy staff was Consul John "Black Jack" McCarthy who saved many lives by getting American citizen, foreign nationals, and Cambodians out before the Khmer Rouge took over.

Perhaps the last man out of the embassy was a communicator who was making sure that nothing was left behind that could be of use to the Khmer Rouge. In a piece of admirable improvisation, as he closed the vault door of the communications room, he placed pieces of communications wire designed to look like a booby trap, leading out of the room. Years later, when Americans were invited to visit the building in hopes that it would again be chosen for our embassy (it wasn't) they found that the vault door had never been opened and the wires were still intact.

Chhay Born Lay, an Associated Press writer, missed the evacuation. Having had no warning of it, he had gone to the Foreign Office seeking passports for his family. By the time he got back to the AP office, the choppers had come and gone. He was alone and the Khmer Rouge were about to enter the city. AP bureau chief George Esper in Saigon reached Lay on the phone who explained the situation. Esper had chartered a Continental Air Service plane in Saigon to fly to Phnom Penh to carry money to the AP staff there. The CAS plane was still on the ground in Saigon when *Eagle Pull* took place. George asked if the plane would go in and get Lay and his family. Captain "Dutch" Brongersma, pilot of the aircraft, said he would give it a try.

Associated Press correspondent Richard Blystone was the only passenger on the plane flying into Phnom Penh. The aircraft landed without incident at the deserted Pochentong Airport and shut down a quarter of a mile from the terminal. Dick went looking for Lay and his family, who had followed Esper's instructions to head to the airport. Dick ran around looking desperately for Lay and finally found them. They all dashed to the aircraft with its engines still running and made it safely to Saigon, where both Dick and Lay filed their stories of the rescue. Two weeks later, it was Saigon's turn for evacuation, an event that did not run as smoothly as Phnom Penh's. Matt Franjola had been moved to Saigon where he stayed until the North Vietnamese Army marched in. He survived the war.

In the wake of *Eagle Pull*, an eerie quiet descended on Phnom Penh. The army, which was out of ammunition, ceased to exist. The air force had only two bombs left in its arsenal. The Khmer Rouge were coming. A handful of journalists, including Al Rockoff, stayed behind to cover the story. Many people who missed the evacuation made their way to the French embassy along with hundreds of French nationals, also many Asians carrying French passports. Before I left, I told my cook, Jeannot, a French-Vietnamese metis with a French passport, to take his wife and children to the French embassy where they would be sheltered. How wrong I was.

The Soviet embassy waited quietly to welcome their victorious fraternal communists, only to have a Khmer Rouge rocket-propelled grenade demolish their front door. The Khmer Rouge frog-marched the protesting Soviets to the nearby French embassy compound and unceremoniously dumped them there. It was hard going for the hundreds of French passport holders, many of them elderly retirees who had no place to go. Several senior Khmer officials, such as Prince Sirik Matak, found their way to the embassy, which sheltered them until the Khmer Rouge demanded their expulsion. The French acceded to the demand and the Khmer Rouge quickly murdered Sirik Matak and others. One of the Americans in the embassy compound was Doug Sapper, who had planned to leave on a commercial plane that never arrived. He told me later that he helped cook for the refugees in the embassy compound where food was scarce, as the French embassy refused to share its food with its citizens. This resulted in Doug cooking some of the pets of the refugees for food. At length, the Khmer Rouge expelled the refugees and French embassy staff from Kampuchea, the new name for the country. They organized a convoy to take them to Thailand. It was a low point in France's long involvement with Cambodia.

Most Americans evacuated from Cambodia were in Thailand. The Phnom Penh embassy had money left over from its commissary fund and decided to spend the money on a farewell dinner aboard the Oriental Hotel's elegant boat, the *Oriental Queen*. Everyone who made it out of Cambodia was invited, not just US embassy personnel. Despite the luxury and fine food it was a somber occasion. We had all lost friends; many were still unaccounted for. We all drank too much, including Ambassador Dean who was sharply critical of the American government for betraying an ally. One journalist assured the ambassador that he would treat the harsh comments as "background." "Print every word," said Dean. And the writer did. It cost Dean his next embassy but not his career. Henry Kissinger did not like being taken to task by his subordinates. Dean went on to serve as ambassador to Lebanon, Thailand, and India. It was my privilege to have known him.

Despite, or perhaps because of, the war and the high metallic content of the air in Phnom Penh, I formed more friendships than I might have if Cambodia had been at peace. Friendships were more intense. I have kept in touch with more people from my two years in Cambodia than from any other postings. Many of the people I knew and worked with were handpicked for their assignments. Some, drawn like moths to a flame, craved the danger and adrenaline rush. A few just had fun. I like the quote attributed to Michael Herr, the author of *Dispatches*, an account of the Vietnam war by a drug-addled voyeur journalist: "I had Vietnam instead of a happy childhood." For some, the same was true of Cambodia.

But in the end, the behavior of the American government was disgraceful, especially the US Congress. We encouraged the small, poorly led army to take on the North Vietnamese invaders, supported them half-heartedly, and then deserted them. Perhaps two million Khmer died in the genocide that followed. It was not America's finest hour.

People often ask me what was my favorite posting in the CIA. I say that I liked them all but each for different reasons. Then I say that Cambodia was my favorite. It was there that I made my first recruitments, handled some of my best agents, and made some of my lasting friends. Because of the war and rockets falling into Phnom Penh every day, life was intense. Every day, it seems that something interesting, dangerous, or fun happened. Sometimes all three happened in one day.

***

When Cambodia fell, I joined BJ in Bangkok while Vietnam, Laos, and Cambodia fell under communist sway. After a two-month trip around the world with BJ to decompress from the trauma of Cambodia, I returned to Thailand. Almost immediately, the station chief assigned me to debrief Americans who were leaving Vietnam. This wide assortment of people included everyone from old Asia hands who had missed the evacuation at the end of April, to army deserters who had been rounded up by the new regime in the south and deported. One of the people I was on the lookout for was Tucker Gougelmann, a Marine veteran of Guadalcanal and later a CIA paramilitary officer who had served in Vietnam. Tucker, who had retired in Thailand with his Vietnamese wife, made a trip to Vietnam in 1975 to help get his wife's family out of the country. The Vietnamese captured him and installed him in prison in Hanoi where he was tortured, probably to death. Though they denied holding him, the Vietnamese released his battered remains to American authorities in 1977. His remains rest in Arlington National Cemetery. When I asked the boss if he really wanted me to work full time with the debriefings, he said, "Only from nine to five. After that, you work for me." It was a busy month and I received a nice certificate of appreciation.

One of the first official diplomatic functions I attended was a dinner in honor of the late Steven Solarz, a first-term Democrat congressmen from New York City who also sat on the House Foreign Affairs Committee. A senior embassy officer hosted the event, which included several leading Thai politicians. Solarz reveled in the spotlight on his first trip to Asia as a congressman. When someone asked him about the alarming developments in Cambodia, Solarz called it a tragedy but incorrectly predicted, "When the shooting stops, the killing stops." Never one to mince words, I told Solarz that he was wrong and the bill that ended aid to the Khmer Republic doomed the country. "The killing is not over. It has just started," I said, as calmly as I could manage, adding, "That bill will probably result in the death of a million Cambodians at the hands of the Khmer Rouge." I was wrong. The final tally turned out to be much higher. Neither Solarz nor the embassy officer who hosted the event appreciated my candor.

It was good to be back in Thailand, where BJ had made friends, learned Thai, and liked her teaching job. We found a nice four-bedroom house with a spiral teak staircase, which was a five-minute drive to work. BJ brought her maid, Sri, a very pleasant Thai-Mon woman who became our nanny and spent 17 years with us.

Thailand has had a long and close relationship with the CIA, dating back to World War II, when the Office of Strategic Services (OSS), forerunner of the CIA, worked with the Free Thai Movement against the Japanese who occupied Thailand. Many OSS officers joined the CIA and a number of them were sent back to Thailand. William "Wild Bill" Donovan, a New York lawyer and Medal of Honor winner in World War I, founded and ran the OSS at the request of President Roosevelt and to the chagrin of the US Army and the Federal Bureau of Investigations. In the early 1950s President Eisenhower made Donovan ambassador to Thailand. During the same period, a former OSS officer, Robert "Red" Jantzen, was chief of station for many years. My first boss was Hugh, an affable and very competent Harvard graduate who parachuted into Laos in 1945 as an OSS lieutenant.

Two old-timers from the 1950s, Bill Lair and Jack Shirley, were still on board when I arrived. Bill, a laconic Texan and one of the original Agency officers in Thailand dating from 1951 spent most of his distinguished career in Thailand and Laos. He helped create a special unit in the Thai police for special operations. Both married Thai women. Bill's wife was from an aristocratic family. King Bhumibol decorated Jack Shirley for saving Thai airmen after a plane crash. Both men had earned the respect of the king who wanted them commissioned in the Royal Thai Police, an action that required the approval of President Eisenhower. Ike signed off and Bill was made a lieutenant colonel and Jack a captain.

Later in my tour, after my old boss, Dan, took over as chief, I observed just how effective Bill could be. At a dinner party where both Dan and I were invited, I saw Dan called away to take an emergency telephone call. Because of serious internal political tensions in Thailand at the time, when Dan got off the phone, I asked if a coup d'état was underway.

"No," he said. "One of our officers has been arrested at the airport attempting to enter Thailand on a false passport, against my orders."

"What are you going to do?" I asked.

"Nothing. I am going to let Colonel Lair handle the matter." Dan made a phone call. Bill went to the airport, sorted out the problem quickly, and left with the officer. No incident, no press, no problem. It was nice to have men like Bill in the station. It was even better to have Dan on board as chief. He knew how to work with the Thai and how to run operations better than anyone I knew. While there was a human crisis on the Cambodian border, there was a political crisis brewing in Bangkok ending with a coup d'état. A Thai friend called me at home saying he was coming to see me. By the time he arrived, Thai radio stations were playing martial music, a sure sign the military had taken charge. My friend, a

Dan Arnold with twins Nicolas, left, and Laura in retirement in Bucks County, Pennsylvania. A Marine wounded in action in World War II, Dan was a mandarin of the CIA's East Asia Division and a mentor to me.

senior military officer, said he would take me to the coup leaders, as he wanted to be sure the Americans knew exactly what was happening. After driving through a number of Thai army checkpoints, he delivered me to the coup plotter who gave me an excellent briefing.

My friend then drove me to my office where people were working late. Bill Lair arrived about the same time I did and we each wrote up our reports. It transpired that two different groups had planned the coup and one was pre-empted by another. Bill's contacts won the day but the station had both sides of a complex situation well covered. I came away with a better appreciation of the unique role Bill played and of the wisdom of letting certain officers spend much of their career in one area.

My friend, Royal Thai Air Force Group Captain Sudhi Lekhyananda, who I had first met in Ohio where he was in graduate school with my father, as a very young boy, attended elementary school with King Bhumibol. Their fathers had studied at Harvard University together. Sudhi's father earned a law degree; the king's father earned a degree in medicine. Because of their family history, the king often invited Sudhi and his lovely wife, Sue, to informal jazz evenings at the palace, where His Majesty performed many of his own compositions. The king rarely invited foreigners, but Sudhi told me he made an exception for Red Jantzen and his wife. To show that the Americans were special friends, Queen Sirikit would ask Red to dance.

Jack Shirley retired in Thailand and was much liked—especially by the Thai military and the Thai police who had served with him over many years in Laos during the war. Jack tended to hang out at the Madrid bar on Patpong road, not far from my old AP office. When Hollywood came to Bangkok to make the film *The Deer Hunter*, the producer wisely hired Jack to be a "facilitator" and facilitate he did. He saved the production several million dollars by renting Thai military equipment at bargain rates, and arranging locations such as the rental of Patpong Road, which was transformed into the infamous Tu Do Street in Saigon for the film.

Jack also made bookings for a senior producer making his first trip to Thailand. In addition to reserving the Somerset Maugham suite of the Oriental Hotel, at the time Bangkok's finest hotel, Jack had the hotel's Rolls-Royce on hand at the airport for the fellow's arrival. Jack personally walked the producer through customs and escorted him to the hotel where he was taken directly to the suite overlooking the Chao Phraya River in the old wing of the hotel. When the Hollywood man walked into the bedroom, he found a young completely nude Thai woman kneeling on the four-poster bed, palms pressed together above her chest in a traditional Thai gesture of respect, or "*wai*" greeted him. The producer missed all his morning appointments the next day. The film won Academy awards for Best Picture and Best Director. The young lady, a dancer from Mike's Place bar on Patpong, is in the film.

Years later, I took a young American helicopter pilot to lunch at the Madrid bar, which was famous for its pizza, among other things. I told him that the bar had been a hangout for CIA and Air America personnel during and after the Vietnam War and was still a favorite for old Thai hands. I pointed to the bar stool closest to the door and mentioned that it "belonged" to Jack Shirley. At that moment, an elderly Briton who was reading the *Bangkok Post* occupied the stool. As if on cue, Jack walked in. The Brit jumped up and said "Just keepin' it warm for you Jack." Shirley nodded a greeting to me, and sat down. Unordered, a Singha beer appeared in front of him. Jack had the staff well trained.

***

Patpong is a little street with a bad reputation. Located between Silom and Suriwongse Roads in central Bangkok, the privately owned street stretches more than 200 meters long. Built in 1946 by Udom Patpong, a Sino-Thai businessman, it has earned a reputation as Bangkok's "street of sin." Closed to through traffic every evening, the street becomes a night bazaar lined with bars filled with girls hawking their services for a price. Touts lure visitors to upstairs establishments featuring illegal sex shows. Here, it is *caveat emptor*—or buyer beware—all part of the tawdry scene.

It was not always so. Before the Vietnam War, Patpong was sedate, commercial, and cosmopolitan. I worked there in 1962 for the AP. The United States Information Service operated a library two doors away. Bangkok's classy nightclub, the Keynote Club, with Narcing Aguilar at the piano bar, attracted an upscale trade. Every year Udom closed the street for a few nights to host the Patpong Mardi Gras, a charity event that raised money for a leprosarium in Chiang Mai.

By the 1970s, Patpong had morphed into a street of bars and restaurants, some of which were owned by convivial expatriates. In addition to offering a variety of tasty food the restaurants were the meeting place and recreational center for Bangkok's growing foreign community. Tourists were rarely seen. The Napoleon restaurant was known for its steak sandwiches and jazz on Sundays, when the best bands jammed. The Barrel, home of American Legion Shanghai Post Number One (Operating in Exile), featured chipped beef on toast, a favorite of veterans, including me. Tourists didn't usually go to Patpong. It attracted expatriates who knew their way around.

Foreign adventurers have long sought their fortunes in Thailand. In the 17th century, a young Greek named Constantine Phaulkon pitched up on the shores of Thailand, then known as Siam, and rose to become Foreign Minister at the court of King Narai in Ayuttaya. Then, as now, adventurers in Thailand sometimes come to an unhappy end. Phaulkon fell victim to court intrigue and was eventually executed. Although no one was executed on Patpong, it attracted some sketchy characters.

One of these lesser adventure seekers was Guillaume Vogeleer, better known as "Jimmy." He had been a young sergeant in the Belgian paratroopers in 1960, when he was sent to the Congo to help restore order following an internal revolt. Following his discharge from the military, Jimmy became a mercenary and served in that capacity in the Congo, Biafra, and Yemen. A short, solid, fellow with a trimmed beard, he could be dangerous when aroused. Actually, he was always dangerous. He was also known as Jimmy the Mercenary or simply Jimmy the Merc; he carried a knife, concealed in this belt buckle.

Violence was part of his way of life, and it was always politic to be on good terms with Jimmy. He had a Thai girlfriend named Daeng who owned the Madrid Bar on Patpong. One day, they had a fight and broke up. Daeng, fearing Jimmy might cause trouble, hired an off-duty Bangkok police officer for protection. Jimmy walked into the bar and saw the cop. As Jimmy dashed the length of the bar, the unfortunate security man fumbled to pull his pistol. Before he could clear leather Jimmy was on him; he wrestled the weapon from the frightened policeman's hand and put the gun in the fellow's mouth. "My friend," Jimmy said gently, "If you are going to work for Daeng you are going to have to be a lot faster than that." The cop resigned and shortly thereafter Daeng made up with Jimmy.

Jimmy's prized possession was his paratrooper's red beret, which he hung proudly behind the bar of the Madrid. One night, Jimmy was drinking with friends at the Madrid when a very drunk and very large German walked in. He ordered a drink and asked about the beret hanging on the wall. Jimmy rose and in a friendly tone said it was his old Belgian paratrooper beret. The Hun then made two mistakes. He first belittled Belgium and then he disparaged the Belgian parachute regiment. Jimmy was fast. In a serious of violent blows, he reduced the hapless German to a weeping heap on the floor. Daeng called the police who arrived quickly, arrested the German, and dragged him out. Jimmy returned to his friends saying, "I'm sorry guys. I didn't know he was a bleeder."

While serving as vice president, Walter Mondale visited Thailand with his wife and son, Teddy. King Bhumibol hosted a state dinner for the Mondales, but Teddy wasn't included. The ambassador, who needed to find something for Teddy to do that evening, asked that I arrange an evening for the young Mondale. "Have a good time," he said and in a low, serious voice, added "Don't get into trouble."

Teddy was a pleasant young man whose hobby was motor cross. He had a two-man Secret Service detail that accompanied him on his night on the town. We also had a four-man security squad from the Thai police's Special Branch under the command of an English-speaking major. Teddy was offered two options: a Thai food banquet followed by a live classical dance performance, or Patpong. Teddy immediately chose the latter. Hearing that, the police major said he had to call his boss, chief of Bangkok police. When asked if Patpong was off limits, he said "No, but if you want to go to Patpong, we need to 'sanitize' the street in advance." Within a few minutes of the phone call, all touts, louts, beggars, and shills on Patpong Road had been dispersed for the evening.

By Patpong standards, Teddy had a very quiet and restrained evening. He grazed at a few watering holes including the Grand Prix bar owned by Rick Menard. You had to be invited by Rick to sit at his private little bar at the back where he resided. Up front was a long oval bar that had an island in the middle with three or more girls in bikinis dancing. Teddy seemed to enjoy the convivial evening from his perch at Rick's private bar. We ended up at Mike's Place, a gin mill run by a German (Mike), famous for the quality of its dancers. Teddy and a few White House staff officers enjoyed themselves until it was closing time. Teddy groaned when the lights went up, signaling last call for drinks. The Special Branch major saw this and approached. "Do you want another drink?" he asked. Teddy nodded. The major had a quick word with Mike who announced to the girls, "Back to work." The lights went down, the girls resumed dancing, and Teddy had another drink.

Some years later, during a layover at San Francisco International Airport en route back to Washington DC after a visit to China, I was drinking a beer at a stand-up bar waiting for my flight to be called. A lanky fellow in cowboy boots was standing next to me. I guessed his age to about 50. We started to chat and he told me he was an oilfield worker on his way home from Borneo to Canada. He bought me a drink. I asked if he ever made it up to Bangkok. He said he had and we talked about Bangkok for a while. I bought him a drink. I asked if he had ever been to Executive Room on Pat Pong. He looked surprised and said "That's my home away from home whenever I'm in Bangkok. How did you know?" I said it was an educated guess. The Executive Room was a well-known haunt of expat oilmen. Owned by an American roughneck and operated by his Filipina wife, Ike, it was the classiest bar on Pat Pong; all the girls wore evening gowns. They were genteel and not pushy. In the course of our conversation, the Canadian bought me another drink. Then my flight was called and I had to leave. I told him I owed him a drink. He said, "Don't worry about it. You can buy me a drink the next time I see you on Patpong." I took out business cards and wrote on the back "Good for one drink at the Executive Room." I gave him the card and said that Ike would honor the card. We shook hands and I never saw him again.

About six months later I was in Bangkok on business and stopped by the Executive Room one evening after work with friends. I remembered the Canadian oilman and asked Ike if anyone had come in with my card looking for a drink. She said yes, a month or two earlier some oilies from Balikpapan dropped in and one of the showed her my card and asked, "Ike, if I give this card to you will you give me a free drink"? She read my note and said yes. He ordered a drink and when

Ike asked for the card the oilman said, "I'll pay for the drink. I want to keep the card."

Over time, Patpong lost all of its charm and become dangerous as expats moved to safer pastures. One night in the 1990s, a fellow I worked with agreed to meet a friend on Patpong after work for a drink. He arrived early and was approached by a young tout.

"Sex show upstairs," he said. "No cover charge." My friend went upstairs and ordered a beer. A young Thai lady came on the stage nude and performed a lewd act.

"How much for the beer?" he asked, when he had finished his beer.

"$50," said the barman.

"Bullshit!" said my friend and several nasty-looking Thai toughs surrounded him.

"I don't have $50 on me," he said, "can I make a phone call to get the money?"

"Do it," said the bar's manager and handed him a phone. My friend dialed a number from memory.

"Colonel," he said, "I'm on Patpong Road and am being charged $50 for a beer." He turned to the manager and said. "It's for you" and handed the manager the phone. My friend had called a senior officer in the Special Branch of the Royal Thai Police.

"*Kup, kup, kup,*" (Yes sir, yes sir, yes sir) said the manager to the cop.

"*Sia jai mock kup,*" (Very sorry sir) added the manager and hung up.

"The beer is on me," said the manager.

"I'll have another one," answered my friend. Don't try this unless you have a good friend in the Royal Thai Police.

***

The United States established diplomatic relations with the People's Republic of China (PRC) on January 1, 1979. This marked a watershed in the history of Agency operations targeting PRC officials. Before the normalization of US–China relations, the Chinese had a strict policy to avoid all direct contact with American officials. This inhibited the ability of our officers, especially our Chinese-speaking officers of China Operations, to spot and develop likely targets for recruitment. The Agency had other avenues of approach, which it exploited fully, but there is nothing better than direct case officer contact, and this had been lacking.

We were all eager to meet the Chinese—especially two of our China officers who spoke good Mandarin—and to make direct contact with Chinese officials. However, every attempt we made to meet the Chinese on the "circuit" met with failure. The Chinese were always polite but invariably said that due to the lack of formal relations they were forbidden to talk to Americans. Finally, we had a stroke of luck. More accurately, through a stroke of hard work we arranged for a neutral third country national to invite both American and Chinese diplomats to a private dinner in a famous restaurant for a banquet with special dishes flown in from Hong Kong.

About eight guests attended including our two China Ops officers, whom we will call Tom and Jerry. Tom, the senior of the two, had an aggressive operational style. A 20-year veteran of the Cold War, his officers called him "Mad Dog," but only behind his back. Jerry, who was younger and smoother, was frustrated that few of the local Chinese could speak Mandarin and the Mandarin speakers at the PRC embassy would not speak to him. When the Chinese diplomats invited to the banquet learned that Americans would be present their love of good food overcame the bureaucratic injunction against fraternization. Besides, with other guests also invited they figured they could avoid speaking to the Americans.

One other American—a journalist who is my source of information for what transpired that evening—also attended the dinner at the renowned restaurant. Located in the bowels of Chinatown where few foreigners ventured, the Chinese considered it one of the finest restaurants in town. Said to have once been an elegant brothel, it offered many private rooms for intimate dinners. Apart from my friend, all the guests were officials from several countries. They were Chinese experts looking forward to the expensive culinary experience. To put everyone in a good mood, the restaurant served fiery Chinese alcohol called *mao tai* in tiny cups kept full through seemingly endless rounds of toasts in fine Chinese tradition. *Mao tai* is considerably more potent that whiskey or the vodka that flowed at Soviet events. The lingua franca for the evening was Mandarin Chinese, to the delight of the PRC guests. Softened by the *mao tai*, they lost whatever inhibitions they had in talking to their American counterparts. For one evening the dictates of protocol would be relaxed in lieu of the opportunity to drink and dine sumptuously.

The dinner did not disappoint. Course after course delighted the diners. Toasts to international friendship, to the cook, to the next meeting, etc., kept pace with the food. Everyone was having a good time. This is what good case officers are always looking for, a great meal with a good target. Or maybe, vice versa. As the evening wore on the alcohol began to take its toll. Liquor can certainly lubricate an evening but it can also be the downfall of the case officer in more ways than one. Alcoholism, for instance, is an occupational hazard of life for American officials—and his or her spouse. Drinking too much risks another danger: giving away a secret. The Soviets, for example, constantly try to drink their American counterparts under the table, sometimes for fun but often hoping to get an edge in the game of spy vs. spy. Perhaps even more unfortunate than giving away a secret would be getting a nugget of important information only to forget it in a drunken stupor. I have seen more than one case officer in the men's room at diplomatic receptions making notes to themselves about information they just received lest they forget it by the end of the evening. Such are the dangers of case officers in the field who only have one liver to give for their country.

Everyone got drunk, except my journalist friend who was a teetotaler. A quiet observer of the revelry, he made up for not drinking by thoroughly enjoying the food. At one point, he noticed that Jerry excused himself to visit the restroom, maybe to make notes. When he did not return, the other guests assumed he had gone home. Ordinarily, it would have been a serious breach of protocol but in the alcoholic haze of the evening, no one noticed the gaffe. In the festive mood, fueled by the *mao tai*, no one missed Jerry.

Tom, his constitution honed by many hours of business dining, thought he could handle the occasion. When the Chinese guests rose unsteadily to take their leave, Tom got up to say goodnight. As he did so, and without warning, Tom vomited explosively on the junior PRC official present. He didn't get a chance to exchange cards with any of the fast-disappearing Chinese diplomats; he saw his chances of a follow-up meeting were seriously diminished. Not the best way to end the evening, perhaps, but these things happen. On that unfortunate note, the evening ended. These things happen.

About three hours after the restaurant closed, Jerry woke up in the bathroom where he had fallen asleep. With some effort, he roused the Indian night watchman, who was fast asleep on the threshold of the restaurant. The watchman finally produced some keys and unlocked the security grille. Jerry's next problem was finding his car, which he had parked somewhere in the warren of streets of Chinatown. With some luck, he found the car, but he couldn't seem to connect his keys to the keyhole. While fumbling with his key that he came to attention of a police officer who offered his assistance and helped Jerry get home. Although it had not been China Ops' finest hour, no real harm was done and some good work was accomplished at a personal level, most of it by Jerry. Needless to say, neither Tom nor Jerry reported fully on all aspects of the evening, which the station hailed as a breakthrough accomplishment

***

One of the many things I like about the Thai is their ability to have fun while doing business. Mixing business with pleasure seems fundamental to their ethos. They call it *sanuk*. A good example happened when an infestation of rats jeopardized the rice harvest in the province of Nonthaburi, just north of Bangkok. The governor mobilized the populace to kill rats, something of a departure for a people who follow Theravada Buddhism. He organized an event he called the Rat Fair. The idea was for thousands of citizens to gather early on a Saturday morning, hunt down and kill rats, and then have a big party. In the afternoon, he arranged classical Thai dancing, paddled boat races on the Chao Phraya River, and a picnic lunch that included fried field rat. There was even a Miss Rat Fair contest. This was *sanuk* in action.

Eating rat with Pulitzer Prize-winning AP photographer Neal Ulevich at a Rat Fair festival in Nonthaburi, Thailand. The fair was organized by the provincial government to kill rats that were eating the rice crop. The event included a Miss Rat Fair contest of which I was a judge.

When the foreign press corps learned of the rodent hunt they decided to cover the event. Neal Ulevich, the Associated Press photographer, alerted me and since I had nothing better to do that weekend, I decided to join in. We did not participate in the early morning rat killing, but joined the afternoon festivities, which drew a huge crowd. The governor, a jovial can-do kind of fellow, oversaw the events. He welcomed the press and when he learned that I was an American he immediately made me a judge in the Miss Rat Fair contest. A bevy of local beauties in swimsuits competed for the title. I don't know how they were selected for the contest, but any one of them could have won. I voted for a shy, slender young beauty who actually won the contest. I only worried about her having to tell people that her claim to fame was winning the Miss Rat Fair contest. It probably looks better on her curriculum vitae in Thai.

The Rat Fair also featured boat racing. Teams of local boys, about 20 rowers per team, fiercely paddled their long, low, boats down the big, busy, and fast-flowing river, the lifeline of central Thailand. They demonstrated more enthusiasm than skill as a number of boats foundered in the choppy river. The mishaps did little to dampen the spirits of the rowers, however, who quickly became swimmers focused on saving their boats. This all happened amid cheers from spectators on the riverbank, most of whom were fortified by local alcoholic spirits.

Away from the river, dozens of young ladies, dressed in their finest traditional silk gowns, performed traditional dancing to slow, classical Thai music in front of an appreciative audience of friends and family. I almost forgot the theme of our bucolic sojourn until it was announced that some rats had been captured alive and would be part of the lunch.

The morning rat hunt had been very successful. Thousands of rats, and some hundreds of poisonous snakes, were killed in the group effort to save the rice harvest. Some hundreds of rodents had also been taken alive. A circle of youths, each armed with a wooden cudgel, formed a circle about 50 feet across. Thousands of spectators surrounded the circle and watched as live rats were released from jute sacks. The rodents ran wild, trying to get away. They were then set upon by the armed youths who seemed to take great pleasure bashing the rats with their clubs. Blood splattered everywhere as the boys warmed to their lethal task.

The day did not end with the grisly dispatching of captured rats. It ended with eating them. The rats were skinned and gutted as teams of cooks skillfully sautéed them in woks seasoned with garlic and Thai spices. Honored guests, including the foreign press and me, were pressed forward to taste the fruit of the hunt. I had never been offered rat before. Our hosts assured us that these were not urban vermin living in sewers. These were country rats (*noo na*), raised on the finest rice in the world. Few refused the honor and I must say mine was delicious. It tasted like chicken.

Visitors needed to be wary. Pickpockets and purse-snatchers were on the lookout for an easy mark. Burglars were also active and often very skilled. My first experience with Bangkok burglars, or *kemoys* as they were known locally, came in 1962 when my father was an adviser to the Thai Air Force. Late one night, Pappy came into my bedroom with a rifle in his hand, woke me up, and whispered "*Kemoys* downstairs." I armed myself with a short Thai sword and we moved quietly to the staircase to see two burglars at work in the living room. My father switched on the lights, chambered a round, and we roared down the staircase brandishing our weapons. It worked. Cat burglars in Bangkok are rarely violent and, true to form, the pair broke through a screen door in their haste to depart. As they ran across the lawn, my father fired a round in the air. Lights came on all over the neighborhood as the *kemoys* were climbing the barbed wire at the top of our wall, leaving pieces of shirt and a little blood on the wire in their wake. Police arrived in less than five minutes. We were not bothered again.

My next encounter with burglars was quite a surprise. We had two servants—a cook, and a maid—who lived in quarters behind the house. Our little Lhasa Apso dog—Tsampa—served as our main defense. He had a distinguished pedigree having been bred in India by Tenzing Norgay, the Sherpa conqueror of Mt. Everest. Tenzing gave the very small puppy to a Swedish nurse en route to visit us, and she left Tsampa with us. Our other dog, a mixed breed, was larger and meaner and lived with the staff. Tsampa slept on our bed and, like most of his breed, had keen hearing and slept lightly. Traditionally in Tibet, Lhasas were paired with mastiffs in the Dalai Lama's palace, the Potala. Intruders woke up the little dogs, who in turn would wake up the mastiffs who would then go to work. The arrangement also worked for us.

Late one night when we were asleep, Tsampa heard a sound and immediately began to bark, waking both of us up and the outside dog, whose bite was worse than his bark. I turned on a light and armed myself with a Russian Makarov pistol, a gift from a Cambodian general. As I descended the staircase, pistol in hand, I saw two young burglars in the process of dis-assembling my stereo system and passing components to accomplices outside. The lights, barking, and possibly my pistol, sent them running away from the house. After they fled, I reported the incident to the local police station, which immediately sent a car full of very cooperative and professional police officers. The only thing I regretted losing was a 12th-century Song Dynasty Chinese vase that had been sitting on one of the hi-fi speakers. After a few minutes searching the grounds, a Thai policeman found the vase, unbroken, on the lawn.

The next day, a Thai friend dropped by to take us out to dinner in a nearby Chinese restaurant. As I prepared a couple of Scotch and sodas I told him that there would be no music with our drinks. The burglars had taken the speakers. I described our recent excitement. He was embarrassed and asked for details. He wondered what I would have done if the burglars had been armed. I said I would have attempted to detain them until the police arrived. "Good," he said. He then asked, "What would you have done if they opened fire?" I told him that I would have fired in self-defense, noting that I was undefeated in gunfights. "Good," he said, but added, "If you shoot a burglar, don't call the police. Call me. My brother is a police general and he will send a team to handle the matter." I thanked him and asked how they would handle it. "Usually, they just throw the bodies in the river. It happens quite often. No need for you to be inconvenienced." Then we went to dinner.

A few months later, Group Captain Sudhi, my father's old friend who had taken me under his arm, invited us to spend a weekend in the Khao Yai National Park, a four-hour drive into the hills northeast of Bangkok. Sudhi, his charming wife, Sue, and the whole family sort of adopted us. We visited their weekend homes in Pattaya and Hua Hin, and played golf, the national passion. Khao Yai (Big Mountain) had tropical jungle with a wildlife population that included 50 tigers and a golf course. The exotic fauna added a special something to a round of golf. Although I never saw a tiger, on one visit, I landed a golf ball in the rough on a large and fresh elephant dropping.

"Lend me your sand wedge, Sudhi," I asked.

"No way," he answered.

"Take a free drop, local rule." The same day a monkey ran onto a green and stole my golf ball.

"Take a free drop, another local rule," said Sudhi.

A Royal Thai Air Force facility that was closed to the public dominated the highest terrain inside. It housed the Khao Khio (Green Mountain) radar site, which provided early warning of attacking enemy aircraft. The radar site was one of the projects Sudhi and my father had worked on together a decade earlier. The air force had rustic but comfortable cabins in the grounds of the site for the use of senior officers and their friends at the site. Here, we cooked for ourselves, sometimes roasting a barking deer over a fire around which we huddled for warmth. Sudhi regularly included Bruce Thompson, the IBM director for Thailand and Sudhi's tenant in a charming house on Klong Saen Sap, a major Bangkok canal on trips to Khao Yai. Bruce always brought a bottle of Jack Daniels whiskey. We passed the bottle around the bonfire, taking sips as we told stories.

My favorite story from Bruce took place in Da Nang, Vietnam, during the war, when he was a young IBM staffer in Vietnam in charge of taking care of the computers used by the Marine Corps in support of their 80,000 men in country. Bruce met with the three-star Marine general in command of all Marines in Vietnam. A softly-spoken southerner, the general asked the young man from IBM:

"Son, have you ever been in the service?"

Bruce replied, "No sir, I was in the Air Force."

The general smiled and said, "Son, I think we are going to get along just fine." And so they did.

On another occasion, Sudhi drove the family Volkswagen bus with plenty of room for his wife, Sue, their three small children, BJ, and me. I sat in front with Sudhi. We turned off Friendship Highway, which was financed by the US and linked Bangkok with Korat, a major town in the northeast and the site of a major Royal Thai Air Force base. It was overcast and rain threatened. Suddenly, a bullet shattered the windshield and exited through my side window. Unfazed, Sudhi kept driving until he thought it was safe to stop the van. "Probably a communist sniper," he said matter-of-factly. "We know they are operating around here because of Khao Khio. That's why security is so tight up there." We kicked out the remains of the windshield just as it began to rain. I zipped my jacket and held a golf umbrella outside the slow-moving van to keep rain off Sudhi as we made our way slowly up the mountain. We made it safely to Khao Khio, where Sudhi reported the incident and opened the bar early.

***

My Swiss artist friend Theo Meier was thriving in Chiang Mai. He married his maid and model Laiad who controlled his drinking, was heavily involved in the construction of his riverside residence outside Chiang Mai, and helped get Theo's career back on track. One afternoon, I received a call from Prince Sanidh Rangsit, Theo's patron and friend. Sanidh had always kind and generous to me. He hosted my farewell dinner in Bangkok in 1963 when I returned to college. The theme was Bali and Theo cooked Balinese food for the occasion. Sanidh had a PhD in Ethnology and a reputation as a hedonist. The French film *Emmanuelle*, which depicted the sexual life of certain French diplomats in Thailand in the 1950s, included a character loosely patterned after Sanidh. He invited me to attend a big birthday party for Theo in Chiang Mai to celebrate his 72nd birthday, auspicious as the "Sixth Cycle" to the Theravada Buddhist Thai. Naturally, I accepted, took annual leave, and bought extra film for the event.

The party lasted three days. Each night a Thai band played until midnight. Then a second band played until people stopped dancing. It was kind of an open house. There were senior guests such as members of Chiang Mai's royal family, an Indian maharajah, and the American consul. But just about everyone in the small village came along to wish Theo happy birthday, and enjoy Thai food and entertainment, which included industrial quantities of Maekhong whiskey. I vaguely recall falling

Swiss artist Theo Meier sketches BJ at his Chiang Mai, Thailand, studio in 1970. Theo was one of the European artists who made their home on the Indonesian island of Bali before World War II. He moved to Thailand in the 1950s where he continued to paint until his death in 1984. I met him when working on a Tarzan film in 1963 and we became close friends.

asleep around four o'clock in the morning on the first day, seeing Theo, 72 years old, dancing vigorously with a young Thai woman.

It was my all-time favorite party, birthday or otherwise. I shot 10 rolls of film; some of the photos appear in the book *Theo Meier: A Swiss Artist Under the Tropics.* Published in 2007, by Didier Hamel, it is the definitive book on Theo and his art. One of my photos in the book is Theo's sketch of BJ and another of Theo making the sketch.

***

During my posting I was saddened to see the destruction of many fine old residences, many of which graced canals that once carried travelers and much of the city's commerce. Developers were tearing down traditional houses to build shopping centers, skyscrapers, and big apartment complexes. Urban blight was replacing the elegant residences that once stood on the quiet, tree-lined streets. I began a project in my spare time to photograph stately old houses to preserve them on film. Aiding me in this project was Pranalee Singhara na Ayuthia, a senior official in the Thai National Security Agency and a member of Thai aristocracy. She opened many doors for me. This led to my first book, *Old Homes of Bangkok: Fragile Link.* Thai and diplomatic friends opened doors for me and made introductions to homeowners as the project progressed.

One of the fine old houses—Krom Phra Chan Palace—had been the family home of Queen Sirikit. The riverside residence was constructed in 1926 for the marriage of the Queen's father, Mom Chao Nakkhatra Kitiyakara. When I photographed the house it was the residence of M. L. Kalyakit Kitiyakara and his wife, Khunying (a bestowed royal title) Arun, a charming lady with a puckish sense of humor. One day, she invited BJ and me for royal teacakes, a favorite of King Bhumibol, she said, which she cooked over charcoal in the garden. As we chatted and enjoyed the delicious Siamese confections, Arun casually asked if I would like to see photos of Queen Sirikit nude. Shocked, I thought she was joking and politely declined. Enjoying my discomfort, the Khunying opened the family photo album, and pointed to a toddler standing naked in a wading pool. "That's the Queen," Arun declared with a grin.

Later, Arun invited us to a picnic at her summer home in Nontaburi on the Chao Phraya River north of Bangkok. She co-hosted the event with her close friend Josie Stanton, the widow of the first American ambassador to Thailand after World War II, Edwin Stanton. White-haired and rather elegant, Josie converted to Buddhism and made Bangkok her home. When she first arrived in Bangkok just after the war ended, Josie selected a residence. Shown a variety of fine old homes she chose one on Wireless Road with a big compound and large stately trees. Because the grounds were full of scrapped Japanese vehicles from the war, officials from the Foreign Ministry urged her to choose another house. However, she prevailed and ultimately moved into the mansion, which had originally belonged to a British businessman and his several Siamese wives. The house, which belongs to the Thai government, continues to be the American ambassador's residence and is in my book.

The house across the street from the ambassador's residence, was a colonial-style mansion with a spacious lawn built in the 1920s by the Anglo-Thai Company. It belonged to the Charter Bank when I photographed it. The land sold for many millions of dollars and the house was torn down. It was a prime example of how leading foreign businessmen lived in Siam before the name of the kingdom was changed to Thailand before World War II. Sited on huge gardens, many of these homes on Wireless Road are gone now, the land too valuable. The quiet canals that flanked the two-lane road were filled in and paved. Traffic moves at a snail's pace.

One member of the Thai royal family who helped me was a war hero, Mom Chao (Prince) Karawik Chakrabandu, the former equerry of King Parajadipok, Rama VII, who was deposed in 1932 and lived out his life in England. During World War II, even though Thailand was considered a belligerent nation, the British commissioned two dozen Thai living in Britain into the British Army to help fight against the Japanese, who were occupying Thailand. The new officers were assigned to the Durham Light Infantry regiment because King Parajadipok had been the colonel of the regiment, an honorific title. Karawik, with the rank of captain, belonged to Force 136, the British counterpart of the OSS, and entered Thailand in 1944 by British submarine. He was close to the king's widow, Queen Rambai Bharni, who lived in Sukhothai Palace in Bangkok. The prince arranged for me to photograph the palace, a stately old 19th-century residence on a klong or canal. The spacious garden featured a putting green. Golf was the queen's passion.

Prime Minister Mom Rajawongse Kukrit Pramoj, a grandson of King Chulalongkorn (Rama V), wrote the foreword of the book, which was co-published by the royally sponsored Siam Society. Kukrit, in addition to being a politician, owned a Bangkok newspaper and was one of the Thailand's leading man of letters. I knew him from my AP days when we were both active in the Bangkok Foreign Correspondents' Club. Kukrit's unique half Thai (upper) and half Western (lower) residence is featured in the book.

A quick note here about Thai royal titles. Because kings had many wives, there was a multitude of royal offspring. To keep the number of princes and princesses manageable, royal progeny lost a title with each generation and after five generations, there was no royal title. So a grandson of a king is a Mom Chao. His children are Mom Rajawongse. Their children are Mom Luang. Later generations are allowed to use the word "na" to indicate royal lineage along the lines of the French "de" and German "von." An example is our friend Pranalee Singhara na Ayuthia, a retired senior official of the National Security Council. Ayuthia indicates that she is descended from King Rama III (1788–1851 CE).

* * *

While Serge Taube shaped my career, arranging key foreign assignments while teaching me how to recruit agents for the Clandestine Service, the man who provided hands-on guidance for much of my time in CIA, and beyond, was Daniel Clay Arnold. Dan belonged to the early generation of CIA "Asia Hands."

In those days, many Agency officers had previous service and Asian experience in the OSS, sometimes said to stand for "Oh So Social" because of the Ivy League pedigrees of its men and women. Thailand attracted its share of these daring souls, who had often operated behind Japanese lines working with local guerrilla fighters. They included: Robert "Red" Jantzen who rescued Americans from a Japanese prison camp in the Philippines, businessman Willis Bird Sr., Alexander McDonald, founder of the *Bangkok Post* newspaper, and James "Jim" Thompson, a Princeton architect with five Bronze Star medals and stayed in Thailand after the war and developed Thai silk into an international brand. Willis Bird Sr. was a colonel in the OSS who had led a mission to meet Mao Tse-tung in China, and settled in Thailand after the war, married into an aristocratic Thai family, and became a leading American businessman.

While these men worked behind Japanese lines, Dan Arnold fought the Japanese face-to-face as a Marine infantryman island-hopping in the Pacific. He saw action on Guam (where he was wounded) and Eniwitok. His brother, also a Marine, was killed in action on Iwo Jima. Dan became one of the mandarins of the East Asia Division, serving as chief in numerous countries including Laos, and Thailand. During his years in Laos he commanded thousands of hill-tribe guerilla fighters, against more than one hundred thousand invading North Vietnamese Army troops operating the "Ho Chi Minh trail." More than two hundred unarmed civilian aircraft of the CIA's Air America, the world's most shot-at airline, were under Dan's command as the war drew to a sad end in 1975.

In the early 1960s, when Dan served as deputy chief of station in Bangkok, under "Red" Jantzen, he pulled off a covert action coup that demonstrates what the CIA can accomplish with a little ingenuity and devious thinking. Dan was an avid reader of the Foreign Broadcast Information Service (FBIS), an overt CIA-supported organization that translates foreign-language radio broadcasts around the world. One day Dan read a translation of a Soviet broadcast in the Burmese language that attacked and insulted the King of Thailand, the royal family, the Thai military and other Thai institutions. The broadcast was aimed at a Burmese audience and played to the historical antipathy between Burma and Thailand. The KGB Active Measures mavens in Moscow must have thought that by attacking Burma's old enemy they would gain favor with the non-aligned Burmese. Dan, a friend of the Thai monarch, decided it was time for some "dirty tricks."

The Soviet embassy in Bangkok published a "news" digest promoting their propaganda agenda. Dan created a fake Soviet digest that included the text of the broadcast aimed at the Burmese. He printed the newsletter on the same Gestetner model the Soviet embassy used, with identical paper, typeface, and ink. He then circulated it to the Soviets' regular recipients as well as other Thai opinion leaders, who widely accepted it as a genuine Soviet product. There was an immediate outcry of protest at the Soviet attack against the Thai monarchy. The hapless Soviet ambassador was summoned by the Ministry of Foreign affairs and reduced to tears by the minister's sharp rebuke. It severely set back Soviet relations with Thailand. The Thai came close to breaking diplomatic relations. It did not take the Russians long to figure out what had happened. They blamed the CIA and asked the Thai to investigate. When asked by the Thai, Dan produced the original Soviet broadcast in Burmese, proving the Soviets had indeed insulted the king and the nation. Dan Arnold 1, USSR 0.

The Clandestine Service is a risk-taking organization but over the years I observed that the higher an officer climbed the corporate ladder, the more risk-averse he became. This was especially true of very senior officers in Langley who had been appointed to their positions. Dan was not one of these men. He never shirked from a tough decision. When I was once turned down when I wanted to "pitch" a sensitive target, Dan reversed the call and let me proceed. The man accepted my offer and reported accurately for years.

***

The borders of Thailand, Burma, and Laos meet at an area that is known as the "Golden Triangle" for the opium-producing poppies that have been cultivated in the hills there for generations. Most of the poppy crop is gown in the remote hills of the northern Shan state of Burma, where opium is chemically refined into far more deadly heroin. By the 1970s the flow of heroin through Thailand had become an international problem for law enforcement and intelligence services.

My friend, who I will call Tommy, agreed we should tour the rather inaccessible hills. This was long before Thailand became a destination for eco-tourism and trekking through tribal villages. The region's few roads were generally in poor shape. There were fewer hotels, but some of the guesthouses had a rustic charm. The scenery, however, was beautiful and largely unknown to westerners, apart from a few missionaries, anthropologists, and people interested in the narcotics trade.

Getting annual leave for our mountain vacation was easy. It was more difficult to persuade BJ and especially Tommy's Thai friend Ott to accompany us on our adventure into the opium hills. Ott wanted to go to Bali. BJ, already a fan of

Chiang Mai, the main city of northern Thailand, was easier to persuade. It had a six hundred-year history that made it older than Bangkok and possessed a slow-moving charm that Bangkok lacked. We used it as our base. We asked a friend in Chiang Mai to lend us a four-wheel-drive Land Cruiser and in exchange promised to report on the state of roads, hotels, and eating houses as well as any mule caravans we might see on our on our little foray into the hills.

We stocked up on bottled water, fruit, snacks, and a bottle of Scotch whiskey in case of a snakebite. Tommy was our driver; I was navigator and photographer. After a night in Chiang Mai we headed southwest early in the morning on a good paved road and in perfect weather, heading for Mae Sariang in an area populated by the Karen ethnic minority. In the hills we saw elephants working in Thailand's rapidly dwindling teak forests and stopped for a noodle lunch. Then we turned north, bound for Mae Hong Son, a charming town with Burmese-style Buddhist pagodas, a reminder of the many mixed cultures in the area. We found an adequate Chinese hotel with Western plumbing and a clean restaurant.

A visit to the morning market confirmed that we were now in hill-tribe country as evidenced by the colorful dress of Hmong, Lisu, Lahu, and Akha women, many of whom walked for hours to do their shopping. Mae Hong Son was the turning point back to Chiang Mai over a road that had not yet been constructed. The fun was about to begin. Signage was non-existent, but there was only one road heading north out of town and we took it. Red laterite, a material whose dust soon covered the car and us, replaced the paved road. Streams that often became wild torrents in the raining season bisected roads. Bridges sturdy enough to accommodate cars were few and far between. Some of the bridges looked so frail that we opted to ford the creeks, with me wading ahead looking for submerged boulders or holes. Most of the time there were no bridges at all.

We had virtually the only vehicle on the "road" and many people we passed asked for a lift. Heading for a village called Pai, in deep jungle with only a few hill-tribe villages, we started asking how far it was to Pai. Every answer was the same: "Six kilometers." All of them were wrong. Along the way we met a young Hmong hunter armed with a homemade, muzzle-loading flintlock rifle. I asked if he would sell it. After some bargaining, he agreed to part with his weapon for 300 baht, about $15. We both thought we had made a good deal.

Further on, we rounded a corner in thick jungle to see a mule caravan crossing the road in front of us. We stopped quickly. It was a tense moment, waiting to see if we were in trouble. I put my camera away and watched as the animals and their handlers crossed from the north and disappeared into the jungle. Each mule carried heavy loads covered with waterproof tarps. No one paid us any attention, and soon the dozens of animals and their muleteers were gone, as quietly as they had come. The lack of an armed escort or confrontation with us suggested that this was not a drug caravan but rather was smuggling other Burmese products, such as jade or other gemstones. The caravan took about five minutes to quietly cross the road. After they had passed, we moved on.

Pai turned out to be a dusty hill town, little more than a wide spot on a bad road. But it did have a funky Chinese restaurant with excellent fried rice, noodles, cold beer, and a bathroom. It was all downhill, literally, after that. The road deteriorated further; soon, we found ourselves on a narrow track with no traffic at all. Tommy sensed danger and stopped. Looking ahead, we found ourselves at the edge of a hundred-foot cliff. Somehow, we had turned off the road. If we had continued, we would have gone over. Tommy very gently turned the car around and we made our way back to the road. We moved more carefully, and more slowly. The rough terrain and stream crossings had destroyed the vehicle's clutch.

We eased out way into Chiang Mai just as the sun was setting and headed for The Pub, a popular watering hole owned by a Briton in the tobacco business. Covered in red laterite dust, the ladies made a beeline for the loo, where they washed off some of it. We enjoyed a fine meal of fish and chips washed down with Singha beer and made it to our hotel, The Chang Puek.

When we checked in, the manager informed us the hot water had run out. Now BJ is the most placid, even-tempered, and sweet lady you will ever meet. Until, that is, there is no hot water. She melted down. It was a rare and not a pleasant sight. After a quick chat with the manager and the passage of a few banknotes, he formed a bucket brigade to hand-carry hot water to our room. BJ hunkered down in the bathtub when I poured the water over her as she washed her hair and body. Whenever I asked how she was doing, all I heard was, "More!" So the buckets kept coming until finally she was clean.

When we returned the Land Cruiser the next morning, my friend did not recognize it. A quick wash fixed that. I mentioned that the clutch needed some looking at and showed him on a map where we had encountered the mule caravan. He thanked us for the info and said, "You were lucky." Smugglers, even those not transporting drugs, can be dangerous and the hills were essentially lawless. I was happy we made the trip, difficult and dangerous though it was. I learned a lot that put me in good stead years later when I was in the same hills plotting the destruction of the leading drug warlord, Khun Sa, just over the border in Burma. But Ott had a point; Bali would have been a lot less stressful.

***

One afternoon I was pleasantly surprised to receive a phone call from my old colleague in the Associated Press, writer Peter Arnett calling from New York. A native of Bluff, New Zealand, the southernmost city in the world, Peter had worked in his youth for the *Bangkok World* newspaper, the same paper that offered me $40 a month in 1962. He soon joined the AP and spent more than a decade in

Vietnam covering the war and winning a Pulitzer Prize. I last saw Peter in 1974 when he visited Cambodia.

We chatted about the old days and Peter asked me what was happening in Thailand. I told him more and more refugees were coming from Vietnam by boat and that many were attacked by Thai pirates. Survivors lucky enough to make it to Thailand were often turned back by authorities. Many died at sea. Peter passed this information to our mutual friend AP photographer Eddie Adams who then flew to Bangkok seeking "boat people" to photograph. He was fortunate enough to find a boat landing on a Thai beach and managed to get aboard before Thai military pushed the boat off. Eddie documented the sad episode and his photos raised awareness of the plight of the Vietnamese.

Thanks largely to Eddie's photos, Peter and Eddie traveled the world for the AP, telling the stories of the ten million homeless refugees worldwide seeking shelter at that time. Thanks to their reporting, thousands of Vietnamese were allowed into the United States as refugees. I was told that Eddie was prouder of his boat people photos than the dramatic Pulitzer-winning picture he took of a Vietnamese police general summarily executing a captured Viet Cong killer during the Tet Offensive in Saigon in 1968.

***

Organizing an operational dinner takes a lot of planning. They are primarily business occasions with a specific operational objective in each event. There must be at least one "target," others could be considered "fillers," rounding out the guest list with people who may be friends, interesting people to ensure a lively evening, or to repay a previous invitation.

Among the many considerations the guest list should not include people whose governments are not always on good terms: Indians and Pakistanis, for example. Cultural issues must be considered, especially when planning the meal. Does the food need to be Kosher, or Halal or, in recent years, vegetarian or gluten-free? In Thailand it was essential to know the political backgrounds of guests because it can be very easy to offend someone without ever knowing you had done so. The Thai would never tell you.

In the "old days" these events could be very formal, often tedious, and usually boring, not to mention risking one's health going to a dinner where hygienic cooking practices might not be observed, e.g. not washing fresh produce in Clorox or making ice with tap water, all hazards of life in the third world. Among her many talents, organizing dinner parties and making people feel welcome, and especially serving Michelin-star quality food are BJ's strong suits. I am certain that people who might have declined an invitation were lured into accepting knowing that they would dine well.

It therefore came as a surprise when we included two men from the state of Maine to a small dinner party in the mid-1970s with sub-optimal results. We included Major Stuart "Stu" Gerald, and his wife, Maggie, who taught English with BJ, with Michael Vickery, a somewhat eccentric academic well known for his extensive knowledge of ancient Cambodian history and his mastery of ancient and modern languages. I did not know him as well as I knew Stu who was a pilot, a Vietnam veteran, and an easy-going and congenial fellow who rose to the rank of brigadier general in his military career. Stu graduated from of the University of Maine. Stu and Maggie had a young son, Jake, who learned Thai by listening to the cook and maid speak. Jake impressed me at a party Stu hosted, which included a number of Royal Thai Army officers. Jake chatted with officers in his colloquial kitchen Thai. He was not only able to communicate with them, he even did a little interpreting for his father.

One day, while I was walking near the river, I heard someone yelling my name from a taxi. It was Michael, who was visiting from Penang, Malaysia, where he taught at a local university. He invited me to jump in, which I did. He had read in a Penang newspaper that a benevolent Chinese society in Bangkok was going to empty its paupers' cemetery to make room for new bodies. He wanted to visit the disinterment. I thought this was a strange reason to visit Bangkok but having nothing better to do at the moment I went along for the ride. The man in charge of the mass exhumation welcomed us to the rather gruesome spectacle during which hundreds of human bones were piled into stacks with skulls on top. It reminded me of the killing fields in Cambodia. Michael asked a lot of questions and was very pleased to have made the trip. I thanked Michael for bringing me along and invited him to dinner.

It turned out that Michael grew up in Maine, although he did most of his studies at Yale and the University of Washington. Because both he and Stu were from Maine, I thought if might be good for Stu to meet Michael, even though I suspected Michael, an unabashed admirer of Pol Pot, the leader of the Khmer Rouge, might be a difficult dinner pairing. Over the years I had several robust but fruitless arguments with Michael about his defense of the genocidal Cambodian communists, but was never able to change his mind.

Knowing that I was playing with social fire, I sought to downplay current politics by stressing their common heritage from the great state of Maine. Stu was easier to persuade than Michael to play this game. After a few minutes of Stu asking about Michael's family, they discovered that they were distantly related. Stu was considerably happier to know of the connection than Michael, who seemed slightly aghast that he might be related to an army officer actively involved with killing Southeast Asian communists. I applauded Michael's restraint and civility towards his recently discovered kinsman as I sought to keep the discussion focused more on Maine and less on the war in which Stu and I had recently participated.

Stu asked if Michael was a football fan. Michael disdainfully responded that in all his time at the University of Maine he had attended only one football game, a Maine–Bowdoin contest held in miserable weather. "What I remember most vividly," said Michael, who was clearly not a sports buff, "apart from the freezing rain that turned the football field into a muddy quagmire, was at half time when some drunken student, pretending that he was rowing a boat, "rowed" the entire length of the field on his back through the mud to the roar of approval of everyone in the stands, except me."

Stu beamed at Michael's description and cried out, "That was me!"

***

Seventeen provinces of northeastern Thailand now comprise the area the Thai refer to as *Isaan*. The poorest part of the country, Isaan's dialect, food, and culture owe more to Laos than to Thailand. This southern tier of northeastern provinces stretches along the Cambodian border. A high percentage of Khmer speakers dating back centuries, to when the whole region was part of the empire of Angkor, also live in this region.

I first went to Isaan in 1962 on assignments for the Associated Press, mostly connected with the military build-up for the coming wars in Vietnam and Laos. Tourists rarely visited this hot, dusty, and impoverished region which was well off the beaten track for tourism, although there are fine Khmer ruins at Phimai and Phnom Rung. However, one tourist event promoted by the government is the annual Elephant Roundup in Surin, a vestige from the times when there were thousands of working elephants in the teak forests of the kingdom. The teak has gone and so have most of the elephants.

The United States Department of State had a consulate in Udorn, the major city of the Isaan, not far from Laos. Tim invited us along with Matt and Emily to the Elephant Roundup. Matt was a Foreign Service Officer serving in the embassy in Bangkok and a classmate of Tim. Matt was a character of the old school. He was a clothes horse favoring white three-piece linen suits with great panache. Matt probably would have been more comfortable serving as a diplomat a century earlier. He had served in Vietnam during the war and was the last US consul in Mandalay, Burma, where old retired local staff remember him fondly.

We planned to rendezvous with Tim in Surin for a picnic in the shade of the ruins of an ancient Khmer temple, before enjoying the spectacle of the elephant roundup. Matt drove to Surin in his very respectable Mercedes-Benz. He brought a huge Persian rug, a souvenir from a posting to Tehran to be used as our picnic blanket. He also brought his Burmese lacquer-ware picnic hamper and service for 12, a souvenir of Mandalay. The Bromans took care of the food. BJ ordered a Virginia ham well in advance. We also brought a selection of international cheeses, fresh

French-style baguettes, and tinned French pâté of foie gras from our pantry. We served red, white, and sparkling wines. A small crowd of local children surrounded our lunch setting and watched at a respectful distance. It looked like a movie set moved from the banks of the Loire to the parched Korat plateau.

The elephant roundup, which was almost anti-climactic, turned out to be—in true Thai fashion—a lot of fun. Scores, maybe hundreds, of elephants gathered in an open field. Mounted mostly by ethnic Kui tribesmen, the elephant wranglers of the Isaan, the elephants delighted the crowd by playing soccer. Two teams chased a huge soccer ball, across the field, batting it around before a cheering crowd. Another event had a line of volunteers, mostly young males, lying in a row as elephants walked over them. No one was injured during the spectacle before a hushed crowd. At the end of the festival, mahouts offered rides on elephants. BJ, Matt, and I climbed aboard a docile pachyderm. Matt, sporting his white suit and a solar toppee hat, looked the very model of a passé colonial factotum. Tim captured the moment on film and the image was later used in a recruiting brochure.

A train trip to Udorn took place in July at Tim's invitation. We traveled first class and BJ and I were reading when a man knocked on our compartment door. He was an American and said, "I believe there is a bottle of Scotch whiskey in this compartment." I responded, "You must be a friend of Tim." It was Stanley Karnow, a well-known and much respected American journalist, who admitted the consul had given him the clue. I invited him in for a nightcap.

Stanley's main reason for the trip was to interview people for an article he was writing for *Geo Magazine*. Over warm Scotch, neat, Stanley explained that he was doing a piece about the Hmong hill tribe that fought for the Americans against the North Vietnamese Army in Laos. He said he had several interviews lined up with Hmong refugees in the Isaan and added that he hoped to also interview Anthony Poshepny, better known as Tony Poe, a legendary paramilitary officer in the CIA from Laos and other wars, and no friend of the press.

I had never met Tony but had heard a lot about him. A close friend, who was killed in Laos in 1972, had worked for Tony in northern Laos and regarded him more like a father than a boss. Tony married a Hmong woman, had four children by her, and led Hmong in battle against the NVA. He sometimes proved the body count of enemy killed by sending in the ears of dead Vietnamese to his headquarters in Vientiane. A heavy drinker, Tony could be sometimes difficult to control. Regardless, the CIA twice awarded him its Intelligence Star. Tony especially disliked journalists. I asked Stanley if he had an interviewed arranged. He said he was working on it. I wished him luck.

Udorn had been an important base during the war in Laos. Air America, as well as many US Air Force aircraft, launched from the town's busy air base. The Udorn airfield was one of the ones my father had worked on a decade before. Vestiges of the war years remained. Uniquely, the CIA base at Udorn fell under the jurisdiction of the station in Vientiane, Laos. The Wolverine Bar, which had been a watering hole for Agency and air force personnel was still open. It featured a mural on the wall behind the bar depicting falling bombs from B-52 aircraft, presumably in Laos. The American Legion had a post there for veterans who never went home.

Stanley was in luck. Tony had mellowed in his attitude towards journalists and wanted the world to know what the Hmong had done for the United States and how badly many of them were being treated after the war. Thousands fled Laos as refugees, and many were eventually relocated to the United States. Stanley had asked me to join him. It was a pleasure to meet Tony who strongly resembled Marlon Brando in his role of Kurtz in the film *Apocalypse Now*. Tony, who was in good form, claimed he was ready to go back and re-take Laos, but the call never came. The interview went well and Stanley wrote an excellent article. I am sure Tony liked it.

***

One summer, an Indian-Thai businessman introduced me to the owner of a Nepalese travel agency. He told me it would be easy and relatively inexpensive to organize a trek in Nepal. He said that Nepal had opened up new terrain for tourism and suggested a gentle seven-day, hundred-mile walk from Jomasom to Pokhara along the Thak Khola gorge, the steepest in the world.

Over drinks at the Barrel Bar on Pat Pong Road, we planned the trip. There was PT Tomaino and Dick Kempshall from the Drug Enforcement Administration (DEA), an ex-Air America pilot "Big George" Taylor, and Dave "the Bear" Spillane, and me from the Agency. We all agreed we needed to forsake the heat and humidity of tropical Southeast Asia for two weeks to stroll through the high country of Nepal. As we came to learn, trekking in Nepal is not a sport, it is therapy—an instant and fairly painless cure for the ills of 20th-century life. We would forget work, traffic jams, and the stress of urban living, and leave roads, telephones, and electricity behind.

My only knowledge of Nepal came from stories told by Agency old-timers who spoke of the days when they supported Tibetan Khamba tribesmen against the invasion of Chinese communists into serene and Buddhist Tibet. The support ended in 1959 when the Dalai Lama, the spiritual leader of Tibet, fled the country.

With only 10 days to make our trek we decided to fly to Katmandu, the capital of Nepal, and then charter an aircraft to take us to the remote town of Jomasom, not far from Tibet. Emil Wick, a Swiss, and one of the few pilots licensed to fly into the short airstrip at Jomasom, took us on a Swiss-made Pilatus Porter single-engine aircraft, a workhorse of Air America in Laos and Vietnam on dangerous short mountain airstrips. I sat in the co-pilot seat next to Captain Wick as we flew up the Kali Gandaki River between mountains like Dhaulagiri and Annapurna I, two of the 10 tallest mountains in the world. The scenery was spectacular. As we approached the tiny landing strip, I asked the skipper if he ever had any trouble getting into Jomason. "Only once," he said, and pointed to the wreckage of a Porter at the end of the dirt strip. "As I set her down a wind came down the gorge and flipped the plane on its back. It took me a week to walk out." Airline pilots usually don't discuss their crashes with passengers, especially on approach to a landing, but Captain Wick smiled and assured me that we would be all right.

As the plane came to a halt in front of the hovel that passed for a terminal, a group of trekkers besieged us. A party of Italians who had been stranded in Jomasom by strong winds for some days hoped to catch a lift back to Katmandu. Captain Wick allowed the five quickest Italians to board the aircraft after quickly arranging the charter flight back to Katmandu.

Happily, we found that our guide and our porters were waiting for us. It had taken them a week to walk to Jomasom, which sat at an altitude of 9,300 feet. The trail to Pokhara was mostly downhill, but with a lot of up-and-down in between. Our guide assigned a porter to each of us. The porters carried our luggage along with tents, sleeping bags, food, and other necessities. They promptly bounded off the trail ahead of us, fully laden, barefoot, and apparently happy to be heading downhill.

It took a day or more for us to catch our breath in the thin but clean air. The mountain getaway proved to be as much of a treat for our lungs at it was for our mental health. We walked for about eight hours a day, stopping for lunch and tea breaks. We made camp in the early evening and sat around a fire enjoying Nepalese cuisine, which was filling, spicy, and delicious. The only Western fare we ate during the trip came at teatime. The cook's assistant, the "tea wallah," produced beautiful English biscuits to go with our English tea every day.

On the third day, sitting on some high ground while the boys broke camp, I saw three Western trekkers moving slowly. It looked like two men and a woman, probably hippies with no porters. As they drew nearer it dawned on me that this was a photo op. The men had long beards and wore the generic dress of impoverished travelers in a country where hashish was legal. I reached for my long 300mm lens and attached it to my black Nikon-F camera.

Seeing me sitting alone with a camera in my hand, the men charged. "No photo, no photo," they shouted in a threatening manner. I switched from a long lens to my 24mm wide-angle lens as they approached and continued shooting. This was becoming interesting. As the longhaired and bearded hippies grew closer, I decided I needed to share this experience with my fellow trekkers. "Dick!" I shouted. Richard Kempshall, a former Marine, and active narc, walked over and saw the situation. Without a further word from me, Dick leaped off the bluff in front of the charging hippies who quickly turned and fled. It was the only untoward incident of our entire trek.

The ancient narrow trail, carved out of rock above the river a hundred feet below in some places, could be treacherous, especially when mule caravans, carrying heavy loads in baskets, passed coming upstream. Mules always took the inside part of the trail; the outside had no handrails, only a long drop to water below. Broken baskets on the rocks below gave mute testimony to the fate of clumsy mules (and trekkers). It all added to the allure of the adventure.

One day, we had to cross an avalanche of large boulders that blocked the trail. Tedious and time-consuming, we finally made it. Our biggest trekker, the Bear, become badly dehydrated so Big George and I went into the nearest hamlet looking for fluids for the Bear while the boys set up camp. We found a dingy joint that resembled the bar of intergalactic miscreants in the film *Star Wars*. A motley group of disheveled and vaguely hostile foreigners eyed us through a blue haze of hashish smoke. Big George stared them down as I purchased the last case of Limu, Nepalese lemonade, and the last five quarts of local beer. The Bear replenished his electrolytes after drinking all 24 bottles of Limu. The rest of us made do with the beer.

The Tatopani hot springs, where travelers could bathe and refresh in walled hot spring waters at no cost, offered a most welcome rest stop. When we arrived we found a young French woman, traveling alone, luxuriating in the hot and healing water. I asked in French if we could join her and she nodded assent. We stripped to jockey shorts and joined her in the large pool, soaking our aching muscles in the heated water.

A highlight of our extended walk was the Poon Hill, also the highest point of elevation. As the sun flooded over the valley below, we walked to the top of the hill at 12,000 feet, to find an eagle soaring above us. In that spiritual moment, none of us spoke as we watched the big bird enjoying the morning, alive and free.

Four days into the trek, we reached the village of Shika. The moment we saw the sign for the Santi's Lodge, we told our Nepalese guide that we would be sleeping under a roof that night. A charming young woman named Santi whose father was a retired sergeant major of Gurkhas, Nepal's legendary soldiers of fortune in the British Army, ran this charming little lodge. For US$1 each we rented a cot in the dormitory upstairs for our sleeping bags. A good deal at double the price. In an unexpected bonus we could see the sun-capped peak of 26,795-feet tall Dhaulagiri peeking through our window in the distance. This majestic mountain, the seventh highest in the world, emerged from cloud cover for the first time in days.

As we walked into the valley not far from our destination, Pokhara, in the banana belt at an altitude of around 2,700 feet, we passed a rug factory, the only shopping opportunity on our trek apart from buying mountain coral stones from itinerant Tibetans. We stopped to shop. The Bear and I could not pass up a chance to buy a wool rug at a US-financed factory to help Tibetan refugees from the Chinese. It was added weight but Pokhara was near and my rug was small. It now graces the floor of my office.

We came to the last bridge, a rickety assembly of bamboo poles lashed together about 10 feet above a shallow stream abounding in large stones. It was the most

Dave "The Bear" Spillane poses for a photo with young Nepalese boys he met during a trek from Jomasom near the Tibetan border down to Pokkara in western Nepal in 1978. The little guys were captivated by the 6-foot-3-inches gentle Bear as we passed their remote village in a seven-day trek through the steepest gorge in the world.

dangerous bridge we had seen on our seven-day trek. Our porters walked straight into the water, giving us a clue as to their opinion of the structural qualities of the bridge. We went across, gingerly, one at a time. The Bear, the biggest, went last. On the far side we could see the major town of Pohkara and trekkers about to start their adventure, and looking fearfully at the substandard bridge. I greeted the Bear after he followed me across the bridge and said in a loud voice, "Well done Bear, that was the best bridge I've seen in seven days." A low moan of horror went up from the nascent hikers.

We walked to the airport hotel at a jaunty pace—we were finally on a flat surface and just getting into our stride—where our car and driver were waiting to carry us back to Katmandu. But first we needed lunch. In the spacious hotel dining room we pored over the menu and eventually ordered two meals. Each. We quaffed industrial quantities of beer while waiting for our food. Finally, I asked, "Where is our food?" "We are waiting for the rest of your party," we were told. "We are all here. Bring the food!" We enjoyed every bite of both meals.

***

On Christmas Day, 1978, the People's Army of Vietnam (PAVN) invaded Cambodia. The move was intended to punish the Khmer Rouge for their repeated depredations along their common border and then to effect regime change. Pol Pot's autogenicidal regime refused to be subordinate, or even to be friendly with the Vietnamese who had put them in power. This upset the Chinese, the only friends the Khmer Rouge had. They eventually reacted by launching a limited invasion of Vietnam, only to be met with heavy resistance by veteran fighters with advanced weapons. After taking thousands of casualties in a few weeks, the Chinese limped back across the border, saying, "Let that be a lesson," though they were the ones who learned the lesson.

When PAVN rolled into Cambodia, I was delighted. How else could Pol Pot be stopped from destroying his own country? The United States had little interest in Southeast Asia, despite the Carter administration's proclaimed interest in human rights. As the Vietnamese advanced rapidly across Cambodia, the Khmer Rouge quickly reverted to their past role as a guerrilla force and took to the bush. While this was happening, many Cambodians, no longer under the Pol Pot yoke, began pouring into Thailand as refugees. This gave us "Cambodia watchers" fresh eyewitness accounts of what was taking place in Cambodia. It was also a shot in the arm for the non-communist Cambodian resistance on the border, who could not focus on the Vietnamese occupying Cambodia as a common enemy.

Tim and I were both very interested to know what was happening on the border. We took annual leave, and I drove up to the border to see what has going on. It was an unusual time and place for a vacation, but it seemed like a good idea. Instead of heading for Aranyaprathet, the principal border town and close to the major refugee camps, we headed south to the Thai town of Chantaburi, famed for its sapphires and the evil-smelling fruit, durian.

The area was under the control of the Royal Thai Marine Corps where I had friends. Armed with photos of me with the commandant of the Thai Marines from my active duty service with the Thai as a Marine reserve officer, I was able to talk our way through the check points that were stopping civilian traffic heading for the border. We turned on to the laterite road leading to the Cambodian town of Pailin, a Khmer Rouge stronghold just over the border. Tim and I had visited Pailin in 1974 when it was still in the hands of the Republic of Cambodia. Now the Vietnamese were there, with tanks, about 15 miles away.

It was quiet on the rutted road, or, as the war novels say, too quiet. There were no more Thai Marines, and pretty soon there were no more Thai civilians. Eventually, we reached a roadblock manned by Khmer Rouge soldiers armed with light machine guns and anti-armor rocket-propelled grenades (RPG). It was a dicey moment that easily could have turned ugly. Fortunately, Tim spoke fluent Cambodian. We got out of the car, Tim with a map and me with a camera. As Tim showed the unit commander that he was on the Thai side of the border, I explained in French to a teenage rifleman with an AK-47 that I worked for the French communist newspaper

With Khmer Rouge soldiers on the Thai–Cambodian border in 1979. The Khmer Rouge were fleeing Vietnamese Army tanks a few miles away. Tim and I were allowed past Thai Marine positions after being warned that there was a Khmer Rouge road block ahead. The Khmer Rouge soldiers were friendly and happy to be out of Cambodia. (Photo by Tim)

L'Humanité. I doubt if he understood me, but he did not stop me taking pictures. The tension abated. We chatted for a few minutes and took some group photos, before turning around and heading back to Thai Marine lines.

This patrol knew that they were in Thailand and that Vietnamese tanks were in Pailin. They were the first line of defense for the Thai Marines if the Vietnamese chose to chase the Khmer Rouge in hot pursuit across the border. The Vietnamese stayed in Cambodia.

We headed north along the frontier road and encountered many Cambodian civilians, including a group of black-pajama-clad young women Khmer Rouge walking along the road away from Cambodia and their suffering of the past four-and-a-half years. There were no soldiers with them, but there were many sick with malaria and some wounded. All were malnourished and starving. Tim spoke to a man boiling leaves for his people and we learned that they had not eaten for days. Thai troops herded the new refugees into a field surrounded by fresh rings of barbed wire. We gave the fellow money to buy food, and I photographed Thai civilians passing food to the Khmer through the barbed wire.

We made it back to Chantaburi without incident and found a hotel for the night. In the morning we headed for the market to load up with durian. Tim and I are both aficionados of this fruit, which is notorious for its obnoxious odor. It is an acquired taste. I am sure there were some people who thought Tim and I had "gone native" because of our affection for this fruit, which is forbidden in all hotels and aircraft in Thailand (its odor tends to linger in the air-conditioning). We filled the trunk of my Toyota Celica with durian and returned to work.

**

It was hard to say goodbye, after four delightful years at post. It was doubly difficult to leave our friends, many of whom are still friends. We wanted to have a memorable farewell party and invite as many people as we could. We decided to host the event in the spacious grounds of a venerable club to which I was a member. An ensemble of students from the Fine Arts College played classical music. Food stations staffed by young ladies in traditional dress offered top local cuisine.

We had about a hundred guests including two princes from the local royal family. The princes were chatting in the verdant grounds enjoying the music when I approached them with Tim. The senior prince gravely said in a low voice "Barry, someone just told me that you worked for the CIA." Before I could utter my standard denial, Tim spoke up. "Your Highness, Barry no more works for the CIA than I do." Instead of being mollified, the prince looked increasingly worried. Because of his many contacts, excellent language skills and a flair for talking to people of all sides of the political spectrum, Tim was often mistaken for being a "spook." No damage was done. The second prince, a bon vivant ethnographer more interested in women than politics, just smiled and reached for another Scotch and soda.

A Soviet embassy officer, well known to us as a KGB officer, arrived uninvited. I stopped him at the door where I was greeting guests. He quickly apologized for not having an invitation but said he wanted to wish me farewell. Before he could hand me the present he had in hand, I said I appreciated his thoughtfulness but due to budgetary constraints we could not let any more people in. He was clearly there to see whom I knew and do some spotting for himself. His chagrin at being turned away was enhanced by the timely arrival of a Chinese embassy second secretary who *was* on the invitation list. BJ and I greeted him and his wife warmly as the Russian beat a hasty retreat.

It was a rather formal event with everyone well dressed in national dress, coats and ties, or in uniform. The guests included a cross section of local society: academics, military, and diplomats. We also had a smattering of the press on hand, who kept the bartenders busy, just as I had when I was in the working press. Our Khmer aristocrat friend Kim was there with her debonair Scottish husband Tony McDevitt. British businessman Mark Graham, a Sandhurst graduate, was there along with his sophisticated Thai wife, Junipha, who added yet another touch of class to the evening, as did French diplomat Bertrand Rault and his charming Vietnamese wife, Kim. One of BJ's friends and a fellow English-language teacher from AUA, Pat Rama, came with her Sino-Thai husband John, whom I confess I introduced to the world of antique collecting.

After we packed out our possessions for shipment back to Washington DC, we stayed at the city's best hotel and some would say Asia's best hotel at the time. Through my friendship with the managing director, I arranged for our last few nights to be in a suite of the original 19th-century hotel. It is amusing to note that when Somerset Maugham stayed in the hotel in the 1930, he was writing his only travel book, *The Gentleman in the Parlour*, which deals mainly with Burma. Maugham was in town having contracted malaria. The German woman running the hotel at the time feared that the famous writer might die at the hotel and thought of having him moved. But the hardy old Brit pulled through.

The suite looked out across manicured grounds onto a busy river. The suite included two rooms, a spacious bedroom with a four-poster bed and walls adorned with Jim Thompson silk, and a sitting room, which we used for an open house event. We invited virtually everyone we knew who might want to help me drink the 20-plus bottles of wine, whiskey, and digestifs that I needed to get rid of before we left town. With the help of the Bangkok foreign press corps, and numerous others, the mission was accomplished. After we said goodbye to the last guests, BJ and I walked for a last dinner at our favorite Indian restaurant, while nanny Sri watched baby Seth, our first son, born in Bangkok in 1978, sleep in the enormous canopied bed.

***

After three tours in the field, I had to do an obligatory Headquarters tour. This was fine with me. It gave baby Seth a chance to see the United States for the first time and for BJ an opportunity to resume her career as a teacher. The Agency gave me a job with supervisory responsibility and exposure to new areas and programs. I also began working with other agencies including the FBI, or, as the Drug Enforcement Administration field officers liked to call them, the Feebs.

The Agency had somewhat rocky relations with the Bureau dating from the days of J. Edgar Hoover, who detested the Agency and OSS before it. At one point, Bureau officers put their careers on the line in cooperating with the Agency against Mr. Hoover's orders. Hoover, always eager to expand his power, mainly fought the Agency over turf. There were also cultural differences. The FBI agents are cops. They arrest people who break the law. Some see CIA case officers as law-breakers as they conduct espionage around the world. The difference is that the CIA breaks foreign laws and not American laws. The culture of the Clandestine Service calls for officers to lead their "targets" into breaking the espionage laws of their country in support of the mission of the Agency to protect the security of the United States.

Despite perceived turf and cultural issues, I found the people I dealt with at the Bureau in Washington DC to be, without exception, professional, cooperative, and appreciative of any information and assistance we provided concerning foreign targets of interest to both Agencies. We had regular meetings in Langley and DC discussing ongoing operations without problem, and I developed a congenial working relationship with my counterparts. On the morning that the Bureau's very successful sting operation Abscam broke in the *Washington Post* in 1980 with the arrest of several congressmen, I was visiting the Bureau with a few colleagues. Abscam went after corrupt politicians at the federal and local levels involving large bribes for favors. One senator and six congressmen were convicted along with lesser politicians.

I showed the story on the cover of the *Washington Post* to one of the FBI officers we were meeting and congratulated him. He thanked me and said, "In the old days it would not have gone down that way. Mr. Hoover would have run the operation the same way but he would not have arrested the crooked congressman. He would have called the man in, shown him the footage of the bribe being taken, and then said, something like, 'I don't want to ruin your career. Don't take bribes. Let this be a lesson. And on the way out, stop by my comptroller's office. We have a few budget suggestions.'"

The agent said Hoover had files on hundreds of officials and ruled by instilling fear. "That's how he lasted so long in Washington." Then we had our meeting, which was a model of inter-agency cooperation. I was beginning to learn how Washington worked.

***

At this point in my career, the Agency had not "declared" me to any foreign intelligence service. That changed in my new assignment when the Agency tapped me to work with the British Secret Intelligence Service (SIS), more commonly known as MI6, or just 6. MI6, the CIA's counterpart, was responsible for foreign intelligence collection while MI5, the FBI's counterpart, took care of internal security.

For reasons I still do not fully understand, the Agency asked me to work with MI6 on a target both agencies had been pursuing separately. I suspect that my English education had something to do with my selection. My success as a "headhunter" in Southeast Asia probably helped. After high-level discussions, the Americans and the British, decided to work together on this "hard" target. In intel-speak, a "hard target" is someone working for an unfriendly country; Soviets, Red Chinese, North Koreans, etc., were "hard targets." In some cases, we went after these targets in cooperation with friendly intelligence services with whom we were in "liaison." Normally, we would pursue targets alone or "unilaterally." In this case, the British suggested a joint operation. Since the target would be in the United States, we took the lead in planning and making the recruitment.

The target was traveling on business and we had a very narrow window of opportunity to approach him. His file revealed that he had real vulnerabilities that we were ready to exploit. A very experienced and senior MI6 officer arrived in Washington DC and was introduced to me as my partner on the operation. From the minute I met Alec, as I will call him, I liked him. It quickly became clear that although I was technically in charge I was the junior partner in the operation. Alec very much resembled Alec Guinness in the role of George Smiley, the quiet, polite, and softly-spoken British spy in John le Carré's book, *Tinker, Tailor, Soldier, Spy*. The senior Agency officer who picked me for the job, as "the pluperfect case officer," described Alec to me. He predicted I was in for the ride of my life. How right he was.

In the weeks we worked on this case I learned a lot. Alec was an excellent teacher and, as our friendship grew, he opened up about his wartime experiences, how he came to be "tapped" by MI6. He also showed his tough side. For one long-running operation, Alex received a serious decoration from Prince Philip personally. When I asked how long it ran, he put a finger beside his nose and whispered, "It's still running." Without going into detail, suffice to say that we tracked our unsuspecting target during his travels and finally were in a position to make "the pitch." We devised an offer that we thought our target could not refuse.

At that point, Alec, who looked a lot calmer than I felt, said, "Perhaps I should tell you my secret instructions." Surprised, I asked, "If you have secret instructions, why tell me?" Alec quietly said, "I think you should know. My instructions are not to let this case end in recruitment." Completely confused, I asked why. Alec gave me a wan smile and said MI6 really didn't want to share the agent with the Americans. They knew he would be traveling abroad again and were planning to pitch him without American assistance. "Why are you telling me this?" I asked. He answered, "Because the time is right. This is our best chance. We need to move now. We need to recruit this chap," he said.

This put me in a bind. I told Alec perhaps it was time for me to share my own secret orders with him. "Why would you have secret orders?" Alec asked, "and why would you tell me about them?" I answered, "My division chief told me that under no circumstances was I to do anything to upset MI6. I think it is only fair that you know." Alec thanked me and suggested we should both forget our secret instructions and get on with the recruitment. "Let's be robust," he said.

We moved ahead. The target, after listening to the pitch, said he appreciated the generous offer, but had to decline. I was disappointed. Alec was not. He told me, "We are in the business of making dreams come true. We know his dreams and we will make them come true." The target was told that if his wife knew what was being offered, and that he had declined the offer, she would kill him. The target thought for a moment, shrugged, sighed, and accepted our proposal.

This turned out to be a major recruitment for both services. Kudos flowed back and forth across the Atlantic. The services shared information from our new agent. The operations strengthened the relationship between the CIA and MI6. In my case, it meant a promotion ahead of schedule as a result of this case, although very few people in the Agency even knew about it. MI6 did not treat Alec so well. A short time later he was retired for failing in his mission to prevent the recruitment. Despite his premature retirement, Alec held no grudge. He expected it. We kept in contact for years. He visited us in the States; we visited him in the UK. He told me he never regretted his decision to "be robust."

***

Early in my career, I made a list of countries where I wanted to serve. Four were in Southeast Asia, the other was in Europe. In time, I served in all of them. Like my

A "Bogart moment" in Europe in the early 1980s.

Cambodian assignment, Serge Taube was responsible for my European assignment. But there was no war going on in Europe and wives could accompany. Serge wanted me on board in time to attend the Fourth of July party at the ambassador's residence, where I could meet a number of people and jump start my new assignment. I arrived alone. BJ and Seth followed a month later. The ambassador had invited a thousand or more of his best friends to the party, which was held in the spacious grounds of his mansion. Looking around at the assembled guests in the garden, I saw a well-dressed Asian fellow, standing alone. I approached him and took a chance. I gave him a very respectful "*wai*" a Thai greeting. He looked surprised and asked, "How do you know I am Thai?" He was the Thai ambassador. Speaking Thai, I told him I thought he looked Thai and added that I had just arrived and didn't know anyone. The ambassador, like many Thai diplomats, was genteel and very professional. The ambassador said I must meet all the Southeast Asian ambassadors from ASEAN and said promised to host a dinner the next week. I was off to a good start.

At the dinner, a waiter asked what I wanted to drink. I asked for a Mekhong—Thailand's best whiskey—and soda. The ambassador heard this and said, "We have good Scotch whiskey. We don't have Mekhong." Knowing that Mekhong was a favorite drink of some Royal Thai Army officers, I asked what would happen if some generals came to town and wanted Mekhong. He had no answer, but the evening helped me get my foot in the diplomatic door and the ambassador became a good friend. Some weeks later, a box arrived for me at the office. It was a case of Mekhong and came with a note from the ambassador. After our meeting he had ordered two cases from Thailand; he kept one and sent me the other. He explained that a high-level delegation of military officers had arrived asking for Mekhong. He had it on hand.

***

I had another stroke of luck because of my friendship with mathematician Moshe and his colleague Daniel who had been friends for years. Shortly after my assignment was confirmed I called Moshe and told him we were heading his way. A few weeks later, he informed me that an elderly neighbor in his apartment building had just passed away and his rent-controlled apartment was available. If I wanted it, Moshe would put down a deposit. I said yes and sent him the deposit.

The apartment was old and elegant. It had four bedrooms, a dining room, sitting room with fireplace, two rooms on the top floor for servants, and a large "cave" in the basement for wine and storage. The rent was $1,000 per month, well within my allowance. I thanked Moshe and asked him to put down the deposit, little realizing what a huge favor he had done for us. I needed one of the servant's rooms for our Thai nanny, Sri, and used the other one for a photographic darkroom.

An early priority was to stock the wine cellar. Our duty-free shop offered a wide selection of wine and spirits. I selected a fine St. Julien wine from Bordeaux. Chateau

Gloria became my house wine for about $4 per bottle. I also stocked a small quantity of good California wines, which I served *en carafe* so as not to give away the wine's provenance, often to the astonishment of wine-wise European dinner guests.

Soon after we arrived, Serge invited us to dinner. Serge, a native French-speaker, said there are three sorts of Americans who lived here: those who love it, those who hate it, and those who hate it but say they love it. The last group is probably the largest. The city is easy to visit but harder to live in. It takes about six months to get settled. Food shopping, especially for Americans used to supermarkets, can be a challenge. We had a small market near us with individual shops for things like vegetables, bread, and seafood.

Local merchants do not allow you to touch fruit. You get what they select for you. It took BJ a while to adapt. However, she soon developed a rapport with the young Cambodian fishmonger, whom she would chat with in Cambodian. Soon, he was picking out the best fish for her. We bought pâté and other gourmet items in the market down the street. Duck liver pâté in port wine became our favorite. The old proprietor was easy to deal with but was often absent. The nice lady with the

Young Seth Broman carrying baguettes in the Luxembourg Gardens of Paris, 1982.

stall next to his would tell us to wait. She would run across the street to pull him out of the wine bar where he had his morning pick-me-up. He always apologized, served us quickly, and went back to the bar.

Every morning, on my way to work, I bought the *New York Herald Tribune* from a stout, elderly women in a news kiosk opposite our apartment. After about six months of this, the lady said she knew I lived nearby and would keep a copy of the paper for me as she only received six each day. In her mind, I had become a "regular." I didn't really appreciate it until the day I was behind an American tourist in line and when he asked for the *Tribune*, she said curtly, "Finished." Then, seeing me, she handed over my paper and I paid. When the tourist started to remonstrate, she cut him off, saying "'e live 'ere." It was the only time I heard her speak English.

We enrolled Seth, age three, in a bi-lingual Montessori school. He loved it from day one. He had Sri and in the afternoons they would visit the large park across the street. There, he would sail his boat in a shallow pool or ride small burros, a special treat. The park had a merry-go-round where riders, holding small sticks, could try to grab the brass ring, literally. If a rider skewered enough rings, he got a free ride.

Initially, we were worried that Sri, who spoke no languages apart from Thai, would have a hard time in Europe. I was especially concerned that living in a small room on the top floors, two flights up, would be a problem for her. The other residents, of the servants' quarters, without exception, were young black African cooks, employed by affluent families, including a past ambassador to the United States. I needn't have worried. Within days, Sri, a Thai-Mon woman in her late fifties, had organized a roster for cleaning the bathroom and picking up garbage. She became a mother to the soft-spoken Africans and taught them to make Thai dishes. Soon after that, one of our distinguished neighbors stopped me in the entryway to express thanks to Sri for teaching her cook how to prepare Thai food.

***

The city offered a target-rich environment. The hard targets, primarily Soviets and Chinese, were there. Although these were fair game, I focused primarily on the Cambodians. We had identified four groups: two hard targets and two soft targets. The hard targets were the Khmer Rouge, the communist Cambodians who were ousted from power by their erstwhile allies, the Vietnamese, who put the Khmer Rouge in power in 1975. It turned out that Cambodians' traditional hatred for the Vietnamese ("Dirty diaper eaters" is a common epithet), outweighed communist fraternity, and by 1978 the Vietnamese had had enough. The few Khmer Rouge in town were generally considered pariahs and were hard to meet. BJ, who had lost many friends to the Khmer Rouge, refused to let any in our apartment. She would host Soviets, Chinese, and even North Koreans, but not Khmer Rouge, which I considered to be fair enough. I met them in small cafés in unfashionable parts of the city.

We also viewed supporters of Phnom Penh's puppet government in Phnom Penh, put in place by the conquering Vietnamese, as hard targets including the People's Republic of Kampuchea (PRK) consisted of a ragged bunch of opportunists who had left the Khmer Rouge to join the Vietnamese. Heng Samrin was in charge in Phnom Penh. Hun Sen, a senior Khmer Rouge officer, later replaced him. The small and motley group of PRK sympathizers were often venal and ready to be bought, or rented.

I spent much of my time with two groups of Cambodian resistance fighters opposed to the puppet administration of Heng Samrin. The first, the Khmer People's National Liberation Front (KPNLF), was founded by former Cambodian prime minister Son Sann in 1978. The second, FUNCINPEC, a royalist faction created by former King Norodom Sihanouk in 1981. In 1982, the two groups formed a coalition of non-communist forces that operated separately from the Khmer Rouge, who survived along the Thai–Cambodian border supported by the Chinese and tolerated by the Thai. Both Sihanouk and Son Sann resided most of the time in Paris, trying to gain support from the United States and other countries.

The non-communists sought to oust Heng Samrin and prevent the Khmer Rouge from returning to power. Sihanouk had been overthrown in a coup d'état in 1970 by his own government led by General Lon Nol. Sihanouk often insisted that the CIA fostered the coup d'état. Although this was not true, the idea resonated after his book *My War with the CIA* appeared, ghostwritten by Australian communist Wilfred Burchett, was published. China welcomed Sihanouk after the coup. In a fit of pique against the new Khmer Republic, and to the delight of the Chinese, he joined his old enemy, the Khmer Rouge. Unlike millions of his countrymen and many members of the royal family, Sihanouk somehow avoided death at the hands of his Khmer Rouge friends.

Sihanouk took up residence at his comfortable villa in Mougins on the French Riviera. He longed to return to power and step back into the political arena, this time as a friend of the United States. I knew him and many of his supporters who were happy to be in touch with an American.

I also had several friends in Son Sann's group from my days in Southeast Asia. I reported on the post-war tragedy that left as many as two million Cambodians dead to a generally disinterested US government, which turned its back on Southeast Asia. Son Sann, a softly-spoken economist and former prime minister, was anti-royalist as well as an anti-communist. He actively sought American support for his cause. He called on the United States to "Give us the means to retake Cambodia." They were also happy to have an American contact.

***

My very efficient secretary, Peggy Ann, surprised me one day saying that the ambassador wanted to see me right away. The ambassador greeted me warmly. He told me that he had bumped into the principal of the American school a few days earlier, who had told him the school was offering a course on the Vietnam War. The ambassador said, "I invited the class for lunch at the embassy and I know you were in the war. Would you mind talking to the class?" I accepted with pleasure.

About 20 high-school students arrived with their young female teacher, and after lunch I gave a two-hour presentation in the library. It was a casual session and I encouraged questions during this casual session. I divided my presentation into three parts: my Vietnam time as an AP photographer early in the war, my experiences as a Marine infantry officer in combat, and my time in nearby Cambodia. I made no judgment about the war.

I fielded a lot of questions from the young Americans regarding the war, and thought the session went well. After the class, the teacher thanked me for speaking to her class and admitted that she feared I would espouse the government position on the war and appreciated my non-political stance. A year later, I received a call from the teacher, who said the course was being offered again and asked if I would be available to speak. I said sure, as long as the ambassador concurred. Then she said, "Frankly, I was a little reluctant to invite you." "Why?" I asked. "Well, after your talk last year, two of the boys in the class joined the Marine Corps."

***

Europe was a dangerous place for official Americans when I was posted there. Although we had close relations with the government where I was posted, there were a number of violent anti-American groups active. One senior American military officer was murdered by terrorists in the city I was posted to, which lead to a number of measures to protect official Americans. Another senior American, who had fought with Free French airmen in World War II, was attacked by a gunman. The officer dodged bullets until the terrorist ran out of ammunition. Another American was wounded by a terrorist elsewhere in the country. Two local policemen were killed when a bomb set under an American's car exploded. Some officials took turns with their wives starting their car engines. Some started carrying weapons with special permission from local authorities. During this period a number of Soviet officials were kicked out of the country.

My old Belgian mercenary friend Jimmy earned his living nearby in the early 1980s as the bodyguard of a Saudi Arabian prince. His main duty was escorting the prince's teenage daughter, Princess Fatima, on shopping trips. She apparently did her best to spend her daily pocket money of $6,000. However, he most enjoyed protecting the prince on his excursions to the country's casinos. The prince gave Jimmy gambling chips, which Jimmy immediately exchanged for cash. Jimmy sometimes supplemented his salary in this manner two or three times in an evening. It was a good gig for Jimmy, until he could go back to Indochina.

Knowing that I was often out alone at night, Jimmy gave me an extendible baton for self-defense. This little weapon looked like a hand microphone but when deployed extended its length to about two feet. Ideally, the baton extended itself during the swing. The lead-weighted rubber-coated knob would do serious damage to any person in reach. An underworld friend had given it to Jimmy, who thought that I needed it more than he did. I carried the weapon at night and used it to good effect on two occasions. Both times I brandished the weapon when I was on a subway train late at night. Each time, an elderly French woman was being harassed by drunken bums, seeking money. The first time, the old lady was in tears and fumbling to find money in her purse. The train was almost deserted, no police in sight. I approached the man, deployed my toy to its full length and said—keep moving—in my best cop impersonation. The second time, the man was younger but smaller. He ran as soon as I pulled out my baton.

A few months later, a senior visitor from Headquarters visited and I was asked to show him around town. As we transferred from one subway train to another at a large and busy station, a group of young Gypsies approached us. Gypsy criminals often worked in gangs that sometimes included a woman with a babe in her arms. They would surround and harass a target, using the distraction to pick a pocket or purse. I saw them heading for us and jumped in front of the division chief, telling him to put his wallet in a front pocket and stay close to me. The band of Gypsies, male and female, in their teens or younger, were all over me as I started punching. It must have been a shock to my companion. Suddenly, out of nowhere two young men in civilian clothes jumped into the fray and rescued us. They threw the young Gypsies off me while the leader of the pack and small children scattered. The men who came to our defense were known as "runners," members of the police anti-Gypsy squad in action.

The visitor from Headquarters headed the division of the Clandestine Service that ran operations against foreign targets in the United States. Before our tussle with the Gypsies, I had asked him if officers were ever sent to their home for family reasons and if they have a strong recruiting record they are likely to get a job. Some weeks later, I received a message from him. He asked if I would like to be a chief for my next assignment. I never thought of serving in a domestic job but knew the promotion would help my career. My parents would enjoy having their grandsons close. I accepted with pleasure. Finally, I would have my own command.

On one occasion I came to the attention of the police and immediately wished I had not. This is a cautionary tale. I was driving along the river one sunny Saturday morning with BJ and four-year-old son Seth in the backseat. We were making a rare shopping trip by car. Suddenly, a police car swept from the rear, and cut in front of me forcing me to downshift to avoid a collision. I cursed as they dashed ahead. Moments later, the car with two police officers inside, stopped at a red light.

I stopped next to it. Unbeknownst to me, little Seth rolled down his window. Seeing this, the policeman riding "shotgun" rolled down his window too. Seth repeated my comment verbatim, "Drive much, asshole?" with as much force as a four-year-old can muster. The policeman turned to the driver and I heard him say, "What a cute little kid. I wonder what he said."

***

Our Europe posting gave me the opportunity to renew a friendship with a favorite author whom I will call Luc. I had been a fan since college when I read his books dealing with the Indochina wars. We first met years before in Asia when he was on assignment for a leading European magazine. I happily discovered we were neighbors. In 1940, Luc was serving as a private in the army when the Germans invaded and captured him. He escaped and with the help of the British joined an allied unit in Africa. He rose to the rank of captain and fought in Italy and France where he won numerous decorations for bravery. Luc fought in the Korean War where he was badly wounded at the battle of Heartbreak Ridge. He learned English in an American military hospital. Medically discharged from the army, Luc became a journalist and an expert on Indochina.

Sitting in Luc's opulent apartment one day, I noticed a silver ashtray inscribed with the name of a past president of the country. Knowing that I had a small collection of ashtrays purloined from places such as the Continental Palace Hotel in Saigon and the Café de Paris in Phnom Penh, Luc handed the silver ashtray to me and said, with a smile, "I give to you, before you steal it." It is a cherished souvenir.

One summer, Luc asked me to drive him to his mountain home near a national park. When Luc became wealthy from his books and films, he purchased a 17th-century fortified stone manor house and land in the rugged hills near his hometown. This remote mountain house, which was cold even in the summer, had a single source of heat, an eight-foot wide fireplace over which Luc cooked in a cast-iron pot.

The drive took all day on winding country roads past striking scenery. We made two memorable stops along the way. We had lunch at a rustic restaurant in a small hamlet. The elderly proprietor, wearing a black beret and with a cigarette dangling from his mouth, had only one thing to offer, a fixed five-course meal of lamb cooked on a spit over an open fire. It was also the inn's only source of heat so we sat close to the fire. Everything was local, including the wine, which had no label on the bottle.

Continuing our journey driving slowly through a winding two-lane road in the mountains, we passed a farmhouse and Luc asked me to stop. Some short tree limbs were hanging from a string outside the farmhouse. Luc spoke to the farmer and bought all five of the sticks. He handed me one and explained that the hollowed-out tree limbs, called boufadou, were the bellows he remembered from his youth. You blow into one end and point the other end at your dying fire. It works like a charm. I still use mine every time I make a fire.

Luc's old stone farmhouse had a framed picture on the wall in the kitchen. It showed an army officer on horseback rallying his men in battle. Luc explained that it was of his father, in action during World War I. He added that his father was virtually the sole survivor of his battalion. In World War II, Luc and his father were on opposite sides and when Luc joined the allies his father never spoke to him again.

Back in the city a few months later, I received an invitation to a dinner from Luc in honor of the writer James Clavell, who was promoting his latest novel. Among the guests were Clavell's local publishers and their wives. I saw this as an excellent opportunity to meet one of my favorite living writers and learn the background to Clavell's first novel, *King Rat*, which describes the experiences of a young British Army officer captured by the Japanese in World War II and imprisoned at the notorious Changi Prison in Singapore. Clavell, an Australian-born naturalized American, told me that the book was entirely autobiographical. He was the young British officer through whose eyes he tells the story. The title character, whom he called only "the King," was an American army corporal who had been thrown into prison with thousands of British and colonial troops. Despite his low rank, "the King" not only had natural leadership skills but he also knew how to wheel and deal. Clavell recalled how "the King" had saved his life by obtaining medicines for him on the black market. Clavell watched "the King" take charge, while senior British officers thought only of themselves and not their men. The experience caused Clavell to immigrate to the United States after the war.

I asked, "What happened to the King after the war?" Clavell said that in 1946 he received a letter from the King with a photo of him standing in front of his brand-new Chevrolet car at his home in Texas. He had no further contact until many years later, when Clavell was a successful writer. During a business trip to New York the hotel desk clerk rang saying a man with the King's name was in the lobby and wanted to see him. Clavell rushed downstairs only to find a journalist with the same name as King Rat seeking an interview. Clavell never heard from the King again. I asked Clavell what he thought about the recent novel, *Noble House*, of Hong Kong. "I never read fiction," he answered with a smile. "I take from everything I read and would not want to be accused of plagiarism."

Luc had arranged two tables for dinner. He placed Clavell, himself, and me at one table with a few wives. He put the French publishers at the other table. Luc's excellent Egyptian cook prepared an elegant Mediterranean meal of couscous and lamb. As soon as the wine was poured, one of the publishers got up and approached Luc saying that a mistake had been made with the wines. "Your table has Chateau Margaux 1966," he said, "and our table has Margaux 1977." Smiling, Luc replied, "There is no mistake. This table is for creative people. Your table is for the bloodsuckers." The publisher sat down, drank his young wine, and sulked all evening. Luc later explained to me that he had once had a bad experience with this publisher and this was his revenge.

***

If you are posted in Europe, it is a good idea to have a restaurant you can call your own. There are thousands to choose from. Before I left Seattle in the summer of 1981 my friend Bob Peterson, a world-class foodie, suggested I try Au Trou Gascon, a one-star Michelin restaurant that came highly recommended to him. It was a small mom and pop place, rustic but classy with great food. I loved it.

When my friend Moshe was a young student from his native Israel, his colleague and close friend Daniel introduced him to the best restaurants in the city. Moshe decided to do the same for the Bromans. We started a temple of classic cuisine. When the elegant dining room heated up later in the evening, to let out smoke and cool off the room, the roof quietly opened up and soon after, closed again. One night we went to a three-star restaurant, famed for its desserts, Moshe's weakness and the reason for our going. However, when it came time for dessert, the waiter told us that the chef had gone home. Moshe said, "No problem. Get him back!" When told that would not happen, Moshe said quietly, "Next year, you will have only two stars." Next year, they had only two stars and we never went back.

Typically, when Moshe invited us to dinner, he told us where he was taking us. The evening always started with Champagne at his and Daniel's apartment three floors below us. But on one occasion he declined to tell us where we would eat. "It is a surprise," is all he said.

With some anticipation, we enjoyed our pre-dinner drink and Daniel drove. We soon found ourselves in an unfashionable part of town and then in front of a restaurant. We went in and were greeted by a woman who took our coats. Then she turned to me and said "You cannot have ravioli with foie gras or baby lamb tonight."

Moshe was shocked at her rudeness and demanded, "Why not?"

"Because he had them for lunch," she replied, with a smile.

Moshe turned to me in shock. "You know this restaurant?" he asked.

I didn't have to answer. The woman answered for me. Pointing to a table for two by the door and away from other tables, she said, "That is his table." We were in my favorite place. Moshe was not happy. He thought he was showing us a new "find" and reverted to taking us to known restaurants with multiple stars.

***

We had a memorable visit of very senior officials from Washington during my European posting. All hands were involved in the visit including me. My very small role involved support at a lunch hosted by an anti-American leftist European woman whose paramour was a member of the communist party and a conservative, protective, and strong-willed American female guest. The women disliked each other cordially and the event was strained. I earned my White House cufflinks that day.

William Casey, Director of the CIA, was along on the visit. Part of the time he was busy with old comrades from the OSS who had gathered for the event. He had been a captain in the London OSS station during the war and was well and favorably known to many senior CIA officers who had served with him during the war. One of the veterans, who took part in the reunion, was a support "asset" of mine who had served with Casey in London. A very successful businessman based in Europe, he told me that he would put in a good word for me when he saw "Bill." I warned him that Bill had no "need to know" that his old buddy was cooperating with the Agency. "You are quite right," he exclaimed "mum's the word." I suspect that this cornerstone of security was forgotten after a couple of dry martinis. Mr. Casey did not mention my friend when we met. He wanted to talk about Cambodia, thanked me for my efforts with the Khmer resistance, and told me that he was getting support for the resistance and that that I would be involved with that project. He was true to his word.

***

One of the most interesting social contacts I made was a European aristocrat with a strong link to the United States and its founding. He was a lawyer by training and also a businessman. One of his businesses was a famous European manufacturer of fine crystal. One highlight of our tour was a weekend at the workshop in the Vosges Mountains. The factory was not open to the public, which made our visit even more special.

The manager of the workshop greeted us cordially, showed us to our suite in the main building and invited us to dinner in the nearby small down. At dinner, over a glass of wine, the manager asked BJ her ethnic background. This is a common question for BJ, who replied that she is from the village of Pepeeko on Hawaii's "Big Island." Her father was Filipino and her mother was born in Hawaii of Japanese parents. When I explained this to our host, he beamed and apologized for his blunt question but he wanted to know if she was part Japanese. He explained American army troops of Japanese ancestry liberated the town in 1944. Two of BJ's uncles had fought in Europe in the famed Japanese-American 442nd Regimental Combat Team. The unit's motto was "Go for Broke." With a tear in his eye, the old fellow proposed a toast to the memory of the Japanese-Americans who gave their lives to liberate his town.

The next day we toured the small private museum where we saw exquisite examples of crystal creations over the past 200 years. In the workshop we watched glass blowers in action. One of the works of art being readied for shipment was a large elephant with all fittings made of crystal, a special order for an Indian maharaja. In the museum we noticed a magnificent set of crystal glassware with Nazi engraving. The crystal was ordered during World War II but they deliberately slowed down the work in anticipation of the arrival of the Americans, so they would not have to deliver the glasses. They were never delivered. The 442nd got there first.

Unlike other glassworks that we had visited, such as Kosta Boda and Orrefors in Sweden, the workshop sells no "seconds." Finished works of crystal move slowly on a conveyer belt past two ladies who inspect them for quality. One by one these ladies pick up each piece and examine it. If an object is placed back on the moving belt, it means it has failed inspection. The belt spills them into a bin, where they crash with a heartbreaking sound. It took all of my self-control to avoid dashing over and saving a piece or two. An inspector smiled and consoled me with the thought that the shards of crystal would be melted down and sent back for recycling as a new, perfect, work of art.

***

Matt, our State Department friend from Bangkok, was serving as a senior officer in the US embassy in Luxembourg and encouraged us to visit. With his ambassador recently departed and the new one not yet arrived, Matt told us that if we came that weekend we could stay in the ambassador's residence. It was a grand chateau where the infamous Pearl Mesta stayed when she was the ambassador to Luxembourg (1949–53) that looked down on Luxembourg City. The Broadway play, *Call Me Madam*, documented Pearl's experience.

We found the ambassador's residence, except for the walls, a sheer delight. The former ambassador had participated in the Art in Embassies Program, founded in 1964 by President John Kennedy. The program promoted American culture and art by allowing ambassadors to borrow works of American art from private collections, galleries, or museums. The ambassador, a fan of modern art, had covered the old walls with large paintings of ribbons in hideous dayglo colors, or bright splotches of paint thrown onto canvas. All were totally out of character with the architecture and history of the building.

Matt chuckled, "Let me tell you a story," he said. "The last week the ambassador was here, he hosted his farewell dinner for the most important leaders of Luxembourg, including the prime minister and the head of the opposition party. I was there. At one point the prime minister got into a quarrel with an opposition politician. The ambassador tries to make peace. The prime minister turned on him. 'Don't tell me what to do. For years I have had to sit in the chair and look at that shit on the wall.'"

This is not the way an ambassador wants to leave a posting.

In 1983 our second son, Brendan, was born. The timing could not have been better. My next assignment was home, where Brendan would find doting grandparents. Brendan was premature. His arrival was unexpected and in the wee hours before dawn on September 15, I found myself racing to the hospital with BJ and fumes in the gas tank. Brendan was born within hours and the little fellow was transferred to a hospital famed for caring for premature babies. The doctor told us we should be prepared for the worst. But, after 55 days in an incubator, we took Brendan home. The doctors and staff saved his life.

Our trip home was not without incident. As I departed the hospital with BJ and Brendan in the back, a bus hit us. The bus, instead of stopping, hit us several more times, pushing the car off the street toward a pharmacy. We stopped short of crashing. People rushed to help us, the police arrived. I put BJ and Brendan in a taxi and stayed to face a very nervous bus driver and the police. No one was hurt but it was a tough way for Brendan to begin life.

In the summer of 1984 with my three-year tour coming to an end, the Agency assigned me home. I looked forward to the challenge of working against foreign targets in the United States. One of the several positive aspects of the assignment was that no one could declare me *persona non grata*, a fate that befell officers serving overseas when the host nation caught them engaged in espionage. During an operational trip to another European city I had dinner with a case officer assigned there. I casually asked the officer's wife how she liked their posting. "I love it," she said, "I only hope we finish our tour." This struck me as strange. "Why do you say that?" I asked. "Because we never have." Although my operation went well, the local government soon asked the officer to leave. The same thing happened on his next assignment. Apart from the political embarrassment and possible arrest of agents, such unpleasant events disrupt lives, families, and careers.

As my tour wound down, we said goodbye to friends and acquaintances in our cozy neighborhood. We gave a generous tip to our efficient Portuguese concierge and a small gift to the rotund newspaper vender across the street who had kept the copies of the *International Herald Tribune* for me. BJ's butcher and fruit sellers took her for coffee. The manager of our next door café, a hot spot for American jazzmen in the 1950s, stopped BJ one morning and offered her a glass of freshly squeezed farewell orange juice.

One lady whose name I never knew but whom I saw regularly was the neighborhood meter maid who made the lives of people with automobiles difficult. Parking was limited and expensive. The stoic ladies are everywhere, quietly ticketing illegally parked cars, deaf to the pleas of the malefactors. I owned a car for weekend getaways or longer road trips including one to Sweden. I parked on the street but was not much worried about getting parking tickets. The trick was to never block access to a driveway. Nor did I ever park in a taxi zone. Taxi drivers took matters into their own hands by "keying" offending cars.

Our pleasant neighborhood parking attendant ticketed my car faithfully and regularly. Whenever I found a ticket under a windshield wiper, I removed it and placed it with the others in the glove compartment. I never got into a dispute with the lady. Late in my tour, I left my apartment one morning to find our meter maid writing a ticket for my car. I was in no rush and waited quietly while she wrote up my offense. When she was through I walked over, wished her *bonjour*, and removed the ticket.

"I know you don't pay," she said, "But it is my duty to write them and I will continue to do so." I don't know what made me do it but I said, "These tickets are paid. I save them and at the end of the year the amount owed is then reduced from your national debt. I estimate that, thanks to your good work, the price of a Jeep is removed from the debt. Keep up the good work!" This was not true, of course, but I wanted to keep her morale high and her attitude towards the United States positive.

***

The result of my casual conversations I had earlier with the division chief of the Foreign Resource Division (FRD) came as a complete surprise. I would have asked for a lateral transfer back to Asia, perhaps as a deputy chief of station. It could take years to be named chief of station in Asia. I was moving ahead faster than I had planned and was told that assignments to FRD were only offered to officers with a record of recruiting agents as that was the main mission of FRD. There is a misconception that the CIA does not operate in the United States. The Agency has a worldwide charter to recruit foreign assets, including foreigners living in the United States. In fact, there are many attractive targets among foreign diplomats, military officers, academics, and students in the United States.

In Langley the chief of FRD, my new boss, welcomed me to the division and briefed me on my duties. The man spoke with a strong upper-class British accent. I asked him about it. His British father, an ambassador in Her Majesty's diplomatic service, had married his American mother. When they divorced my new boss had moved with his mother to the United States. For years, his father didn't know his son worked for the CIA. His father referred to officers of MI6, more correctly the Secret Intelligence Service (SIS), the British intelligence counterpart of CIA, as "chaps with false noses." During a visit to London, his father invited him to lunch at his club. He decided it was time to tell his father where he actually worked. He told me he said, "Father, I feel I should tell you that I wear a false nose." Unperturbed, his father replied, "Oh really, may I see your gun?"

I arrived at the post alone to find a house. BJ and the boys were still on vacation with her family in Hawaii. I found a realtor and went shopping for a house. On the first day I found a cozy five-bedroom house close to a large lake. It had a nice deck looking out through cedar trees. With four bedrooms up and one downstairs for our Thai nanny, Sri, it suited our needs perfectly. The house had been on the market for four hours. I bought it, one of my best financial moves ever. We still live in this house, which now has the Broman art, book, and map collection. Over the decades the lake view has largely been lost to the growth of trees, but the deck gives the impression of being part of a tree house.

One of my first meetings was to pay my respects to the Special Agent in Charge (SAC) of the local FBI field office. In certain instances, the Agency coordinates with the Bureau to ensure both agencies are not pursing the same target, and I wanted to get off on the right foot. During my Headquarters assignment I had worked closely with the Bureau and saw no reason why that should not be the case here. I made an appointment and presented myself to the SAC at his large. I opened by saying that for once I had an assignment from which I could not be kicked out by the host intelligence service. "Don't be too sure of that," the SAC told me, with no humor in his voice at all.

"So you're the guy with the good view," he said. He had mistaken me for my Agency counterpart in the Domestic Contact Service (DCS), an overt CIA office that worked in those days with American businesses to gather foreign intelligence. Although some American companies did not want any part of the espionage business, most happily cooperated with the Agency when they could. One of my DCS friends used to tell the story about his "account" with the CEO of a Fortune 50 company. Once a month my friend would have an appointment with this titan of industry in his New York City office. The CEO treated him to an upscale lunch after every meeting. No one in the office, including the CEO's personal assistant, ever knew my friend, a young officer, worked for the CIA. He never told. "It's the office mystery," the CEO told my friend, "I love it."

***

Bill Casey, Director of the CIA (DCI), visited us and held a meeting for all hands. After making some general remarks to the assembled CIA officers, Mr. Casey dismissed the others and had a one-on-one chat with me. We talked about current cases, including a promising hard target case in a nearby state. As always, Mr. Casey wanted to talk about Cambodia. He told me the Agency was working closer with Cambodia's non-communist resistance who were fighting Vietnamese-installed puppet regime of Heng Samrin. I told him I was keeping an eye on Cambodia and had just made a recruitment against that target.

Casey also told me that East Asia Division would be getting a new chief. He gave me the name of the man, but asked me not to tell anyone because the appointment had not been announced. I promised. Although disappointed in the choice, I held my tongue. Not only did the fellow lack experience and knowledge of East Asia, he had a reputation for being arrogant. Two days later, my secretary told me that Mr. Casey was on the phone for me. This was a first for me. I took the call wondering if I was in trouble.

Mr. Casey said, "Barry, do you remember I told you not to mention who would be the new Chief/EA?"

"Yes, sir," I replied.

"Did you tell anyone?" he asked.

"No, sir," I answered truthfully.

"That's good," he said. "I made a mistake. He is not getting the job." Then he told me the name of the new chief, a good man, and hung up.

It came as a surprise to learn that no one from FRD had ever been to Alaska. I checked with my counterpart at DCS, an excellent fellow who did not share the reticence of some of his colleagues in the Directorate of Intelligence (DI) to cooperate with the Directorate of Operations (DO). He made regular trips to Alaska and offered to take me along on his next trip and make some introductions. Headquarters agreed, and off we went to Anchorage on a balmy summer day.

We checked into the Captain Cook Hotel, the city's finest at the time, and I was stopped in my tracks when a burly fellow loudly greeted my colleague in the lobby with the words "What is the CIA doing in Anchorage?" I had forgotten that my friend could tell people where he worked. I couldn't. Hearing the initials of the Agency blared out in public came as a shock. As it turned out, the fellow was a former governor of Alaska and a social contact of my colleague. He smiled as he shook my hand and said, "Son, there are only 10 men with vision in the state of Alaska, and you're looking at one of them." I told him I was delighted to meet him and to be in Alaska. I used one of my aliases and never saw him again.

Our first stop was the FBI field office, which had one Foreign Counterintelligence (FCI) officer assigned to look out for spies. His job was to arrest them when committing espionage. My job was to recruit them and send them home to spy for us. I enjoyed working with him. He didn't get many counterintelligence visitors and we cooperated on a few interesting cases. We sometimes met for drinks at the Great Alaska Bush Company, a favorite hangout of oilmen working on the North Slope and a lively place when "oilies" came to town. He also introduced to me Gwenies, an Anchorage food institution where I habitually had breakfast on my way home. They served huge meals that featured caribou sausage. I usually made a couple of orders to take to friends and family.

In Fairbanks, my FBI contact took me to the Malamute Saloon, which sometimes hosted readings of the poems of Robert W. Service, the "bard of the Yukon." The place looked like the saloon Service wrote about in his famous opus, *The Shooting of Dan McGrew*. One of my favorites, the poem embraces the ethos of Alaska and the men – like my maternal grandfather and uncle –who sought their fortunes there, It begins:

A bunch of the boys were whooping it up in the Malamute saloon;
The kid that hands the music box was hitting a jag-time tune;
Back of the bar, in a solo game, sat Dangerous Dan McGrew,
And watching his luck was the light-o'-love, the lady that's known as Lou.

Once, on a chilly spring morning, the counterintelligence man, whose hobby was hunting with a bow instead of a rifle, drove me to see the oil pipeline that ran from north of Fairbanks headed to Prudhoe Bay. As we approached a stream, a moose walked onto the road from the creek bed. "I thought it would be larger," I commented. "That's the baby," he said, "here comes mama." A huge female moose soon emerged from the bush. The fed stopped his SUV well away from the animals. "They charge sometimes," he said, "and then their limbs collapse when they hit the car and they land in your lap." Eventually, they moved on, and we drove north to the pipeline.

My most memorable trip to Alaska took place one cold winter day when I made a long overnight automobile ride with a support asset from Anchorage to Juneau, the state capital. There is no road to Juneau, and to reach it by land required passage through the Yukon Territory of Canada to the town of Haines, Alaska. From there travelers needed to take a ferryboat down to Juneau.

Although Juneau is south of Anchorage, the trip starts with a long drive north to the village of Tok on the Alaska–Canada Highway. We spent that Friday night in Tok where it was minus 40 degrees Farenheit. Tok Lodge, where a country band was providing music in the dining room, had a full house. The only space available was at a table occupied by four Athabascan fur trappers and one pleasant young Athabascan woman, Ramona. Members of a major indigenous group in Alaska, they welcomed us to their table for the evening.

I opened the conversation by talking about the weather.

"Sure is cold, 40 below," I said.

Roy, a 30-something wolverine trapper replied, "40 below not cold, 60 below cold."

"What's the difference?" I countered.

"At 60 below you die," he said.

Roy and the others were drinking beer with peach brandy. Roy said the most dangerous thing about being out in minus 40-degree weather was falling asleep on his snowmobile. "You fall asleep, you die. Next year I am going to get my dog team back. They will take you home and if you are asleep they will howl when you get home. You don't die." Sage words, I am sure.

The next morning we filled up with gas to begin the long ride into the Yukon. A young man pumped the gas and said a strange thing had just happened to him. "I was changing a tire on a pickup and my hands were cold. I dropped the tire and it broke. That can happen at 40 below." We drove off in the dark heading for Canada. The sun came up and through clear blue skies heated and raised the temperature to a balmy minus 12 degrees. We drove over 50 miles per hour on packed snow with no traffic. We saw one vehicle, a pickup, stopped by the road. The unwritten rules of the north country require drivers to stop and assist motorists. A young man sat in the driver's seat, his engine was running. We rolled our windows down at the same time. "Thanks for stopping," he said. "I'm fine, just taking a break." We started up again. My friend looked in the rear view mirror. "I just saw the head of a young woman appear in the pickup. Probably they thought they were alone." I smiled. "Just taking a break."

We drove on across the frozen north. Fresh snow weighed down the pines. Towering mountains loomed large in the distance. We crossed a corner of the Yukon where my Canadian ancestor participated in the gold rush of 1898. He ended his days farming in the Fraser valley of British Columbia. Some hours passed before we re-entered the United States and headed for the small town of Haines, Alaska, where we would catch the ferry to Juneau. Reaching Haines at dinnertime, we found a funky restaurant called the Calypso and enjoyed our meal. Fine photos, mostly of bald eagles, covered the walls. The waitress told me that Manfred von Stauffenberg, her husband and co-owner of the Calypso, had taken the pictures.

Hearing the name, I asked her if her husband was any relation to Colonel Claus von Stauffenberg the man who tried to kill Hitler in 1944. With some surprise she said, "You are the first person who ever asked," adding, "He is a son." The assassination attempt failed and thousands of people, including the colonel, were executed in the aftermath. I met Manfred, who said he was not a legitimate son of the colonel. He escaped into Switzerland as a child and later made his way to America. Apart from his interesting family story, Manfred impressed me as an excellent wildlife photographer. He introduced me to the Alaska Chilkat Bald Eagle Preserve, an organization he supported. He also said he was a smoke jumper with a team of Tlingit Native Americans. "If you speak German," Manfred told me, "Tlingit comes easy."

Manfred took me to see the eagle preserve, which runs for six miles along the Chilkat River. The Chilkat valley, home to several hundred eagles year round, attracts as many three thousand bald eagles in the winter when the salmon are spawning. One tree in the preserve might hold as many as 60 eagles, gathered to feast on the spawned-out salmon. Wearing wading boots, Manfred strode into the frigid water to drag salmon carcasses out of the water to attract eagles to swoop down on them as I snapped photos.

We concluded our trip taking an Alaska ferryboat to Juneau. We flew out in the middle of the night. Meeting Manfred, hearing about his family history and seeing the eagles impelled me to return later for a longer visit. On the second trip I took a perilous flight from Haines down to Juneau with a bush pilot in a small aircraft. The weather turned bad just as we lifted off from Haines and the pilot kept losing altitude to stay under the clouds. We were skimming the waves of the north Pacific when we touched down in Juneau at last light. I complimented the skipper for the thrilling ride and asked why we flew over beaches much of the way. "I was looking for a place to put down in case we ran out of visibility." I was reminded of the adage an Air America pilot once shared with me. "There are old pilots and bold pilots. But there are no old bold pilots."

***

I enjoyed a correct and often convivial relationship with the FBI. They had numerous small one-officer posts in this region, who were by and large a pleasure to work with. On one occasion, the Bureau made initial contact with a Middle Eastern target of considerable interest to us and turned it over to the Agency. We recruited the man, one of the few clandestine assets from his country, and he proved to be valuable when he returned home.

Relations with the Bureau got even better when I hired a retired FBI officer, a bluff and friendly fellow whom everyone liked. I put him in charge of liaison with the Bureau. In far-flung Bureau offices where our officers might be put on hold or where the wheels of cooperation might have turned slowly, having our new man on the case made a world of difference. Everyone knew him and opened their files to him.

Our only problem came from an FBI field office that was not in my "turf." It not only poached my targets, people the FBI had already conceded belonged to the CIA, it poached in territory assigned to other FBI offices. The first attempt by the FBI to poach one of our cases that had already been approved as a CIA target by FBI headquarters. When it came to my attention, I spoke to my counterpart in the city involved. He knew nothing of the matter and assured me that his officers were not pursuing our target. After a little sleuthing, it became clear that a sister Bureau office was the culprit. Caught with its hand in my cookie jar, the Special Agent in Charge apologized and backed off.

The matter didn't end there. Sometime later, the same office targeted a man we were after in Alaska. This wasn't a coincidence; it was a pattern. After the offending office backed off again, I decided to visit the aggressive field office. I met with the officer responsible for both the poaching efforts. He grudgingly promised it would not happen again. I asked to see the Special Agent in Charge, his boss. This seemed to worry him and I assured him I wanted to make a courtesy call and would not be discussing the poaching issues. Reluctantly, he made it happen.

The SAC's brother, an officer in the CIA, was a good friend of mine. I opened our meeting by saying how much I enjoyed working with his brother on a foreign assignment. The brother was an analyst from the Directorate of Intelligence on a rare posting abroad. He was so good, in fact, that the deputy chief of station and I convinced the man to move to the Directorate of Operations and he went on to have a distinguished career in the Clandestine Service. When I mentioned my part in his brother's career change, the SAC turned nasty. "So you're the son-of-a-bitch who turned my little brother into a spook!" I was taken aback. I thought I did the brother a favor. I still do.

***

My assignment gave me the opportunity to serve as a chief in a new area division. It also gave the boys a chance to see how Americans lived and get to know both sets of aging grandparents. The assignment also gave BJ a chance to open her own business, East-West Catering, with my sister, Jenny, as her partner. Always an excellent cook, BJ expanded her horizons in Paris at the Cordon Bleu culinary school. The ladies cooked high-end meals in the homes of their clients. They did very well and BJ flourished with avid corporate clients with deep pockets and an appreciation for fine Asian and European cuisine. They could have gone far. But when I received orders for a new Asian posting, BJ gave up her business and followed the flag with me.

In the fall of 1986, I received an offer to be deputy chief of station (DCOS) in Southeast Asia. It was just the job I was looking for. This was one of the countries in which I wanted to serve. I accepted with pleasure and asked if I could hire a tutor locally for some language training. Headquarters concurred. We found a very pleasant female graduate student who agreed to come to the house twice a week to teach BJ and me one of the world's easiest languages to learn.

Our teacher, I will call her Wati, was a single professional woman in her thirties. Petite and pretty, she came from an aristocratic family. Our ability to speak her language improved steadily under her expert tutelage. We also became friends with Wati, who had few American friends apart from her fellow graduate-school students. One day she announced she had met a young American businessman at a graduate student party and he asked her for a date. She had never been on a date and didn't know what to do. We asked if she liked the fellow. She did, and added that he drove a sports car, was very polite, and everyone liked him. We said that a dinner and movie should not be a problem, so she accepted the date. She reported the following week that the date had gone well. He was a complete gentleman and her meal was delicious. She wrote to her mother back home about her first date and the mother immediately wrote back that she had sent her daughter to the United States to get an advanced degree and not to go on dates with Americans. As a result, when the young businessman asked her for a second date, she turned him down.

We left for Asia with a good language foundation and Wati returned home with her master's degree and an important government position. I wonder if she knew that her erstwhile suitor became a billionaire, married happily, and was a captain of industry and philanthropy. I don't think Wati ever married.

***

The timing of our posting could not have been better. As the deputy chief of station, or number two, I worked for a legendary chief, an Asian American who had been decorated for valor during hazardous postings in the Middle East. For the first time, I deployed as a "declared" officer, which means the local security services knew that I worked for the Agency. I functioned in a "liaison" capacity with the intelligence service on targets of mutual interest. In spook-speak, I was in a "target-rich" environment.

BJ landed a plum job with the State Department as the Community Liaison Officer (CLO), a sort of an embassy ombudsperson. She helped newcomers adjust, conducted cultural tours, organized shopping events, and was the person whom embassy personnel went to when they had problems. Everyone knew BJ. I became known as "Mr. BJ," a title I bore with pride. When a burly USAID Hawaiian hosted a luau, BJ danced a classic Hawaiian hula, a crowd-pleaser. When Vice President Dan Quayle visited, BJ, in her capacity as CLO, served as the official greeter. Our old friend Tim and his wife, Vicki, whom BJ introduced to Tim at an earlier posting, were also at post. Our antique collecting continued.

The intelligence service hosted a welcome dinner for us shortly after we arrived. The host seated me next to an attractive woman who spoke excellent English. Her husband, a general, sat opposite us in a private dining room of a major hotel. I opened the conversation by asking if she was a member of the leading ethnic group. "Good lord, no," she said, quickly adding, "My husband is from that group. It is easy to tell. He is cold and quiet with no sense of humor. I am from another group. We are easy going and friendly." As she spoke, her husband glowered at me from across the table. My education in the peoples and customs of my new posting had begun.

The Soviet Union, a hardy perennial target of the CIA, was very active here. The Soviets had run a successful Soviet operation against us in the past, so we had to be alert for counterintelligence threats even as we fished for new recruits of our own. While the Agency considered Soviet diplomats fair game, our favorite targets were the KGB, the CIA's counterpart agency, and the GRU, Soviet military intelligence.

By the late 1980s, relations with the USSR, our Cold War enemy for decades, began to thaw. Soviet leader Mikhail Gorbachev had come to power with glasnost, a new open and transparent regime. At the same time, the Soviet Union began to self-destruct. This was a period when building relationships with Soviets was easier than before and presented opportunities for recruitment. We harbored no illusions about each other. More Soviets officials than Americans probably knew I was a CIA officer, which was fine with me. It can be helpful for Soviets who want to defect to know who to look for. Many of our best agents started out as "walk ins."

Someone arranged a US–Soviet "friendly" soccer match. Although we had a strong pool of players, it wasn't strong enough. Soviets played soccer, and often played it very well. We knew we wouldn't win but viewed this as an opportunity to make new contacts. But we didn't want to disgrace ourselves. Our team had one major asset, a big fellow who had been drafted by the Green Bay Packers professional football team out of college. He also played an aggressive game of soccer, which drew the respect of our opposition and cut their margin of victory. We made a few good contacts at the event, which was our purpose all along.

An opportunity for sustained one-on-one contact with the Soviets came from the Ministry of Foreign Affairs on an upcountry trip for selected international guests. Trip sponsors included the American oil company that had oil rigs operating in coastal waters. I was invited along with a small group of Americans on the trip. About 30 assorted foreigners participated including a few Soviets. Among them was a fellow who may have been my counterpart. I will call him Boris.

The well-organized trip turned out to be a lot of fun. We were given VIP treatment while visiting offshore oil rigs, looking down on circling barracuda that gathered to eat scraps of food from the rig's galley. We also traveled up a local river to visit a wood-processing factory, and lived very well thanks to the oil company's largesse.

BJ, as the embassy Community Liaison Officer, greets Vice President Dan Quayle and his wife during a visit.

One evening featured singing after dinner. A young, good-looking KGB officer gave an incredibly talented version of the old New Orleans song, "The House of the Rising Sun," in unaccented English. It was a hard act to follow, but one of our young officers gave it a try. He sang the full theme song of the television program *Rawhide* that launched the career of a young Clint Eastwood. Competing with the Soviets was not confined to the arms race and space.

Boris and I spent some quality time together on our field trips. We discussed the rapidly changing politics of the USSR and the portent for the future. Boris was worried, with good reason. It turned out that Boris was a great joke-teller, a talent I modestly feel I shared with him. One of the things I like about Russians is their sense of humor and the quality of their jokes. Some nationalities, like the Irish, are famous for their joke-telling prowess. Others, like England and France, are not. Soviet jokes often poked fun at the establishment, sometimes brutally. I usually heard these stories from low-level apparatchiks after too much vodka. But Boris surprised me. He was a senior officer and not drunk when he told me the following joke:

Early one morning Comrade Leonid Ilyich Brezhnev, Secretary General of the Central Committee of the Communist Party of the Soviet Union, rose from his bed. He threw open the curtains of his bedroom to greet the new day. The sun was just rising. "Good morning sun," said Brezhnev. "Good morning, comrade Brezhnev," replied the sun. "Have a nice day." Brezhnev left for a full day of work at the Kremlin. He returned home just as the sun was going down. "Good night sun," said the Secretary General, "see you in the morning." "Fuck you Brezhnev," said the sun. Offended and hurt, Brezhnev replied, "Why do you say such a thing to me? This morning you were so nice." "This morning," said the sun, "I was in the East. Now I am in the West."

I hope Boris is enjoying his retirement somewhere in the West.

***

On the morning of the August 27, 1883, the deadliest volcanic eruption in recorded history blew up the island of Krakatoa in the Sunda Strait between Java and Sumatra. The explosion was heard in Perth, Australia, two thousand miles away. A tsunami 150-foot high hit the west Java coastal town of Meruk and killed more than 36,000 people. The explosion destroyed most of the island. In 1900 a new island dubbed Anak Krakatoa, or baby Krakatoa, emerged from the underwater crater. Soon after its birth it measured 30 feet above sea level.

We learned of an ocean-going 37-foot ketch for charter skippered by a young Englishman with a strong sailing pedigree, a gold earring, and a live eagle on his shoulder when he was at sea. With Tim and Vicki, we chartered the boat and set off to have a look at Anak Krakatoa that was rising from the sea and over six hundred feet high. The skipper's mate was a fierce-looking, lithe Balinese fellow named Budi with a mane of wild hair and a reputation for seducing young Japanese female tourists.

Although the skipper usually charted the ketch for voyages around Java with a stop in Bali, we didn't have time for a long trip. He agreed to take us over Anak Krakatoa and make a stop at the Ujung Kulon National Park on the west tip of Java, accessible only by boat and home of the nearly extinct Javanese rhino.

Our young boys loved their first time on a sailing boat in Asia, Vicki, not so much. *Mal de mer* set in immediately on the choppy waters that separated the Indian Ocean from the Pacific, and the poor lady spent much of the time at sea in distress. On deck, 10-year-old Seth kept a tight grip on five-year-old Brendan as they relished being inundated by waves over the bow under the watchful eye of Dad and the fearful eye of Mom.

We sailed over to Anak Krakatoa and dropped anchor in the lee of the island, out of the wind. We went ashore and found that life had taken hold on the new island; vegetation sprouted up the sandy slopes. Steam rose from the young volcano's caldera and a misstep on the rim could have had dire consequences. We survived the climb, peeked into the abyss, and slept soundly through the night despite rough seas that dragged our anchor.

The next morning we sailed back to Java and landed at the national park where there were no other visitors, not surprising given the choppy water that made landing ashore inordinately hazardous. Park rangers welcomed us and proudly led us to a herd of pretty tame-looking wild deer grazing on the lawn of the park headquarters. When we inquired about the whereabouts of the rare Java rhinos, the ranger told us that he regularly saw rhino droppings, but had never, in all the years he had worked there, seen a rhino. We decided we didn't need to venture into the dense and malarial jungle, and after some effort made it back to the boat. We sailed up the coast to Anjer without incident.

In December 2018, Anak Krakatoa, now about one thousand feet high, erupted violently, sending a tsunami wave into the coast of west Java killing more than four hundred people.

***

Among the most remote yet fascinating Indonesian islands, is the Banda group, located 1,500 miles east of Jakarta. These islands were on the southern edge of the Spice Islands and were the home of nutmeg and mace, which attracted traders from Europe more than three hundred years ago. In the 17th century, Great Britain and the Netherlands fought wars over control of the spice trade. In 1616, English interlopers threatened the Dutch monopoly of nutmeg when they occupied the tiny island of Rhun in the Bandas. Nutmeg purchased in Banda for 1,000 guilders fetched 86,000 guilders in Amsterdam as long as the monopoly held. To ensure their monopoly, the Dutch negotiated the Treaty of Breda in 1667, giving the English a small, remote, and virtually worthless island in exchange for Rhun. It was the island of Manhattan on the Hudson River in North America. For years the Dutch had the better of the deal.

I had the good fortune to meet Des Alwi, a charming fellow known fondly as "the King of the Bandas." He had played many roles over the years: former freedom fighter against the Dutch, a diplomat, rebel against Sukarno, Indonesia's first president after gaining independence from the Netherlands. Des was born in the Banda Islands, where Mohammad Hatta, the first vice-president of Indonesia, who had been exiled to the remote Bandas by the Dutch, adopted him. Des, long retired from politics when I met him, spent most of his time in Jakarta. He made documentary films and promoted travel to visit Banda, which was far easier said than done. Only two commercial flights a week flew from Ambon to the Bandas. Des invited me and three Sino-Indonesian friends of mine to visit his islands. They wanted to scuba-dive in the pristine waters of the Banda Sea. I wanted to see Rhun.

We timed our 1988 visit to coincide with the annual inter-island *kora kora* boat race. Each of the islands of the Banda chain sponsored a long war canoe seeking to bring fame and honor to their home islands. Des offered us berths on his small inter-island steamer, a confiscated Taiwanese fishing boat that supplied the Bandas from Ambon 150 miles to the north. We opted for the boat over the infrequent aircraft and spent a delightful 24 hours cruising over the glass-like surface of the Banda Sea, watching whales breach as we headed for the smoke of Gunung Api, a very active volcano. Des arranged accommodation in tiny cabins near the boat's bridge. Dozens of islanders made themselves comfortable on mats on the main deck.

To my surprise, there were two Americans on the boat. The man was a journalist on a working vacation with his girlfriend. They were traveling leisurely around Southeast Asia and said that they needed to touch base with an American when they returned to civilization. "What's his name?" I asked. "Barry Broman," he replied. I produced my calling card and handed it to the journalist. "Small world," was all he said.

To be in the Bandas when Des Alwi was in residence made the difference between a good visit and a great one. He owned and operated a small, comfortable, hotel on the waterfront of Bandaneira. The hotel offered no frills but the price was right. Over the years it had a number of distinguished guests including Lady Diana and Mick Jagger (not at the same time). It looked out at the nearby island of Gunung Api, aptly named Fire Island, an active volcano that had recently blown its top and burned down much of the foliage of the island. Ancient canons set in the cement, barrel down, formed the bollards on the quay, where boats tied up outside the hotel.

Des organized the food and entertainment. Among other things, he served hyper-fresh raw tuna, which he billed as the world's cheapest sashimi. It sold in the nearby market for 10 US cents per pound. With a little wasabi and soy sauce, it tasted delicious. At night, he had a white sheet hung across the street. The sheet was the screen for the films he showed after dark. Des invited everyone on the island to the free alfresco film. With only four cars on the island, traffic posted no problem. Des owned two of them.

Des arranged for a boat to give us a tour of the islands, including, to my delight, the remote and now-famous island of Rhun. Unlike Manhattan, the skyline of Rhun remains unchanged. No structure on the tiny island is higher than a palm tree. It still lacks plentiful fresh water, which bedeviled the British when they were there. I suspect the total value of the island is worth about the same as a brownstone building on the upper East Side of Manhattan.

We thoroughly enjoyed the boat races that took place off Banda Neirea, the largest settlement in the islands. In the background was the island of Guning Api. Hundreds of islanders gathered to watch the long boats, each with about 20 paddlers. At the end of the frenetic nautical dash, an ebullient Des awarded trophies to the winners.

The remains of the old Dutch forts and the many colonial villas offered mute testimony to the past glory and importance of this little island chain. The Bandas sill produce nutmeg but life moves at a slow pace. The Bandas are but one example of how many great places—each with a story of its own—lie hidden in this vast archipelago. Des Alwi, a man who had done much for his young country while remaining a loyal and loving son of the islands that gave the world nutmeg, made our trip there very special.

***

Towards the end of my tour, a Dutch friend, Loek Pasmans, invited me to accompany him to Irian Jaya, formerly Dutch New Guinea and now called Papua, the largest province of Indonesia. Loek, a longtime resident of Jakarta, was publishing a textbook on the geography of Indonesia for the Ministry of Education and needed photos. So I took one week of annual leave, acquired malaria medication, and packed my rucksack.

Two countries, Indonesia and the country of Papua New Guinea, share the island of New Guinea, the fourth largest island in the world. The western half belongs to Indonesia where more than three hundred languages are spoken. Among our stops was Wamena, located in the fertile Baliem Valley, deep in the interior and at an altitude of 5,000 feet. The Dani people, one of the province's largest ethnic groups were only discovered by the outside world in 1938 by an American aviator.

I looked forward to a chance to put my anthropology training to good use. The Dani, once headhunters, still engaged in violent inter-village "play" wars. These fights sometimes end with fatalities. Dark-skinned Melanesians, the Danis wear few clothes. Men usually wear only a penis sheath called a *koteka*, usually made from a long, pointed gourd. One size fits all. Women often wear only a grass skirt. In the Wamena market I saw a woman selling vegetables in the poorly lit building. While she conducted business, she nursed a baby on one breast and a baby pig on the other. Low light prevented me from taking a photo but I doubt it would have made it into the geography book anyway.

During our trip we met a young Indonesian man wearing a tee shirt with the word Harvard on it. It turned out he spoke excellent English and had worked for Harvard anthropologists. A font of information about the Dani people, he explained that pigs played a central role in the local economy. As prized possessions, owners bring them into the huts to sleep. When we visited, the going price for a Dani bride was four pigs.

The Dani played a small role in helping the Allies in World War II when a C-47 transport aircraft went down in the unexplored mountains near their plateau. The survivors included US Army nurses. Search aircraft located the crash site and paratroopers with medics parachuted in easily enough but faced a serious problem getting the injured out of the mountainous area. It would take weeks to try to walk out. With the help of local Dani who were paid in salt for their labor, the Americans hacked a rough airstrip out of the jungle. Too short and rough for a C-47, it proved adequate for a CG4-A combat glider. Captain Henry Palmer, a friend of my father, piloted his glider into the valley and picked up the survivors and rescuers. His glider was "snatched" by a low-flying C-47, which carried a cable that hooked the nylon towrope of Palmer's glider on the ground. It took three flights to get everyone out. The Dani were delighted to have their salt brought in by air. It was a 30-day walk to the coast, one way.

I needed a photo of Jayapura, the coastal capital of Irian Jaya. The Dutch had called the town Hollandia. American forces captured it in 1944 as they fought their way westward under General Douglas MacArthur, who made Hollandia his headquarters for a while. A high hill looking down on the port provided the best view of the town. We followed a dirt road to the radio station at the top. Not only did we have a spectacular view of the city, the port, and villages on small islands offshore but we could also see the remains of American landing craft and tanks that didn't make it into battle when MacArthur's troops took the city. I began taking photos, with the sun dropping fast. As I worked and Loek watched, an elderly man walked up. He was gathering firewood with a machete. He looked at Loek and greeted him in Dutch. Amazed, Loek engaged him in conversation. It transpired that the old fellow was a Christian from Ambon who had served in the Dutch army. He said he was a teenager when the Americans conquered Hollandia and he gave us a detailed description of the battle and American occupation, which included 11 open-air cinemas that delighted all of the children in town.

We had made a friend. I told Loek that we had lost the good light and needed to come back the next day for better sundown light. Loek said OK and told the old fellow that we would be back the next day and that he would bring a Dutch cigar for the old soldier. We arrived the next day in perfect light to find the old fellow standing there dressed in his Sunday best clothes. Delighted to see him, Loek presented him with a cigar while I poured a couple of Scotch whiskies to celebrate the occasion. But not until I had all the photos I needed for the book.

***

My third posting with Tim allowed us to continue the antique collecting that we had begun together more than a decade earlier. The hills south of the capital were a good place to spend weekends away from the torrid tropical coast and we both has access to charming villas where we could relax on weekends. The boys could ride ponies through a large tea plantation nearby. The area was also a gathering point for antique dealers who would scour the hills during a week and then descend on the capital to sell their finds. We befriended some of these fellows who would spot our cars on a Saturday morning and set up their wares on the lawn.

Some care needed to be taken. Local craftsmen made ceramic pots and plates, often replicas of older colonial pottery. The low prices the dealers asked were a clue that these could not be originals. Tim, ever the diplomat, handled the issue of authenticity deftly. He would heft a large plate and ask "If this was real, how much would it cost?" Unfazed and unoffended, the dealer would quote a large figure to let us know what an opportunity we were being offered. When it came time to pay we would hand over the payment but never received change. Instead, the dealer always offered us attractive and authentic 19th-century Chinese tea dishes priced at $1 each. Over time we amassed sizable collections. Today, we use these dishes as drink coasters. Eventually, we limited the amount of cash we took to the hills on weekend to prevent over shopping. If something broke, usually one of the brass lamps that had been cannibalized from old lamps, we could return it or have it repaired at little or no cost. We learned a lot from these roving entrepreneurs who could be spotted at a distance carrying their large bundles over their shoulders.

We brought steaks and red Bordeaux wines to the cool hills where we would grill steaks on fires of old tea wood. After dinner we played board games such as Monopoly or Pictionary. We did not miss television or the Internet. It was a simpler time. The only disconcerting intruders we had to deal with at our mountain getaway were the fruit bats that lived in the eaves. These huge creatures, although harmless, hung upside down and looked at you like they wanted to suck your blood. We did not spend much time on the verandah under the eaves, as bat droppings were also an issue.

The embassy owned a colonial period house built in Art Deco style, not far from our A-frame. The house had lovely grounds that bordered jungle and was reserved for the ambassador and senior officers. Tim was one of them and he sometimes invited us as his guests. We all enjoyed playing croquet on the villa's lawn. Our boys, Seth and Brendan, liked the villa because they could pitch their tent near the jungle. One night when the boys were asleep in their tent, Tim and I quietly crept up to the tent. Tim, an accomplished big game hunter from his tours in Africa, made the low grunting sounds of wild boars.

The sound woke up the boys. "Did you hear that?" said Brendan. "What do you think it was?"

Seth, five years older, answered "Maybe an animal."

At that point, Tim, Seth's godfather, spoke up. "That was me making the sound of a wild pig. Back to bed now. Sleep tight." And so they did. Imagine our surprise, however, when we woke the boys up for breakfast the next morning and found tracks of small feral pigs around their tent. I suspect Tim's porcine grunts attracted them.

This posting was both personally and professionally satisfying. We made a few new friends and I made a few good recruitments. It is important not to confuse or combine the two. I learned how to work as a liaison officer, not only with my counterparts but also with other sister intelligence services. During my tour the chief, the consummate ops officer who was decorated for valor earlier in his career, rotated out and was replaced by a very different sort of boss. The new fellow had been an ops officer in his youth, but decided that he didn't want a career abroad. So he switched to the Directorate of Intelligence (DI) and became a very successful analyst. When Bob Gates, also a DI officer, became director of CIA, he planned to move many analysts into chiefs of station positions around the world. My new boss was the test case. Gates probably selected him because of his past operational experience and his leadership skills. However, Gates didn't last long in the job, and the chance of having analysts in COS slots ended with his departure. I found my new boss to be very easy to deal with. He let me continue to run the station's operations. When I asked if he wanted to make any changes he only said, "If it ain't broken, don't fix it." We got along fine. When I was preparing to leave, he said in my fitness report. "I want to thank this officer for teaching me how to be a chief of station."

BJ had also enjoyed a very successful, if at times trying tour, as Community Liaison Officer. The position proved particularly challenging after our first ambassador, an outstanding fellow and a huge success despite not being a career Foreign Service Officer, left. Ironically, the man who replaced him *was* a career Foreign Service Officer but not a very good one. He had reached his Peter Principle level of incompetence and it showed. Moreover, he and his wife seemed to be trying to save as much money

Brendan Broman holds his croquet gear after a match at the American ambassador's weekend cottage in Indonesia. Seth and Brendan loved weekends in the cool highlands where they could ride ponies in a tea plantation and camp in the jungle grounds of the ambassador's art deco house where wild boar roamed at night.

as possible for retirement. Not to put too fine a point on it: he was a cheapskate. In fact, his wife was so stingy that she asked some guests coming to community functions at the embassy to bring their own sugar. At dinners, some turkeys appeared more than once. His wife and her antics can charitably be described as "wacky."

We were sorry to leave our large, modern home that had a three-story high wall of glass looking out on the swimming pool. Our Thai nanny Sri got along well with our local staff, which included a cook, and her husband, the gardener, who almost always succeeded in keeping venomous snakes from getting into the house. Our administrative counselor, Dave, a salty old fellow with many years' service in third-world countries, liked to take me aside and inform me that my house won again as the most expensive residence to air condition. I always pointed out that he rented the house and assigned me to it. Dave told me a story of being on home leave in the States with his small children after a hardship tour somewhere in Africa. Grandma was making breakfast for this kids who just sat and watched their cereal in milk. She told them to eat up. "We have to wait, Grandma," said the little girl. "We are waiting for the weevils to rise up. Then we will rack them off and eat our cereal. That's how we did it in Africa." I could see grandma, in her comfortable mid-western American house, run shrieking from the kitchen. Ex-pat kids, like service brats, learn fast and roll with the punches. What doesn't kill you makes you stronger.

***

By the time my posting ended in 1990 I had been in the field for nine years. It was time to return to Langley and ride a desk until I could get another foreign posting. The Agency offered me a good position as chief of the Indochina Operations Group. The job would raise my profile, put me in daily contact with senior Asia hands in the intelligence community and advance my career. I accepted the offer with pleasure.

No sooner had I agreed to return to Langley than Billy Huff, the newly assigned chief of station elsewhere in Southeast Asia sent me a message. I had worked for him before and we got along well. A China hand and former Marine, Billy had an opening for a senior officer to manage a project dealing with Cambodia. He knew I spoke Thai and French and had long experience in the area. I told Billy I had already accepted an offer in Langley but that I would also like the job he offered. The job seemed to be something for which I had been in training for over the past decade. Billy contacted Headquarters. They said I could take my pick of assignments but that the Langley job would be more career enhancing. Nonetheless, I opted for Billy's offer and never regretted it.

Things had changed a lot for the Cambodian resistance since I left Europe. The two non-communist groups, the Khmer People's National Liberation Front (KPNLF) and the royalist group under Norodom Sihanouk known by its French acronym (FUNCINPEC) had grown in strength with the support of the Association of Southeast Asian Nations (ASEAN) friends, led by Thailand. The Thai put pressure on the United States to increase support to the non-communists. The Chinese were continuing their support for the ousted Khmer Rouge hiding in camps along the Thai–Cambodian border. The Thai army controlled the flow of weapons to the Khmer Rouge but preferred to back the NCR. At no time did the Americans provide any support to the Khmer Rouge.

The Thai army supported elements of the NCR from its inception, starting in 1975 after Phnom Penh fell to the Khmer Rouge. General Chavalit Yongchaiyut headed this program and sought armed support from other members of the ASEAN. Ken Conboy, in his encyclopedic book *The Cambodian Wars: Clashing Armies and*

CIA Covert Operations, wrote: "Chavalit remained the linchpin on Cambodia. Specifically, he was leading the effort to coordinate a covert ASEAN cabal to support the noncommunist resistance. The first was Singapore … The second was Malaysia. Starting in late 1979, the intelligence representative at the Malaysian embassy in Bangkok … attended his first coordination session with Chavalit and SID (Singapore's Security and Intelligence Division)."

Still suffering from what was known as the "Vietnam Syndrome," the American government hesitated entering into any covert action in Southeast Asia in the wake of its ignominious withdrawal from the region in 1975. We reported on the activities of the NCR, recruited assets to keep us informed on developments, but were reluctant to get involved. With the election of President Reagan in 1981, and his appointment of William Casey as Director of the CIA (DCI), things changed. Reagan made it clear that he wanted to defeat the USSR and reverse its gains around the world. Paramilitary programs blossomed, notably in Afghanistan, but also in Nicaragua and Angola.

It was a start. America reentered the game, and over time its contributions grew. At no time did the United States, or its ASEAN allies, support the Khmer Rouge who were also part of the resistance to the Vietnamese-installed regime in Phnom Penh, the People's Republic of Kampuchea (PRK). The Chinese with the cooperation of the Thai who were secretly supporting both sides, provided the bulk of foreign assistance to the Khmer Rouge. The Thai favored the NCR, sometimes siphoning Chinese weapons away from the Khmer Rouge to the NCR. The Thai also withheld heavy weapons such as tanks and artillery from the Khmer Rouge, to the chagrin of the Chinese. Sometimes NCR forces, mostly Sihanouk's men, cooperated with the Khmer Rouge, but only when hard pressed by the PRK.

The group in charge of the project was called the Executive Committee (Exco). By the time I arrived in 1990, the Exco had become the Cambodia Working Group. American funding came from the US Agency for International Development (USAID) and from a special US Congressional fund established thanks to Congressmen Stephen Solarz who had become a champion of Cambodia.

***

I knew the target and liked the mission. I also knew many of the players from my years in Phnom Penh and elsewhere. I had discussed this possibility with director Bill Casey several times and was happy to get the job. The Agency was conducting similar projects in Angola, Afghanistan, and elsewhere.

After the US government evacuated us from Phnom Penh in 1975, one step ahead of the Khmer Rouge, it turned its back on Indochina, especially Cambodia. The bloodbath that followed the victory of the Khmer communists seemed to cause little concern to the Carter administration despite its vaunted interest in human rights. Probably two million Cambodians died in the four years that Pol Pot ruled Cambodia. Ironically, it was his former ally Vietnam that ended the reign of terror in 1979. Vietnam had shed a lot of blood putting the Khmer Rouge in power, and assumed that the Cambodian communists would accept Vietnamese hegemony in the region. The Vietnamese were wrong. The Khmer Rouge were radical communists, but as Cambodian nationalists, they also retained historical hatred for the Vietnamese. Before the 18th century, the entire Mekong River delta, today in southern Vietnam, belonged to Cambodia. France halted Vietnam's regional advance in the 1860s, when it made southern Vietnam (Cochin China) a colony and declared Cambodia as French protectorate.

Vietnam endured a tough year in 1979. The Khmer Rouge provoked their Vietnamese "comrades" to the point where it became unbearable. Vietnam invaded the country it had earlier "liberated" and forced the Khmer Rouge leadership into exile in Thailand. The Vietnamese installed a puppet regime led by some turncoat Cambodian communists led by Heng Samrin, whose regime was known as the People's Republic of Kampuchea (PRK). Many people, including me, welcomed this invasion. Anyone willing to remove the Khmer Rouge had my respect. It was the lesser of two evils.

The Chinese, however, were not amused by the Vietnamese invasion of Cambodia. The Khmer Rouge's only friend, the Chinese, decided to "teach the Vietnamese a lesson." They invaded Vietnam along its northern border and took a few towns, including the old French hill station of Sapa. The Vietnamese, annealed by decades of war, fought back. They fought a brutal but short war against China, inflicting many thousands of casualties on the Chinese, who somehow failed to remember that the Vietnamese were tough, experienced, and well armed. The Chinese pulled back to lick their wounds. It was they who learned a lesson.

The international community wrestled with the question of what to do with the Vietnamese. Hanoi had not altruistically invaded Cambodia because of the genocide perpetrated on the Khmer people by their former ally. They wanted to control Cambodia, by brutal conquest if necessary. China responded by continuing to support the Khmer Rouge in exile. Prince Sihanouk reacted by changing sides again.

Meanwhile, Cambodian resistance to the Khmer Rouge had begun in 1975, almost as soon as they took power. But it would be years before the United States gave any support to anti-Khmer Rouge forces. The resistance received help from the Thai who were nervous about having the Khmer Rouge on their border. This nervousness only increased when the Thai saw the People's Army of Vietnam (PAVN) appear on the Thai border in 1979. Toan Chay, a former fighter pilot in the Khmer Air Force (KAF) and one of the early leaders of the Cambodian resistance, organized a small unit of patriots on the Thai–Cambodian border in 1975 to fight the Khmer Rouge. Later a former Cambodian army general named Dien Del appeared on the border and set up his own resistance force, also with clandestine Thai army support. I knew Dien Del, a much-respected commander of the Second Infantry Division in Phnom Penh in 1974. He came from a group known as the Khmer Krom, ethnic Khmer, born in South Vietnam, where about a million Khmer Krom lived in the Mekong Delta. He was heavily decorated, brave, and an aficionado of Remy Martin Cognac, who dedicated himself to the removal of first the Khmer Rouge and later the Vietnamese.

Gradually, the US government acceded to requests from the Thai and other ASEAN countries and began limited support for the two non-communist factions that waged low-level guerrilla against the Vietnamese-installed regime in Phnom Penh. Heng Samrin nominally led the pro-Vietnamese government in Phnom Penh, but it also included a former Khmer Rouge division commander named Hun Sen.

Conboy notes: "CIA Director William Casey on looking beyond the past and as early as 1981 had argued that the United States should provide weapons to anyone fighting communists—the Cambodian noncommunist resistance included." Initial efforts were rebuffed, but he tried again in 1982. "Casey made a fresh pitch for covert lethal aid. Getting a whiff of Casey's request, the Department of State balked. But Reagan by now saw merit in at least symbolic assistance."

Guns and ammunition would come from the other three countries—Thailand, Singapore, and Malaysia—that formed the coalition known as the Working Group on Cambodia. I walked into this active little war in the summer of 1990. My deputy was Bob, a senior ops officer (GS-15 or full colonel equivalent). He was a former Recon Marine and a man of few words. Bob was blessed with common sense, an attribute that I find not at all common. He also spoke good Thai. The team also included a Merle, a Vietnamese linguist, whose language skills came in very handy. There was a no-nonsense finance officer who kept tabs on every penny of money and a sharp young logistics officer who did a marvelous job. In addition, I had several paramilitary officers, all ex-military, and all very good at their jobs. We provided no "lethal" assistance and did no fighting.

We often visited the Thai–Cambodian border to visit the leaders of the two non-communist factions who were based in northwestern Cambodia's so-called "liberated zone." We used an aged Pilatus Porter aircraft to get closer to the fighting. Later, we had a Huey that could take us to our safe house, known as Eagle House right, on the border.

I was appalled to learn that Americans on the Working Group did not go into Cambodia because the ambassador deemed it unsafe. I felt this was completely inappropriate. How can you fight a war if you cannot see it? I took my concerns to my boss. He supported me, and the ambassador relented. We could go in but we could not spend the night. Although it was not what I wanted, it was better than nothing. Now we could visit the KPNLF headquarters at Boeung Trakun near the Thai border town of Aranyaprathet. We would fly further north up to Surin province to visit the Royalist forces of ANKI. A rough road cut through the Dangrek escarpment led into the plains of Cambodia. It was good to be back in camouflage utilities again and meeting with our brigade commanders in the field.

In addition to supporting the effort to force the Vietnamese to withdraw from Cambodia and set the scene for free elections, my team also reported on developments in Cambodia. We focused on the activities of the PRK puppet government and Chinese support of the Khmer Rouge. We gathered intelligence through liaison activities in the Working Group and from the NCR factions we supported. We also had unilateral agents who had been recruited to report secretly to CIA. As a result, the bulk of reporting came from the American team on the Working Group.

We were especially fortunate to have a handpicked team of senior Royal Thai Army (RTA) officers on the Working Group, along with excellent officers from the Malaysian intelligence service and Singapore intelligence and army. After years of growing pains, especially with the disparate and often ineffective Cambodian resistance groups, things seemed to be coming together and we began to see results. Conboy wrote:

> The RTA assigned to the Working Group were some of it best and brightest. Named chairman was Major General Surayud (Chulanond) … Special Colonel Ayupoon (Karnasuta) … now had oversight for all logistics and funding for the noncommunists. Special Colonel Teerawat Putamononda, a graduate of Virginia Military Institute (VMI) … was named politico-military liaison with the Ministry of Foreign Affairs. Finally, Special Colonel Naruenart Kampanatsanyakorn, a Sandhurst graduate, was named advisor for public relations.

Each of these officers retired from the army with the rank of four-star general. They were indeed the best and brightest. Surayut later served as commander-in-chief of the RTA before being named supreme commander. Later, he served as prime minister, before becoming a member of the King's Privy Council. Surayud's rise to high office was all the more incredible due to the fact that his father was a senior official of the Thai Communist Party, a fact that adversely affected his junior years in the army. He rose through sheer competence, honesty, and devotion to his king and country.

In contrast, Ayupoon was cut from a wealthy family and was politically well connected. Educated in the United States with a degree in finance, Ayupoon could be unusually abrasive and brutally frank, for a Thai. His directness, along with his competence and honesty, made him a favorite of Americans who worked with him. We played tennis, my favorite sport, at the Royal Bangkok Sports Club, and golf, his favorite sport, at the Royal Thai Army Golf Club.

Ayupoon was also a favorite of Prime Minister Suchinda Kraprayoon, which also helped the Working Group who received memberships in the army golf course which was also run by General Ayupoon. We conducted a lot of work on Sundays on the golf course. I don't care much for golf but I always enjoyed playing with senior Thai officers, who tend to have one caddy carrying the clubs and another carrying an umbrella for the sun and a folding stool. The club had seven hundred lady caddies. Numerous kiosks, set up around the course, sold snacks and drinks, making golf a leisurely pastime. A round of golf could take five hours. Things speeded up on the par five 12th hole, which abutted an army pistol range; sometimes ricochets bounced overhead. The caddies usually worked the 12th hole at the double time. A lot of good-humored banter accompanied the golf matches, along with numerous small bets to make the game more interesting. The round of golf always ended with a sumptuous Thai lunch at the clubhouse.

On one of our visits inside northwestern Cambodia, we traveled over a new 10-mile road funded by the United States Agency for International Aid (USAID) and built by Thai civilian contractors to the town of Thma Pouk, which was under KPNLF control. We named this rustic road after the very capable USAID officer, Bill Erdahl, who was in charge of the project. Enemy land mines constituted his biggest challenge to building the road lay in enemy land mines. The large bulldozer working on the road exploded seven hundred anti-personnel mines. The bulldozer met its match the day it drove over an anti-tank mine, which flipped the big machine over on its back. The driver survived but was deaf for two days.

After observing KPNLF civic action projects in and around Thma Pouk, we drove north to the ancient Khmer ruins at Banteay Chhmar. This 12th-century temple built by the great Jayavarman VII was never fully excavated or restored, unlike most the sites around Angkor Wat. We lunched near the ruins with senior KPNLF officers. The World Monument Fund lists Banteay Chhmar, heavily looted during the war, as one of the top one hundred most endangered sites in the world. Although they were active in the area, the Khmer Rouge kept their distance from the non-communist resistance. The main danger was land mines, many of them planted by the Khmer Rouge. Cambodia still has about five million unexploded mines and every year they kill innocent civilians.

On our visit to the royalist forces of ANKI, we travelled to Surin and usually stayed at the Tharin Hotel. We would breakfast with Thai officers from Task Force 838, which was responsible for supporting the Khmer resistance and senior ANKI officers. My favorite ANKI general was Chief of Staff, General Toan Chay, a quiet native of Siem Reap who began his military career as a fighter pilot in the Khmer Air Force (KAF). An early resistance leader on the border, he rose in rank by dint of his brains and bravery. He once suffered a heart attack during an offensive against PRK positions. He was evacuated to a Thai hospital, from which he quickly discharged himself to return to the battlefield.

Toan Chay so impressed an American civilian friend of mine, Warren Hoffecker, that Warren would take annual leave from his job in Saudi Arabia and fly to Thailand to support Toan Chay in the field. I first met Warren, a Princeton graduate and a US Army Special Forces officer in Vietnam, in Phnom Penh in 1973, when he was

In the ruins of the ancient Cambodian temple of Banteay Chhmar of northwestern Cambodia with two bodyguards from the Khmer People's National Liberation Front (KPNLF) during the war against the Vietnamese-installed puppet government of Heng Samrin, 1991.

working for Catholic Relief Services. Without official status or any remuneration, Warren worked diligently to help Toan Chay and ANKI in the malarial jungle of northwestern Cambodia while on vacation.

On one memorable visit to Cambodia with Billy Huff and other senior members of the Working Group, we witnessed a live-fire exercise of captured PRK artillery by KPNLF gunners. Arriving at Eagle House on the border, we changed into camouflage uniforms, left all pocket litter behind, and picked up M-16 rifles. We met with senior KPNLF officers including my old friend General Dien Del at Boeung Trakoun, inside Cambodia, where we participated in a ceremony to lay wreaths on an impressive memorial to the KPNLF war dead. Later, we inspected captured PRK T-54 tanks and other vehicles being put back into service against their previous owners.

We then walked single file through a minefield until we came to a clearing where captured PRK artillery pieces were lined up, and after a briefing for the VIPs we saw some high-quality shooting by KPNLF artillery and their ASEAN instructors. In the final demonstration of the day, the KPNLF demonstrated using a West German mine-breaching Komet MRL-80 to destroy mines. The weapon, powered by a small rocket, fires a line of explosive det-cord across a minefield. The det-cord explodes, destroying any mines nearby and allowing troops to assault through the breach. After this impressive demonstration we discovered that the Komet had actually blown up a landmine that was planted in the field. There were no casualties but everyone walked a little more carefully until we returned to the base.

On my last trip inside Cambodia together with many senior Thai officers from the Working Group, I attended a promotion ceremony for KPNLF officers. Generals Sak Satsukan, Dien Del, and Pann Thai presided over the event. Young ladies from a large refugee camp nearby performed classical Khmer dances before hundreds of troops on the parade field. I took the opportunity to say goodbye to several old friends including Dien Del, who became Inspector General of the Royal Cambodian Armed Forces in 1994 and was elected to the Cambodian National Assembly in 1998. A Cognac-loving, heavily decorated, hard-fighting soldier, whom I was happy to call my friend, Dien Del died in 2013.

While the Working Group was making solid progress with their Cambodian allies, the Soviet Union was falling apart. The two events were related. For years the United States supported anti-communist groups around the world at considerable cost to the Soviet Union in treasure and lives. The Russians supported the Vietnamese, now enemies of China. Conboy reported that the Vietnamese admitted losing 10,000 troops in fighting Cambodia between 1982 and 1988 at least 10,000 killed in action. During the same time frame, the Soviets lost 15,000 of their own killed in Afghanistan. The Working Group and their Khmer allies were winning.

Singapore and Malaysia had supported the Khmer resistance for years, and they sent top-quality officers from both intelligence and military branches as their representatives on the working group. Singapore primarily provided lethal aid to the NCR, while Malaysia focused on training Cambodians at a secret jungle training facility.

After the last Working Group meeting in Singapore, Billy and I were invited to attend the graduation of Cambodian resistance officer class training in Malaysia. Singapore and Malaysia cooperated congenially on the Cambodia project but had bilateral problems at the time. No Singaporeans were invited to the jungle visit in Malaysia. So when Billy and I were driven to the jungle warfare school in Malaysia in the early hours of the morning, our car stopped midway across the causeway separating Singapore from Malaysia. We got out of the Singaporean car and got into a Malaysian car to continue our journey. It reminded me of spies being swapped at Check Point Charlie in Berlin.

By the end of 1990, things were going well for the Cambodian resistance, and Washington began scaling back support. After lengthy and complicated negotiations, a set of agreements were signed in Paris in October 1991. Peace was finally restored

Cambodian girls perform a classical dance in the "liberated zone" of Cambodia in 1991 at a memorial service of the Khmer People's National Liberation Front, for men killed in action.

to Cambodia. This led to the arrival of United Nations Transitional Authority (UNTAC) in Cambodia. Free and fair elections were held, and the largest winners of the vote were the royalist faction led by Prince Norodom Ranariddh, Sihanouk's son.

Ken Conboy ended his book:

> Stephen Solarz, who had been the strongest congressional supporter for the KPNLF and Funcinpec (ANS), felt more than vindicated. "The peace process worked out better than anybody could have expected," he would later assess. And the noncommunists got the most votes. Barry Broman, the senior CIA representative on the Working Group, agreed, "The US could declare its policy objectives were met," adding, "In Cambodia we could finally declare victory."

With peace restored to Cambodia, my team disbanded and I needed to find something else to do. Billy Huff put me in charge of counter-narcotics, a hardy perennial mission. At the time most of the world's heroin, an opium derivative, came from poppies grown in Southeast Asia. Opium poppies thrive in mountainous altitudes above 3,000 feet. They don't require good soil or much labor. When the poppies mature, the round bulbs are "scored" with small blades, usually by women, in the morning. The sap oozes out during the day and in the afternoon the sap is collected. This is raw opium. This can be smoked in a pipe and is addictive. In the 19th century a British chemist created a new drug derived from opium, 10 times more addictive. In the 20th century the German company Bayer trademarked the drug and named it heroin. During my years in Asia, rebel groups in Burma at war with the junta in Rangoon produced much of the world's heroin.

The Golden Triangle is the name given to the confluence of the borders of Burma, Thailand, and Laos, where much of the world's opium originates. Under colonial British regimes in Burma, French in Laos, and independent Siam, opium was a state monopoly and a lucrative one. Much of Southeast Asian heroin passed from Burma through Thailand en route to drug users around the world. The two main trafficking groups were the United Wa State Army of the tribal Wa on the China border and the Mong Thai Army of Khun Sa on the Thai border.

There has been much written accusing the CIA of being involved in the drug trade in Southeast Asia. None of it true. The false charges fall into two categories: misinformation and disinformation. The latter describes efforts of state organizations such as the Soviet KGB to plant false stories in the news media and books as part of their worldwide Active Measures program designed to attack the United States, and especially the CIA. The Russian government continues these activities today.

For decades we worked closely with the Royal Thai government, to contain opium production and the flow of drugs into and out of the kingdom. The US State Department provided assistance to Thailand to encourage crop substitution to replace opium-producing poppies. The Thai government, with support from the United States, built roads in the remote tribal hills of northern Thailand to enable farmers to transport more perishable agricultural products.

We also worked with the American Drug Enforcement Administration (DEA), a law enforcement organization. Billy particularly wanted me to improve relations with the DEA. Like the FBI, there was a "culture" problem with DEA. Trained as cops, DEA agents viewed their primary job as putting bad guys in jail. In contrast, the CIA preferred to recruit bad guys and provide intelligence on more important bad guys.

As a first step, I was asked to make friends with the DEA chief, a tough former police officer. I approached him at a cocktail party to break the ice. He was polite but reserved. I named some of my old DEA buddies, including two, Pete Tomaino and Dick Kempshall, who I trekked with in Nepal. He knew them all and began to shed his reserve. Then I mentioned a DEA secretary I remembered. Tall, blonde, and attractive, she held the record for drinking Brandy Alexander cocktails at a well-known watering hole. "I wonder what happened to her?" I mused. "I married her," he replied.

My main mission, however, was going after one of the world's leading heroin traffickers, Chang Chi-fu, a Sino-Shan from the Shan state of Burma better known as Khun Sa. He portrayed himself as a freedom fighter seeking independence for the Shan people from the oppressive Burmese. In reality, he was a drug warlord, the head of a force of more than 10,000 men in what he called the Mong Tai Army (MTA). With these men, he dominated much of the region. With the proceeds from heroin trafficking he operated some legitimate business, including jade and timber enterprises in Thailand. He also had a payroll of bribed Thai and Burmese officials who facilitated his nefarious activities.

In my new role, I contacted an old friend in the police. Now a senior officer with a reputation for bravery and honesty, I had known him in the 1970s when he was a colonel. He had worked in liaison with the Agency for years. I told him I wanted to mount operations against Khun Sa, and asked for his assistance. He readily agreed and put together a trusted team. A few weeks later he informed me Khun Sa would be moving a very large heroin shipment through Thailand. Khun Sa planned to put his 999-brand heroin on a Thai fishing trawler and then transfer to a ship at sea. We had to move fast.

The general told me he had to find money to pay his source, a man who would need a new identity as well as funds to start a new life after the drug bust. I suggested we bring the DEA into the operation. The DEA had a budget to pay sources based on the amount of drugs seized; we would ask them to fund the agent's new life. The general said he didn't trust the DEA. He suspected Khun Sa had penetrated

A young "Long Neck" lady of the Padaung hill tribe in Burma bathes in a pond on the Thai–Burma border not far from the headquarters of Khun Sa, a leading opium warlord in 1991. There are very few Padaung women wearing distinctive brass coils these days although some make good money having their photo taken with tourists.

the DEA network. I said we could just bring the DEA in at the last minute, and let them ride along on the bust. Reluctantly, he agreed. I set it up with DEA.

The general led the raid personally. His team intercepted the heroin as it was being loaded onto the boat. The Thai arrested a number of Khun Sa's men and seized more than 1,100 pounds of heroin. The front page of the *Bangkok Post* the next morning featured a photo of the successful Thai police raiders and a smiling DEA officer. This bust yielded more heroin than the total amount DEA had intercepted cumulatively in all their years operating in Thailand. They shared credit for the bust with the Royal Thai Police. Another person smiling, but not on camera, was the general's source. He walked away with more than $100,000 of DEA money to start a new life. From this operation I enjoyed two successes: the largest drug bust of my career and a much more congenial working relationship with the DEA.

It was my great pleasure and privilege to work with the general and forge a friendship that has now spanned four decades. We worked on other successful drug busts, all to the detriment of Khun Sa. The general once offered to have Khun Sa lured into Thailand from his headquarters at Ho Mong, just inside Burma, not far from Mae Hong Son, Thailand. For a modest sum paid to his asset, the general would then arrest Khun Sa who was wanted not only in the United States, but also in Thailand. The general told me that we would only have a day or two at most to keep the drug lord in custody. After that Khun Sa's "friends" would get him released. We needed to have an aircraft to take Khun Sa away quickly, as we had done earlier with one of Khun Sa's senior aides. The operation never got off the ground. For reasons I still don't understand, Langley was not interested in paying to have Khun San lured into Thailand. We would have to come up with a better plan.

***

Prime Minister General Suchinda Kraprayoon supported American action against the Vietnamese in Cambodia and drug lord Khun Sa in Burma but he was mainly focused on holding power. His February 1991 coup d'état against the elected government of Chatichai Choonhavan, under the auspices of a group that called itself the National Peace Keeping Council (NPKC) was a setback for democracy in Thailand. It also put Suchinda at odds with the United States government, which frowned on the removal of elected governments.

Following a general election in March 1992, a five-party coalition named Suchinda the new prime minister in April. This immediately led to large-scale demonstrations by pro-democracy protectors opposed to a power grab of yet another military government. As the protests grew the situation worsened. The Thai government brought army units into Bangkok and established a curfew. Matters came to a head in May when mass rallies took place in Bangkok near the Grand Palace.

On May 17, more than 200,000 protesters gathered at the Sanam Luang grounds near the Grand Palace in Bangkok. In the crowd I bumped into my friend Nate Thayer from the Associated Press. I knew Nate well from our days working in Cambodia. He knew exactly what I was doing in Thailand with the Cambodia Working Group and publishing the story would have given Nate a scoop, something that few journalists could pass up. But Nate, the son of an American ambassador, kept the secret, and I appreciated that. A smart fellow and a risk taker, Nate was also first and foremost a newsman and he had my respect. I considered him a lineal descendent of Matt Franjola, the AP chief in Cambodia I had known during the war. We decided to stick together at the Sanam Luang protest.

The crowd was in a rather festive mood as their numbers grew. Finally, protest leaders set off on the short walk to Government House to demand Suchinda's resignation. I had friends among the army leaders on the scene and wanted to know what they would do. One army general assured me he would not order his men to fire under any circumstances. But, he cautioned, other officers closer to Suchinda might. Another general whom I respected told me before the protest that he would take annual leave and not be in Thailand during the protests lest he be ordered to fire on the protesters. He missed the fighting and preserved his career.

Nate and I moved with the crowd down Rajdamnoen Avenue, past the Democracy Monument, to find that police behind barbed wire blocked the Phan Fa Bridge. This prevented the crowd from reaching the parliament building, and this is when the confrontation began. The happy mood at Sanam Luang earlier evaporated. Demonstrators began throwing rocks at the police, who responded with water cannons. Some in the crowd tossed Molotov cocktails at the police, who responded by charging into the crowd with batons. Protestors set fire trucks alight and casualties mounted. About midnight, Nate asked if I could hear rifle fire. I heard M-16 single shots. I had heard a lot of M-16 fire in Vietnam but, for the first time, they were aimed at me. The situation turned ugly. Only Thai army troops had M-16s. It was time to report to Washington. I left the scene while Nate was on the phone filing his report to the AP. As I walked away looking for a taxi, I saw army troops standing by, ready to confront the protesters.

I sent a FLASH precedence situation report to Headquarters. Things were getting out of hand. Later that night, I received a phone call. The caller said in perfect English "We know who you are. We are watching you," and then hung up. There was no direct threat and I took the call as a warning from the right wing of the military not to interfere with the crackdown that was coming. I did not report the call. It might have been taken as a threat against me and I did not want to be pulled out of Thailand. I was not bothered again.

The next day events escalated. The Thai government brought the army and scores of people—perhaps hundreds—were killed. Thousands were arrested. Many others just disappeared. Thailand was in full crisis. We called on our contacts, many of whom risked their careers and lives to keep us informed. One sensitive asset sought refuge at an embassy residence and, fearing for his life, asked to be evacuated from Thailand. I met with him, calmed him down, and promised to keep him safe. I asked him to wait out the storm. He agreed, and two days later returned home.

The situation also revealed how our agents would react in a full-blown crisis. In Vietnam I had seen how people behave under stress on the battlefield. Some men who perform well on the parade deck can't handle combat. On the other hand, some men who are constantly in trouble in the rear show their true colors when it counts most. The situation was similar here. Some, notably the female officer in charge of reports, performed admirably, staying at her post throughout the crisis. Some assets and developmental contacts risked their lives to report what was happening during a watershed moment in modern Thai history.

On May 20, King Bhumihhol intervened, a rare instance of royal public involvement in politics and one of His Majesty's finest hours. The king went on television

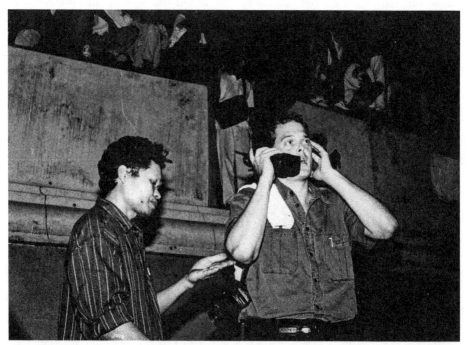

Associated Press correspondent Nate Thayer calls in a report to his office in Bangkok on May 17, 1992 when Thai army troops opened fire on pro-democracy demonstrators on Rajdamnoen Avenue. Hundreds were killed in the brutal one-sided fight. King Bumiphol intervened, brought an end to the bloodshed, and accepted the resignation of Prime Minister General Suchinda Kraprayoon.

in the evening with General Suchinda kneeling in front of him along with a leader of the protesters. The king quietly scolded them both and told them to think of the people and the country. The crisis was over. Four days later Suchinda resigned as prime minister and I went back to chasing drug lords.

***

After a year of war in Cambodia, and running operations against Burmese narcotics traffickers, I was ready for a break. It came thanks to Thai businessman, Krisada "Nit" Kampanatsanyakorn, an old friend. He invited me to accompany him on a three-day trek in the hills of northern Thailand. Intrigued I asked where we would be going and why. "To the remote mountains of Chiang Mai province near the Burma border into Karen hill tribe country," said Nit. He explained that a good friend of his was a district chief in Chiang Mai province where some hill tribe villages had no roads or electricity. Nit had donated five solar-powered television sets to five Karen villages in an effort to help bring them into the 20th century. In appreciation, the district chief invited Nit to be on hand when he turned the power on for each of the television sets. I asked how we were going to get to the villages. "That's the good part," said Nit. "On elephants."

He made it sound like an everyday experience. Maybe a hundred years ago it was. But without roads, parts of northern Thailand were only accessible on foot or by elephant. I signed on. It turned out that this trip was going to be a gala event. Nit invited along his wife and three small children, plus a few of his close friends to join in the expedition. The Thai always know how to have a good time and this would be no exception. We took the night train to Chiang Mai, first class, of course. Nit had cars waiting at the railway station to take us into the mountains. He brought his guitar along for entertainment at night.

The district chief had planned the expedition well. He assigned each adult to an elephant with a Karen mahout. Advance teams set up tents and dining tables at each nightly stop of our elephant safari. In good weather we headed into the mountains not far from the Burma border. The forest was not dense, mostly second or third growth timber. The area had no roads and few trails but it did have plenty of streams that we forded. Elephants like to take a quick shower when crossing a stream. They suck water into their trunk and then spray it over their backs. Riders get to share in the shower so an umbrella would have been useful. Elephants also like to descend hills on their rumps and no seatbelts are provided, so be warned.

My small elephant had been trained to haul teak logs to rivers, not to carry passengers. Teak, however, was scarce and a job was a job. My young Karen mahout spoke little Thai but was enthusiastic about the adventure. He warned me that his elephant liked to scrape passengers off its back by passing trees closely.

He vigorously kept us away from big trees but let his beast of burden do what it wanted when it came to crossing water. In time, I came to enjoy the refreshing showers.

At the end of each day we camped near water so the elephants could bathe, the high point of the day for an elephant. Nit and his family donned their swimsuits and also jumped into the water, always upstream of the elephants. One of my favorite photos from the trip shows Nit, a captain of industry in Thailand, lounging in a shallow steam surrounded by his children splashing in the water while his wife washed his hair.

The most memorable part of the trip was visiting the Karen villages where the TV sets had been set up, solar batteries working, waiting for the day when they could be turned on. That day came when we arrived. The reactions on the faces of young Karen children watching television images for the first time were priceless. The look of awe, joy, and amazement on the faces not only of the kids but also the adult Karen was well worth all the rough, cross-country travel.

***

After 11 years in the field, it was time to return to Langley. Some officers sought assignments in Langley, where the work load was less onerous than in the field and a workday lasted only eight hours compared to 10 or often more overseas. Officers experienced far less stress at Headquarters and could appreciate all the amenities of being home. It is easier and safer to live in the Washington DC area than in hardship posts, where you can't drink water from the tap, and do not have to deal with a hostile government, and face terrorist threats.

To my delight the Agency made me chief of the Thai-Burma branch in the East Asia division. I was going to a job I was qualified for and happy to have. The area division took care of its own. Throughout my career I was fortunate to have "rabbis," senior officer mentors, who looked after my career advancement. This became easier as my reputation as a recruiter or "headhunter" grew, making me attractive to chiefs of station in the field. In this case I aimed at getting in line for a final Asia posting to the last of the countries I had on my operational "bucket list."

We bought a house in suburban Reston, Virginia, and BJ returned to her career as a teacher. Instead of giving weekly dinner parties, she happily embraced a more normal social life. The boys, both born abroad, were delighted to finally be "home" where they could drink water from the faucet.

President Bill Clinton, like Jimmy Carter, was no friend of the CIA. Carter had done real harm to the Agency through his Annapolis crony Stansfield Turner, who in a major disservice to the country, had fired hundreds of seasoned and experienced case officers. When Clinton belatedly deigned to visit CIA headquarters in Langley, a message circulated throughout the Clandestine Service

Standing next to my elephant during a three-day excursion in the hills of Chiang Mai province near the Burma border. The trip was made to inaugurate solar-powered television sets in three remote Karen villages. Across the Salween River to the west, Burmese Karen were fighting for independence.

informing us that the president was paying a visit and that each branch of every area division should submit short blurbs on top cases being run in the field by our stations. I recall that the Agency would select a total of six cases worldwide for the briefing to President Clinton. At the Thai-Burma branch we submitted two cases for consideration. I cannot say more about the operations except to say they were world-class. Of the six cases briefed to the president, two belonged to the Thai-Burma branch.

Out of the blue, as I was getting settled in, I received a phone call from a CIA legend, Anthony "Tony Poe" Poshepny, retired in California, asking for a favor. My only meeting with Tony was in Udorn, Thailand, many years before. He achieved fame for taking part in several of the CIA's little wars, including support for the Khamba tribesmen in Tibet that resulted in the rescue of the Dalai Lama. He also supported the PRRI, a rebel group on Sumatra. Most importantly, however, he had earned his fame as a jungle fighter in northern Laos leading Hmong and other tribal groups against North Vietnamese invaders and their Lao communist allies. Tony, a Marine who saw action on Iwo Jima during World War II, married a Hmong princess and lived on his tapioca farm in northeastern Thailand before retiring from the CIA and moving to California.

Tony had a simple, and reasonable, request, I thought. He wanted the decorations he had earned while serving in the CIA to be released. He explained that the Central Cover staff at CIA had ruled that since he had been under non-official cover (NOC) while in Laos he could not receive or display his awards for heroism. This was nonsense. Tony was one of the most famous, some would say infamous, of the CIA's paramilitary officers. I told Tony I agreed with him and promised to see if I could get the medals released. He thanked me, and said his elderly mother wanted them mounted next to his late father's decorations in California.

I wrote a memo requesting the release of Tony's medals and sent it up the chain of command. Weeks went by. One day I received a call. The man identified himself as the DDA, the Deputy Director for Administration of CIA. "Barry," he said, "I have your memo in front of me. It has been read by a number of senior Agency officers and each of them has recommended that Tony not receive his medals. I was once a case officer. I know who Tony is and what he has done. I agree with you and want you to know that I will be getting Tony's medals released." Tony's medals made it to the wall of his mother's house next to those of his father.

***

The Clinton years were a time of upheaval in the Agency. It quickly became apparent that he was not a fan of human intelligence, HUMINT in our jargon. He was persuaded that the United States should place more emphasis on technology collecting intelligence from sources such as satellites and signals collection or SIGINT from our Cold War enemies. The years of taking the fight to the Soviets ended. The aggressive paramilitary operations that characterized the Reagan years and the term of President George H. W. Bush, a savvy Washington insider and a former Director of CIA, were over. The years of taking the fight to the Soviets ended.

The Clinton administration put emphasis on diversity and gender equality. The Congress passed the Civil Rights Act in 1964 and President Johnson signed an executive order on equal employment opportunity in 1965. Clinton now mandated that officers undergo special Equal Employment Opportunity (EEO) training. I thought this a little strange given the numerous highly qualified female and minority officers I served with over the years. Nonetheless, I was one of a selected number of middle-to-senior officers assigned for EEO training. I knew we were in for a long week when the woman-of-color in charge of the course opened with an attack on the CIA, which she called a "racist and sexist organization." A political appointee, she obviously had not been with the Agency long. She was short on knowledge and long on attitude.

We endured a litany of accusations from our keynote speaker until a woman taking the course interrupted her. A case officer from Africa division, she wasn't afraid to speak her mind. "Don't call them racists," she said. "Some of these men serve in countries and speak languages you never heard of. We in the DO work overseas and respect the cultures and customs of the people we work with. They might be Asian or African, Moslems or Hindu. Some of our best officers are minorities or women. Don't lecture us on something you do not understand."

She sat down. We could have kissed her. But that would be called sexist.

On a brighter note, the Clinton administration threw a lot of money at the Agency for training, and East Asia Division spent a pile of it for off-site training on the Pecos River in New Mexico. The Division used the weeklong course for "team building." Having spent much of my career in the field, I found that I didn't know many of the people in my group. The exercise gave me the opportunity to meet a lot of people fast. The course, run by civilians whose normal clients were senior corporate officials, was divided into classroom sessions best described by an officer I had served with on the Cambodian border as "psycho babble."

The outdoor portion, which resembled a Marine Corps obstacle course without the possibility of getting hurt, was the most fun. The exercises, cleverly designed to force people to work as teams, featured such challenges as climbing a wall using handholds. The organizers roped together teams of three people making it impossible to climb to the top without teamwork. The physical training did bring us together. Fortunately, we had safety ropes in case of falls. Another exercise had us roped together in threes, walking on narrow wooden beams 20 feet in the air. When my friend from the Cambodian border, an army Vietnam combat veteran, lost his balance on a high beam, a frail-looking woman who appeared more at home running a library than defying gravity walked out on the beam, leaned over and pulled my buddy back to safety. We all applauded her pluck. Team building was working. The final outdoor test required jumping off a cliff and zip lining across the Pecos River. People pay big money for fun like this, and I thank the Agency for the training. The desert facility, not far from Santa Fe, provided high-end Southwest cuisine. We paid for any alcohol consumed, and after dinner broke into groups around hot tubs in the Spanish-style houses nestled into the hillside for more tequila-fired team building.

***

After two years it was time to return to the field. The posting I sought came through. We would be going back to Southeast Asia and back to chasing drug traffickers.

At the time, 90 percent of the world's illicit opium and more importantly, heroin, came of the hills of northern Burma. Operating unilaterally or in cooperation with the DEA and Burmese government, progress was being made.

Various ethnic groups have grown opium in the hills of northern Burma for centuries. During much of that time, the colonial British Indian empire controlled the opium trade as a state monopoly. The father of writer George Orwell, once a police officer in Burma, was an opium revenue officer. The British did not restrict opium poppy cultivation in Burma until 1912. Under British rule, parts of the country were administered directly by the Brits. These were the "Divisions" where the majority of the population were Burmans, the ethnic Burmese. Highland areas where more than one hundred minority groups lived, were designated "States," which were administered indirectly by the British. A good example was the Shan State where feudal Shan princes ruled the Tai-speaking minority with British advisors. After Burma achieved independence from Britain in 1948 it was immediately wracked by insurgencies, some communist-inspired, others by ethnic groups such as the Shan, Karen, and Kachin seeking independence. These struggles continue.

Drug trafficking organizations emerged in the chaos of fighting, most of them led by ethnic Chinese or tribal groups connected to Chinese criminal enterprises. Three main groups, each with their own army, dominated the opium and heroin trade. They included the Mong Tai Army led by my old nemesis Chang Chi-fu, who called himself Khun Sa; the United Wa State Army operating in the Wa Hills of the northern Shan state; and the Kokang, another Chinese tribal group operating on the Burma–China border.

Due to poor relations between Burma and the United States in the mid-1990s over human rights and democracy issues, there were only two issues: narcotics trafficking and international terrorism. The State Department considered Burma to be a pariah state after the regime put down pro-democracy protests in 1988 in a bloody wave of repression that ended US aid to Burma. US politicians praised Nobel peace laureate and Burmese opposition leader, Aung San Suu Kyi, the symbol of hope for democracy in the troubled nation. The embassy openly supported "The Lady," as Suu Kyi was known. Numerous congressmen visited Burma in hopes of getting a photo op with her.

In the 1980s the State Department ran a very successful counter-narcotics program in Burma, considered by many to be the best of its type in the world. In addition to training in the US and assistance on the ground sharing intelligence, the United States provided helicopters to assist operations against the drug lords in the north. After US assistance ended in 1988, drug production rose tenfold. Despite the loss of assistance, the Burmese continued to cooperate with the DEA and CIA. The most visible proof of this cooperation was a series of opium yield surveys conducted in Burma. I directed the American team on one of these operations in 1995. The idea was to scientifically sample opium poppy fields to estimate the size of the crop. I ran a similar operation in Thailand in 1991, and found dealing with the Burmese to be easier and considerably less expensive than the Thai.

The Burmese provided an infantry battalion to give security to the teams as they sampled more than one hundred opium fields in the northern Shan state, part of the region known as The Golden Triangle. None of the selected fields were under the control of the Burmese government, who informed the trafficking organizations that they were coming in to sample opium and warned against any opposition. There was none. Funding for the project came from the Counternarcotic Center at CIA

headquarters in Langley, Virginia. The United States Department of Agriculture supervised the science and sampling.

It has been widely but erroneously reported that Burma's military regime controlled the drug trade. While there were corrupt individuals in the government who profited from the trade, narcotics trafficking was not a state enterprise, as it was elsewhere in Southeast Asia. The drug warlords, some of them former members of the Burma Communist Party (BCP), which had self-destructed in 1988, commanded thousands of tough, tribal fighters who controlled the rugged and inaccessible hills that straddled the Burma–China border. The Wa, known to the British as the Wild Wa, had been headhunters in colonial days and were never brought under British rule. In the mid-1990s the Wa had at least 20,000 men under arms, most of whom came from the Chinese government, which had previously funded and armed the BCP for decades.

Our team for the survey was composed of American officers from State, DEA, US Department of Agriculture and the CIA. Military Intelligence (MI), directed the Burmese side. The Myanmar Agriculture Service did the scientific and lab work. The Burma Army provided an infantry battalion for security during visits to the poppy fields under the control of the Wa or Khun Sa. The Burma Air Force provided American-built Huey helicopters to transport the teams more cheaply than the Thai had charged earlier.

The incursion into forbidden parts of the northern Shan state gave me a rare opportunity to see opium fields in production. We encountered armed United Wa Army and Khun Sa's Mong Tai soldiers watching us as we cut plants from their fields. We appreciated the presence of young but tough Burma Army soldiers armed with Heckler & Koch rifles, who provided our security. Liaison even arranged a lunch with Wa leaders. It was a tense and unhappy bunch sitting across from us. The DEA Burma chief, sitting next to me, identified some of the Wa leaders to me from their WANTED posters. The US government had a one-million-dollar reward for the capture of the Wa leader. He was a no-show at our meeting.

For a few days, we operated out of Keng Tung, an ancient town and the largest of the old Shan state. It was founded by Mengrai, who also founded Chiang Mai, Thailand, in 1296. The last feudal lord of Keng Tung, Sai Sao Long Mengrai, was a friend of mine. He lost his power in the 1962 military coup. A charming, English-educated fellow, when I first met him, he said "Call me Shorty." The ruler of the region was an English-speaking Burma Army general who had received infantry training in Fort Benning, Georgia. He was our host.

One afternoon, the general was waiting at Keng Tung's airfield as we returned in our rented choppers from a day of opium sampling in the hills. I asked him how long it would take to reach Loi Mwe, a hill town on the road to Thailand. It had been a hill station under the British and boasted several interesting colonial buildings and churches. The general pointed to a far-off mountaintop and said that was Loi Mwe.

He estimated it would take five or six hours by car on a good day. "Or," he added with a smile, "ten minutes in that helicopter," pointing to one of our Hueys. Minutes later the chopper set us down on a pad at Loi Mwe, which was the base of a battalion of Burma Army infantry. A car was waiting for us and the general gave me a quick tour of the old British district chief's home and two Christian churches that still had flocks of adherents. He treated me to a quick Scotch and soda in lawn chairs under pine trees in the cool mountain air at the officers' club. With daylight fading, we hurried back to the waiting helicopter and had a safe trip down into the valley and dinner.

A few days later, we headed to the remote hills of Wa country. The Burmese troops cut a clearing in the middle of a poppy field, not far from our helicopter landing pads. They constructed a makeshift picnic ground where we ate spicy

With Nobel Peace-Prize laureate Aung San Suu Kyi in 1995 after she attended a tea in her honor at an American embassy residence in Rangoon. The daughter of General Aung San who guided Burma's independence from Great Britain after World War II, Suu Kyi led the democratic movement against Burma's military government and eventually led her party to victory after years of house arrest.

curry washed down with Johnny Walker scotch whiskey or local beer, surrounded by acres of blossoming opium poppies. Curious Wa tribeswomen watched us eat, fretting over their trampled opium field and wondering when they could get back to the harvest.

Back in Rangoon, with samples from more than one hundred opium fields, we turned our attention to drying the poppy bulbs. Several bags of poppies were given to me with instructions from the Myanmar Agriculture Service how to dry them carefully in the sun. I delegated this smelly chore to a junior officer, who clearly thought this was below her status. I suspect she didn't add opium drying to her list of skills on her curriculum vitae. I am thankful that no one, especially a foreign journalist, knew that my driveway and parking area was used to dry recently harvested opium poppies.

***

My best Burmese friend, U Ye Htoon, was known to his friends as Roland. I met him through his sister Sunda Khin who lives in northern Virginia. Roland graduated from Bucknell University in the US and took his law degree in England, following the footsteps of his late father who had been Minister of Justice of Burma. Roland owned a law firm in Rangoon, among other things, and was smart, witty, and articulate. I learned a lot from him about Buddhism and the ways of the Burman.

Roland's career in law and politics was dashed by Burma's military dictatorship. His student activism and pro-democracy sentiments resulted in numerous prison sentences over the decades. When I met him in 1994 he was free, after agreeing not to engage in politics. One of his clients was the American embassy. Roland's wife, Onma, a quiet, dignified lady, was the daughter of Dr. Ba Maw, Burma's first prime minister. She also prepared the best food I tasted in Rangoon and was Burma's only taxidermist, trained at the Smithsonian Institute in Washington DC.

One area where Roland was most articulate and informative was on Theravada Buddhism, the religion of most Burmese. His father had once been president of the World Fellowship of Buddhists. He told great stories, some sad, some funny, all interesting. During one of his incarcerations as a political prisoner in the notorious Insein Prison, he was housed in a small house inside the prison. It was one of four houses for important prisoners. A next-door neighbor was drug lord Lo Hsing Han, an ethnic Kokang-Chinese from the Shan state. One night Lo, who had his meals catered from outside, invited Roland for dinner. Roland could not pass up a good meal. After dark and against the strong urging of his fellow inmates not to go, Roland snuck out, evaded the guards and searchlights, and knocked on Lo's door. He enjoyed the food and successfully made it back to his house undetected. They remained friends after both were released.

Roland lived in a small bungalow on a waterfront property on Inya Lake in an inlet directly opposite former strongman General Ne Win's compound. Although Ne Win gave up power in 1988, he still enjoyed influence, as seen by the tight security surrounding his house. If a boat strayed too close, a few bullets across the bow could be expected. During the years Roland was in prison, his very competent and very attractive daughter, Yuza, ran the family's affairs. Roland's only son died of malaria when he fled Rangoon to join pro-democracy activists in the jungle. It was a loss Roland never got over.

***

Aung San Suu Kyi was the daughter of General Aung San, a founder of independent Burma who was assassinated in 1947 while serving as prime minister. She rose to prominence as leader of the National League for Democracy (NLD) which won 81 percent of votes cast in the 1990 elections. The military junta refused to accept the will of the people, and she spent more than 15 years in and out of house arrest. In 1991 she was awarded the Nobel Peace Prize.

Suu Kyi was an international symbol of the quest for democratic government for Burma. She spent much of her time under house arrest. Once a week she would speak to her followers at the gate of her house over the closed gate. She gave hundreds of interviews, when allowed to, and had a huge international following that included members of the American Congress. Numerous politicians traveled to meet with her and express support for her political agenda, while savoring the mandatory photo op with her.

One senior senator, Arlen Specter (R-Pa.) came to town and arranged to have breakfast with The Lady at the lakeside residence of the American chargé d'affaires (the US did not have an ambassador due to the strained relations with the military regime in Rangoon). The senator, who was also an avid antique collector, asked for a Burmese antique dealer to bring silver objects to the residence that morning for his inspection. Ernesto, an ethnic Kayah and a Christian, was widely known as an honest fellow with excellent pieces of old Burmese and Shan silver objects for sale. Ernesto arrived on time, giving the senator plenty of time to shop before the scheduled breakfast with The Lady. Senator Specter, however, was so taken with the items for sale that he blew off The Lady when she arrived and let a fellow senator meet with her. Business concluded, very successfully for Ernesto, and the senator managed to make it to the table in time for his photo op with Aung San Suu Kyi.

Another visitor from Washington, a congressional staff assistant, asked to see me privately for a briefing and I agreed. Before I was able to begin my situation report on what was happening in Burma, the young staffer jumped to the reason for the meeting.

"A few of us in Washington are worried about the safety of The Lady. She may be under house arrest now but could be thrown back into prison any time. We have a plan," he said.

"May I know the plan?" I asked.

"Of course. In fact, we will need your help." This did not sound good.

"We want to rescue The Lady," he announced. This did not sound good at all.

"We know she lives in a house on a lake. Right?" I nodded.

"We would send in a team by air to land on the lake. They would overcome the guards in her compound. And take her out by air from the lake." I told him there were a number of armed Burmese security personnel in the compound. They would put up a fight.

"But," I added, "there is only one person who you really have to worry about."

"Who," he asked?

"The Lady. The military have been trying for years to get her out of Burma. She won't go and has said so. The junta wants her to go back to her husband in England and help raise the kids, not bring down the military regime in Burma."

Taken aback, this is not what the staffer wanted to hear. He said he would report what I told him and be in touch. I never heard from him again.

Who is briefing these people in Washington, I asked myself? The incident reminded me of another senator who asked me "When are these people going to realize that socialism doesn't work?" As gently as I could, I told the senator, another with aspirations for the White House, "They learned that a long time ago. That's why they dropped their 'path to socialism' program in 1989. Now they are trying to rebuild their economy through capitalism." He changed the subject.

Fortunately, not all senators came so ill prepared. Senator John McCain (R-Ariz.), a man with a long and painful experience of Southeast Asia, particularly impressed me. When we met, he said the US needed to establish a "road map" of steps leading to improved relations. He had followed a similar and ultimately successful approach to repairing relations with Vietnam. Given his harsh treatment at the hands of the Vietnamese as a prisoner of war in the "Hanoi Hilton," his determination to rebuild the US relationship with Vietnam struck some as ironic, but it also showed his political acumen and human side. Senator McCain also impressed a Burmese who opened a fine Burmese restaurant in Rangoon, the Padonmar, and named one of the private upstairs rooms, the John McCain room.

In 2015 the NLD won a landslide electoral victory. Suu Kyi became Burma's first female Minister for Foreign Affairs and later de facto prime minister. But the army never gave the NLD full power to rule, further depriving Burma of a truly democratic government.

***

In June 1942 President Franklin Roosevelt established the Office of Strategic Services (OSS) and put New York lawyer, Colonel William J. "Wild Bill" Donovan, in command. Against the wishes of the military and the FBI, the OSS was to engage in special operations behind enemy lines. They were the forerunner of the CIA. With assistance from our British allies, the OSS organized resistance to the Nazi occupation of Europe. With notably less British assistance in Asia, the OSS was pretty much on its own against the Japanese.

The OSS conducted its first, longest, and many say best, operation in Burma. OSS Detachment 101 operated from 1942 until the end of the war in the mountains of the Kachin state of northern Burma. Although the unit never had more than eight hundred Americans assigned to it, they recruited, armed and trained more than ten thousand guerrilla "rangers" from the Kachin hill tribe who operated behind Japanese lines with great effect. The Kachin were natural fighters who had already proven their worth in the colonial British Army including service in Mesopotamia in World War I. Tough and resourceful, many Kachin were also Christian thanks to the work of American Baptist missionaries among the hill tribes dating to the 19th century. They detested the Japanese for the atrocities inflicted on the Kachin people after they conquered Burma in 1942.

In 1995, a group of Detachment 101 veterans visited Burma for the 50th anniversary of the end of World War II. Despite the strained US–Burmese relationship, the Burma Army gave these veterans the VIP treatment, including taking them on a trip to the Kachin state, in thanks for their wartime service to Burma.

The informal leader of the group was Pete Lutkins, a tall and poised gentleman from Mississippi who served throughout the entire existence of Detachment 101 in Burma. He rose to command a battalion of rangers with 1,500 Kachin rangers and a small herd of elephants. Although badly wounded by Japanese machine gun fire, he survived the war, rising to the rank of major. At the end of the war, the OSS detachment and their Kachin rangers were credited with killing more than 5,000 Japanese soldiers, rescuing 425 downed Allied airmen, blowing up 75 bridges, and detailing 9 trains. They provided the bulk of intelligence to Allied ground units in northern Burma to provide targets for the 10th Air Force. After the war, Detachment 101 veterans felt they owed a debt of honor to the Kachin rangers who fought and died in the war. They raised money to support a Kachin school and orphanage, among other good works for their Kachin friends.

The OSS veterans were invited to meet a group of Kachin. Pete Lutkins walked up to the young Kachin girls wearing the distinctive and beautiful formal Kachin dress, a woven skirt of red wool with intricate designs, black velvet tunics adorned with silver jewelry, and red turbans.

Pete started speaking to them in Jingpaw Kachin, their native language. He was 74 years old and had been away from Burma for 50 years but he still remembered his Kachin from years in the jungle with his rangers. The teenagers could not believe it. Then he told them his "bush name" bestowed on him by Kachin elders. It was Ka'Ang Zhau Lai, "He who was in from the beginning to the end." The girls immediately knew who he was. Pete had become part of the oral history of the Kachin people. The girls began to weep with joy at their meeting a legend. The veterans teared up.

Pete Lutkins passed away in 2014 at the age of 93. He never forgot the Kachin. And they never forgot him.

**

Ethnic minorities have been at war with the Burmese since the country achieved independence from Great Britain in 1948. Large parts of the country are not controlled by the government. When I arrived at post there were 16 active insurgencies. A lack of infrastructure made many areas difficult to reach. The river transportation system, for example, never recovered from the loss of the Irrawaddy Flotilla Company's ships. Hundreds were scuttled in 1942 to prevent their falling into the hands of the invading Japanese. Some were refloated, but most were never replaced. For these reasons, large parts of Burma were off limits to foreigners.

In the mid-1990s Burma experienced a small economic boom and the government relaxed some of its travel restrictions. American cooperation with the Burmese in countering terrorism improved, creating opportunities that hadn't existed before. One of the places I wanted to visit was Mrauk-U, the capital of the Arakanese kingdom from the 15th to the 18th century in western Burma near the border of Bangladesh. I asked if I might be able to visit the Arakan, which had been renamed Rakhine State in 1989.

The request was approved. "It would have to be an official visit," I was told.

"What official reason would I have to visit the Rakhine state?" I asked.

"The Rohingya," the intelligence officer said.

"Why should we be interested in the Muslim minority group in the Arakan?" I asked.

"Because they are receiving weapons-training at fundamentalist Islam camps in the Middle East and are smuggling guns into and through Myanmar."

"Can you arrange a briefing for me in Sittwe?"

"No problem," he answered. So, the trip was on, the first of its kind.

At that moment I became interested in the Rohingya, a group that had migrated into Burma from Bengal India over hundreds of years, especially after the British took control of the Arakan in 1826. The Burmese considered them illegal immigrants and did not include them as one of the 132 ethnic minority groups in the country. Aung San Suu Kyi regarded the Rohingya in the same way as the generals did.

Getting to the Rakhine capital Sittwe (formerly Akyab) was not easy. The few flights per week were always booked. Before my trip I mentioned to a European physician that I would be going to Sittwe.

"You must visit my Italian friend there," he said. "He is one of the few white men in Sittwe and is starved for company."

A Burmese lieutenant met my flight and told me that I would stay at a government guesthouse. It was an old British colonial wooden bungalow with no air conditioning. This was not a problem since there was no electricity in the city either. I found the place actually quite charming. The old quarters could probably tell some tales of the days of the Raj. It consisted of one large room with teak plank flooring and mosquito netting over the camp bed, with a candle on a small table next to the bed. The lieutenant informed me that I was expected for drinks and dinner at the Italian's villa, which he pointed out to me down the street. It was 105 degrees Fahrenheit.

I walked to the house at the appointed time. I brought a present, a ball of mozzarella cheese packed in ice in a wine caddy normally used for picnics. Charming and effusive, the doctor was in his thirties and spent his time fighting malaria, a serious threat in the Rakhine state. When I presented the cheese to him I thought he would cry with joy. He rubbed the wrapped cheese all over his face; it was the coldest thing he had seen in days. He welcomed me to his home and served a fine Scotch whiskey and soda. He apologized profusely for the lack of ice. There was still some ice in my wine cooler and I deposited the remains in our whiskey glasses. I could see the ice melt before my eyes. He grew tomatoes and basil in his garden. Now he had mozzarella he made a Caprese salad as our first course.

The next morning I received a briefing from the Burmese on their two perceived security threats, the Rohingya and the Arakan Liberation Army. Community relations with the Rohingya deteriorated after World War II, and in 1982 General Ne Win denied the Rohingya citizenship.

The Arakan Liberation Army (ALA), sought to restore the independence that the Arakanese, an ancient Buddhist civilization, lost when the Burmese conquered them in 1784. Small and relatively ineffective, the ALA was considered more of a political nuisance than a military threat.

Business concluded, I was delighted to learn that my Burmese hosts had arranged for me to visit the ancient city of Mrauk-U up the Kaladan River. I had been fascinated with Mrauk-U, also known as Myo Haung ("ancient city"), since reading *The Land of the Great Image* by Maurice Collis. Collins tells the story of a Catholic priest's visit to the city in the 17th century when it was a major power in the region. The Great Image referred to the Buddha image that was later captured by the Burmese and transferred to Mandalay. It rests today at the Maha Muni pagoda in Mandalay It is the most revered image of the Buddha in Burma and the Arakanese want it back.

I was taken to the river and introduced to an Arakanese fellow who was to be my guide on the overnight trip to Mrauk-U. Then I saw my boat. It reminded me of the broken-down vessel featured in the film *The African Queen*. The small commercial craft was used for hauling agricultural produce up and down the river, and had seen better days. A little table and a few chairs had been added for the ease of passengers making the trip. There were only three of us. A junior officer with limited English acted as my "minder" on the excursion. He did not look too happy about his assignment. Immediately after we cast off he curled up in a corner and went to sleep for the entire six-hour chug up-river.

My guide, a jolly fellow, who spoke excellent English, laughed when I asked him how long he had been a guide. "I am not a guide," he said, "I am a businessman. There are no people to guide here."

"How were you chosen to be my guide?" I asked.

"Because I can speak English. The army asked me to guide you." I apologized for the inconvenience to him.

"Not at all," he laughed. "I am delighted to be chosen. I have never met an American and I have more questions for you than you have of me. When we get to Mrauk-U you will have a real guide." Steaming upstream against a moderate current on the wide and calm river, we saw a number of large sailing boats hauling goods as they did for centuries. It was as if time stood still in the Arakan.

The passage was smooth but hot. About half way, the mate of the two-man crew served tea with local biscuits. I didn't see a lifeboat or any life preservers on board but did not want to look like a wimp by asking. After about five hours we left the river and entered a small stream. "Eight more miles to go," said my new friend, who was a font of knowledge about the situation in the Rakhine, including the worsening relations with the Rohingya. "They will have to go back to Bangladesh," he assured me. Apparently, the Arakanese and Burmese were in agreement on that point.

We cruised up to a landing in the small town of Mrauk-U where a party of local officials greeted us. An elderly but spry fellow who spoke fluent English in a crisp Oxbridge accent was my guide to the ancient city. I asked if there were many foreign tourists in Mrauk-U. He smiled, "Today, you are the only one. Actually, the only one this month." The town, was normally off limits to foreigners, had no hotels, and very few tourists. I found the government guesthouse spartan but adequate. What I really missed was electricity. I enjoyed a full day of touring the old ruins, which were interesting but paled in comparison with the hundreds of ancient temples at Pagan on the Irrawaddy or Angkor in Cambodia.

My guide apologized for the dilapidated state of many of the ancient buildings. "We have no budget for repairs or restoration. The money all goes to Pagan," he said in low tones. "It will be much nicer when we restore the city to her past glory and bring the Maha Muni Buddha home."

***

In 1994, James "Jim" B. Sherwood, an American who amassed considerable wealth from his shipping company, Sea Containers, and founded the Orient-Express Company, decided he wanted to bring five-star tourism to Burma. Jim already operated world-class trains and hotels. He wanted to add a boat. My old friend Bill Warren, a Bangkok-based writer, with whom I did a book on the spirit houses of Thailand, introduced me to Jim. Bill wrote for the *Orient-Express* magazine. He said Jim lived large, jetting around the world in his private plane expanding his empire of luxury-living venues, and wanted me to meet him.

Jim bought and refitted a Rhine River cruise boat, which he renamed *The Road to Mandalay* to sail the great Irrawaddy River. We hit it off when we met at the venerable Strand Hotel in Rangoon. Jim asked BJ and me to join him and a number of his senior staff and their wives from London, Singapore and Bangkok on his "shakedown" cruise between Pagan (now Bagan) and Mandalay, 90 miles away. BJ and I were the only non-Orient-Express couple on board, and I shared my rapidly expanding knowledge of Burma and its people. Our party took a commercial Air Mandalay flight to Pagan. When a tourist who was not a member of our group, looking out the window at the scores of ancient temples, asked if we were in Mandalay, I said no, we had made an unscheduled stop in Pagan. Jim had diverted the aircraft for his party.

Jim brought Thai staff from his Orient-Express train that operated between Thailand and Malaysia to help train the newly hired Burmese boat staff. The Burmese trainees included a dozen attractive young ladies, who had just graduated from a teachers' college in Mandalay and found they could make ten times more money waiting on tables on board the boat than they could make teaching school. Burma's educational loss was the Orient-Express's gain. To help skipper the long boat Jim coaxed an old British seaman, Brian Hills, out of retirement. Earlier, Brian had captained Jim's first pleasure boat, the *MV Orient Express* in the Mediterranean Sea.

Brian looked worried when I approached him on the bridge. He explained that the Irrawaddy is a treacherous river, especially at low water. He said *The Road to Mandalay* needed at least six feet of water and might have trouble handling sharp bends in the constantly changing channel. Jim hired skilled Burmese river captains and experienced crewmen but his large, heavy boat was not built for these waters and the crew had not handled such a large boat before. Brian told me that in the old days of the Irrawaddy Flotilla Company, the Scottish-owned colonial company operated over four hundred boats on the rivers and coasts of

Burma. The river boats had stern or side paddles that created their own channels. With the passing of the Irrawaddy Flotilla Company after World War II, so went the channels. He also told me that the old company's iron rule was that if a boat went aground on a sandbar, the skipper had to stay on board until it was refloated. Depending on the season, that could take many months. I am sure it was a great motivator.

As always happens, the shakedown cruise experienced a number of problems, magnified in importance by the presence of Jim and his charming English wife, Dr Shirley Sherwood, a noted botanist. The most dangerous moment came when a large framed painting on the bulkhead in Jim's stateroom fell down on him in the night due to faulty framing. Jim or Shirley could have been badly hurt but they emerged intact and unfazed. More humorous but still vexing was the problem posed by the remote-controlled televisions installed in all their staterooms. The remote signal was so strong that guests in one stateroom could control TVs in the next stateroom, leaving passengers startled to find their TV mysteriously rising up from its hidden location without being summoned. Overall, however, we thoroughly enjoyed the trip.

I later received a note from Jim asking if I would entertain a friend who would be traveling on *The Road to Mandalay*. He said that he and Shirley had enjoyed their dinner with us and wanted to give a similar colonial-era experience to their friend, Sir Peter Ustinov. What a treat! Of course I said yes. Sir Peter was doing a travel film on Burma, and part of his itinerary was on board *The Road to Mandalay*. At the dinner I put my Shan friend Sai Sao Long Mengrai or "Shorty" as he liked to be called next to Sir Peter. Shorty was the last feudal lord of the Shan state of Keng Tung. English-educated (King's School Canterbury), as were many Shan royalty, Shorty was famed as a wit and raconteur.

Charming and very entertaining, Sir Peter, fresh from an evening of wit and storytelling at the Oriental Hotel in Bangkok, was still performing to the delight of all of us at dinner. The only person who could keep up with Sir Peter, a two-time Academy Award winner, was Shorty. He seemed to one-up Sir Peter, effortlessly, at every turn. Finally, Sir Peter, stopped the discussion and addressed me. "Who is this little fellow? He keeps topping me, and that is not easy." Shorty smiled his pixie smile. He was the perfect person to joust verbally with Sir Peter Ustinov.

Sadly, I didn't have the time or opportunity to have much one-on-one time with our guest of honor. I wanted to know more about Sir Peter's father, a one-time press officer at the German embassy in London in the early 1930s. He later began working for the British counterintelligence service, MI5, stayed in England, and took British citizenship. During World War II, Sir Peter served as a private in the British Army. At the time he was writing a film to star David Niven, who was serving in the army as a lieutenant colonel. To allow fraternization between the private and the colonel in the very class-conscious British military, it was decided to assign Sir Peter to Colonel Niven as his batman. I didn't have a chance to ask Sir Peter about his often quoted definition of a diplomat. "A diplomat these days is nothing but a head waiter who is allowed to sit occasionally." Perhaps, but not in the United States.

***

At the top of my list of places to visit in Burma was the seaside town of Mergui, a small island in the south on the coast of the Andaman Sea. This ancient city, now known as Myeik in Burma and Mergen to the Thai was once a powerful seaport belonging to the Siamese (Thai) kingdom of Ayuthia in the 17th century. I had always wanted to go to Mergui after reading *Siamese White*, another book by Maurice Collis. It recounts the true story of Sam White, an English freebooter (some say pirate) in the pay of Siam and the port master of Mergui. The fascinating story, which I won't spoil for future readers, is made more interesting by the fact that Collis himself was once the chief British colonial administrator in Mergui before World War II.

In 1995 I got my chance to go to Mergui while on a visit to an off-shore oil rig. There I met Anglo-Burman Bill Gil, a retired rubber grower and son of a British sea captain. He was the most prominent and possibly the only British citizen in Mergui. Bill, who was full of useful information about Mergui, the most important town on the Tenasserim Coast, urged me to return. The person he wanted me to meet, he said, was an old Irishman living on nearby King Island. During World War II, the Irishman successfully evaded Japanese invaders when they captured Mergui in 1942. Bill warned me that we would need to give some advance warning of our visit to the old rubber planter, "because he normally doesn't wear any clothes."

My brief visit to Mergui whetted my appetite for another trip that would give me more time to explore and enjoy the historical town. I arranged a trip and flew down on a bi-weekly flight aboard an aging Myanma Airways Fokker aircraft and was met by a young Burmese intelligence officer. He asked what I wanted to do in Mergui. I said I wanted to visit the city with my friend Bill Gil, tour around the island and perhaps visit King Island nearby. He said I was invited to enjoy a harbor tour on the harbormasters' launch. This was an unexpected treat. Then he said a visit to King Island was not possible. One thing that struck me immediately in Mergui was the large-scale and totally overt offloading of high-value cargo, notably cigarettes and Scotch whiskey over the beach without any Customs and Excise control. Obviously, free market enterprise reigned, with customary payoffs to local officials. I wondered if it was like this when Sam White ran the port for King Narai of Siam. Mergui was Siam's window to the West with goods portaged across Tenasserim to the Gulf of Siam in both directions for centuries saving weeks or months traveling through pirate-invested Malacca Strait.

My intelligence escort told me about drug routes that brought heroin produced in the Shan state south to the sea and then by boat, to Thailand and Malaysia. He said smugglers also moved quantities of weapons through the area to insurgent armies as well as to Muslim rebels in southern Thailand. However, he said, Thai fisherman poaching in Burmese waters posed the main problem for the local authorities. With Thai waters badly overfished, the Thai had moved into Burmese waters, which were still rich with fish and lobsters. At any given time, the Burmese had hundreds of Thai fishermen in Burmese jails. Help was on the way; China was providing new patrol boats.

Mergui's role as a trading hub has resulted in a very mixed population that includes Indian, Thai, and Chinese minorities along with other lessen known groups, such as the fast-disappearing Moken people called "Sea Gypsies." These nomadic sea rovers were here before any of the others and were greatly feared as pirates or "Salateers" during White's days. Much reduced in numbers today, they live off the sea, moving through the islands in small open boats.

In the oddest stop on the tour, we visited an undistinguished shop house residence on the quay. I wondered what the attraction was. It quickly became apparent as we entered and found the house filled with swallows' nests, hundreds of them. Birds flew in and out, completely ignoring the human residents who had installed nets to catch the bird droppings. The swallows' nests ended up in expensive Chinese restaurants in Hong Kong or Bangkok specializing in bird's nest soup.

While the Burmese generally disdain seafood, preferring fresh water fish, the country does have a thriving export industry in lobsters. In Rangoon, Burmese friends advised me to buy lobsters in Mergui. Bill Gil knew where to go. He made our last stop the lobster merchant's seaside operations. Before heading for the airport Bill gave me a quick tour of the town. I photographed Mary White's gravestone but not her grave. The stone was mounted near the beach, unmarked and difficult to read. She died in Mergui in 1687. British historian J. S. Furnivall discovered the stone in 1910 when he saw an Indian washer man (dhobie) beating clothes against the stone. I found Collis's old and rather dilapidated wooden house. It appears in my book *Myanmar Architecture: Cities of Gold*, with text by Ma Thanegi. It is probably the least attractive photograph in the book but I put it in as an homage to Mr. Collis.

Mergui's airport, a vestige of the British, featured a short airstrip and a humble shed that passed for a terminal. The Myanma Airways clerk informed me that I was in luck. The plane was en route. This gave me the impression that the airline did not scrupulously follow schedule. I was right. Their airfield had no instruments to assist with landings at night or in bad weather. Like many things in Burma, airline schedules were advisory only.

The helpful Myanma Airways clerk suggested that I might be more comfortable waiting at the nearby golf course, another relic of the Raj. He said I could enjoy a drink there and when I saw the plane approaching I should return to the airport. So I checked my bag and walked down to the pleasant if impoverished nine-hole course. Here I was greeted as if I were a member and invited to sit on the verandah for a drink while waiting for the plane. It was a Sunday and a group of military officers were in the middle of an army golf tournament. As I enjoyed my snack, a tepid Myanmar beer with local cashew nuts, I kept an ear cocked for the sound of incoming aircraft.

I watched Burma Army officers putting out on the 18th green. One officer handed his putter to a caddy and sat down at my table. I introduced myself and the officer said he knew who I was. He was the local military intelligence chief and said he regretted not being on hand to meet me when I arrived. He asked how the visit had gone. I thanked him for the harbor boat tour and the assistance of his young intelligence officer. I also told him that I would let his boss in Rangoon know about the fine reception I received in Mergui. That seemed to be what he was waiting to hear because his next comment was, "The next time you come, we will take you to King Island." I never made it to King Island and regret not hearing the story of the old Irish nudist and how he evaded the Japanese during the war.

***

In 1994 Rangoon was a decaying gem of colonial architecture. The poverty that had crippled the country's economy for decades under General Ne Win's misguided "path to socialism" left the country in something of a time warp. Once the city was a venerable vestige of the British Raj, graced with parks, tree-lined boulevards, and stately homes. Instead of being torn down as happened in other colonial cities like Singapore and Kuala Lumpur, most Rangoon mansions and government buildings just went to seed.

During my years in Asia, I saw the widespread destruction of many fine old homes to make room for high-rise buildings, which destroyed much of the charm and history of the region. It spurred me to preserve the buildings on film as much as I could and, in 1981, together with the Siam Society, we published a book, *Old Homes of Bangkok: Fragile Link*. Most of the houses in the book are now gone. The colonial architecture in Rangoon faced the same fate as the old houses in Bangkok. In the early 1990s a new Burmese government encouraged foreign investment, ushering in economic boom. Money poured in, land prices spiked, and many old homes were torn down. On my very first day in Rangoon I had my driver take me around the city to get my bearings. I took a camera along and began my quest to record the fading glory of one of Southeast Asia's finest cities.

At one stop I was photographing an elegant old home from the street when an elderly Burmese woman approached me from the house. I asked her if she spoke English and in a deep gravelly voice said, somewhat indignantly, "Of course I speak English" as if all Burmese did. I explained that I had just arrived in Rangoon and hope she didn't mind if I photographed her charming home. "You must be Barry," she said. She was virtually the first person I had spoken to in Rangoon. How did she know who I was? These are the kinds of things that concern CIA officers operating under cover.

She introduced herself as Kyi Kyi Myint Toon and said that her good friend Sunda Khin in Washington DC had written to say that I was en route to Burma and that I took pictures in my spare time. Sunda tutored me in the Burmese language before I left Washington and made several introductions to friends and family in Rangoon. Kyi Kyi (pronounced chee chee) was one of them. The widow of a renowned Burmese jurist, she invited me in for a cup of tea and told me where to find other old homes to photograph. I persuaded one of Burma's leading writers and painters, Ma Thanegi, to write a book on Burma's architecture, which I illustrated with photos. Kyi Kyi is pictured in the book in front of her home. Ma Thanegi was once the private secretary of Aung San Suu Kyi and spent time in prison with The Lady. A tenacious and talented women, Ma Thanegi became my guru on the arts and crafts of Burma and our art collection is graced by a number of her water colors. One shows the finely worked iron grille of an old Rangoon window. Painted in 1994, it could have risked more jail time for the feisty artist because it shows iron bars, perhaps a reference to the military regime.

When Britain added Rangoon—a sleepy town dominated by the ancient and imposing Schwe Dagon pagoda—to its Indian empire in 1853, it made it the capital of British Burma, which it ruled from Delhi until 1935 when Burma became a separate colony. The British immediately set about creating a city modeled after a model of a modern English city. They laid it out on a grid checkerboard with streets 60-feet wide. They built the broad Strand Road that runs along the Rangoon River. The city's finest hotel, The Strand, had a place of honor on the road and still exists amid the growth and change all around. A young Scot, Lieutenant Alexander Fraser of the Bengal Engineers, implemented the final city plan. It is perhaps fitting that a Scotsman was involved with the creation of British Rangoon as many of the commercial enterprises that sprang up in Burma over the next century were run by Scots.

The Burmese people lived as a minority in Rangoon. As part of the Indian empire, Rangoon saw the arrival of many thousands of Indian officials, business-men, and laborers. Many other ethnic groups, including Chinese, Armenian, and largely Christian minority groups from within Burma such as Shan and Karen, worked and lived in Rangoon. For a country in which the overwhelm-ing majority follow Theravada Buddhists, Rangoon had a surprisingly large number of Christian churches including two cathedrals, one Anglican, one Catholic. The city even has an Armenian church, badly in need of repair and parishioners.

I began photographing old buildings and residences in my spare time, just as I had done in Thailand two decades before. Foreign embassies had saved and refurbished some of best structures. The Indian ambassador's stately mansion, for example, once belonged to the Imperial Bank of India. The American ambassador has a similarly grand residence on 10 acres on Inya Lake. The British snapped up the house called Belmont, the most exquisite gem of colonial residences. The old home of the director of the Irrawaddy Flotilla Company (IFC), Belmont, now houses Her Majesty's envoy. In front of the house stands a bronze statue of Sir Arthur Phayre, the first British commissioner of Rangoon. Dedicated in 1899, the statue was rescued from the Rangoon zoo and transferred to Belmont.

Early on, I learned that the Burmese government forbade taking pictures of any government building, a drawback when documenting old Rangoon's architecture. In addition, the government also barred foreigners from even entering the grounds of the University of Rangoon, let alone taking pictures. I mentioned this to a senior officer one day after a vigorous set of tennis.

"What do you want to photograph?" he asked, and I named half a dozen buildings including the stately and massive, Secretariat, once home of the British government and now the headquarters of the Burmese government.

"Give me a list." I presented my "wish" list of 10 buildings.

"Next Sunday a major will be here at 9AM to pick you up and take you to nine of the buildings on your list, which you can photograph."

"What about the tenth building?" I asked.

"We sold it," he answered with a smile. "It will be a hotel. Wait six months and it will look a lot better." I did and it did.

Perhaps my favorite colonial structure in Burma is Candacraig, the old chummery of the Burmah-Bombay Trading Company in the hill station town of Maymyo (now Pwin U-Lwin) east of Mandalay on the Shan plateau. A chummery was quarters for British bachelors working for commercial enterprises, in this case a teak company. Named for a place in Scotland (of course), the Candacraig became a hotel after independence and the British left. It had about 10 rooms nestled amid whispering pine trees away from the bustle of town. In its heyday as a hotel, it featured prime rib of roast beef with Yorkshire pudding for dinner. Those days were long gone when BJ and I stayed there in 1994. "Decayed elegance" best describes how it looked. It was on hard times. We were the only guests. It had no menu, never mind roast beef. When asked what we wanted for dinner, we settled on a fine chicken curry with fresh marrows (large squash) from the garden.

After dinner we sat at the small table in front of the hotel so I could smoke a cigar and sip some elderly single malt Scotch whiskey in the cool evening air. Suddenly, a man appeared out of the dark in front of us. I had not seen or heard him and was startled. He stopped in front of us, turned to face me, and said in a loud voice as he saluted, "Sah!" A fine fellow, the Gurkha night guard making his round was another relic of the Raj. Many Gurkha soldiers stayed on in Burma after World War II.

Many years later, when I was on an assignment for *Forbes Magazine* in the far north of Burma at Putao (British Fort Hertz), I met an elderly British woman at the airport. The widow of a colonel of the Burma Rifles regiment during the war, she said that her husband had worked for the Burmah-Bombay Company. When I mentioned the Candacraig, she beamed and told me that her late husband spoke fondly of his many visits to the old chummery for officers passing to and fro from the teak forests. She lowered her voice and told me, "The young officers would find girls in town and bring them to the Candacraig after dinner for parties. Sometimes the girls would slide down the bannister leading to the second floor stark naked." I didn't ask for details. I suspect shenanigans like that never took place in the Scottish Candacraig. Hopefully, I am wrong.

BJ stands at the entrance of the Candacraig Hotel in the old hill station Maymyo (now Pyin Oo Lwin) not far from Mandalay, Burma. Its architecture is typical of the colonial buildings still found in remote parts of the country.

In the summer of 1996, a senior intelligence officer asked if I would give a slide show of old Rangoon buildings I had photographed to the city fathers of Rangoon. He wanted to promote the need to preserve the architectural heritage of the city by preventing the destruction of many grand old buildings that had taken place in cities like Bangkok and Singapore. We held the talk in a government-owned hotel, formerly a British bank, and a prime example of the type of building that needed to be saved. Army officers in charge of the administration of Rangoon made up more than half of the audience. The others were friends of mine and included a number of Burmese homeowners who had allowed me to photograph their homes. When the colonel introduced me, he said "Mr. Broman has probably been to more places than any of you during your military careers." Possibly true, and in my opening remarks I said, "If that is true, it is only because the colonel allowed me to do so. And I thank him for it."

***

If you ever have the urge to attend the annual Water Festival (Thingyan) in Burma, I encourage you to resist it. Many people love it, but don't say I didn't warn you. This ancient New Year festival takes place in several Southeast Asian countries around the middle of April. Traditionally, this festival calls for the old year to be washed away and the New Year anointed with water. In Burma, the origins of Thingyan began when Thagyamin, king of the spirits, or nats, descended to earth to bestow his blessings riding a winged golden horse carrying a water jar, a symbol of peace and prosperity. In ancient times, the water festival also featured the public washing of the Burmese king's hair, a ritual purification. This elegant event has morphed into alcohol-infused fun as the country lets its hair down. Sarongs and *longgyis* are put away and out come tight jeans and tee shirts.

The Thai celebrate this holiday as Songgran. It has somewhat gotten out of hand in recent years in Bangkok, thanks to drunken foreign tourists armed with outsized water pistols. In Burma, the water festival is even more boisterous, bordering on dangerous.

Rangoon essentially shuts down for four days. No one does any work and it is almost impossible to move around town. The way I see it, the Burmese divide into two teams: the sadists and the masochists. The first team abuses the second team, zealously throwing water at them. The second team revels in the abuse. Burma has a long tradition of conservative restraint in its culture. Young people are generally polite, quiet, and respectful. That all changes during the water festival when the cork in the bottle of cultural restraint pops off, unleashing a water-throwing frenzy.

This mayhem is semi-organized. Corporations, government institutions, even private families sponsor stands, called *pendals*, along the major streets. Rock and roll bands perform at the *pendals*, while friends, family, and employees hose down

A high-power water hose douses celebrators of the Water Festival in Rangoon, Burma. The country lets its hair down during this wild three-day event.

anyone who cares to approach. Cars line up with people hanging from every window, on the roof, and in the trunk, waiting to get soaked. Modest *pendals* arm their people with small hoses to greet the passing parade. Bigger *pendals* have more waterpower, including high-pressure fire hoses that can break the eardrum of an unlucky reveler. The upside to this over-the-top festival is that it gives people a chance to have a socially acceptable four-day release from the pressures of everyday life. This was especially welcome in the decades of harsh military rule, when there was very little to celebrate. Also, the event is very photogenic. Photographers are a magnet to water throwers; so some caution and preparation is needed. In my case, I used a 300mm telephoto to good effect and rarely got close to the action. I decided one water festival was enough and took BJ to Angkor Wat in Cambodia where the water festival was much more subdued and we stayed dry.

***

Drug lord Khun Sa had a bad year in 1996. Things had been going poorly for the narcotics' trafficker since our joint operations against him in Thailand in the early 1990s. Despite his private army of more than 15,000 men in the Shan state, Khun Sa was under a lot of pressure and his days were numbered. I ran my first operation against this Chinese-Shan drug lord in the early 1980s. In Thailand the Royal Thai

Police interdicted more than 700 kilos of his 999 Brand heroin and probably would have put him out of business in the early 1990s but for Washington's reluctance to support the Thai army's Suchinda Plan, which called for lethal measures against the drug trafficker.

The Thai leadership was fed up with Khun Sa's massive heroin operation, which he ran out of the village of Ho Mong just inside Burma. Its only road linked it to the Thai town of Mae Hong Son nearby. The Burmese, with encouragement from the CIA and DEA, were also ready to move against Khun Sa, their one-time friend when he had led militia forces against the Burma Communist Party (BCP). That friendship ended when Khun Sa used his private army to enforce his drug business and landed him in a Burmese prison for a few years.

A softly-spoken Burmese intelligence officer, Lieutenant Colonel Kyaw Thein, became the main player in Khun Sa's downfall. For years this officer had worked closely with ethnic minorities and had gained the trust of several insurgent groups. He had a plan. Just as he had been involved in wooing Buddhist Karen away from the Christian Karen insurgents, he thought he could split Khun Sa's Mong Tai Army in Burma's Shan state. Khun Sa liked to style himself as a Shan "freedom fighter" against the Burmese government. He played on his mother's Shan blood, claiming that he fought for Shan independence. In reality, the Burmese armed force had permitted Khun Sa to expand his drug business against rival tribal drug traffickers, notably the United Wa State Army.

Taking a page from organized crime in the West, Khun Sa established numerous legitimate businesses. He owned timber and jade businesses in Thailand, where he owned property and maintained a stable of bribed officials, some of them very senior. As I noted earlier, an offer was made to lure Khun San into Mae Hong Son where he was wanted by the Thai police. But we had to move fast. If we didn't move Khun Sa out of Thailand within 24 hours, his "friends" in the Thai government would arrange his release. Khun Sa was also under indictment in the United States with a $2 million reward on his head. Headquarters quashed the plan.

Kyaw Thein persuaded 5,000 Shan in Khun Sa's "army" that they had been duped and that their boss had no real interest in seeking independence for the Shan people. As the noose tightened, a senior Royal Thai Army officer visited Burma in 1995 for discussions with the Burmese on counter narcotics cooperation. Thailand wanted to help Burma take down Khun Sa. With a joint plan in hand, the drug lord's days were numbered. The Burma army went on the offensive against the Mong Tai Army tucked away in Ho Mong, which was easy to reach from Thailand but difficult to approach from the rugged hills to the West.

Under attack, the disaffected Shan deserted Khun Sa. The Thai army blocked the escape avenue, which also served as a resupply route to Ho Mong into Thailand. Khun Sa was running out of time, friends, and money. Heroin drug lords did not have money on the scale that their cocaine-peddling brethren enjoyed in Latin

America. The Latinos often owned their product throughout its life cycle from coca leaf to the homes of Hollywood cocaine buyers, making the cartels vastly wealthy. Heroin, on the other hand, typically changes hands many times before it reaches the streets of Vancouver or New York; with each sale the price doubles and the potency of the narcotic is cut. Khun Sa and his fellow traffickers in Burma saw a relatively small profit for their drug. At the same time, they had heavy overhead expenses maintaining their "armies" and paying off "friends" in the governments of Burma, Thailand, and China.

Khun Sa formally surrendered his shrunken forces to the Burma Army in May 1996. Twelve thousand men surrendered and turned over more than 7,000 weapons at a lavishly orchestrated and publicized event in the Shan state. Suddenly, thousands of unarmed men found themselves out of work. Many felt cheated by their leader. Already under sentence of death by the government of Burma, Khun Sa sold out his men and cut a deal with the Burmese, who dropped the death penalty and promised Khun Sa that he would not be handed over to the United States. If Khun Sa thought he was going to live out his life in luxury with his ill-gotten gains, he was wrong. He was not allowed to return to Ho Mong, where his four mistresses lived. He spent the rest of his life under virtual house arrest near Rangoon.

***

By 1996 my career in government was coming to an end. With 30 years of service, it was time to move on. The Clinton administration was not much interested in HUMINT and was cutting back on clandestine operators. Many of my peers accepted the "buy out" program offer of $25,000 to take early retirement and I joined them. Of course, the downside of letting go of hundreds of experienced officers with thousands of useful contacts and many with rare language skills, is that it creates a vacuum. This is the kind of vacuum that leads to situations like 9/11. Satellites are fine but that cannot give you terrorists' plans and intentions. Human assets can.

Looking back, I reflected over my years with the Agency and thought about the dozens of men and women I had recruited. None was ever caught. None was a fabricator. Every case officer has a favorite agent. Mine was a European gentleman almost old enough to be my father. A State Department friend introduced him to me with the warning "I doubt very much he is telling the truth about what he has done. He is too good to be true, so be careful." Fabricators, or "paper hangers" are the bane of case officers. In some countries fabricating intelligence is a cottage industry.

I met the fellow and immediately liked him. He spoke several languages, traveled widely, and claimed to have done some impossible things and survived to talk about it. My suspicions were allayed when he produced photographic evidence of what he had done around the world. His history of surviving tough situations and meeting high-profile enemies of the United States impressed me. He answered all my questions and provided additional photographic proof of his stories. He acted like he wanted to be recruited and I accommodated him. I will call him Leon. With Headquarters approval, I made the pitch. It came as no surprise to him. He even breathed a sigh of relief.

"I am very happy to be working with CIA."

"Why?" I asked.

"You need me. I am a risk taker and love America. I have only one demand," he said.

"What's that?" I asked, fearing the worst.

With a straight face, he responded, "I only want assignments that are life-threatening."

Leon also told me that he did not want to receive a salary. "I want to be paid by the job," he said, "and only paid what my work is worth." I never met anyone like him, before or after. Among the 40-plus recruitments I made in my career, no one ever said they wanted to risk their life, or eschewed a salary. I told him that I could not guarantee he would risk his life on each assignment but I would try my best. I asked if there was someone I could contact in the event that he was killed on an operation. "I have no family," he said, "just a girlfriend and she has no need to know what I do. If I am killed, bury me where I fall." I know it sounds melodramatic, right out of a cheap spy novel. But he said it and from the look in his eye I believed he meant it.

We decided to test Leon's capability and nerve. A field station needed to infiltrate a major drug organization and track the movement of an important trafficker. The station warned that if he was caught, he would certainly be killed. When I relayed this information to Leon, he smiled and acknowledged the station was probably right. "But," he said, "I have no intention of getting caught." We provided special training and equipment for his mission and he disappeared for months. Eventually, he surfaced and was debriefed in the field. To the surprise of everyone involved, including me, the operation was a complete success. Leon received a princely sum for his work. The full story, which would make a good book, or a film, can never be told. One of the realities of working for the Clandestine Service, is that the public often hears about the disasters, but rarely learns about the successes.

I felt considerably more confident, and relieved, sending Leon on his second assignment. Another station needed an agent who could go behind enemy lines in a war zone to report on the situation. Again, the station warned that if Leon was captured, he could expect no mercy. Leon thought he should go, despite the risks. He was not a young man and the terrain and climate were daunting. But he did five hundred pushups before breakfast, abstained from alcohol, and said he could live off the land, if necessary. He disappeared for two months and we feared he had been killed in action, if not captured and executed. Finally, he emerged with dozens of reports from the front. Along the way he had engaged in several firefights and captured at least one town while leading insurgents. The ruling government had put a large reward on his head. Leon also arranged, on his own initiative, to generate international publicity for the plight of the rebels he worked with. Showered with accolades, he also received a generous cash payment from Langley.

Flushed with success, Leon then volunteered to contact a notorious terrorist organization through a friend who was persona grata with the terrorists. The station, located in a country where the terrorists had killed hundreds of people, said that it had tried to infiltrate the organization, but no agent had ever come back alive. It did not want to risk Leon's life and politely declined the offer. When I informed Leon of the decision, he shrugged, smiled, and said he was going anyway. He said he would pay his own expenses but would expect fair compensation if he survived. I urged him not to go but he said this was the kind of thing that motivated him. He liked living on the edge. He then told me about his youth during World War II when he saw his first combat and where he won his first medal. "To really live," he said, "you must nearly die."

Off Leon went again, despite my pleas to stop him. Weeks later, I received a phone call. "I'm back," was all he said. He returned again loaded with intelligence for a grateful and very generous station. By then, Leon was becoming a legend among the very small fraternity of case officers who were involved with his operations around the world.

When the Agency transferred me to a new assignment, I turned over Leon to a very savvy case officer who I knew would enjoy working with a daredevil agent who had a death wish combined with the luck of the Irish. Years went by and I never heard from, or about, Leon. Towards the end of my career, I was at Headquarters and received a phone call from a case officer in the building. He asked if I was the officer who had recruited Leon. I said yes. "We need to talk," he said, "let's have a cup of coffee."

The case officer worked in a different area division and shook my hand vigorously. "I always wanted to meet the man who recruited Leon." He told me that Leon was still alive and well and had continued his hazardous lifestyle in the years since I recruited him. He had been captured several times in war zones, escaping once and talking his way out another time. He had been in high mountains and hot deserts and made a number of friends in the Agency and in several rebel groups along the way.

The case officer said, "I handled Leon long after you did. He is about to retire and has been invited him to Langley to receive a medal from the Agency. He asked about you and wants to see you."

"Why?" I asked.

"You are the guy who recruited him. You gave meaning to his life. He wants to thank you. And we want your help writing the citation for his award."

"He was the best agent I ever handled," I answered.

"Mine too," he said.

I provided more detail about key events in Leon's early and dangerous life on behalf of the Agency. His years of service spanned a time when the Agency was involved in several wars, some public, some not. It seems Leon was a veteran of most of them. On the day of the ceremony, CIA officers brought him into the headquarters building "black." He didn't enter through the front door, past the statue of General William Donovan and passed the wall of honor with engraved stars depicting Agency officers killed in the line of duty. Rather, he came in through the underground garage and was taken up in the director's private elevator to the 7th floor where a very senior officer read the citation and presented the medal. Leon looked 20 years younger than his actual age. He barely had a moment to hold the medal before he returned it to the officer for safekeeping. This was the CIA and he was a clandestine asset. He could not keep the medal and knew it. No one took photos. Leon left quietly the way he had come. Thus ended a most distinguished career.

Later that night, a few of his old case officers, including me, took him out for a valedictory meal. Reserved and quiet, as usual, he didn't talk about his daring deeds. At the end of the meal he thanked each of us and we all thanked him. After I retired from the Agency I heard from Leon, who had finally married his longtime paramour and was living quietly in retirement. She never knew about his secret life with the CIA. He told me that a cinematographer wanted to make a film about his life, not knowing that he had been a CIA agent. It would have made a great film, even if the CIA spying component was left out. He declined the offer. I never saw him again. But we kept in touch up to the end of his life. He was a man of courage who saw America as the country he wanted to help regardless of the risks. We need a few more like him.

***

By the time my last tour ended I had served in all of the five countries on my Agency bucket list. Our son Seth was heading for college, having graduated from an international school in a class of 10. In his college essay, he wrote about growing up around the world, He described seeing the sights of the world, and dining with princes, generals, and prime ministers, but never having a place to call home. He worried about his brother, Brendan, five years younger, who had to look forward to more years of travel until he, too, could go to university. That convinced me that it was time to hang up my cloak.

With the collapse of the Soviet Union, the Agency was in a transition mode. Targets were still there, including the Russians, who never really went away. Declining morale and weak leadership in the Directorate of Operations also contributed to my decision to truncate my time with the Agency. By definition, the Clandestine Service is a risk-taking organization. Lives are sometimes lost. An example of increasing leadership "shyness" came when I tried to get an outstanding young officer assigned to my station. I watched the officer achieve incredible results against hard targets at another station; he was a born headhunter. One of his cases was briefed to President Clinton. My division chief turned down the request. He told me the man was "not a team player." I responded that espionage is not a team sport. Few case officers ever make really important recruitments. He seemed to make them routinely. Yet his singular style and passion that worked so well with hard targets was not appreciated by the appointed masters of the Agency. He resigned and it was the Agency's loss. Clearly, it was time for me to go.

A mentor suggested I set up a consulting firm, which I did. An old friend who owned a number of companies was my first client. No more boring National Day receptions trolling for disaffected Soviets. BJ could return to her teaching career and not worry about hosting a dinner party every week. The boys could get back to being Americans, and I could watch sports on television with my aging father.

BJ was also happy to end her wandering life following the flag. Because of my career she had lost several opportunities to shine as a caterer and also as a writer. She taught at several international schools and enjoyed her time with the State Department. With my buyout money I bought a new car in Seattle and drove leisurely across the country, visiting friends along the way to Langley to formally end my government career. At headquarters, the East Asia Division hosted a small farewell gathering with old friends and colleagues and gave me an attractive clock with an Agency plaque of thanks. The Agency later mailed me a medal and several citations. I took a large cardboard box down to the ground floor of the Agency and packed numerous antiques on loan from the Broman collection. They constituted a large part of East Asia Division's display of Asian art.

On a farewell visit to the State Department I was surprised to be invited to call on a senior state officer whom I did not know. The fellow greeted me warmly and wished me a happy retirement. He said he wanted to thank me for our reporting at my last post. I was somewhat surprised because our reporting was mainly on narcotics issues and not political. He said "I know that, but your internal reporting was balanced, insightful and useful. I am afraid the mission only told The Lady's story."

I said my goodbyes in Langley and turned in my badge. My last stop was at the memorial to officers of the CIA who had fallen in the line of duty located on the north wall of the headquarters building. By 2018, there were 129 stars on the wall, many more than in 1996 when I retired. Of the people belonging to the stars, most are named in the Book of Honor in front of the wall. Some identities remain secret, even in death. I paid my respects to one officer, Johnny, a good friend who was killed in action in Laos. Then I exited the building and the Agency.

CHAPTER 5

Latter Years

Retirement suited me. More correctly, retirement from government service suited me. I soon found I was working harder than ever but enjoying it more. Now I could travel where I wanted without seeking permission, and did. I returned to my old vocation, photography, and began publishing photo books, most dealing with Burma. I wrote articles for *Arts of Asia*, the Hong Kong-based bible for Asian art dealers and collectors. I wrote and photographed stories for *Architectural Digest* and some travel magazines. I reconnected with my old houseboat roommate from college days, Neil Hollander, now living in Paris writing books and directing films. He introduced me to the world of documentary filmmaking. I made regular trips to Southeast Asia on business and, increasingly, for pleasure, especially in Burma and Thailand. I was finally happy to be my own boss and be able to take advantage of interesting travel opportunities off the beaten track.

One of these trips came in 2001 when I received an email from my French friend in Rangoon, Patrick Robert, alerting me to a planned New Year celebration of the Naga tribe in the remote hills of northwestern Burma. The Ministry of Tourism came up with the idea. Patrick invited me to join him. The Naga, famed for their prowess as headhunters, are one of the most interesting and least visited tribal groups in Burma. They live in the hills bordering of Assam in India, a region that had been off limits to visitors for decades. Interested in Anthropology since graduate school, I jumped at the chance to visit the Naga at home.

Most Naga reside in India across a remote and undemarcated border. During colonial days, the British studied, pacified, and largely converted these Naga to Christianity. In contrast, no one paid much attention to the one hundred thousand Naga living on the Burma side of the border. They remained little studied, Christianized, and pacified. Colonial maps identified the areas where Burmese Naga lived as "unadministered." In many respects, not much has changed since then.

I flew to Rangoon ready for another adventure, only to find a distraught Patrick who informed me that the festival was cancelled. Apparently, the military-led Ministry of Tourism had not cleared the event with the army commander responsible for

A Naga tribesman dances at the New Year festival in a colorful costume that includes a cane helmet of sun bear fur, wild boar tusks, and a hornbill feather. The tribesman carries a machete (*dah*) and wears a necklace of tiger claws. These remote hills are usually off limits to foreigners and the custom of head hunting still occurs in remote hills far from Burmese governmental controls.

Nagaland in Burma, who correctly pointed out that there was no infrastructure to take care of the two hundred foreigners that the tourist ministry wanted to bring. It looked like a wasted trip for me but I told Patrick that I would make a phone call. I rang an army general who was a friend and explained the situation to the senior intelligence officer. He welcomed me back to Burma, thanked me for the call, and said he would get back to me. Two hours later he called, and said we could go. He had spoken to the army commander-in-chief and explained that Burma would lose face if the entire event was cancelled. The commander then phoned the regional commander and told him to let a few people come to the celebration. We were in that small group.

Patrick led our party, which included his vivacious Shan wife, Claudia Saw Lwin, and a grown son from a previous marriage. We were in the hands of an intrepid Japanese tour operator in Rangoon, Shota-san, who specialized in mountain trekking in upper Burma. The festival was to take place in the Thankul Naga village of Layshi about 20 miles west of Chindwin River, which demarcates the eastern boundary of Burma's Nagaland. The Burma Army arranged for Naga from various sub-groups, such as the Thankul, Keomingun, and Konyak, to converge on Layshi for a few days of rare interaction, dancing, singing, and especially drinking their homemade beer. As an incentive, the government gave the Naga valuable gifts such as tons of rice.

It was clear from the outset that this festival, the first of its kind, had been poorly planned. The regional army commander had wisely limited the number of foreign guests, as there was indeed no infrastructure for tourists. We flew into the small town of Hkamti on the Chindwin River. We found one small inn with seven rooms, already fully booked. Thanks to a bit of luck and Claudia's fast thinking, we found a place to sleep on the floor of our taxi driver's family. The next day we sailed down the Chindwin in a long-tail boat to the river town of Tamanthi, where we spent the night sleeping on the floor of a Buddhist temple, thanks again to Claudia. The next day we crossed the Chindwin where a dump truck was waiting to carry us over a very bad road into the mountains. The rest of Shota's party—high-rolling Japanese tourists unused to "roughing it," were not amused by the jolting truck ride uphill at a snail's pace. The Imperial Japanese Army climbed these same hills in the spring of 1944 in their unsuccessful invasion of India. In what became one of the war's turning points, the British and Indian armies stopped them at the Naga village of Kohima, to the west of Layshi. After Kohima, Japan went on the defensive.

Our visit took place in December and we climbed the Paktoi range that separates India from Burma in the cool weather. In the monsoon season the road would have been impassable. We arrived at Layshi, a large Naga village that was also housed a battalion of Burma Army troops, with a helicopter-landing zone. Our party of four slept on the floor in the office of the Myanmar Agriculture Service. The event itself, however, was very well worth the inconveniences. Naga groups had been walking along jungle trails, some of them for more than a week, to reach Layshi. As they arrived, the Burmese Army gave the women and girls tee shirts by the Burma Army to cover their bare breasts. They gave the men and boys soccer shorts to replace their loincloths. The Naga, magnificent and attractive in their tribal finery, happily received the gifts of modern clothing. I was disappointed.

The Naga adorn themselves with elegant body cloths, their main apparel, which serve to protect them from the cold nights at altitudes of 6,000 feet or higher. The unspoiled surrounding jungle has few roads. Large hornbill birds fly overhead, semi-feral wild oxen called *mithan* provide protein, and tigers can be heard growling in the night. The Naga, who are armed with long knives, incorporate the region's fauna in their headgear. A typical Naga warrior might wear a cane helmet decorated with wild boar tusks, hornbill feathers, and monkey fur. A lucky few wear necklaces of tiger claws over their heavily tattooed chests. Fewer will wear brass necklaces indicating how many heads they have taken. The British authorities outlawed head taking but they rarely ventured into the Burma hills leaving the Naga pretty much to themselves. Their isolation continues today.

The highlight of every day of the festival, after a dinner of *mithan* and home-brewed "beer" or Mandalay rum for the wealthy, came when the various Naga tribes vied to outdo each other in spirited dancing around a huge bonfire, the only source of heat. Chanting songs interspersed with what sounded like war cries, the warriors in all their finery resembled 19th-century American Indians preparing to go on the warpath. A Naga teenager from Dimapur, India, who spoke English, befriended me. He identified the various sub-tribes by their distinctive garb and adornment. While I was photographing the dancing, the boy came up to me and in a low voice said, "This is a song about cutting off Japanese heads after the battle of Kohima." Turned back by British and Indian troops, the Japanese fell back into Burma in disarray. At that point the British who had outlawed head taking, released their Naga militia with their long knives to pursue the Japanese. I suggested that the teenager not mention the song to Shota and his Japanese clients.

Despite the hardships we experienced reaching this remote and unique festival, we all had a great time. I literally bought a body cloth off an inebriated Thankhul Naga whose equally soused buddies told him he was crazy to turn down the sum I offered. He assured me he had more cloths at home and said that he thought I was offering too much ($10 in Burmese kyat) for the finely woven woolen textile in the traditional red and white colors of the Thankhul. Fierce Konyak Naga, who had walked all the way from the Indian border far to the north, demonstrated their prowess with long spears. Some wore monkey skulls around their necks. The drinking and dancing lasted for three days. Then Burmese officials gave gifts to the assembled tribes and as much rice as they could carry home to their mountain villages. All agreed that the festival had been a huge success, but that it could have been better. I wrote a list of recommendations on how the next year's festival could be improved and gave it to the general with my thanks for arranging our visit.

The following year, 2002, the Burmese held the festival in Lahe, north of Layshi, where different Naga tribes gathered. This time I brought with me my film partner, Neil Hollander. The Jim Thompson Foundation in Bangkok funded us to make a short film on Naga textiles to accompany a photo exhibit of mine on the Naga. It was the first film we made together.

A larger number of tourists attended and the festival was much better organized. I noted with satisfaction that every one of my recommendations had been adopted. For example, the organizers prepared 20 outhouses, including four that featured porcelain toilets. They constructed living quarters made entirely of freshly cut bamboo including bed frames and bedside tables. It was cold at Layshi but we were well prepared. As the sun went down, Neil and I watched a van arrive with a new group of tourists. One of them, an elderly European, looked around and spotted us. He walked up and asked, "Mr. Broman?" I nodded and he said, "Here is your mail," and handed me a sheaf of mail. He was a German publisher and a friend of Patrick Robert who could not get away from Rangoon for the festival. Patrick told the German to look for us and deliver my mail. I offered him a glass of Scotch whiskey and lent him a sleeping bag, which he appreciated when the temperatures began dropping that night.

We also met a Scotsman from South Africa, Jamie Saul, an expert on the Naga. Each year Jamie visited the Naga, mostly in India where they were more accessible. He gave me current information on the Naga and the low-level war they were waging in India for independence. He also cited instances where headhunting still occurred in the high country between warring clans. When Jamie died some years later of a sudden heart attack during a visit to Burma, Naga warriors lined the path in the village of Tamanthi as Jamie's body was carried down to the Chindwin River to be returned to South Africa.

Before traveling to Nagaland, I paid my respects to my intelligence friend who had been so helpful the year before. He assured me Lahe would be more pleasant than Layshi, and he was right.

"How are you going to return to Yangon (Rangoon) after the festival?"

"We will fly back from Hkamti, that's the only way I know of," I said.

"Why not come down the Chindwin?" said the general puckishly.

"Because it is forbidden to foreigners," I said, finally understanding what the general was getting at.

"You can if I say you can." He gave the necessary orders and we made a rare trip down the shallow river with our interpreter and a military intelligence "minder." Along the way we passed a gold field with hundreds of miners hard at work sifting the river sands for gold dust. Pulling into the gold camp, we came upon a middle-aged Burmese woman quietly panning gold in the river just south of Hkamti, the main town on the upper Chindwin. I asked if she found any gold. She nodded yes. How much money did you make last year? $60,000 she answered through our interpreter. Neil turned to me. "We have a film here."

Suvarnabhumi means "land of gold" in Sanskrit. It is also the name of the Bangkok International Airport, which may lead people to think that the term refers to Thailand. It actually refers to the land watered by the Irrawaddy and Chindwin rivers of Burma. It dates from a millennium ago, before the Burmese migrated south from Tibet. The Pyu and Mon people ruled the land. It was rich in gold and many other precious minerals and metals. It still is.

As a consultant for a Canadian mining company, I learned something about the gold of Burma. A Canadian geologist and I had access to data regarding areas in Burma rich in gold. Most of the areas of interest were near one of the major rivers or in remote mountains. A senior Burmese geologist tapped a map and pointed to an area in the rugged mountains of the Kachin state in the north. "This is where the gold comes from," he said. "The British never explored these mountains properly, and we don't know exactly where the lode is. But we know gold is carried by gravity down the rivers of upper Myanmar and much of it ends up in the Chindwin and Irrawaddy rivers."

We ended up taking a close look at the Bawdwin mine, a silver and zinc mine near the Chinese border that had been in production since the days of the Ming dynasty emperors five hundred years ago. When the British took the area in the late 19th century, they brought in new mining methods and new miners. One of these was a young American mining engineer, early in the 20th century. He soon made a fortune for himself and his British employers when he sank a shaft into a rich lode of silver. His name was Herbert Hoover, later a president of the United States. In the end, the Canadians decided not to invest in the mine. The British burned it out in 1942 to deny it to the Japanese invaders and it was deemed too costly to put it back into proper running condition.

Neil was active in Paris and found a French producer, François Le Bayon, who put up funds to make our film. Getting permission for a foreign company to film in Burma can be difficult and expensive. Some of the places we needed to visit were off limits to foreigners. We needed special permission, which was given. Finding the right place to film was also a challenge. The location of gold fields changes constantly depending on where and how much gold the annual flood season brings down from the high country and where it is deposited. We knew where the current gold fields on the Chindwin were located, and we learned of another, larger, field on the Irrawaddy, just below the second defile of the river south of Bhamo.

I approached my friend Roland, who owned a travel agency among other things, and asked if he could assist with the necessary logistical arrangements for our crew to visit gold camps on both rivers and film them. We also needed to interview gold miners, and people involved with the production chain, mostly in the river town of Mandalay. Roland assigned the project to Yin Min Htay, a tall, softly-spoken Sino-Burmese woman who worked for his travel company, Shambhala. Yin Min was not only a supremely competent travel guide, she was a national heroine. She won a gold medal for Burma in rowing at the Southeast Asia Games. Yin Min was perfect person for this difficult assignment; she went on to assist me with other films and books.

We organized the film team. Neil was our director and cameraman. I was the producer. Our French backer, François, came along as executive producer. My son Seth was our production assistant. Roland recruited a jovial retired Burma Air Force colonel as interpreter, and Yin Min made it all happen. She went upcountry in advance and rented a 60-foot boat that served as an Irrawaddy waterbus to take us from one town to another. We removed the seats, set up sleeping quarters with mosquito nets up front, and installed a small round table midship to use for meals. The skipper's mother was our cook. She organized her galley in the stern just in front of our "head," or toilet, that hung suspended above the water at the aft end

Film crew for our documentary, *The Golden Road to Mandalay*, on our Irrawaddy River boat. From the left: Seth Broman, production assistant; Yin Min Htay, arranger; U Soe Myint, interpreter; Francis Le Bayon, co-producer; Neil Hollander, director.

of our sleek craft. The boat was covered, and in a brilliant move Yin Min created a platform above the bridge complete with chairs and a large umbrella, where we could mount a camera. We would be filming in style.

We spent most of our time on the Irrawaddy River, either in the gold fields or in Mandalay, where gold is smelted, pounded into leaf, or crafted into jewelry and sold. We began our trip in Bhamo, the northerly most navigable town on the river. In 1287 Kublai Khan's army marched into Burma through Bhamo, just 40 miles south of the Chinese border, on its way south to destroy the Burmese capital at Pagan, after the Burmese king had made the mistake of killing a Mongol envoy and his entourage.

In a stroke of good luck, our departure from Bhamo coincided with the visit of a Pandaw river-cruise boat. My Scottish friend Paul Strachan owned the Pandaw Company, and his riverboats were all built along the lines of the riverboats of the Irrawaddy Flotilla Company that plied the rivers of Burma in British colonial times. I had traveled on numerous Pandaw boats as photographer and sometime lecturer. Paul was on the boat on this upriver cruise, and invited our film crew to join a chartered flight bringing passengers for the downstream cruise of the *Pandaw*. I accepted with pleasure, and saw Paul briefly as we crossed paths at the airport.

Yin Min had moored our boat next to the *Pandaw*. I exchanged a few quick words with Paul, who sailed upriver on the *Pandaw* and with his passengers was flying back to Rangoon. We quickly boarded our boat and settled in with sleeping bags and all our film gear, to the amusement of the onlooking *Pandaw* passengers who would truly be traveling in style. Paul invited me to spend the night on the *Pandaw*, where I gave a short talk on the river and on Burma. As a seasoned traveler on the Irrawaddy, and on Pandaw boats, I quickly noted what a great treat they had ahead of them and gave them some of the river's history over the past millennium. I ended my brief talk saying that Neil, our film crew, and I would be setting off the next morning on our boat to the gold fields. That information led to a cry to adjust the *Pandaw*'s schedule to visit the gold fields. The key to the success of Pandaw boats is flexibility.

Life on our new boat was pleasant. With one charcoal stove our cook turned out tasty meals, including a dinner of fried river shrimp in peppers. We moved quickly down the river and had no trouble finding the gold field. There were scores of large gold dredges, boats that brought up the river sands containing gold. An average dredge would carry a crew of 8 to 10 people, including women, who would pan the sands brought up for gold. The dredges were tied up alongside each other, making a floating community of several thousand people. Small shops set up on shore, and sold food and drink to the gold miners. We started filming immediately, and thanks to the colonel quickly made some friends who invited us aboard their dredges to film the gold mining process. A day after we arrived we saw the *Pandaw* steaming towards us. It maneuvered close to our boat and dropped anchor. My comments to the passengers sparked the unscheduled stop. I gave them a quick tour of the gold camp and two hours later they sailed on.

Gold fever permeated the atmosphere. Like the lady we met on the Chindwin River the year before, everyone working the gold field wanted to strike it rich. Even small children would pan for gold along the riverbank. I was reminded of my maternal grandfather, Tom Foley, who left his father's farm on Prince Edward Island, Canada, for the gold rush in the Yukon late in the 19th century. He didn't find much gold, but made his money selling dry goods to miners, and bought a nice farm in British Columbia where my mother was born. It worked the same in Burma; people selling goods and services to the miners made the money.

After a week of shooting on the Irrawaddy, we shifted west to the Chindwin, a more remote and shallow river. Neil and I were already well and favorably known to the Chinese lady who owned the river-view restaurant in Hkamti. On a lucky day, one could eat wild sambaur deer from the jungles of Nagaland across the river. We traveled down the Chindwin on an open boat, and found the gold dredges sucking up gold sands along the river. After two days of shooting, Seth and I went back upriver to Hkamti and from there on to Mandalay to arrange for the translation of interviews. Neil, François, the colonel, and Yin Min continued down the Chindwin.

The entire team rendezvoused in Mandalay, the center of the gold business in Burma. We filmed gold being smelted into small ingots using an ancient method that is as dangerous as it is polluting. The smelter sold some of the small ingots to jewelers, others to gold-pounding shops where strong young men pound gold into gold leaf. Producing gold leaf is back-breaking work. Laborers wielding 14-pound hammers worked six hours a day producing pure gold leaf; 35,000 pieces per inch of gold. Buddhists faithfuly purchase the gold leaf and make merit by applying the leaf to images of the Buddha.

The Maha Muni Pagoda near Mandalay holds the most famous Buddha image in Burma. Over 12 feet high and thought to have been cast in the 2nd century CE, the Burmese took the image when they conquered the Arakan in 1784. They brought it in pieces to its present site and reassembled it. So much gold leaf has been put on the lower body of the image that it has become obese with gold. A successful miner makes merit by adding gold to the Maha Muni (Great Sage) before heading back to the gold fields for more.

Seth designed t-shirts commemorating the film, and before the team broke up we took a group photo on a riverbank. All the men wore Burmese sarongs (*longgyis*) while Yin Min, the lone lady, wore trousers. Everyone wore the souvenir t-shirts. At the end of the shoot Neil and François returned home to Paris to edit the film, while Seth and I headed for Bangkok for some R&R. We especially needed food different from the fried rice and noodles that was our main fare for weeks.

***

In 2002, the editors of *The Foreign Service Journal*, the house publication of the State Department, asked me to write an article about the drug trade in Southeast Asia. They had decided to focus on the worldwide narcotics trade for an upcoming issue of the magazine and saw me as a natural choice to write an article about Burma. In the article, "Rangoon: Key to Stopping the Opium Trade," I argued that poor US relations with the military regime in Rangoon hurt our joint efforts to curtail the flow of drugs from Burma.

Shortly after the article appeared, I received a phone call from a well-connected consulting firm in Washington DC. I wondered why a lobbying company would contact me. The caller said they had read my article and asked if I would be interested in working on a project funded by the government of Burma. I asked what the work would entail. The lobbyist, I'll call him Tom, explained that the prime minister of Burma, General Khin Nyunt, wanted to improve relations with the United States, and that counternarcotics was one of the few areas where we currently worked together. Khin Nyunt, considered a moderate in the ruling junta, was also the head of Burma's intelligence service. Khin Nyunt had hired the Washington firm to gain State Department "certification" that Burma was helping in the "war on drugs." With certification came additional assistance for counternarcotics programs. Having worked with the Burmese against drug lords in Burma, I thought Burma deserved to be certified. More importantly, so did the State Department and the Drug Enforcement Administration (DEA). My job would be to assist the firm in bringing the message to leaders in Washington DC. I said that I might be interested, but first they should run my name past Khin Nyunt, whom I had never met, to make sure that he was comfortable with me working on his behalf. Tom called back the next day; I was the guy the general wanted.

Things moved fast. The Burmese had scheduled an important drug burn for the next week in upper Burma and wanted me to attend as a guest of honor. The Burmese used drug burns as public relations events designed to show that they were serious about eradicating illegal narcotics. I took a flight from Seattle to Bangkok, where the Burmese consul general and two other officers from the Burmese embassy met me at midnight. The consul general handed me a ticket to Rangoon early the next morning. A junior Burmese whipped out a Polaroid camera to take my photo for my visa, which the consul general produced on the spot. Normally, it would take one to two days to get a visa at the embassy. The whole thing here took about 20 minutes. They dropped me at the airport hotel, and as I thanked the group for their assistance in getting me to Rangoon so quickly. The senior man enquired in a low voice, "May I ask who you are? I don't usually give visas at the airport at midnight." I referred him to Prime Minister Khin Nyunt for an explanation.

The next morning, after a one-hour flight in the first-class section of a Myanma Airways flight, I enjoyed a VIP welcome in Rangoon. Colonel Hla Min, the government spokesman and a senior intelligence officer and an old friend, met me at the foot of the plane. "Today," he said in his fluent English, "you will take the red carpet to the VIP arrival hall. Enjoy it, Barry," he said, with a smile, "it may never happen again." He was right.

I joined a distinguished group of senior American, Australian, and United Nations officials involved in counternarcotics programs in Burma for the showcase excursion into the northern Shan state, the main drug-producing part of Burma. Ethnic minorities, many of them former supporters of the Burmese Communist Party, which fought the central government for decades before it collapsed in 1989, still controlled much of this area. We visited several cities in the region where the Burmese authorities had confiscated large amounts of narcotics. Khin Nyunt hosted the event, which kicked off with a burning of opium poppies in Lashio. As a guest of the Burmese government, I took precedence over the invited ambassadors from China and Japan and the American chargé d'affaires, who ranked lower because the United States did not have an ambassador in Burma at that time.

The Burmese treated us to a rare visit into a part of Burma that was usually off limits to foreigners. Even Burmese troops were denied access to some areas as a result of ceasefire agreements in 1989. Rebel groups including the United Wa State Army, the Kokang Chinese, and other ethnic-minority opium growers largely controlled this area. In perhaps the most bizarre stop on the trip, our hosts took us to a drug museum on the China border in the area controlled by the Kokang. The museum provided a history of opium and heroin production in the area as if it was a thing of the past. One of the museum dioramas depicted the shooting down of a CIA aircraft in Burma in the 1950s. The shoot down happened, but the plane had not been supporting drug traffickers. The Burmese knew this, and so did we. At a welcoming ceremony hosted by Kokang leaders, the Burmese minister of interior, a congenial army colonel, leaned over and whispered to me, "We fought that son of a bitch for years when he was a communist. Now we will fight him as a drug lord."

The campaign to obtain certification from the US Congress was focused on officials who were involved with narcotics suppression. The lobby firm opened many doors. I gave detailed briefings on the cooperation that the Burmese had provided over the years, and at times Colonel Hla Min came with me to provide details. We briefed leading members of Congress and other opinion leaders in Washington DC. Our pitch was simple and direct: help Burma stop the flow of heroin from the Golden Triangle to markets in the West. While many officials expressed sympathy and support for the Burmese, assisted quietly by the State Department and DEA, we faced an uphill battle because of concerns over Burma's dismal human rights record and dictatorial military rule. In the minds of several elected officials, and especially their staffers, this overrode achieving greater cooperation on counternarcotics. As the aide of a senior senator put it to me after a briefing, "Your points are all good but you are wasting your time. US policy on Burma is controlled by Aung San Suu Kyi, and she wants no cooperation with the generals." He was correct. The lobbyists told Khin Nyunt that he was wasting his money and the project ended.

In 2004, hard-liner generals ousted General Khin Nyunt as prime minister and head of intelligence. They placed him under house arrest for the next seven years. His efforts to build bridges with the West had failed, and the hard-liners tightened their grip on power. Things began to change in 2010. In 2016 Aung San Suu Kyi's National League for Democracy ostensibly took power but in name only.

***

After the success of our gold mining film, and my work with the Burmese on counternarcotics, Neil and I received permission from Burmese intelligence to go where few filmmakers had gone before, into the Wa Hills of the northern Shan state, the heart of the area known as the Golden Triangle. This small remote area on the border with China was ruled by the United Wa State Army (UWSA) from the town of Pangsan right on the border. We wanted to tell the story of the tribal poppy growers in the remote China–Burma border country. We faced some serious challenges. The Burmese government forbade virtually all travel by foreigners, especially Westerners, in the area. Thanks to a 1989 ceasefire between the Burma Army and the United Wa State Army, even the Burma Army was not allowed in the rugged Wa Hills. With the demise of Khun Sa's drug operation, the Wa became the most important narcotics organization in the Golden Triangle. It had more than 20,000 men from various tribal groups under arms. I approached the Burmese with the idea of producing a film that would depict the hard life of an opium cultivator and the efforts of the United Nations, with support from the Burmese, to introduce new crops to the region. They approved our plan, as did the United Nations team in Burma.

The British colonial officials who first encountered the fierce "Wild-Wa" fighters in the late 19th century, wisely did not seriously attempt to bring this hill tribe under full submission, possibly due to their penchant for head hunting. As with maps of Nagaland, maps of the Wa hills were marked "unadministered territory." If the Brits had been less eager to paint more areas red on the map of the world, they would have put the Wa area in China where it probably belonged. After independence from Britain in 1948, the Burmese Communist Party (BCP) in their struggle against the Burmese government recruited many Wa on both sides of the border. These tough little hill men fought for decades as foot soldiers for an insurgency, which was heavily supported by China. That ended in 1989 when the BCP self-destructed and a fragile peace broke out. Many of the tribal groups were still armed, living in regions designated as Special Zones where they enjoyed a large degree of independence and turned to narcotics smuggling as a new source of income and enjoyed a large degree of independence.

In the 1980s, the State Department ran a very effective program with Burma resulting in the United States giving Burma helicopters to assist in the war on drugs. The Burmese were motivated to work with the Americans and the UN because groups like the UWSA who challenged Burma's sovereignty controlled much of the area under cultivation. I approached my old counterpart and explained what we wanted to do. He liked the idea and gave us permission to proceed. The UN narcotics office in Rangoon also liked the idea and offered critical logistics support.

We flew to the Shan town of Keng Tung. Bad weather forced the vintage Myanma Airways Fokker-28 to fly over Keng Tung and landed at Tachilek on the Thai border. While waiting for the weather to clear, I asked our veteran pilot what he thought the chances were of getting into Keng Tung.

"Not too good," he said. "You might enjoy a day or two in Tachilek shopping and sightseeing."

"If we can't get in today," I said, " please radio the tower at Keng Tung and have them tell the DDSI officers who are waiting for us that we will have to delay our trip."

"DDSI?" he asked. "They are waiting for you?" Few Burmese want to get on the wrong side of Military Intelligence.

"Yes but safety comes first," I nodded.

"No problem," he said. "We will fly under the weather." And so we did.

Several senior intelligence officers as well as a UN van and driver were waiting to welcome us to the Shan state, the largest of the Shan states. We were introduced to the army major who was to be our "escort." He seemed none too happy to have the honor. As the counternarcotics chief for the Shan state, he had just been ordered into the den of the largest drug trafficking organization in Burma, if not the world. Sensing his unease, I thanked him for his support and said that once we get to Mong Pawk it might be best if he stayed in the UN compound, where he would not come to the attention of the Wa. We would rely on the UN for security as we filmed in the hills and conducted our interviews. He concurred.

The UN—the lone international presence in the Wa Hills—had 72 local workers from at least six ethnic groups, under the direction of a tireless and savvy Frenchman named Xavier Bouan, whose main task was to persuade farmers to switch from poppies to other crops. Given the importance that opium plays in the local economy and

Soldiers of the United Wa State Army, a major drug-trafficking organization in Burma, buying raw opium from a woman in the Shan state. They forced her to sell before she arrived at Mong Pawk where she would have received a better price.

the firm control that the UWSA has over the growers, Bouan faced an uphill battle. The UN team hosted us during our two weeks filming in the beautiful hill country.

The drive north took eight hours over bad roads, away from the lush valleys and into a region controlled by remnants of the Burma Communist Party (BCP), an area with virtual autonomy from Burmese control and little, if any, Burmese government presence. A good example was the town of Mong La, which we passed on our drive north. After five bone-jarring hours on the road we crested a hill in the dark, to find a brightly lit town with a searchlight scanning the sky. This in-area electricity is a rarity. The town, right on the border of China was full of gambling casinos, massage parlors, opulent Chinese restaurants, and a vibrant nightlife, all for the benefit of Chinese tourists who did not need visas to visit this Special Zone (number 4). It was Las Vegas in the jungle. We were now nearing the Wa Hills where Burmese money was not accepted (only Chinese RMB), the Burmese flag was not flown (only the Wa flag), and where the Burma Army was not allowed. Products in the markets seemed to have all come from China. The principal products going out seemed to be narcotics and timber.

Luckily, our trip coincided with Lahu New Year, which the hill tribes marked with a particularly large, boisterous and photogenic festival in Mong Pawk. Since most of the Lahu tribesmen were in the Wa army, they walked around in uniform. Recalling the earlier Lahu devotion to the BCP, girls danced around a hammer-and-sickle flag of the old communist party. People from all over the region—the Wa, Lahu, Paluang, and Kachin—all dressed in their colorful traditional clothes filled the markets. An anthropologists' dream—it was a policeman's nightmare. Hill tribe farmers openly traded their raw opium with smugglers in exchange for Chinese currency or, as had been more common in the past, old silver rupees from India. Wa soldiers, armed with guns, kept a watchful eye on the scene. The Wa army recruited from all tribal groups and some of the soldiers appeared to be in their early teens. The USWA was the only buyer. As the only buyer, the USWA set the price and often intercepted tribeswomen heading to town to force the sale of their opium.

We spent one night at a mountaintop Lahu village during the festival, which coincided with the opium harvest. We slept in the village medical dispensary quite comfortably, despite the cool night. At dawn we looked down on clouds covering the valley below. The village chief, a senior officer of the Wa army and a former BCP officer, invited us to join in a New Year's breakfast. The Lahu were all dressed in their finest tribal clothes. They served us one of the best breakfasts of my life. Certainly, it was the best meal I ever ate with opium-growing communists on a mountain top. It included Chinese delicacies, many of them new to me, all of them delicious. We washed the food down with several brands of aged Cognac, a breakfast first for me. Our hosts provided tea for the ladies in the party.

After breakfast I asked the chief if there would be any opium-harvesting that day. The grizzled old fellow, who clearly had been ordered to take good care of us, obliged by telling several young Lahu maidens to harvest a few poppies for us. Two minutes later, we followed them over the household fence to an opium field. Wearing their best blue silk finery, the girls scored poppy bulbs for our cameras, letting the milky sap ooze out. In the afternoon they would return, probably in their working clothes, to scrape off the black sap that had hardened. Locals smoke this raw opium but most of it would be transformed into heroin for the export market.

Another day, we visited a Paluang village, where a village elder greeted us and allowed us to film him smoking the first of his many pipes that day. The UN and Wa leaders were trying to suppress opium smoking, but our host's age and status exempted him from the program that required tribesmen addicted to opium to attend a month-long rehabilitation program. Habitual smokers are easily identified by their thumbs, which are stained black by repeatedly affixing sticky raw opium to their pipes. The old boy invited us to smoke his pipe. Out of courtesy, I had a few puffs of the thin fumes but I didn't inhale. We left the old smoker to his dreams and followed two of his daughters into one of his opium fields to film them scoring poppies.

All of the cultivators we filmed and interviewed were friendly and cooperative. One particularly affable Kachin lady—perhaps about 80 years old—identified herself as Xavier's "girlfriend." With the help of a Kachin interpreter, we recorded an excellent interview with her on the verandah of her bamboo hut, while the young French UN chief beamed off-camera. With incredible clarity she gave us a quick rundown on the history of her village over the past 70 years, including the wartime Japanese and Thai occupations and the return of the British. On the subject of opium, she became very serious. She said she would never give up opium cultivation or smoking because she needed to "chase the dragon."

Early on during our visit to Mong Pawk, Xavier informed me that I had an appointment with Pao Yu-hsiang, commander in chief of the United Wa State Army, at his headquarters in Pangsan on the China border, a few hours away by car. I was taken aback. We did not request an interview with the drug lord and had hoped to make our film in the Wa Hills as quietly as possible. I wondered why Mr. Pao wanted to see us. I hoped he had never heard of me, and my government background.

We dutifully appeared at the heavily guarded headquarters of the United Wa State Army, located only a few yards from China. Pao Yu-hsiang's men cordially welcomed our team, including UN-provided interpreters, and escorted us to a reception room. There we found a group of unsmiling men, seated on the opposite side of a table with a green tablecloth. I recognized Pao Yu-hsiang from his wanted poster. Kevin set up his camera on a tripod while Neil and I sat opposite the USWA leaders. Pao welcomed us in his tribal tongue. The interpreters translated his comments from Wa into Burmese, and then English. His comments were translated from Wa into Burmese, and then English. It was going to be a long interview. I responded by

With Neil Hollander and drug warlord Pao Yu-hsiang, Chairman of the Wa United State Army at his headquarters in Pangsang in the northern state of Burma on the border with China. Burmese military intelligence arranged for us without our knowledge to interview Pao for our documentary film, *Flowers of Death*, about drugs in the Golden Triangle. At the time, the Wa army had a 20,000-man armed force.

thanking him for granting an on-camera interview and explained that our film sought to document the efforts of the UN to help farmers substitute poppies with other crops in the Wa Hills.

Pao nodded his approval and then asked who we were. I said we were from Adventure Film Productions and introduced Neil, the director, and Kevin, our cameraman.

"I know all that," Pao said. "But three days ago I was celebrating Wa New Year with my mother in my village and I got a call from DDSI saying that I needed to get to Pangsan to be interviewed for a film. So tell me again, who are you?"

"I am very sorry," I said. "When DDSI gave us permission to make this film I did not ask for the interview. The general must have thought it would be better if you were interviewed so here we are."

"You know the general?" he asked.

"I know him well," I said.

"OK, no problem, let's do the interview," said the warlord.

Throughout the lengthy interview, Pao Yu-hsiang insisted that he was getting out of the heroin business, blaming high overhead and low profit margins. He complained about the high cost of maintaining a large armed force to protect his "state." He claimed to have more than 40 other businesses, including an airline, a bank, fruit plantations, and several jade mining operations, all of which were less troublesome than trafficking heroin in a hostile environment. He didn't mention the price placed on his head by the Americans. I asked about his involvement in the growing methamphetamine trade that was causing major problems in Thailand, where the drug, known there as *yaba* (crazy medicine), found a ready market with Thai youths. He denied making meth (a lie). Since all the precursor chemicals needed to make the drug had to be smuggled into the Wa hills, he argued it was easier and cheaper to make the meth in Thailand.

At the end of the freewheeling interview, Pao asked, "When are you going back to Burma?"

"We are in Burma," I responded.

"No," Pao said tartly. "You are in the Wa State." I didn't argue with him and we ended the interview. It sure looked like the Wa State to me; no Burmese government presence, no Burmese flags flying and no Burmese currency accepted, only Chinese.

***

To counter the less-than-accurate comments of the drug lord, we obtained permission from the American Drug Enforcement Administration (DEA) to interview their chief in Burma, John Whalen, whom I had met earlier on the drug burn hosted by General Khin Nyunt. John knew a lot about Pao and his drug trafficking. A fluent Burmese speaker, John gave us a concise and accurate account of the true state of affairs with the Wa traffickers. Later, John told me that the Wa army had grown to 30,000 men to protect their illicit activities.

***

There is a saying, undoubtedly of Scottish origin: the blood and sweat of Scotsmen built the British Empire and the English lost it. This is especially true of Burma, and a good example is the Irrawaddy Flotilla Company (IFC), a company formed in Glasgow in 1865 that was destined to have the largest fleet of privately owned boats in the world. In its heyday the IFC employed more than 11,000 men, about 200 of them Scotsmen. The largest of the IFC fleet were the Siam-class boats, 325 feet in length and licensed to carry 4,000 passengers. Alas, the fleet met an ugly end in 1942, when more than 600 vessels were scuttled in the Irrawaddy and Chindwin rivers to deny them to the invading Imperial Japanese Army.

The fortunes of Scots in Burma improved when Paul Strachan revived the tradition of Scottish enterprise on the rivers of Burma. I met Paul in Rangoon in 1995, who walked in the footsteps of his Hibernean forebears, when he saved an aging IFC boat, the RV *Pandaw* from the knackers yard near Rangoon and established the Pandaw River Cruises.

Over the years, mostly after my retirement from government service, I traveled on many of Paul's boats that sailed the rivers of Southeast Asia and India, usually as a working photographer and sometimes as a lecturer. Whether it's on the Irrawaddy, the Chindwin, or the Ganges, traveling on a Pandaw boat takes you back in time. There is no finer way to enjoy the great rivers of Southeast Asia than on the teak deck of a Pandaw boat watching the passing landscape. Waiters announce haute cuisine meals, both Eastern and Western, with the gentle sound of a Burmese brass gong. Whenever I am with Paul on a Pandaw voyage I rest easy. He is a master of problem handling, fast thinking, and being decisive in challenging situations. It's chaps like him who used to build empires.

Every trip on a Pandaw vessel provides adventure, albeit one couched in luxury with an international staff making the experience an elegant one. I had about as much adventure as I could handle in 2002 when Paul invited me to accompany him on the maiden voyage of the RV *Mekong Pandaw* up the Mekong river from Saigon (Ho Chi Minh City to some) in Vietnam to Angkor Wat in Cambodia via the Tonle Sap River and the Tonle Sap Lake. We rendezvoused in Saigon, where I had installed myself in the old colonial Majestic Hotel at the end of rue Catinat, later Tu Do Street, now Giai Phong, still the classiest street in Saigon. The new name of the city is Ho Chi Minh City but I still go with the old name as many of the locals do.

We set off from the port of Saigon on the first, and only, voyage of the RV *Mekong Pandaw* from Saigon. Our planned route took us down a canal under the My Tho Bridge, into the Mekong River, across the Great Lake of Cambodia (the Tonle Sap) to Siem Reap, and then back to Saigon. We made a good start along the Cho Gao Canal, enjoying shoreline scenes of Vietnamese at work and at play. All kinds of boats were chugging up and down the canal. We faced our first challenge at the town of My Tho where the canal met the Mekong. We saw immediately that clearance under the My Tho Bridge was going to be tight. Paul had built the boat so that the railing on the upper deck could be lowered for this very situation. Unfortunately, thanks to several layers of paint, the railing wouldn't budge.

We reached the bridge at full tide and realized we would not be able to sail under it. Paul arranged an impromptu excursion ashore while we waited for the water level to drop. That happened late at night. Paul and I stood on the bridge with a seaman with a measuring tape in his hand watching the boat inch toward us against the current. The boat pulled into the middle of the canal where the bridge was at its highest. Paul talked to the skipper of the *Pandaw* on a mobile phone as it approached the bridge. I had a camera in hand. It was going to be very tight. The boat passed under the bridge with a clearance of 4 inches (10 centimeters). We breathed a sigh of relief as we scrambled back on board. Later, we learned that everyone on the crew had wagered a bet on whether we would get under the bridge. The odds were against our making it, but for Paul this was just another day at the office.

From the Mekong Delta we motored north towards Cambodia. On this maiden voyage into Cambodia we encountered delays at the border putting us further behind schedule. When it became clear that we were not going to make the provincial town of Kompong Cham before dark, Paul instructed the reluctant Vietnamese skipper to put in at a small town. Pandaw boats, in the finest tradition of the old IFC, do not require piers or docks to put in to shore. As the boat nudged the river bank, an agile seaman leaped ashore and a large rope was thrown to him. Other lascars followed with stakes and a heavy mallet. In a few minutes the boat was moored fore and aft to the stakes, and the gangplank was run out. There were no steps up the riverbank so crewmen swiftly dug steps out of the soft soil and we were ready to go ashore.

By this time quite a crowd had gathered, looking at the strange, large unexpected boat. We went ashore and I used all my Cambodian and some French to explain to a local official that we would like to walk around town before proceeding up river to Kompong Cham the next morning. No problem. Serendipitously, we had landed on the day of the Bon Om Tauk festival, known in Thailand as Loy Krathong. This delightful event takes place on the evening of the full moon of the 12th lunar month, when locals pay respect to the river spirits. Small containers, traditionally made of banana leaves, filled with offerings such as food, incense, and candles, are then floated on rivers, canals, or ponds. The town officials invited the passengers of the *Pandaw* to participate in this colorful ancient ritual, to the delight of all concerned. Our passengers had a rare opportunity to take part in a festival without planning or fanfare.

After a short visit to Kompong Cham the next day we proceeded to Phnom Penh, the capital of Cambodia, where we spent the night. Phnom Penh sits at the confluence of the Mekong and Tonle Sap rivers. The Tonle Sap River is the world's only river that reverses course during the year. When the Mekong, fed by snow melt in the Himalayas, is high it pushes water up the Tonle Sap River to the Great Lake of Cambodia called the Tonle Sap. The new water fills the lake, which triples in size every year. In the dry season the lake water drains away, reversing the flow of the river.

In Phnom Penh, Paul arranged a small cocktail party on board for the passengers and some VIP Cambodian guests, including a few friends of mine from the royal

Scotsman Paul Strachan, founder and owner of Pandaw River Cruises, pulls away from the RV *Mekong Pandaw* in the Great Lake of Cambodia (Tonle Sap) on the maiden voyage of the boat from Saigon in Vietnam to Angkor Wat in Cambodia in 2002. Due to dangers of the shallow lake and high winds, this was the only time the boat crossed the lake. (Bob Peterson)

family. A troupe of classical Cambodian ballet dancers performed on the teak deck. Paul also laid on a quick cruise around the confluence of rivers for his Cambodian guests, who were all delighted to see such an elegant boat in Cambodian waters.

After Phnom Penh we cruised up the Tonle Sap River, which was bustling with commerce. Villages dotted the river banks. Most Cambodians follow Theravada Buddhism and almost every village had at least one temple, its gold spires sparkling in the sunshine. However, we also passed a number of villages with mosques built by the Muslim Cham minority. The Cham have a long and distinguished history. A thousand years ago they controlled much of southern Vietnam, and in 1177 CE they conquered Angkor. The Khmer Rouge, who ruthlessly tried to wipe out the Cham, destroyed many of the mosques along the river in the 1970s. The 5th Brigade of the Khmer Republics army was composed almost entirely of Cham, and fought well after the war in the losing cause.

At length, we arrived at the Great Lake. Wide but very shallow, the lake hosts a number of floating villages of fishermen. Its waters provide rich nutrients as the lake expands in flood. The lake produces a prodigious quantity of fish, including catfish weighing more than 50 pounds. Cambodians make a fermented fish sauce from the lake's bounty, esteemed by the people of Cambodia as a national treasure.

I love *pra hok*, but it is an acquired taste and I have rarely met a foreigner who has made the acquisition.

After a pleasant and uneventful crossing of the lake, we made our way through a floating village and moored near the provincial town of Siem Reap near the ruins of the great Cambodian civilization of Angkor that flourished for hundreds of years before falling to invading Siamese (Thai) in 1431 CE. This was the end of the trip for Paul and me.

I spent a few days photographing sites in and around Angkor Wat. On the voyage I met a Japanese tour operator leading a group of tourists. He stayed to guide a new group down to Saigon. When I returned home and was editing film from the trip, I sent a few photos to the Japanese tour operator. He wrote back and thanked me and reported the near disaster befell *Mekong Pandaw* on its return across the Great Lake. A freak storm blew up on the lake and heavy winds hit the boat broadside. It caused considerable damage to the boat and much distress to the passengers, who were just beginning their Indochina adventure. The boat never ventured onto the lake again and as a result of the challenges of passing under the My Tho Bridge in Vietnam, all future sailings started at My Tho and not Saigon.

***

At my last posting I was introduced to the ancient, arcane, and complicated fascination by the Burmese with the pre-Buddhist practice of spirit worship. The spirits are called *nats* who are propitiated in harmony with observance of Theravada Buddhism. In retirement, I had time to spend more time to study both the Burmese spirits and their Thai cousins. Most Burmese both venerate and fear *nats* and communicate with them through mediums called *nat kadaw*. In Thailand, spirits called *phi* are honored by daily offerings to small houses in the grounds of their homes and businesses. I photographed a book on this topic with Bill Warren, *Spiritual Abodes in Thailand*.

The Burmese deal very differently with their spirits who are more dangerous than their Thai counterparts. *Nat* worship operates at many levels. Ma Thanegi identifies three main groupings. The highest, the celestials, reside at the mythical Mount Meru. Guardian *nats* occupy the second level. They are pervasive, protecting individuals, villages, even trees. A house will often have a shrine for its guardian *nat*. The third level of *nats* are deceased human beings. The Burmese have identified 37 such *nats*, each of whom died violently. These *nats* are the center of cults that include two brothers, the Taungpyone brothers, whose annual festival is a national event, the largest of its type in Burma.

In 2003, my friend Roland encouraged me to attend Burma's largest *nat* festival in the town of Taungpyone in upper Burma near Mandalay. I suggested to Neil that we film the event. He was up for it, and brought his wife, Regine, with him from France. Our production assistant was Brendan, our younger son. Roland arranged interviews with experts on *nat* worship who would assist us at the festival. I touched base with my friend in military intelligence to let them know what we were doing. In this case I didn't ask for any assistance, the festival was open to the public. We made Mandalay our base because the small village of Taungpyone increases tenfold during the festival, when worshippers of the Taungpyone brothers descend en masse making lodging difficult to find. As with every trip I make to Mandalay, I hired my old friend Ko Ko Gyi ("call me George"), an excellent driver and guide.

Communications with *nat*s must go through a medium, or *nat kadaw*. Traditionally, the mediums were mainly women, but in recent decades male transvestites have essentially made the profession their own. Hired mediums will dance, usually after or while imbibing alcoholic beverages to please the *nat*s. They do not pass messages to the spirits. Their job is to make the *nat*s happy. Mediums with well-heeled patrons may quaff Johnny Walker whiskey, neat from the bottle, while a medium operating on a smaller budget makes do with Mandalay rum or even moonshine. Drinking is common but not mandatory, except when propitiating the Min Kya Nat, the patron *nat* of gamblers and drunkards. He rides a nut-brown stallion and is my personal favorite.

The festival lasts nine days. Taungpyone becomes one extremely large party. Hundreds of stalls spring up selling food, souvenirs, statues of *nat*s, alcohol, and offerings for the *nat*s. Offerings include bunches of *dawna* leaves with their heady aroma or *thalwe*, thought to be the most auspicious of leaves. In the first major event of the festival, worshippers parade wooden statues of the two brothers—each about two-feet high, gilded, and with each brother brandishing swords—through town. Legend says that the brothers were princes in the court of 11th-century King Anawratha of Pagan. Pampered and spoiled, they were known for living wild and seducing young ladies. One day, the king ordered a pagoda to be built at Taungpyone. He demanded that each of his men contribute one brick for the construction. The brothers were off partying and did not obey the order. Vexed, the king had them executed. Their statues reside in a shrine all year and when the festival begins in the lunar month of Wagaung (August or September) they are brought out and paraded before thousands of admirers who have assembled to pay homage.

We arrived early in order to film the parading of the brothers' statues. Neil and Brendan were busy with the camera and tripod and I set off shooting still photos and scouting sites for the camera. A young man wearing dark glasses approached me. He had "cop" written all over him. He spoke to me.

"Camera OK. No video," he said pointing to Neil and Brendan who were setting up a tripod for filming.

"Are you police or DDSI"? I enquired.

Taken aback, he answered, "DDSI." Military intelligence.

"Good" I said. "Please ask your senior officer to inform DDSI headquarters that Mr. Broman and his party is here safely and that you have made contact."

He quickly disappeared but was back 15 minutes later. "Video OK," he said. It was fortuitous that I had let the general know we would be filming at the festival. The lieutenant attached himself to us in a friendly way. What did we need? What did we want? That night the *nat kadaw*s went to work, and so did we. Mediums dance and speak to the brothers in 15-minute increments throughout the festival, with groups of up to 50 allowed into the small shrine. Cameras are not allowed inside the shrine. I needed to find a site where we could set up the camera to film the mediums at work in front of the brothers. The lieutenant approached.

"Can I help," he asked?

"We need a place to set up our camera to film the brothers," I answered.

"Why not go inside?" he said.

"Cameras are not allowed," I explained.

"Allowed," he said. The problem was solved. We went inside and set up close (but not too close) to the stern-looking statues of the brothers and filmed *nat kadaw*s dancing and drinking while communicating with the brothers.

The action at the festival takes place at night when dozens of mediums perform throughout the town in makeshift theaters filled with images of the brothers (and other *nat*s) while thousands of adherents look on. The whole event dissolves into one huge block party fueled by alcohol. Everyone treated our little group as honored guests. We were constantly invited to film and interview *nat kadaw*s, who were delighted to be immortalized on film. The dancing and drinking went on until the wee hours. We experienced a unique opportunity to witness and document one of Burma's most interesting, and least understood, cultural traditions. I never saw any tourists during the festival. This was the real deal. Of course, things might have changed since then.

As we said our goodbyes, I thanked our DDSI watchdog, who had almost become part of the crew. I told him I would put in a good word with the general when we returned to Rangoon as I slipped him a carton of 555 brand cigarettes, a small but appreciated gesture. Alas, the film was never finished. I published the photos in Ma Thanegi's book *Nats: Spirits of Fortune and Fear.*

***

I kept in contact with my barrister Roland after I retired and in my incarnation as a consultant introduced him to a number of foreign companies and people interested in investing in Burma. He continued my education into all things Burmese. Always fun to be around, I saw Roland's Puckish side the day he took me to a hole-in-the-wall restaurant featuring the food of Madras in India. The place looked one step up from street food but Roland assured me I would not get sick. Every dish threatened to be spicy beyond my comfort zone. Roland insisted I try some small skewers of round meat in a fiery sauce. They were chewy but delicious. With a smile, Roland informed me they were goat testicles. He seemed disappointed when I did not run screaming from the room.

Roland was very helpful in putting me in contact with senior officials for business projects. One time, I needed to meet senior mining officials for a client. Roland immediately telephoned General David Abel, a particularly pleasant and effective fellow who was the economic czar of Burma during the 1990s. A Burmese of mixed blood, Abel was a graduate of the British Royal Military College at Sandhurst, and had served in many senior posts, including minister of commerce and minister of finance. Two hours after Roland's call, we were seated in Abel's office in the Secretariat, the seat of Burma's government. When I told the general I needed to speak to senior people involved with mining, he picked up the phone, spoke to the minister responsible and said I would be coming to see him the next day. Mission accomplished. Then, hearing that I was a Burmese history buff, the affable general walked me down the corridor and into a room where a meeting was in progress. "Don't mind me," he said in English to the startled military men. "Just showing my friend where Aung San was murdered," and proceeded to give me the gory details of the death of Burma's leader in 1947 who was shot to death by rival Burmese politicians six months before the country achieved full independence from Britain.

Roland flourished in the new millennium and in time he left his humble cottage for an impressive four-story mansion he built 50 yards away, looking out at Inya Lake toward the dilapidated residence of General Ne Win, who was living in penury and disgrace under house arrest. The guns that once kept intruders out, now kept Ne Win in. The worm had turned. Sometimes, there is justice in the world after all.

On May 2, 2008, Cyclone Nargis, the worst natural disaster to hit Burma in its recorded history, struck, killing more than 138,000 people, most of them in the Irrawaddy Delta. I was in Rangoon at the time. The day before the cyclone hit, I gave a talk at the American embassy on traveling off the beaten track in Burma. I was staying with my French friend Patrick Robert, and when the cyclone hit, spent the night trying to save Patrick's art collection after the roof blew off his house in Golden Valley. Big trees were going down all around us. The heroine of that long night was Patrick's young daughter, Belle. Speaking Burmese, French, and English, she handled the panicked staff with coolness and courage. Her Shan mother, Claudia, was away on business so Belle stepped in and did what Claudia would have done.

The next morning, I began photographing the damage and aftermath of the storm. With great difficulty, I made my way to Roland's house on Pyay Road. The house was intact, but the lawn was strewn with limbs from trees and hundreds of unripe mangoes. Despite the damage all around, Roland insisted in driving me slowly around Rangoon, where I documented the damage and the cooperative spirit of the city's population pitching in to clear the debris of thousands of downed trees,

U Ye Htoon, also known as Roland, practicing his chipping at his lakeside home in Rangoon. The American and British-trained lawyer was a son of a former minister of justice of Burma and was imprisoned for opposing military rule in Burma. He didn't live to see democracy return to Burma, still a dream yet to happen.

all without the benefit of any power tools. I made it to Bangkok on the first plane out when the airport reopened. My first call was to Denis Grey at the Associated Press. The AP had no photos of the disaster. I went straight to his office, made a quick sale and my photos went around the world with the byline AP Photo by Barry Broman. I received dozens of emails from friends around the world asking why had I returned to work for the AP after a hiatus of 45 years.

In 2013, I wrote and photographed a book titled *Myanmar: The Land and its People*. It is dedicated to Roland. The photo on the dedication page shows Roland chipping a golf ball onto the putting green of his lawn across an inlet of Inya Lake in Rangoon across from the home of Ne Win, the man who caused Burma, and Roland, so much pain. This time Roland was alive and prosperous while Ne Win was disgraced and alone. I view this as an example of karma in action.

***

Kipling's "Road to Mandalay" was actually a river, the Irrawaddy. This mighty river rises in the mountains of the Himalayas and waters the heartland of Burma. In 2004 I embarked on a new book project to photograph this extraordinary river. My friend John Stevenson wrote the text. John, an Englishman and Oxford University graduate, was a true Asia hand. He spent much of his career in Hong Kong and Southeast Asia, first as a businessman and then in the publishing world. He was very supportive of many of my various projects. To produce the book, *Irrawaddy: Benevolent River of Burma*, we traveled much of the treacherous river, in part on a luckless government boat that ran aground and on a luxury cruiser that cruised in circles to avoid sandbars and disaster.

Our trip started in Bhamo, near Burma's border with China. We steamed slowly down the river heading for Mandalay on a newly built boat operated by the Burmese government. We traveled first class for $30 and were the only passengers on the upper deck. Several hundred passengers, including small children, crowded below on an open deck. Surrounded by products and live animals they would sell downstream, they slept on grass mats. The boat had no restaurant, but vendors on the lower deck turned out tasty meals of questionable sanitary quality all day long.

John, a seasoned birder, had an active time identifying a variety of migratory birds on the picturesque upper Irrawaddy. One languid afternoon, he bounded up observing ruddy shelducks on a sandbar and observed that these could have been the same birds he had seen in Mongolia earlier that summer.

We had the run of the upper deck, a perfect platform for photography. The only other Western passenger on board was a Greek named Nick who paid for a second-class ticket but dared to climb to the upper deck, reserved for first-class passengers, i.e. John and me. Nick was on vacation from Crete, where he owned a small bed and breakfast hotel. He said he was on assignment taking pictures and writing for his hometown newspaper. The portly skipper, who never cracked a smile, largely ignored us as he navigated the ever-changing river. We kept out of his way as he continually paced the deck, keeping his eye on navigational aids on shore. The Irrawaddy is an unforgiving river, with a channel that changes daily and water levels that can rise or fall many feet without warning.

The skipper had good reason to pay close attention to the vagaries of the river. We were traveling in winter, when water levels on the river were at their lowest. As we made ready to land at the sizable river town of Katha, the boat stuck fast in the sandy river bottom. We had missed the channel and run aground only a few hundred meters from the city. The captain was franticly shouting orders to the engine room while giving other orders to his harried crew, to no good effect. Gradually, passengers bound for Katha gave up hope for an on-time arrival and began jumping onto enterprising small craft that had put out from Katha as impromptu ferries.

John Stevenson examining a small butterfly that landed on his finger while we were working on our book about the Irrawaddy River.

We spent the night on the sandbar under clear skies filled with a million stars. Large boats summoned to our rescue pulled us off the sand in the morning. We put into Katha in glorious early morning light and took in a scene right out of old Asia. As some laborers ferried goods off the boat, other loaded it with new wares. Dozens of food vendors sought to sell their wares alongside the boat, while locals casually bathed or washed clothes in the river a few feet away.

For a photographer, it was a visual overload, and I moved quickly around the upper deck recording the vibrant river scene around me. One digital Nikon camera had an 18–135mm zoom lens, while the other had a 70–300mm zoom lens. In hog heaven, I kept both cameras busy documenting the colorful, controlled chaos around the boat. Nick noticed my rapture and shadowed me, occasionally taking photos of scenes I had taken moments before. When I finally rested to wipe the sweat out of my eyes, Nick said a strange thing.

"You piss me off!"

"Why?" I asked.

"Because of you, I have taken six photos."

"So why does that upset you?" I asked.

"Because I have only one roll of film and it must last me all month." With that, he went below to conserve film and I resumed shooting.

Katha is famous among Westerners for two things. First, a young Eric Blair worked there as a British police officer in the 1920s. He later wrote a novel based on his unhappy experiences in Katha under his *nom de plume*, George Orwell. As we walked around the town, I could find no one who had ever heard of Blair or his famous book, *Burmese Days*.

Katha's other claim-to-fame was as the site of the mass scuttling of many of the boats of the Irrawaddy Flotilla Company fleet in the spring of 1942. The British destroyed the boats to deny them to the invading Japanese army, which was rapidly pushing the British out of Burma into India. Hundreds of beautiful riverboats had their bottoms riddled with machine-gun fire as they settled into the mud along the riverbank. Today, a few salvaged ships' bells can be seen at the Katha fire station.

Behind schedule, we continued down river. At a small town the boat put in to offload and take on new passengers. I saw Nick on shore and called out, asking where he was going. "Mogok," he answered, a town famous for being the source of the world's finest rubies. "It's off limits to foreigners," I shouted. In response, Nick shrugged his shoulders, waved goodbye, and started walking away from the shore. I hope he still had some film in his camera.

I was worried that the boat would not make it to Mandalay on time for John and me to catch the Orient-Express boat *Road to Mandalay*. We were invited to join a two-day cruise down to Pagan. The former Rhine River cruise ship was the finest boat afloat on the Irrawaddy but was heavy and had difficulty negotiating the river at low water levels. The sun had fallen when we put into Kyaukmyaung, a river town known for its large ceramic water jars. The captain announced that it was getting too dark to navigate the treacherous channel, a lesson he had learned the night before in Katha. If we stayed with the boat we would miss our ride in Mandalay. We grabbed our gear and jumped ship. By luck and with a fist full of Burmese currency, I arranged passage for us on a goods truck heading for Mandalay.

The driver was nice enough to drop us at the old US consulate in Mandalay. Although the consulate had closed years before, the embassy maintained the building for the use of embassy officers, and friends, visiting Mandalay. I was in the latter category and gladly paid my $25 fee to stay at the stately old colonial mansion. Unfortunately, we discovered that the caretaker had gone to Rangoon to collect his pay and that the keys to the house went with him. Undeterred, we walked the short distance to the charming and inexpensive Swan Hotel, which looks out on the old palace moat.

The next morning we learned that we had not needed to jump ship after all. Because of low water, the *Road to Mandalay* was unable to steam up to Mandalay. We decided to drive to Pagan and board the boat there. My favorite driver in Mandalay, Ko Ko Gyi, was available and he whisked us down to Pagan in about five hours. We had no trouble finding the boat, which was cruising slowly in circles up and down the river. A small boat ferried us out. We spent the day on board drinking Champagne as we cruised past hundreds of surviving temples of the ancient city, heedless to the complaints of paying passengers who were unable to cruise to Mandalay. In the end, the boat's owners bused them up on the real road to Mandalay.

The finest jade in the world comes from Burma and the best Burmese jade comes from the area around Hpakant in the Uru Valley of the Kachin State. This is jadeite, coveted by Chinese emperors for centuries as "the stone of heaven." In 1784 CE, the emperor Qianlong extended the power of the Middle Kingdom into the remote and malarial valley and took possession of the jade mines. Today, the Burmese military controls the area but Chinese enthusiasm for jade is still enormous and the Chinese are still at work in the mines. For decades, Hpakan was off limits to foreigners. Even the world's top buyers had to have special permission to visit the area. The Burmese government, however, made an exception for the Chinese who under special deals made with the military junta brought thousands of Chinese miners with heavy equipment into the Uru valley.

Some years ago, I asked a Burmese friend with connections to see if Neil Hollander and I could visit Hpakan. After some negotiating, we were allowed to spend two nights in the valley and had permission to film and photograph jade mining. Getting

A Chinese jade buyer examines a large jade boulder in Hpakant, Burma, the center of the finest jade in the world. Normally, foreigners are not allowed to visit Hpakant but this does not count Chinese jade dealers and miners who have made special deals with the military rulers of Burma.

to Hpakan is easier said than done. It is a bone-jarring seven-hour drive from Myitkyina, capital of the Kachin state, in the dry season when the road is passable. In the monsoon season the road is often washed out and the valley is cut off.

We traveled in the dry season. With some effort and a little luck we made it to Hpakan, to find a bustling community of Kachin tribesmen working side by side with thousands of Chinese, both of them competing for jade. The native Kachin had only hand tools. The Chinese had heavy, modern equipment, explosives, and deep pockets. There was an uneasy standoff between the two groups. The Kachin wanted independence from Burma and had fought a decades-long bloody insurgency that ended in ceasefire in 1994. (Two decades later the ceasefire was broken and in 2018 heavy fighting broke out in several parts of the Kachin state including Hpakan where the Chinese were still active.)

My friend in Rangoon put us in contact with a Burmese jade-mine owner in Hpakan who opened his doors to us and generously allowed us to film and photograph his operation. We had similar good fortune with Chinese mine owners, one of whom invited us to film the dynamiting of jade deposits. His staff arranged a table and chairs and a pot of tea while miners prepared explosives. We looked down on a level spot where dozens of holes had been bored by hand into the ground and filled with explosives. Our host gave the order "Fire in the hole!" when we were ready to film. The whole area erupted a foot in the air as broken rock and smoke emerged. Chinese miners began moving the broken rock away in large trucks. As part of their arrangement with the Burmese army, the Chinese moved raw jade including huge boulders weighing more than two tons overland to China. No taxes were paid and none of the profits reached the pockets of the Kachin who owned the valley.

A friendly Burmese mine owner who was operating a rare, and dangerous, underground mine, invited us down into his mine, obviously not expecting us to take him up on his offer. He was half right. I had no intention of going into a deep underground mine operating under medieval conditions. But Neil, a man who had survived many life-threatening adventures around the world, jumped at the offer. The mine owner, reluctant to lose face, went down with Neil. I photographed Neil as he began his descent, telling him I would give it to his widow, Regine, if things went wrong. Neil survived, as he always has so far, and obtained some stunning footage of jade mining at its most hazardous.

We met some friendly Kachin miners at their small, primitive jade mine in the village of Mowange not far from Hpakan. They became friendlier when they learned we were American. The young English-speaking pastor of the local Baptist church, which overlooks down on the mine, approached us.

"Will you come for Sunday services?" he asked.

"We would be delighted," I replied, although neither Neil nor I were churchgoers. "Do you have a choir?"

"Of course, and a band," said the pastor.

"Could we film in the church?" I enquired, seeing an opportunity presenting itself.

"We would be honored," said the young prelate.

"Do you know Amazing Grace?" I ventured.

"Yes we do, but all the hymns are in the Jingpaw Kachin language." This was getting better and better.

So there I was, speaking in front of a crowded Baptist church in upper Burma. The girls and the ladies had dressed up in their traditional, colorful woven red wool skirts and silver-adorned black velvet tops; the men wore traditional sarongs or longyis. I spoke in English while the young pastor translated. I greeted the congregation in the name of President George Bush (Junior) who, I reminded them, was a fellow Baptist. This was the only time I had spoken so kindly about the president, whose father I had once worked for and admired. When I passed on the regards of the veterans of OSS Detachment 101 to their Kachin comrades, the congregation perked up. As soon as I mentioned OSS and Detachment 101, they knew what I was talking about. There were families of former Kachin rangers in the room and they knew everything about Detachment 101. There wasn't a dry eye in the house, except Neil's, and he was busy filming.

The trip was a success. Once back in Seattle, I proposed writing a story about Hpakan to *Arts of Asia* magazine, the Hong Kong-based magazine, important to Asian art collectors and dealers. Over the years I had done a dozen or so articles for the magazine, but doubted they would be interested in a visit to open-pit jade mines. I was wrong. They wanted the story to go in an issue featuring jade. My account of visiting the rarely seen mines of Hpakan would fit nicely. The article ran in the July–August 2005 issue. The editor added a photo of a jade necklace, a single strand of 27 perfectly matched jadeite beads. The necklace sold at Christie's auction house in Hong Kong in 1997 for US$9.3 million.

***

The lack of infrastructure, such as roads and airfields has made visiting the remote hills of the Kachin state difficult for decades. The insurgent activity of the Kachin Independence Organization (KIO) who seek independence from Burma further complicates travel. Most of the large state, which is more than twice the size of Switzerland, is off limits to foreigners. The northernmost town in Burma is Putao, known as Ft. Hertz under the colonial British, and the only town in Burma not captured by the Japanese in World War II. Located only 70 miles from Tibet, Ft. Hertz and its airfield became a major base of the American OSS Detachment 101 behind Japanese lines during the war.

I was allowed to visit Putao briefly in 1995 with a friend who spoke Burmese. We made our first stop the Christian Morse mission. After seizing power in 1962 the

Burmese Army expelled the American Morse family, along with other missionaries. Rather than leave Burma, the Morses retreated into the jungle with much of their flock. After evading Burmese authorities for years, they decamped to Thailand. Their mission and some of its Lisu congregation stayed in Putao with Lisu pastors.

On a crisp December day, we found the mission chorus practicing their Christmas pageant hymns. We were the first Americans to visit the mission in years and it was a touching moment when we introduced ourselves. In addition to the mission and the singing, we found another tangible reminder of the Morse family contribution to the area: fruit trees. They had introduced apple trees from Washington State as well as grapefruit, which were particularly sought after in Rangoon. Grapefruit in Putao cost one US penny each. After seating all the passengers on our plane leaving Putao, the airline lined the aisle with bushel baskets of fresh grapefruit, making visits to the toilet challenging.

In 2006, *Forbes Magazine* hired me to travel to Putao to photograph a new eco-lodge at Mulashide, not far from Putao. The very posh lodge offered mountain trekking in pristine mountain forests in the foothills of the Himalaya Mountains at $800 per night. The brainchild of an Englishman, it had 10 thatched bungalows each outfitted with a Finnish wood-burning stove and a large round wooden hot tub overlooking the Nam Lang River. The three-person European staff included a Swiss chef with a Michelin-starred restaurant in his résumé. Lisu tribesmen and women made up the rest of the staff who outnumbered their guests at a ratio of 4:1.

Magnificent rhododendron trees reaching 40 feet in height stand out in the forest surrounding the lodge. In the early 20th century the British botanist, Kingdon Ward, collected a number of plants, including "rhodies" from these hills. Many of the finest "rhodies" found today in Europe and America are descendants from the plants brought back to England by Ward.

The lodge made elephants available for those who found trekking in the clear and crisp mountain air on foot too taxing. Elephants came in particularly handy for those who wanted to cross streams frigid with the snow melt from the nearby Himalayas. If exploring the mountains at an elephant's pace is not exciting enough, the lodge introduced white-water rafting, a first for Burma. Pat O'Keefe, a burly Australian and a master rafter with a wry sense of humor, ran the rafting operation. Together with a group of athletic-looking Australian businessmen, we were his first group to run the river. "No problem if you go in," he told us, referring to the rapids that can upset the fragile rafts in rock-filled gorges. "We will pick up your body downstream in 10 days at Myitkyina," he added, referring to the capital of the Kachin state many miles south. We were pretty much on our own and it didn't seem to bother Pat, so it didn't bother me. It turned out that Pat had only run the rapids once, some years before.

The adventure began with a long drive followed by a 10-mile hike to the launch point for the rafts. A crew had gone before to set up camp and prepare the rafts.

Pat had done reconnaissance of the river but this was the first trip with paying customers. We immediately fell behind schedule when a flat tire slowed our move to the start of the trek. We spent some hours climbing in the jungle on an unimproved trail used mainly by hill men hauling long rattan vines downhill at full tilt. Anyone going up had to get off the trail or get run over. We were losing the light and rain clouds were forming, when Pat came up to me and said we needed to move faster. The oldest in the party by 15 years and somewhat slowed by humping my camera gear, I had fallen behind.

I told Pat to move ahead with the clients. I said I would take my time getting to camp. He kindly left a Lisu rafting trainee with me, a very pleasant young member of the Morse mission flock. The rain clouds opened up, which didn't worry us at first. The shower cooled us off but it made the steep trail slippery. As the rain increased, night fell. The trek ceased to be fun. By my count, I fell 26 times before I told my young minder that I needed rest. The rain came down harder and I couldn't see the trail, which had become a streambed.

As I sat in the mud trying to protect my cameras from the rain, the thought came to me: What would Chesty do? I was thinking of Lieutenant General Lewis "Chesty" Puller, the Marine's Marine, winner of five Navy Crosses, and the guy you want to be with when the shit hits the fan. Or when you are exhausted in the Burmese jungle in the dark, in the rain and attracting leeches. I told my young Lisu friend to proceed to camp alone, and return with a headlamp and a gallon of fresh water. He was reluctant to leave me, but I assured him this was the right thing to do. He departed, and I curled up protecting my photo gear and immediately fell asleep in the rain.

White-water rafting on the headwaters of the Irrawaddy River in northern Burma.

An hour later, the boy was back with water, headlamps, and Pat, who seemed relieved that tigers hadn't dragged me away for dinner. They woke me up and I quickly drank most of the water. I then put on my headlamp, and walked into camp as the rain abated. The Aussies greeted me warmly and put something alcoholic in my hand that disappeared in an instant. My pitched tent beckoned. The first thing I did was dry my camera gear, take off my wet clothes, and pull off a dozen or so leeches that were quietly and painlessly sucking my blood. I find the best way to get rid of leeches is to put "bug juice" on them. That's what we did in the mountains of Vietnam. The old method is to burn them off with cigarettes. It works, but affects the flavor of the butt. I joined the Aussies, good blokes all, who plied me with industrial quantities of Australian wine and Dinty Moore stew.

The next morning Pat put me in the raft that carried all the camping gear and the Lisu trainee rafter. From our lead raft I photographed the second raft full of Aussie adventurers under the expert care of Babu Lama, a Nepalese and Pat's main rafting man. A young American from Idaho—Pat's fourth crew member—followed behind the rafts in a kayak. His job was to go after anyone who fell overboard. We got a chance to see the young Idahoan in action when we rounded a bend in the fast-flowing river and found a huge tree had fallen across the river. We put in quickly and portaged the rafts around the blocking tree. Before we resumed rafting, Pat pulled out his camera and called me over. "Here's a shot for you." I took a series of photos documenting the young American rushing towards the tree, which hung about one foot above the river. The kayak suddenly flipped over, scooting under the tree underwater and then just suddenly flipped back up after clearing the tree. The kayaker, having demonstrated his extraordinary skill, waved to us. The rest of the trip down the Nam Lang passed mostly uneventfully. A whirlpool trapped us for a few minutes, but with brute force Pat pushed us out and averted what could have been a disaster and a busy day for "kayak man."

Notwithstanding the heavy rain, the leeches, and dodging boulders in the Nam Lang, we all enjoyed the trip through the pristine jungle, home to rarely seen fauna. Although we didn't see them, snow leopards still prowl the snow-capped high country along the Tibetan border. In 1966 scientists discovered the leaf deer, the oldest known species of deer. More as-yet unknown species may be out there. Hopefully, when the fighting with the Kachin ends, more of this magical land where cloud leopards still roam free will open to the outside world.

***

On May 8, 1954, the French surrendered more than 11,000 personnel, about half of them wounded, to the Viet Minh. This brought an end to the French Indochina war that had raged between 1946 and 1954. It also signaled the beginning of the American Indochina war that ended with the fall of Saigon in 1975, although

American combat forces left the country several years earlier. During the battle of Dien Bien Phu, a CIA-owned airline, Civil Air Transport (CAT), with presidential approval, flew 682 re-supply missions to the French garrison at Dien Bien Phu. A total of 34 pilots flew propeller-driven C-119 "Flying Boxcars" painted in the colors of the French Air Force. Their last mission came on May 6, when James B. "Earthquake McGoon" McGovern and his co-pilot, Wallace "Wally" Buford, were shot down and killed by heavy anti-aircraft fire. The garrison fell shortly after McGovern's mission. He was a much-liked character, big and sometimes boisterous. His nickname came from a hillbilly comic strip character from Li'l Abner. Buford received two Distinguished Flying Crosses during World War II. In 2005 the French government posthumously awarded the Legion of Honor to McGovern, Buford, and other CAT pilots for their heroism at the last battle of France's colonial empire in Asia.

In 2008, I visited Dien Bien Phu overland from Hanoi with two American friends, Colonel Michael Eiland, a West Point graduate and a Special Forces officer with multiple combat tours of duty in Vietnam, and Colonel John Hasemen, also a Vietnam veteran, who later served as US military attaché in Indonesia and Burma. Mike was posted to the American embassy in Hanoi and arranged our trip to the old battlefield as part of a one-week swing west to Dien Bien Phu, then north to the China border, then east to the old French hill station of Sa Pa, and back to Hanoi.

Mike, a fluent Vietnamese speaker, had arranged for a car and driver for the trip into the T'ai highlands west of Hanoi, a large mountainous region in northwestern Vietnam populated by a number of hill tribe, especially T'ai who were linguistically related to the Thai and Lao. We spent our first night in the pleasant White T'ai village of Pom Coong, at Mrs. Chung's Homestay, comfortable for a hill tribe village, but spartan. We slept in sleeping bags in a long house that could accommodated 50. Luckily, we had the large room to ourselves. The T'ai food was spicy, featuring curries, similar to Thai food in Bangkok. We drank a home-brewed beer-like beverage through long reeds in large earthenware jars. Fairly weak, the drink was an acquired taste, but it was safer than the potent moonshine for sale in upland shops that featured snakes and other reptiles in recycled whiskey bottles. For upland travel I normally stick to good Vietnamese beer. After dinner our hosts treated us to Red T'ai dancing. We also had an opportunity to buy locally woven tribal textiles. The local elementary school possessed an empty American bomb casing. It used it as the school bell, a reminder that other Americans had passed this way before, usually at around 20,000 feet above or higher, and at high speed, in B-52 bombers.

The road west took us to the site of the Son La hydroelectric dam that has changed the local scenery for ever. As we passed by, we saw many local communities, mostly ethnic minorities, were being relocated to escape the inevitable rising water level when the dam was completed. The path to progress is often painful and many tribal people were dislocated.

A day later we arrived at Dien Bien Phu, a Black T'ai village that became a 20th-century Waterloo for the French. In the spring of 1954 the French chose it as a base from which to prevent a Vietnamese invasion of Laos, a poorly defended French colony nearby. The French garrisoned the town and its airfield and established strong points on a few low hills in the valley. The French forces consisted of a mixed bag of Indochinese troops—mainly ethnic Vietnamese or Cambodian—and other colonial troops from Africa, including a small detachment of North African women who were assigned to a mobile French Army brothel, and a strong contingent from the French Foreign Legion, many of whom were battle-hardened Germans, survivors of World War II. Many T-ai tribesmen from local militia units served under French officers and NCOs. French soldiers were in the minority.

The Viet Minh communist forces under General Vo Nguyen Giap surrounded and outnumbered the disparate collection of French units. General Vo Nguyen Giap's tough and resourceful soldiers managed to move artillery through the rugged mountains of the T'ai highlands, much to the surprise, and regret, of the French. Armed to a large extent by the nearby communist Chinese, the Viet Minh absorbed huge losses in their siege of the French, whose supply lines were too long and their air and artillery resources too few.

Today, Dien Bien Phu looks more like a bustling Vietnamese town than a T'ai village, although there are still plenty of tribal people as seen by the wide array of colorful ethnic dress in the morning markets. We stayed in the Dien Bien Phu hotel where we enjoyed an excellent lunch of grilled venison glazed with honey. Reminders of the famous battle are everywhere. The old French airstrip is still in operation, and facilitates regular flights to Hanoi. The Vietnamese have preserved the old bunker of French commander Colonel Christian de Castries not far from the end of the airfield. The main battlefield attraction, however, is not in the town but in the hills some miles away looking down on the valley. General Giap's headquarters have been largely restored. Visitors, mainly Vietnamese, crowd the site. Over-enthusiastic T'ai girls, who fiercely vie with one another in their zeal to sell souvenirs to tourists, pose the greatest danger today.

A large and impressive statue commemorating the Viet Minh fighters, male and female, who won the battle stands in Dien Bien Phu. Not far away, the Vietnamese have preserved one of the hilltop French positions complete with its trenches and barbed wire. From there a captured American-built tank overlooks the airstrip. The hill also looks down on a large cemetery for Viet Minh killed in action. There is also another, smaller, memorial to the fallen of Dien Bien Phu. Harder to find is the site that commemorates French losses. A German survivor of the Foreign Legion that suffered heavy casualties in the battle erected it. A plaque contains a short, bitter message that says the French would have won the battle if the troops had all been Germans.

Dien Bien Phu has a small museum dedicated to the battle. In addition to a few battered relics from the fighting, visitors can see an excellent documentary film with

A young boy plays on top of an American-built tank captured by the Viet Minh from the French in 1954. The tank rests on "Elaine" a hilltop strong point of the French Army during the battle for Dien Bien Phu that now looks down on the town and a large cemetery for Viet Minh war dead.

excellent combat footage from both sides. A large sand table of the battlefield with French positions in blue lights and Viet Minh positions in red stands in front of the screen. As the siege moves to its bloody conclusion more and more red lights replace the blue ones. According to our guide a steady trickle of increasingly elderly Frenchmen come to pay homage to their fallen comrades.

Driving north from Dien Bien Phu, we passed through Black T'ai and other ethnic minority villages in the T'ai highlands. We stopped for local coffee in one picturesque market town that was crowded with various tribal women in full regalia. A lone Vietnamese vendor wearing her conical straw hat saw us taking photos. She could have played the role of Bloody Mary in the musical *South Pacific*.

"Are you French?" she asked Mike.

"No," he answered in Vietnamese, "We're Americans."

With a broad grin she enquired, "Are you going to bomb us again?" Mike assured her our visit was peaceful.

We made our way through the tribal country along the mountainous borders—first, with Laos and then with China—on a good two-lane hardtop road. We passed dozens of minority groups but saw not one tourist. After a couple of days, we arrived at the old French hill station of Sa Pa. This delightful Hmong town enjoyed a cool climate at an altitude of around 5,000 feet. It once boasted hundreds of French villas for the colonial officials who sought relief from the torrid lowlands. Many of these were lost in the French Indochina war of 1946–54 and the

Chinese incursion of 1979, when the town was occupied for a month. The People's Republic of China wanted to "teach a lesson" to the Vietnamese for their invasion of Cambodia, ousting the Khmer Rouge regime that was supported by the Chinese. The People's Liberation Army walked into a buzz saw when they faced off against the battle-hardened People's Army of Vietnam. After a few weeks of fighting along the border and with a loss of more than 20,000 dead, the Chinese decided they had taught the Vietnamese enough of a lesson and went home. I suspect they learned a lesson rather than taught one.

Sa Pa, now a thriving center of tourism, boasts more than 85 hotels to accommodate every budget of foreign visitors. Tribal Hmong and Yao women offer excellent textiles in street stalls around the town that overlooks down on terraced rice paddies. We stayed nearby at the Victoria Hotel, a charming European-style place located near the Old Catholic church. Staying at the hotel, which seeks to capture the colonial history of the hill town, assures you of getting a seat in the VIP carriage that the hotel owns on the night train down to Hanoi from the border town of Lao Cai, down the hill from Sa Pa. The hotel owns the train. The elegant VIP cabin, with its attentive staff and well-appointed bar, reminded me of an Orient-Express train minus the high cost. Mike's car and driver were waiting for us in Hanoi the next morning.

That was not my first trip to northern Vietnam. In 1998, I visited Hanoi after an assignment I completed for the Orient-Express Company in Laos. Mike was in Hanoi and invited me over for a few days. On the second day, I walked around the old town photographing colonial architecture. Crossing streets presented my biggest challenge. I was told, (a) never look a cyclist in the eyes, and (b) never stop while crossing the road. I recommend crossing next to an elderly Vietnamese woman on the offside of the traffic flow.

Having spent a pleasant morning taking pictures and dodging cyclists, I found a nice-looking pho restaurant near a lake. I was enjoying a bowl of my favorite beef noodle soup when I noticed a Vietnamese man about my age looking at me. Finally, he spoke in French. "How's the soup?" he asked. I said it tasted fine. He then joined me at my table. I feared he was going to try to sell me something. Instead, he introduced himself as a medical doctor and asked if he could practice his French. I told him fine, but added that I was American, not French; I waited for the other shoe to drop. He only smiled and then asked if he could practice his English. Fine with me.

The doctor had worked for eight years in Algeria practicing medicine and pocketing only 10 percent of what the Vietnamese government charged the Algerians for his labor. Now he was home.

"Is this your first visit to Vietnam?" he asked.

"No, I said, "I was a journalist in Saigon many years ago."

"Were you in the war?"

"Yes, I was a Marine Corps officer in Quang Nam in 1969. How about you?"

"I was a captain in the medical corps," he said, "but I didn't go south."

There was no hint of hostility in his voice. On the contrary, the doctor proceeded to suggest what I should see in Hanoi. This beautiful city has trees and lakes and vestiges of an ancient culture sprinkled with strange things like a French Opera House and a ballet where puppets perform in water. At length, he said he had to get back to work and gave me his card. "If you get sick, please call me and I will treat you. Free. We have socialized medicine here," he laughed.

In contrast, several times when visiting Saigon, I have been braced by *cyclo* (pedicab) drivers after hearing that I had served in the war. They were invariably veterans of Army of the Republic of Vietnam (ARVN) and had suffered at the hands of the conquering northerners. The asked bitterly "Why you leave us?" It is a fair question for which I have no answer.

We had such a good time on our trip to Dien Bien Phu in 2008 that Mike invited John Haseman and me back the next year for another trip to the China border, this time to Ha Giang in the mountains and on to a wartime hideout of Ho Chi Minh. This trip required special permission to travel to the sensitive China border area. We met tribes I had never seen before, including the Dzao, Lolo, and Man. Near Ha Giang we visited the "palace" of the last Hmong king, Vuong Chinh Duc, who had grown opium for the colonial French monopoly. The state took over the property and turned it into a museum. A descendent of the king, a young woman named Vuong Thi Cho, guided us through the rustic palace.

The northern scenery with its misty crags seemed to have been borrowed from ancient Chinese paintings. The rain added an element of drama came as we crept along rough mountain tracks in the rain with a broken windshield wiper. We drove very slowly until we reached Minh Yen, where we could have the wiper fixed. Driving north from Cao Bang, we arrived at a place of bucolic beauty: the famous Pac Bo Cave. Ho Chi Minh used the cave, tucked in very close to the China border, while fighting the Japanese during World War II. He once shielded an American airman there, who was rescued behind Japanese lines, and later smuggled him over the border to reunite him with the 14th Air Force.

"Uncle Ho," an early member of the French Communist Party and a founder of the Indochinese Communist Parties, had an interesting relationship with the Americans, who probably saved his life in 1945 during a visit by the OSS "Deer Team" mission. The OSS, operating in southern China, first approached Ho in 1944 and asked him to provide intelligence on the Japanese and also help rescue downed American aircrews. In exchange, the OSS offered weapons and training. During a visit to Kunming, Ho Chi Minh met with Major General Claire Chennault, famed founder of the American Volunteer Group, the "Flying Tigers," and later commander of the 14th Air Force. The meeting went well, with Chennault giving Ho an autograph and six .45-caliber pistols, to the delight of the quiet Vietnamese revolutionary.

When the Deer Team parachuted into Ho's headquarters in July 1945, they found Ho at death's door, too ill to receive the American guests. He was suffering from malaria, dysentery, and maybe hepatitis. OSS medic Private First Class Paul Hoagland dosed Ho with quinine and sulfa drugs. Ho rallied and survived. Later, the Vietnamese claimed that herbs from the jungle saved Ho, but my money is on PRC Hoagland's ministrations.

A rustic pond sits at the mouth of the Pac Bo Cave. The guide claimed it was Uncle Ho's fishing hole. The Vietnamese are turning this idyllic refuge into a major tourist attraction. I fear it has gone the way of the shrine to General Giap near Dien Bien Phu. I was happy that we got there when we did. On our way back to Hanoi we stopped at the Ba Be National Park, a delightful mountain getaway. We took a boat ride, one of the trip's highlights, on Ba Be Lake, which runs through Puang Cave, a huge cavern.

I took full advantage of Mike's lengthy tenure in Hanoi and brought BJ with me on another trip to Hue where I was on an assignment for *Arts of Asia* magazine to write about the restoration of the citadel that was badly damaged during the Tet offensive of 1968 where my battalion had lost many Marines. We also visited Da Nang and Hoi An where I had served. We didn't try to visit An Hoa or the Arizona Territory; there were too many bad memories.

Mike's Hanoi-born wife, Chan, also an embassy officer, made our visit to Hanoi special. Chan's family, Roman Catholics, went south in 1954 when the French left Indochina. She met Mike in Saigon when she was working for a bank. Chan knows all the best places to shop, visit, and dine in Hanoi and shared them with us. A fitness buff, Chan also took us to the park where she exercised to music early every morning. It was charming yet somewhat strange to watch our old enemies waltzing or dancing rock and roll to American music. At the end of the session, Chan introduced us to two of her friends, a senior couple that danced with skill and enthusiasm. The grey-haired husband sported a French beret and was very friendly. Later, Chan informed me that, during the Vietnam War, the old fellow commanded a squadron of MiG-21 fighters.

***

In 2009, Neil and I decided to make a film that would probably result in the Burmese government putting us on the "Black List" of people not allowed into Burma. The military junta disliked negative portrayals of their regime. Up to that point, our films had been non-political. All of my photo books or magazine articles on Burma focused on culture or history. Now, we decided we needed to take the gloves off and make a film that documented the abuse that the military had inflicted on Burma since Ne Win seized power in 1962.

In the past, I had made sure I had the blessing of military intelligence (DDSI). This time I sidestepped seeking official permission to travel and film. We decided not to tell anyone, not even our friends, what we intended to do because it might put them at risk. Several had already been in prison and had no wish to go back.

Neil was making a film about world hunger in Thailand with an American, Henry Rollins, narrating. Henry was a punk rock star in the 1980s who had moved on to acting and "spoken word" presentations. Neil thought Henry could be good as the narrator of our film and made a deal with him. We assembled a film crew quickly and flew to Rangoon. We planned to shoot the film surreptitiously and hoped not to get caught. We had a little bit of luck on our side. The DDSI had been disbanded in 2003 when the hard-liner generals under Than Shwe ousted the moderates under the DDSI commander Khin Nyunt. For decades the DDSI had kept tabs on political dissent in Burma with a disciplined and effective force. With that force gone, we had a better chance of quietly filming.

We worked fast and moved around the country filming Henry on the fly. Nevertheless, I felt we were in trouble from day one. While shooting in a Rangoon park on Inya Lake opposite Aung San Suu Kyi's house in the background, I briefed Henry on what we wanted him to say and trusted him to ad lib on camera without working from a script. We hoped we could shoot with one or two takes and move on, keeping under the radar. Henry, however, needed more prep time and there was none available. As time dragged on a crowd gathered. One man in particular, who was looking on intensely, worried me. It was pretty clear what we were doing as Henry repeatedly pointed to The Lady's house across the lake as he spoke. Finally, finished, we headed for our car and the man approached me. I thought the jig was up before we had really begun. If he worked for the government, we were in trouble. But he clasped my hand and shook it vigorously. He knew what we were doing, and approved. It was our luck that the man was an NLD supporter.

It got worse. Shooting on the run wasn't Henry's thing. He needed a level of comfort and coddling that we couldn't provide. Operating on a shoestring budget, with no backers, we hoped to sell the film later. Our crew consisted of two young Americans, Kevin Chapados and Phelps Harmon, enjoying the lark of their life. While Neil and I were used to roughing it, Henry wasn't. He liked his creature comforts and brought along most of the food he ate. It turned out Henry had a passion for two things: rock and roll music and snakes. Henry sounded like a skilled herpetologist when he spoke of his various pet snakes in Los Angeles. Later, he would prove it.

We motored into Pagan, a wonderful ancient city of two thousand pagodas, most of them in ruins or badly restored, on the east bank of the Irrawaddy River. While filming in the sprawling complex, I noticed that two young men on a motorbike were following us. They kept bumping into us whenever we stopped to film under the pretext of trying to sell us cheap paintings. Neither surreptitious, nor very professional, the boys were just keeping an eye on us. Since it is neither unusual nor illegal to film in Pagan, I urged everyone to be friendly to the boys.

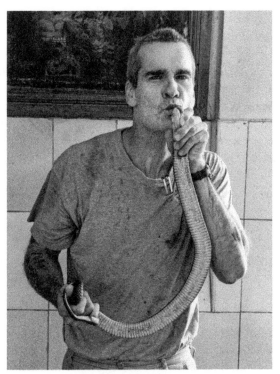

Henry Rollins kissing a live cobra in the Rangoon zoo. Henry did not work out as narrator for a documentary film on Burma but was interesting to travel with while attempting to film incognito.

Henry proved incapable of taking sound advice. Before we could stop him, he ran up to one of the boys and started shouting abuse at him nose-to-nose. Even if the boys weren't government agents, no self-respecting Burman would not put up with such rude behavior. Fortunately, the boys jumped on their bike and made a getaway. Henry calmed down when he realized that he could have blown what paper-thin cover we had. The boys could have gone for help. If they had been DDSI officers, we would have been arrested, possibly beaten, cameras and film confiscated, and prison a distinct possibility. We beat it out of Pagan on an unpaved back road and headed south.

Eventually, we made it to Burma's new capital, Nay Pyi Taw, still under construction and off limits to foreigners. The Burmese government made a mistake of biblical proportions in building this city. Spending scarce resources this way typified the poor decision-making of the ruling junta. The city had avenues 12-lanes wide and few cars on them. There was a full-scale replica of the Shwe Dagon pagoda in Rangoon but few worshipers. Government officials dreaded being posted to Nay Pyi Taw and usually left their families in Rangoon with the best schools and medical facilities.

The only part of the city open to the public was the zoo and we wanted to film it. We pulled up to the entrance to the zoo and I got out to buy tickets only to discover that the zoo was closed on a Sunday. We didn't want to lose a day in the heat of Nay Pyi Taw. Neil, a world traveler and veteran problem-solver, stepped up. Some money changed hands and the gates opened.

The zoo was beautiful and as close to a natural setting for most of the animals as could be imagined. I found the penguin house, an igloo-shaped structure painted white, particularly amusing and symbolic of the general's frivolous waste of money. Here, in a country very short of electricity, they had created an air-conditioned enclosure for animals not native to Burma. It also struck me as strange to see penguins from the far southern hemisphere paired with igloos, iconic symbols of the far northern hemisphere.

"I will handle this," Neil said. "Get Henry over to the penguin house and start shooting." We took off as Neil greeted the zoo director and his assistants. We managed to get a few feet of film of Henry speaking in front of the penguin house before Neil arrived with his new Burmese friends. Neil rushed over to me and said, "I told them you are with the Seattle Zoo on a tight schedule and want very much to see the Nay Pyi Taw Zoo." I told the director that this was the most natural-looking of any zoo I had ever seen (true), and thanked him for letting us in on a Sunday. With that, the director called up a golf cart built for 16 and gave us a royal tour of the zoo. Henry distinguished himself by picking up a wild snake as we approached the reptile house. It turned out to be a harmless snake but the way Henry handled the reptile impressed me, and more importantly, it impressed the zoo's director. Our bona fides were firm.

We made it back to Rangoon without further incident, but it was pretty clear that we didn't have enough to make a film. We needed to interview Aung San Suu Kyi, the Nobel laureate who was a national symbol of defiance to military rule. Unfortunately, we had no way to approach The Lady in Rangoon for an interview.

Making the most of a bad situation, we took Henry to the Rangoon Zoo. We thought we could make Henry happy by taking him to the reptile house. Henry hit it off with the elderly attendant, who took Henry inside to see the snakes. Suddenly, Kevin Chapados, our cameraman, called us over in an urgent voice. There was Henry fondly holding a young cobra. I could see the headlines in my mind's eye: "ROCK STAR KILLED BY SNAKE" and the sub-head "Film makers arrested." What should I do? With an instinct drilled into me by Horst Faas, I grabbed my camera determined to make the last photo of Henry Rollins a good one. I snapped a few frames and Henry saw me. He quietly and daringly kissed the snake on its head. The photo looks good.

We parted on friendly terms with Henry at the end of the shoot, but we knew we couldn't use much of the footage we had taken with such great difficulty.

I considered it a minor miracle that we had not been arrested. In addition to charming snakes, Henry does some writing. I sent him photos from our adventure and he asked permission to use one of them in a book titled *A Mad Dash*. He later sent me an autographed copy of the book, which features my photo of him photographing a hornbill at the Nay Pyi Taw Zoo on the back cover. Inside, Henry provides an account of our Burma sojourn. He refers to Neil as The Director (TD) and to me as the Company Man (CM). He wrote: "After CM's informative and interesting briefing on Burma's history (he's an amazing authority on the place), we set out. I now fully understand the purpose of our trip and why I was invited." A few pages later, while complaining about the work conditions, he adds: "CM is a very good photographer. I was looking at some of his photos today, great work."

Despite his discomfort and general unhappiness, Henry had some good things to say about Neil and me when we were confronted with the closed Nay Pyi Taw Zoo. After Neil bribed a guard to let us in, Henry wrote:

> Some officials came out and explained that the zoo was closed. TD didn't miss a beat. He points at CM and claims that he's from the Seattle Zoo and is here to inspect the place ... I see CM wince and then go into one of the smoothest raps I have ever heard. He knows a lot about a lot of things anyway so he just starts talking about local animals in Burma, and the zoo official was totally taken in by it. Within minutes we are in a golf cart and being given an all access tour of the facility ... TD was brilliant.

Our setback with Henry did not end the project. Neil eventually found a backer for the film, and a Hollywood celebrity with deep affection and respect for Aung San Suu Kyi. Back in business with a reasonable budget and a new crew we started in Thailand. My contacts with Burmese exile groups, rebels, and a humanitarian organization proved extremely helpful. Some even donated excellent footage on the atrocities of the Junta. In northern Thailand, we filmed at a hospital whose only patients are elephants. One had lost a foot to a land mine in Burma while logging. This was the first of many amputees we saw along the border, all victims of the Burma Army.

We also made contact with dissidents from the Karen ethnic minority who were seeking independence from Burma, as promised by the departing British, since 1948. The Karen are mostly Christian, which accounts for their high level of education, fluency in English, and a friendly attitude towards the British and Americans. Unlike the Karen I had seen in the hills of northern Thailand, many of the Burmese Karen were well-educated thanks in large part to American missionaries in Burma since the early 19th century. Today, thousands of Burmese Karen languish in refugee camps in Thailand, forced to flee the fighting across the border. Our new Karen friends smuggled us into the camps to interview and film refugees. A Karen army leader invited us to visit one of his base camps inside Burma. Taking unmarked back roads and avoiding Thai border guards, we made our way into Burma, through a

Soldiers of the rebel Karen National Union (KNU) army set up a captured heavy machine gun in a KNU camp in the Karen state of Burma. The mainly Christian minority has been in rebellion since 1948 seeking greater autonomy from the military Burmese regime. Many Karen have been killed and thousands languish in refugee camps in Thailand along the border with Burma.

minefield to the Karen camp, where we filmed and interviewed combatants as well as civilians who they protected. We made it safely back to Thailand through the minefield, all limbs intact.

Then we planned our last trip to Rangoon to interview The Lady. Through friends in Rangoon and Washington DC, I made contact with her people. Suu Kyi was not under house arrest at the time but she was closely watched, and we had to be very careful. A friend of our backer accompanied us. He was carrying gifts for The Lady. The only person in Rangoon who knew what we were doing was an old friend, Larry Dinger, the American chargé d'affaires, the senior American in the country. When I called to make the appointment to see him, he said, "Paula collects your Burma books. I will have them with me for you to sign." I told him we wanted him to know what we were doing in case the Burmese arrested us. He wished me luck.

We timed our interview with Aung San Suu Kyi so that we could go directly from her office to the airport and leave Burma before the authorities were on to us. The Burmese authorities had the NLD headquarters under constant surveillance from a coffee shop across the street, where plain-clothes agents photograph people coming and going. Fortunately, it was a busy day with numerous other foreigners visiting the party offices.

Aung San Suu Kyi, charming and articulate, as always, welcomed us to her office. We gave her a few gifts and took photos. I reminded her that we had met before and mentioned some mutual friends who were instrumental in arranging the interview. Then I conducted the interview, the last one we made for the film.

At the conclusion of the interview, we hastened to the airport and made it out of Burma without incident and all film in hand. Neil went to work with my younger son, Brendan, editing the film. Academy award-winner Anjelica Houston, a fan of The Lady, narrated the film pro bono. The film, *Burma: A Human Tragedy*, gained some modest acclaim. Around the time the film came out in 2011, Burma experienced significant political change and took steps to restore democracy. In 2012 the NLD won 43 of 45 seats in parliamentary by-elections. The Lady joined the government but could not serve as prime minister as she had been married to a foreigner. She became the "shadow prime minister" and the first woman to be Burma's foreign minister.

Thanks to the changes in Burma, many political prisoners were released. The press, although under pressure, has significantly more freedom. Americans can get visas on arrival or even via email. Neil and I still are able to visit Burma. However, there is a great deal still to be done. The army still controls the country and ethnic

An Adventure Film Production crew preparing to film in Pagan, Burma. From left, production assistant Brendan Broman, director Neil Hollander, producer Barry Broman. We used footage from Pagan in our film *Burma: A Human Tragedy* narrated by Anjelica Huston.

strife, mainly in the Rakhine (Arakan) and Kachin states, continues. True democracy is still a dream in Burma.

***

In 2013, I was invited to participate in the production of a major coffee table book on Burma titled *Seven Days in Myanmar*. The project was the work of Frenchman Didier Millet, whom I have known for years. Based in Singapore, Didier had produced a number of fine photography books in Southeast Asia. These large books required sponsorship, which is not much of a problem in Bangkok or Jakarta but was a challenge in Burma (or Myanmar), just emerging from decades of mismanagement, international pariah status, and internal conflict. Nevertheless, Didier and his team made it work.

Because I had worked in Burma and had taken the photographs for more than 10 books on the country, Didier asked me to work with his team in selecting the most important and photogenic places. In addition, he invited me to be one of the 30 photographers, which included a mixed bag of the internationally famous, young Burmese looking for a chance to make a name for themselves, and people like me who had modest reputations.

One of the top shooters and a longtime friend, Englishman Michael Freeman, was an Oxford man who had spent much of his career photographing some of the world's most remote areas. He had a keen interest in ethnic minorities, and years of experience in Southeast Asia. He told me he wanted to go to some new place in Burma. I suggested he cover the little-visited Chin state on the border with India. I had been there once and told Michael that some Chin women wore facial tattoos and that Chin music included the nose flute. Didier assigned Michael to the Chin Hills.

I requested to shoot in Mandalay, the cultural heart of Burma. Bruno Barbey, a Frenchman and the senior photographer for the Magnum photo agency, was also going to Mandalay. I knew of Bruno and his work but had never met him. He had photographed the Vietnam War and we had mutual friends among the photographers who covered the war. Bruno was with US Marines in the Gulf War and we hit it off quickly. Didier wanted me to photograph "culture," and Bruno to photograph "religion" in and around Mandalay. My "shoot list" included the artist Sein Myint, Burma's top tapestry designer and the Mandalay Marionettes, a national puppetry group, one of Burma's cultural icons and one of the few remaining puppet troupes in Burma. They performed nightly in a tiny theater in the city under the direction of a master puppeteer.

When the director of photographers saw the Maha Muni Pagoda on my shoot list, she informed me that one of the internationally known photographers had already asked for the Maha Muni. I told Bruno about the Maha Muni and its revered bronze image of the Buddha and about a photo I wanted to make there. Early every morning, a team of Burmese monks wash the face of the image in a special ceremony. I had never seen photos of the face washing and didn't even know if we would be allowed to take photos. When I told Bruno the Maha Muni was off limits, he laughed. "No problem," he said, "We can all shoot it. Let the photo editor make the final decision." The photographer who asked to shoot the Maha Muni, something of a prima donna, had not yet arrived in Burma and was not with us in Mandalay.

I introduced Bruno to my old friend artist Sein Myint at his Mandalay studio and workshop where he produced Burma's finest tapestries (*kalaga*). One of his most impressive works, a massive 17-foot long *kalaga* hangs in the United Nations building in New York City, a gift of the people of Burma. When I asked him if it was possible to photograph the face-washing ceremony of the Mahi Muni image, he said, "I don't know, let's ask." He then told us that he was on the board of directors of the pagoda, and made a phone call. "It is all arranged," he said as he hung up the phone. "Be at the Maha Muni tomorrow at four in the morning. You can photograph the face-washing ceremony."

Bruno and I arrived at the temple at the appointed hour, took off our shoes and socks, and walked to the image, a 12-foot high bronze statue of the seated Buddha. The body had grown fat from the daily application of pure gold leaf, which over the centuries made the Great Teacher look obese. The face, however, remained unchanged and waiting for its daily washing. Historians believe that artisans of the ancient kingdom of the Rakhine (Arakan) in southwestern Burma cast the revered image sometime in the 2nd century CE. In the 18th century, after defeating Arakan, the Burmese moved the Maha Muni to Mandalay.

Even at the early hour, a small crowd of Buddhist faithfuls had gathered to witness the washing. A senior monk greeted us, took us to the image, and told us we could photograph the ceremony from anywhere we liked. I stayed close to the holy bronze statue as the team of specially trained monks arrived to perform the ceremony. Bruno disappeared to find his own vantage point. It was a great privilege to be allowed to witness, let alone photograph, the rite so close up. In the end, both Bruno and I took quite spectacular photos of the senior monk carefully washing the bronze face of the image with the assistance of his crew. I had never seen photos of the ceremony and realized that this could be a highlight of the book.

May is the hottest time of year in Mandalay and temperatures reached 104 degrees Fahrenheit during our visit. For a few days Bruno and I split up. He sought religion while I sought some culture. On one of the lower rungs of culture I found the Moustache Brothers, Burma's leading comedians performing at their tiny and modest theater/home in Mandalay. For years they were persecuted for their satirical humor that often poked fun at the military regime. Free to perform as they wished,

Washing the face of the bronze statue of the Buddha in the Maha Muni pagoda in Mandalay, Burma. This is the most revered image of the Buddha in Burma and the ceremony is held daily at four in the morning.

they had created a special program in broken English for Burma's burgeoning tourist population. When I told my driver, Ko Ko Gyi, that I had heard that the brothers were performing again, he said, "I will introduce you to them." When I asked why he had never told me about them before, he said, "It was too dangerous. You could have gotten into trouble and they could have been put back in prison. Now it is OK. You will like them." And I did. Ko Ko Gyi made the introduction and I took a portrait of the brothers. Later, I photographed their inimitable performance and understood why they are considered national heroes.

When I was finished shooting my assigned list, I teamed up with Bruno and we spent a few days shooting together. In just a few days, I learned a lot from watching him work. Bruno had worked for Henri Cartier-Bresson, the father of photojournalism. I told him that Theo Meier had given me a letter of introduction to Henri when I left Thailand in 1963 and visited Paris en route to university in Seattle. I called the number Theo gave me, but Henri was on assignment and I never met him. One day, Bruno and I were photographing a Buddhist nunnery in Sagaing, a former capital of Burma near Mandalay. In Sagaing, renowned for its many Buddhist pagodas and monasteries, I took one of my best photos of the shoot. It shows Bruno walking across a road followed by a string of very young

Buddhist nuns. It reminds me of a mother duck leading her ducklings. The image was in the book.

Back in Rangoon after the shoot, we turned over our images to the photo coordinator, and shared notes of our adventures with our colleagues. Michael Freeman had tales from the Chin Hills and showed me an outstanding photo of an elderly Chin woman with a deeply tattooed face. She was playing a nose flute. It is one of the best images in the book. Bruno who also shot the cover photo had more photos in the book than anyone else. This did not surprise to me. Sadly, none of our photos of the face-washing ceremony at the Maha Muni made it into the book, something I still cannot understand.

***

In the new millennium BJ and I began a tradition of annual vacations with Tim and his vivacious wife Vicki. It started with a visit to a game park in Namibia, a special place to celebrate Tim's sixtieth birthday in 2004. He is a big-game hunter, an avocation that developed after he served in South Africa. His favorite spot is Byseewah, a 70,000-acre private conservation area that offers ethical hunting. Wild animals outnumber guests by several thousand to one. We enjoyed the finest game cooking I have ever tasted. BJ earned kudos for her zebra with green Thai curry sauce she made for our last dinner.

A few years later we spent a memorable fortnight in the south of France, ending with a week in Bordeaux and its wine country. For decades, Tim and I have been enthusiasts of Chateau Gloria, a small and relatively new but high-quality chateau in the commune of St. Julien in the Médoc. Not open to the public, the owners invited us in for a tasting after Tim wrote and explained our loyal consumption of their product over the years. In what can only be described as overwhelming kindness and a true treat for two aging oenophiles, they shared a tasting of their 2009 vintage, a very good year. In Médoc's finest wine shop, the proprietor bemoaned the fact that Russians, Chinese, and Brazilian millionaires were running up the prices of French wines. To make his point, the affable old fellow picked up a bottle of new Chateau Petrus going for thousands of collars. Sadly, he said many of his loyal, long-time French clients could no longer afford their favorite wines.

On a visit to England, our photographer friend Michael Freeman led us on a one-day visit to his alma mater, Oxford University. He arranged for us to have tea with the dons in his old college, Brasenose, across from Radcliffe Camera, an iconic 18th-century library. It is a place quickly recognized by enthusiasts of the Inspector Morse series of television mysteries that were filmed in Oxford.

A week later, Paul Strachan from Pandaw River Cruises hosted us at his manse, Stobhall Castle, outside Perth in Scotland. The castle in its present form dates from 1578. The River Tay, famous for salmon fishing, runs through the property.

An alfresco Berber lunch in the High Atlas Mountains of Morocco in 2018. From left, Vicki, BJ, Barry, and Tim.

We sampled the local "water of life" in the Scottish tongue, Erse, better known to Americans as whiskey. That set us up fine for a drive through the highlands to the Hebrides Islands and eventually to Plocton, which some say is Scotland's prettiest village.

Looking for something a little more "edgy," we were convinced by my friend Chris Andrew, an old Istanbul hand, that we needed to experience Turkey. We went and loved it. Istanbul offers excellent food and shopping. We enjoyed just walking around the old quarter. An unexpected highlight was Cappadocia on the Anatolian Plateau, where we stayed in a charming hotel literally cut into a mountainside—my only stay in a four-star cave. All it lacked was a view, which we got the next morning when we went ballooning at first light. One hundred and fifty balloons lift off daily when the weather is good. I had ballooned before in Burma, but the karst topography of Cappadocia and the skill of our skipper, who bumped a neighboring balloon in a friendly greeting, made this a truly memorable experience.

For an even edgier experience, we decided to visit Russia. The State Department didn't think it was a good idea. US–Russian relations had cooled after Russia's annexation of Crimea, and official Americans in Russia were being harassed in ways not seen since the end of the Cold War. Tim, a veteran of the Tet Offensive in Saigon in 1968 and numerous other crises, had no concern. We evacuated Phnom Penh together in 1975. He survived a stint in Somalia at the time of Black Hawk Down,

Bromans at the Church of Spilled Blood in St. Petersburg, on our river cruise of Russia in 2015.

and after ambassadorial postings to Haiti and Sudan, he thought Russia would be a breeze. And so it was.

We are not cruise people, but Russia is not the kind of place you want to run around on your own. So we took an 11-day Viking River Cruise from St. Petersburg to Moscow and loved it. The skipper and most of the crew were Russian, but most of the wait staff were Filipinos and, thanks to BJ's Filipino heritage, we received royal treatment. Two excellent female Russian guides who spoke fluent English explained the history of the place while at the same time letting us know how much Russians hate Gorbachev and Yeltsin for destroying the Soviet Union and how much they love Putin for "trying to make Russia great again," a catchy slogan.

We crossed Lake Ladoga, Europe's largest, and stopped at Mandrogy, whose finest feature seems to be the vodka museum where the $5 entrance fee included three shots of Russia's favorite tipple. Maybe a little excessive at 11 in the morning, but "when in Rome …" We stopped at Kizhi on Lake Onego, Europe's second largest, and visited elegant old wooden churches at the UNESCO heritage site. In the pretty city of Yaroslavl, I took my favorite photo of the trip. It shows a very cute young lady of about 10 years of age at the World War II memorial. She stood with parents and grandparents in front of a somber statue remembering the 20 million dead from the Great Patriotic War, as the conflict is known in Russia. I asked the parents if I could take her photo. They nodded agreement. The image shows her smiling shyly and giving me a little wave.

In the town of Uglich we visited a school where girls sang folk songs for us. Then, upstairs, our guide took us to the Wall of Heroes, dedicated to teachers and students who died defending Russia, mostly against Germans. The wall also had photographs of people who died in Afghanistan and Chechnya. I couldn't help myself.

"Where is the Ukraine section?" I asked Tanya, our guide, referring to the 2014 invasion of Ukraine when Russia annexed the Crimea and supported separatists in eastern Ukraine.

"There are no Russian dead from Ukraine," Tanya said tersely.

"Of course there are," I said, "and there are Russian prisoners in the hands of the Ukrainians. Maybe the bodies of the dead have not been returned yet. It took years for many of the dead soldiers from Afghanistan to come home." She walked away and was not happy.

Moscow was no St. Petersburg, but buying an 85-cent ticket to ride its incredible subway is money well spent. It is huge, deep, and in places beautiful. In a dramatic display of the best Socialist Republic Realism art, the Ploshchad Revolyutsli station features 76 bronze statues extolling the workers and fighters of the Soviet Union in a dramatic display of the best of socialist realism art. My favorite statue shows a Soviet soldier holding a rifle in one hand with his other hand resting on his war dog. The dog's nose is shiny and bright. Russians believe that rubbing the dog's bronze nose will bring luck, and thousands of subway goers pause to shine the dog's nose every day.

I have a Russian friend whom I will call Sasha. I had not met Sasha face-to-face before our Russia trip but communicated with him often, especially during his visits to the United States. Educated in the United States, Sasha had held senior positions with major American and European firms in Russia. When I told him we were coming to Moscow and had a day free from the cruise, he immediately offered to give us a private tour of the city, and invited us to a traditional Russian meal at his impressive apartment with a view of the city. We accepted with pleasure.

Sasha offered to pick us up at the boat and I asked how we would recognize him. "Easy," he said, "I will be the only one waving an American flag." We did indeed spot him easily and he showed us a Moscow not seen by many Americans. We went to a market off the beaten track where BJ and Vicki bought beautiful scarves and Tim bought a real Astrakhan fur hat. We ate lunch at a hole-in-the-wall restaurant serving delicious borscht and dumpling, not together. In the afternoon, Sasha took us to Fallen Monument Park, where, after the fall of the USSR in 1991, the Russians dumped statues of past Soviet leaders like Lenin and Stalin. They stand upright and mingle with hundreds of non-political statues in Moscow's largest open-air park.

I had my photo taken in front of the statue of Felix Dzerzhinsky, once leader of the Cheka, the secret police of the Soviet Union and forerunner of the KGB. The 15-ton statue of Iron Felix, as he was known, used to dominate Lubyanka Square in front of the KGB headquarters. The authorities transferred it to Fallen Monument Park on August 22, 1991, just after a failed coup by communist hard-liners in Moscow, and the day before the government outlawed the Communist Party. Today, Felix stands in the park looking down on a statue of former dissident and human rights defender, Andrei Sakharov, a Nobel Peace Prize winner. Andrei is seated. There is a certain poetry here.

We hosted Sasha at lunch at the "new Russian classic" restaurant Café Pushkin, the go-to place for a taste of 19th-century aristocratic Russia. Housed in a renovated 18th-century mansion, this charming restaurant serves a variety of traditional favorites. The borscht is famous. We had mushroom pierogies, stuffed Georgian meat dumplings, and pan-seared duck breast, among other things. We did a lot of sharing. Sasha said this was the real deal.

At dinner that night, Sasha and his wife, who I will call Tatiana, served a classic smorgasbord dinner of traditional Russian culinary delights, including caviars, smoked sturgeon, sausages, and, of course, Russian Champagne and vodkas. We spent most of this delightful evening in their elegantly furnished apartment learning about Russia. There was little political talk until Sasha casually mentioned that he fully expected Donald Trump to be the next American president. We were stunned, especially by the confidence with which Sasha made his remark. This was 2015, and Trump was still an underdog upstart in the Republican Party. At his diplomatic best, Ambassador Carney patiently and carefully burst Sasha's bubble assuring him, Trump could never be elected president. At that point, Tatiana, a college professor, backed up her husband and declared her own certainty that Trump would win. I would have lost a lot of money that night betting against Trump. Fortunately, I am not a betting man. Now I ask myself if Sasha and Tatiana knew something that we did not.

***

It was only a matter of time before we decided to visit the "ould sod" of Erin. My mother, born a Foley, traced her Irish lineage back to New Waterford on Prince Edward Island, Canada. Tim Carney also had Irish roots and had visited many years earlier. I had no family links in Ireland but needed to make a stop in Connemara to pay tribute to a fallen comrade.

After three days in Dublin, which we found convivial, low-stress, and rather inexpensive, we headed south to Ballymaloe House, an elegant old manor house near Cork. Tim and Vicki had stayed there 30 years before when it was at the forefront of a revival in fine Irish cooking. We based ourselves at Ballymaloe for a few days and enjoyed its haute cuisine. Especially proud of its locally sourced butters, the inn offered a choice of several—each labeled with the name of the farm that churned it—at the sumptuous breakfast buffet. The pond at the back of the main house is home to stately swans, which added elegance to the wooded estate.

I particularly enjoyed meandering through the 19th-century English Market in Cork, where hanging pheasants vied with pigs' heads for the viands on offer. One could graze while shopping. A short line formed for oysters in the half shell shucked in front of you. I also had the tastiest pork-sausage-on-a-bun I ever ate. While waiting my turn, I experienced a touching moment at the sausage stall. An elderly woman, obviously a regular customer, placed her order, a carryout sausage. When the young man handed her the wrapped food, she tried to pay.

"No charge, missus," he said. "Next time."

"Take my money or I won't be back," she announced. He shook his head, as she stomped away with her sausage in her basket.

"She'll be back," he said, smiling at me, then made my sausage. I suspect the young man knew the woman had little money but was proud and did not want to take charity. I also suspect this little drama had played out before and would happen again. It was a nice peek into Irish life.

A few days later, in the charming little seaside town of Dingle on the west coast ("the next parish is Boston," they say to visiting Americans), I sought live Irish music, a specialty of the quaint town. First, I was advised to have a pint at Dick Mack's. A sign on a gate next door to this landmark pub reads: "Where is Dick Mack's? Opposite the church. Where is the church? Opposite Dick Mack's." When I went in for my pint I found that the pub occupied the right side of a small room. The left side was a leatherwork shop with a craftsman fashioning a belt. At night the entire room becomes a convivial pub with standing room only.

After priming myself at Dick Mack's, I moved on to the An Droicead Beag, a pub that offered traditional music. I arrived early to get a seat near the band, two men, one a fiddler, the other a guitarist. I sat next to a peat fire and chatted with two burly Irishmen who were on vacation from England and touring Ireland by bicycle. The band eschewed the songs of Irish riot and rebellion I grew up with and mostly played lively instrumentals. During a break, I asked if they took requests. "If we know them, we do," said the guitarist and lead vocalist. I asked for the "Garry Owen," famous in the US Army as the song of the 7th Cavalry from the days of George Armstrong Custer, whose military career came to a sudden end at the battle of the Little Big Horn in 1876. The musician said he didn't know the name, so I hummed a few bars. He laughed and said he knew it by its Gaelic name and they both broke into a rollicking version that brought the house down. I guess the boys in the band like to see Irish Yanks of the diaspora happy. They were as happy as I was when I bought them a round.

We made our way up the rugged west coast of Ireland where the locals still speak Gaelic. Abandoned stone huts without roofs sit in rock-filled, wind-swept, hillsides, mute testimony to the hard life that led to the flight of generations of Wild Geese, Irishman who left their native land to fight for new countries. One of them was Peter Nee. I knew him in 1969, as a much-liked member of H Company, 5th Marine Regiment in Vietnam. Full of Irish charm and wit, he died too young when one day he tripped a booby trap and was killed instantly. Peter's death affected me, and I tried to reflect this in the condolence letter I wrote to his sister, Mary, in Boston.

Years went by, and in 2012 an ex-Marine named Cottrell "Cot" Fox was vacationing in Ireland. In the bleak hills of Cashel, Connemara, looking down on Atlantic Ocean, he found the Marine Corps headstone of Peter Nee. Fox didn't know Nee in Vietnam but both were Marines and that's all it takes. Seeing Peter's gravestone, Cot realized that Peter served the Marine Company that probably saved his life in 1968 when the North Vietnamese Army overran his unit en route to attack Hue in the Tet Offensive, an action that earned Cot both a Silver Star Medal and a Purple Heart. Cot made contact with Peter's family and later organized a fund to erect a memorial stone next to Peter's grave. Many of Peter's comrades from H Company, including me, contributed.

I made a point of including Cashel on our trip in order to put flowers on Peter's grave. I contacted his sister in Boston and we made plans to rendezvous in Connemara. We stayed at the Cashel House Hotel, a charming old manor house looking out at the ocean and about two hundred yards from Peter's grave. The manager of the hotel, a classmate of Peter, was particularly solicitous. We met the

At the grave of Lance Corporal Peter Nee in Cashel, Connemara, Ireland. Peter was killed in action in Vietnam in H Company, 5th Marine Regiment, in 1969.

Nee family and visited the thatch-roofed stone cottage where Peter was born. The family hosted us at lunch before we visited Peter's grave, where I placed flowers. The site is perfect for a Marine. He is on the high ground, looking west to the Atlantic with the United States beyond, the country for which he gave his life. We walked slowly down the steep hill and hosted the Nee family to high tea at our hotel.

Peter, the twelfth of 13 Irishmen who volunteered for the Marine Corps and were killed in action in Vietnam, died on March 31, 1969. The world lost not only a fine Marine; it also lost a poet.

We drove back to Dublin, our last stop. We stayed at a pleasant hotel not far from where we dropped off our rental car. Using her formidable Internet skills, BJ found a restaurant nearby, The Gravediggers, rated #5 out of 900+ restaurants in Dublin. It also happened to be the oldest pub in the city and famed for having the "best pour" in Dublin, meaning they served the best pint of Guinness beer in the city, a serious plaudit in those parts. We were initially disappointed to find a rather seedy-looking pub adjacent to a large cemetery, hence the name Gravediggers. Dark inside, it probably looked just as it had when it first opened in 1833. Its patrons, all elderly men, looked local. We found a "snug," a cubbyhole away from the bar that offered some privacy. We started chatting to two Irishman, drinking nearby. One turned out to be Cieran, an eighth-generation Kavanagh. This was his family's pub.

Cieran explained that the restaurant was next door and he made sure there was a table for us. He also bought us a round of drinks, which confirmed, in my mind at least, that this was indeed the best pour in Dublin. Cieran, it turned out, had worked as a chef on the mainland of Europe, married an Italian girl, and returned home to bring new fame and honor to the family business. He mentioned that Anthony Bourdain, an American who traveled the world looking for good food, drink, and interesting people had featured the Gravediggers in one of his television programs. After our pints we adjourned to the restaurant next door, an upscale, modern establishment that brought a sigh of relief from BJ. The Irish fusion proved to be one of the best meals we had in Ireland. The next morning we told our cab driver we had been to the Gravediggers the night before. "Ah, 'tis a fine place," he said. "They serve the best pint in Dublin." It's got my vote.

***

In the 1980s a belly dancer with a history of CIA connections and Middle Eastern experience facilitated my first encounter with show business in the person of playwright and screenwriter, William Mastrosimone. A New Jersey native, Bill was playwright in residence at the Seattle rep and preferred living in the Pacific Northwest to Hollywood. His rustic home was a roomy, custom-built log mansion in rural Enumclaw, Washington, with an up-close and awe-inspiring view of snow-capped Mt. Rainier.

What attracted me to Bill was the film *The Beast*, for which he wrote the screenplay based on his play *Nanawatai*, a strong and moving film, shot largely in the Negev Desert of Israel. It is the story of a Russian tank crew fighting in Afghanistan. Bill and I quickly became friends. Over drinks one night, I mentioned the tragedy of the "boat people" seeking to escape communist rule in Vietnam and Cambodia. Instead of finding freedom after evading government boats, many families in fragile and sinking craft found themselves attacked by pirates, most of them from Thailand, who not only robbed thousands of people seeking freedom, but also killed and raped many women. I told Bill we should do a film on the subject. He said, "Give me a 10-page treatment,"

I wrote it, and Bill tweaked it, before giving it to his business partner in Hollywood. He shopped it around and found some interest from actor James Coburn, who wanted the role of the OSS veteran in Bangkok who helped a group of Vietnam veterans rescue a Vietnamese girl from pirates. At that point, I was transferred abroad and the story went no further.

Over the years, I kept in touch with Bill, whose career was doing well. He wrote a play, *Bang Bang You're Dead*, about violence in American schools. The screen version won two Emmy Awards, one for writing and one for producing. He always encouraged me to write, and after I retired from government I wrote another treatment about capturing a drug lord in Southeast Asia for the reward money, a story loosely based on a real villain. Again Bill helped me, and started by saying that I needed to write the screenplay myself. I wrote a draft and Bill put me in contact with a serious producer in Hollywood. He said the story had merit but would cost a lot to film on location. Then he told me about one hundred films would be produced in Hollywood that year and that there were more than 50,000 screenplays registered with the Screen Writers' Guild. That is the harsh reality of the odds of success in Hollywood. The project went no further.

Meanwhile, Tina Sinatra, Frank's daughter, wanted Bill to write a mini-series about Frank Sinatra's life for television. She approached Bill who agreed. The next hurdle was to get Frank's approval for Bill as writer. The two Jersey boys of Italian heritage met and struck a deal. Frank liked two of Bill's plays, *The Woolgatherers* and *Extremities*. In the course of hundreds of hours of taped interviews, Bill really got to know the leader of the Rat Pack.

Among the things that Frank revealed was that Mafioso Sam Giancana was the man who put the hit on President Kennedy. This was explosive stuff. So explosive, Bill could not use it in his series. Years later, Bill wrote another play, *Ride the Tiger*, that linked Giancana with Kennedy's assassination. According to Sinatra, Giancana helped Kennedy get elected president at the request of Joe Kennedy, Jack's father. When Kennedy took office, he named his brother Bobby Attorney General. Bobby went after the "Mob." Giancana took this as an act of betrayal, and had Kennedy killed. Sinatra feared Giancana would also come after him as he had introduced Giancana to Kennedy.

The closest that Bill and I came to a successful Hollywood project was a story about a retired CIA officer penetrating an ISIS terrorist cell operating in the United States. Bill liked my treatment and arranged a meeting with HBO in Los Angeles at which we made the "pitch." The 30-minute scheduled meeting went on for several hours, but in the end HBO passed on the project. Bill then took the treatment to another cable channel that also turned us down and then stole the idea for the story (with changes that made the story silly). The series lasted one season.

My attitude regarding dealing with Hollywood is summed up in a quote attributed to H. L. Menken: "You can take all of the integrity in Hollywood and fit it into the navel of a flea, leaving enough room for a caraway seed. And an agent's heart."

***

The disappearance of American James "Jim" Thompson, the "Silk King of Thailand," in 1967 is one of Southeast Asia's great mysteries. A wartime hero, he won five Bronze Star Medals for his work with the Office of Strategic Services (OSS) in North Africa. He ended the war as the OSS chief in Bangkok; where he settled and founded the Thai Silk Company, which transformed a cottage industry into a worldwide brand. The urbane Princeton graduate lived in a remarkable Thai-style "house on the klong" that housed his extensive collection of Asian art. Dinner at Jim's house was the most sought-after invitation in Bangkok. He entertained the international jet set of visitors; Ethel Mermen once sang "Hello Dolly" to Jim's cockatoo, Dolly.

While on vacation in Malaysia's Cameron Highlands on Easter Day 1967, Jim went for a walk in the jungle-clad mountains and disappeared. Despite a huge manhunt and the offer of a large reward, no one ever found him. Jim had no wife or children. His heir was his nephew, Henry Thompson, who inherited his assets. He also founded the Jim Thompson Foundation and turned Jim's house into a museum, one of Bangkok's most popular tourist destinations. The silk company continued to flourish under Bill Booth, an American who spoke fluent Thai, something Jim never did, and grew the company into an international brand. We became friends and over the years I produced four films funded by the foundation. One of the films commemorated the centennial of Jim's birth in 1906. I interviewed people from around the world, including Jim's friends, family, and colleagues. The foundation told us not to discuss Jim's disappearance and we didn't. But I ended every interview with the question, "What do you think happened to Jim," and received a wide variety of opinions. These ranged from death-by-tiger to assassination by a rival silk company. Not one of the comments were used in the film.

A number of books were written about Jim's disappearance. One author even suggested that the CIA killed Jim Thompson because of his opposition to US foreign policy in the region. My friend Bill Warren wrote the best one, *Jim Thompson: The Unsolved Mystery*. It offers many theories but no solid conclusion. Privately, Bill told me he thought Jim had fallen into an animal trap in the jungle and either died in the trap or was killed by the trap's owner.

We had a breakthrough in 2013 when a Thai friend of mine, Xuwicha "Noi" Hiranpruek called and said, "I think I may have solved the mystery." Noi said that a Singaporean friend of his, Teo Pin, told him that the Communist Party of Malaya (CPM) had assassinated Jim. I met with Teo Pin in Singapore. He said that his uncle, Teo Pok Hwa, a senior cadre in the CPM, had made a deathbed confession to Teo Pin. According to the uncle, Jim Thompson, during his visit to the Camerons, attempted to contact Chin Peng, the secretary general of the CPM and the most wanted man in Malaysia. Chin Peng cooperated with the British in fighting the Japanese during World War II and was awarded the Order of the British Empire (OBE) for his service. The decoration was later rescinded when Chen Peng led a brutal insurgency against the British and later the Malaysians.

According to Teo Pin, the Cameron Highlands was a hotbed of communist activity and Jim's effort to contact Chin Peng caused immediate suspicion. After a bit of due diligence, the CPM learned that Jim had been in the OSS during the war and immediately suspected him of being a CIA spy. The CPM in the Camerons had no radio to communicate with their headquarters in Thailand or with China, where Chin Peng lived in exile. Local leaders made the decision to kill Jim. I told Teo Pin and Noi that this was important but we needed corroboration.

As a civilian and enjoying his life as a businessman as well as being the toastmaster of Bangkok, Jim maintained close friendships with senior Thais and Americans from his OSS days. For example, during the war, a Thai prime minister, Pridi Panomyong, had cooperated with OSS under the code name Ruth. Pridi remained in power until he was ousted in a coup d'état in 1947 by his archrival Pibulsongram, a right-wing military officer who had cooperated with the Japanese. Pridi remained a close friend of Jim's until he fled to China in 1949 after a failed counter-coup.

A senior Agency officer at the time of Jim's disappearance, Robert "Red" Jantzen, had also been in the OSS. I interviewed his wife, Jane, for the film *Jim Thompson: The Man and the Legend*. She was more than 90 years old and asked me how long the interview would take. No more than one hour, I said. "That's good. I have a tee time at two." A lifelong golfer, Mrs. Jantzen's name can be found on lists of women's golf champions at a prominent Bangkok sports club. Jane and her British husband were interned by the Japanese when they captured the Philippines in World War II. While in prison, her husband died. She met Bob Jantzen when the OSS liberated her camp in 1945 and she married him. Jane was also a close friend of Jim Thompson and suggested he open his house, already a museum of sorts, to the public. He agreed and all proceeds from the modest entrance fee went to the School for the Blind.

Two OSS veterans, Army Brigadier General Ed Black, senior US military officer in Thailand and Willis Bird Sr., a wartime OSS colonel, retired in Bangkok and remained very close friends. Ed had recruited Jim into the OSS. Willis married into an aristocratic Thai family and became a leading businessman in Thailand. His brother-in-law, Royal Thai Air Marshal Sitthi Sawetsila, had been a member of the Free Thai resistance and later foreign minister.

In the spring of 2017 Noi called again. "I have a second source," he said. The game was afoot. Noi mentioned his interest in the Jim Thompson mystery to his old friend Willis "Billy" Bird Jr. Noi said Billy was quiet for two or three minutes. Then he said 'I will tell you something that I have not spoken to anyone about for 50 years.'" Billy described a conversation he had with his father, who said that in 1966 Pridi Panomyong, in exile in China, invited Will senior to visit him in Beijing. Willis, a firm supporter of the war Vietnam, wanted nothing to do with Pridi, his old friend who had falsely been branded a communist by Thai government when he fled Thailand in 1949.

Colonel Bird told his son that he mentioned Pridi's invitation and his decision to decline it to Jim Thompson. Then Pridi invited Jim to visit China. Against Bird's advice, Jim accepted the invitation. Loyal to his wartime ally, Jim was willing to take a chance to see him. When Jim went missing in Malaysia on Easter Day, 1967, Billy said that his father told him, "He must have been killed by the Malayan communists."

The conversation with Billy Jr. suggested the reason why Jim wanted to meet Chin Peng in the Cameron Highlands. With two sources in hand we decided to move ahead with the film. I congratulated Noi for solving the mystery even if we still had many unanswered questions. We also signed up editor Adam Goldschmidt from New York and the team headed for Thailand. We went to Chiang Mai, Thailand, to interview Billy Bird Jr. Helpful, but somewhat reticent to divulge a secret he had kept so long, he found it painful to tell the story. Billy thought of Jim as his godfather. "All my life I called him Uncle Jim," he told me. "Jim was a very special person. He was like a member of the family."

From Chiang Mai we shifted south to the Cameron Highlands and the Moonlight Cottage in Malaysia. The Moonlight Cottage where Jim stayed has been refurbished and renamed the Jim Thompson cottage. Part of our crew stayed there while we filmed the comfortable colonial cottage and the surrounding jungle from a drone. A few of us stayed at the Ye Olde Smokehouse, a fixture in the old British hill station since 1937, and still the best place to stay. It was one of Jim's favorite haunts because it was the only place to get a good beef Wellington. It still is. It may have been Jim's destination on his last walk in 1967.

Teo Pin joined us there and we interviewed him in the garden. He seemed much more relaxed than when I first met him in Singapore a few years earlier. It probably helped a lot that his good friend Noi Hiranpruek and Noi's talented daughter, Pimprae, our executive producer, had come with us. Teo Pin was on a personal quest to learn more about his uncle, Teo Pok Hwa, a wanted "terrorist," who had deserted his wife and children to fight against the Japanese, then the British, and finally against the Malaysians for the Communist Party of Malaya. After decades on the run and in poor health, Pok Hwa emerged in the 1980s, destitute and bitter over China's abandonment of the ethnically Chinese movement. Just before he died, Pok Hwa said that Jim Thompson had been under surveillance by the CPM. Unable to contact Chin Peng or other senior CPM cadres for guidance, the local CPM decided to kill him. He assured his nephew that Jim's bones would never be found.

The Thai premiere of the film was held at the Foreign Correspondents' Club of Thailand to a packed room. I was a working member of the club in 1962 when there were only a few members; our meetings were infrequent and usually held at Mizu's Kitchen, a humble restaurant on Pat Pong Road near the AP and UPI bureaus. The Q&A session after the screening ran longer than the 47-minute film. I was happy to have Noi, Billy, and Teo Pin help answer questions. Somewhat to my surprise we did not face much skepticism and was surprised that there were no challenges to our conclusion that Jim was killed by the CPM.

I still have questions myself and view the film as a work-in-progress. Why did Pridi want to see Bill Bird or Jim? Why did Jim try to contact Chin Peng? I suspect that Pridi wanted Jim's help in getting out of China. Eventually, Pridi did get out and moved to Paris, where he died in 1983. I consider Pridi one of Thailand's great men of the 20th century and had the good fortune to meet him in Paris. We met twice, on the occasion of the birthday of King Rama IX at the Thai embassy where Pridi met friends privately in a reception room. I was mainly interested in learning about Pridi's wartime adventures and he was very forthcoming. I only wish that I had asked him about Jim Thompson.

***

I would be remiss if I wrote a memoir and did not mention an avocation I developed in Asia that has given me a great deal of pleasure over the years. Some people become obsessed, even addicted, spending much time and money doing it; others develop a passion that surpasses reason. Strong emotions can result: jealousy, envy, and greed. I speak of collecting art.

Cambodia at war was not the best place to buy arts and crafts. For one thing, the high metallic content to the air—from dozens of Khmer Rouge rockets landing inside the city on any given day—dampened the art and culture scene. Phnom Penh did not have any real antique shops. Cambodia did, however, have a rich tradition of crafts, notably silk weaving and silver working for the Khmer elite. A few shops survived near the Grand Palace on "Silver Street" where, with patience and a little luck, interesting pieces could be found.

There on "Silver Street," I began my initiation into collecting Asian art. I became more informed and focused over the decades. I was fortunate in my early shopping forays to have a kindred spirit in my friend Tim. As the noose tightened on Phnom Penh, many Cambodians fled the country, and this exodus brought a number of interesting pieces onto the market. A minor member of the Norodom royal family dropped by my house one evening and asked if I was interested in purchasing the French-made dinner service of 19th-century King Norodom. Many of the plates were chipped or cracked and nothing appealed. Then he offered a small stone head of a Hindu deity, and I made my first purchase of ancient Khmer art. Similarly, I bought a 19th-century, two-handed Cham fighting sword with a long bone handle from a young Cham heading for Paris.

After Cambodia fell in 1975, my collecting of the arts and crafts of the region moved into high gear. In a small shop in the Gaysorn Arcade I bought two reasonably priced Thai covered jars several hundred years old from Sawankaloke and Sukothai. The prices were reasonable and I was proud of my first purchases in Thailand. A few days later, I showed my treasures to Horst Faas, an antique collector of some renown after more than a decade of photographing war in Southeast Asia. He examined the bowls closely, said they were genuine and agreed they were a good buy at $15 each. But he observed that one had been repaired and the other had a small chip, which accounted for the low prices. I learned my first lesson. Never buy broken or repaired ceramics.

Horst then gave me a quick course in collecting, starting with the need to know and trust your dealer. He introduced me to Chai Ma, a quiet and much respected Sino-Thai dealer on Silom Road. Over the years I spent many hours learning from Chai Ma how to identify good pieces from bad, genuine from reproductions, broken from repaired. Early on, Chai Ma sold me a stone Khmer torso of a woman, probably dating to the 12th or 13th century, somewhat rough but also charming. He said that if I didn't like a piece I could always bring it back. Or I could trade pieces with him. I once bought a rare and beautiful Ban Chiang bronze bell dating from before the Christian era. I liked it very much, but later decided to swap it for a Khmer bronze conch. I still have the conch. The bell is in a national museum in Southeast Asia.

Chai Ma also sold me a life-size Angkor-period stone hand of a Buddha image in a classic *mudra* gesture that suggested the Buddha signaling OK with his hand. The hand was in perfect condition. According to Chai Ma, a woodcutter in a northeastern Thailand forest found the hand. The statue of the Buddha had fallen over and the hand broke off. The woodcutter could not carry the stone statue, so took only the hand. He sold it in a provincial town and it made its way to Chai Ma's shop. Chai Ma immediately told the seller to find the woodcutter and take an ox cart into the woods to locate the rest of the stone image. When I bought the hand, it was with the understanding that if the rest of the statue was found, I would sell it back to Chai Ma at double what I paid. The woodcutter looked and looked, but never found the Buddha image. I still have the hand.

Chai Ma also introduced me to Thai painting. I purchased a number of oils from the 20th-century artist, Somnuk, who painted mostly village scenes in classic Siamese style. Another, and earlier, buyer of Somnuk's art was the late American Jim Thompson. Jim bought beautiful Somnuk paintings depicting silk weaving in Bangkok and he displayed the paintings in his shop and iconic House on the Klong. I have a few of Somnuk's silk weaving village paintings. My favorite Somnuk shows three elephants sporting fish tails swimming in the ocean. The inspiration for this piece of fantasy came from the wall murals of Wat Kongkaram, a Mon temple in Rajburi, west of Bangkok. It hangs over my fireplace in Kirkland, Washington.

Fortune smiled on me one day during lunch with a friend on Pat Pong Road in Bangkok. A man visiting from Rangoon who knew my friend walked into the restaurant and joined us. He was in a foul mood; he told us that he had brought a few antiques from Burma to a fellow in Bangkok who balked at the already agreed upon price. The antiques included two wooden Buddha images and two lacquer Buddhist texts. He said he would take $100 for everything. I bought them sight unseen and went straight to his hotel to pick them up. I didn't care for one of the Buddha images and immediately sold it. The remaining image, a large 19th-century Buddha seated on five elephants, today sits in a place of honor in our living room.

True collecting takes more than finding a good dealer. Sometimes you need to go to the source. And it never hurts to be lucky. In that regard, BJ and I made a field trip to Ban Chiang in northeastern Thailand, a village where, a decade earlier, archaeologists discovered pottery ancient civilization. Ban Chiang, is now considered an important culture site dating well before the Christian era. The civilization covered thousands of square miles and practiced wet-rice cultivation, forged bronze artifacts, and produced a vast array of low-fired pottery with distinctive patterns.

After a long and tedious drive from Bangkok, we drove into town and asked about buying pottery. We were directed to the humble house of a woman who invited us in. Speaking Thai, we asked if she had anything to sell. She said yes, but before talking business, she served us tea. Communication was a little difficult because our hostess spoke Lao as her first language. Eventually, the lady produced a number of small pots with the distinctive brown and cream circular patterns of Ban Chiang ware; some were broken but most were intact. As we handled the items on offer, more local ladies arrived with bundles of their own Ban Chiang pots. Soon a dozen ladies with pottery, some bronze artifacts, and clay rollers used to print designs on cloth surrounded us. Excavated pieces included everything from small beads with holes for stringing, and pots to a human forearm bone with fused bronze bangles attached. The ladies were polite and waited their turns for their goods to be inspected. After some gentle negotiations we bought a number of small pieces at very low prices. The human bone was not one of them. Today, Ban Chiang is a World Heritage site and excavations continue.

A few years later, I took my large Ban Chiang bell to the British Museum in London. The curator who came to meet us said he had never seen such a fine Ban Chiang bronze. He then showed us the museum's small and undistinguished Ban Chiang holdings. I suggested that the dating was far too recent and suggested a much earlier date, gleaned from my Bangkok experience. Without batting an eye, the fellow changed the date on the card and thanked me.

Our collecting moved into high gear when we arrived in Indonesia. It began with a piece of good luck. A top European art dealer, when he learned we were off to Indonesia, said, "I am going to do you a favor," meaning he would introduce me to his major source of Indonesian antiques. The source turned out to be a softly-spoken young man who dealt out of his home and supplied a small group of Indonesian collectors along with the European dealer. Over tea in his Dutch colonial villa, the dealer explained that he would show me a small group of statues, all of them made of white limestone tuff from the Majapahit Empire of East Java, dating from the 13th to 16th century. He would allow me to choose one piece. The rest would be sent to Europe the next day. The objects, mostly small statues of women, were sublime. I had seen nothing like them published or in museums. I would make my choice, learn the price, and pay. And was happy to do so. The dealer never haggled, but the prices of the items sold in Europe were marked up tenfold. Over time, he offered me Majapahit terracotta statues and Chinese ceramics recovered from sunken ships, all in top condition.

Years later, I heard that the white tuff statues might actually be reproductions. Very fine and beautifully crafted, but not old. Ordinarily, I would have been upset, but not in this case. The low price I paid should have been a clue. The fact that museums had nothing better in their collections was another clue. But I loved them, and still do. I wish I had been allowed to buy more. They are among our most treasured pieces; each one a work of art.

Indonesia is a cornucopia of fine arts from its vastly different and far-flung 13,000 islands. From sophisticated and detailed batik cloth hand dyed in the royal cities of Jogjakarta and Solo on Java, to primitive woodcarving from Stone Age tribesmen of West New Guinea (formerly Irian Jaya), Indonesia has treasures for every taste and budget. Indonesians consider Jogjakarta (Jogja) in central Java the cultural center of the island, and by extension the country. It has strong textile traditions thanks to royal patronage. We have a 19th-century wooden panel from a screen depicting bolts of colored cloth. It now hangs on the wall of our dining room opposite a large, round dinner table of rare Ambon wood on a teak base, also a purchase from Jogjakarta. If something happens to our screen, I have only to visit Tim Carney. He has the other half of the screen in his collection.

Jogja is also home to a lively contemporary art scene, especially painting. Through a group of Sino-Indonesian collectors in Jakarta, Tim and I were invited to meet some of the top painters of Jogja. One of these was Sukamto, a quiet fellow from a small village outside Jogja. Trained at the fine arts college in Jogja, he developed his own style of naïf painting with oil crayons. The inspiration for his paintings derived from actual events that he had witnessed in his village. One of the first paintings I bought depicts the wedding of an elderly widower and a widow of about the same age. The painting showed them as a beautiful young woman with her young husband. I asked Sukamto why they looked so young. "Because that is how they see themselves," he explained.

I commissioned a painting from Sukamto that showed him at work while I photographed him. The result was honest and amusing. The artist portrayed me with my Nikon camera in hand, dressed in Javanese clothes, complete with a *kris* (knife) in my belt, displaying the chalky white face and pointed nose of a European. I love it. Just before we left Indonesia I visited Jogja and paid a call on Sukamto in the countryside. I made a portrait of him with his mother and learned that he was in the chips having been "discovered" by Didier Hamel, a top art dealer in Jakarta. He wanted me to see his car. Sukamto sat in the driver's seat of his second-hand sedan and rolled the window down. Striking a jaunty pose with an elbow on the windowsill, he asked me to photograph him at the wheel. I complied and asked him how often he drove into town. "Oh, I don't drive," he said. "The car is just for show."

Tim and I would occasionally visit Surabaya, a large port city in eastern Java. Our main target was the antique shop of "Surabaya Bob," a charming Dutch-Indonesian fellow whose rustic establishment, Barang Lama (Old Things) was a 45 minute drive from the city. We found the journey well worth the time. For one thing, his prices were about 75 percent lower than Jakarta prices. For another, he had many items not found or rarely seen in the shops along Jalan Surabaya, the antique street of Jakarta. We discovered he had a surplus of antique oil-burning lamps in the Dutch style from the 19th century. While we were there, the government was expanding electricity across East Java and Indonesia and no longer needed the lamps. In top condition they cost $30 and for a few dollars more could be converted to an electric lamp. One hangs over our dining room table now.

On one trip we learned that Bob had purchased two hundred 19th-century Chinese bowls with a brown external glaze and a blue-and-white floral pattern inside. Known as chocolate Ch'ing, pieces in good condition went for about $50 in Jakarta. Bob told us that virgin girls sitting outside the workshop in coastal China painted the patterns to attract passing boys who might want to marry a talented artisan. I hope the story is true. Bob, who carried a large selection, charged us $18 apiece. The only thing that stopped us from buying more was the sad fact that we could hand-carry only 12 bowls each aboard the aircraft back to Jakarta. When an American friend in Surabaya saw our haul, he immediately drove to Bob's to augment his own collection. We gave some away as wedding presents but still have about six, which are sometimes called into service to serve steamed rice at dinner parties.

The island of Bali, off the east coast of Java, has perhaps the most multi-faceted and creative set of artisans anywhere in the world. Everyone seems able to dance, paint, carve, weave, sing, or cook, usually a combination of all of the above. Unique in Indonesia as a bastion of the Hindu religion, Bali's many religious ceremonies give full throttle to the arts and crafts of the island.

We became friendly with John Hardy, a Canadian jewelry designer on Bali, who created beautiful objects from gold and silver employing artisans from a variety of shops around the island. We met him at a one-man show in Jakarta where I bought a silver letter opener with an antique *kris* handle, and began collecting his art. On several occasions I flew to Bali to photograph the production of John's art. One session included taking pictures of a young Balinese model adorned with John's silver necklaces and bracelets. BJ was the main beneficiary of this project, as John paid me in silver jewelry. John also gave me a wine coaster of finely woven silver strands. It was one of two prototypes. The other went to John's friend David Bowie, an aficionado of Bali.

I was fortunate to meet Nyoman Gunarsa, a leading Balinese painter and a lot of fun to be around. I bought a pen and ink sketch of dancing Balinese girls, one of his favorite motifs. We became friends and in the early 1990s he commissioned me to photograph him at work and at play for a book he was producing on his life and his work. Vicki Butler, Tim's wife, was hired to write the book. She, BJ, and I spent two weeks in Bali working on the project. My assignment basically called for hanging out with Nyoman and photographing in the style of a *LIFE* magazine assignment. He met with clients, dealers, and family. He treated us to the finest of Balinese cuisine, found only in homes. One night he arranged for an all-night puppet performance for his village that he wanted me to photograph for the book. This followed an elegant banquet he hosted for the boys in the band. The band in this case was a full gamelan orchestra of great local repute. I limited my intake of fiery *arak*, the alcoholic beverage of choice of the fun-loving Balinese, so that my photography did not suffer. The performance lasted until dawn, longer than I did, but the pictures came out fine.

During a short visit to Hong Kong a leading European art dealer took me along on a buying excursion to one of his Chinese suppliers. We entered a back-alley bare room with a floor covered with treasures from the Han, Tang, and Ming dynasties. We spoke no common language, so my friend and his dealer communicated by hand calculators, which did the talking. My friend made an offer for an item with his calculator. The wizened seller made a counter offers with his calculator. This happened twice and the final price was made. We bought a number of pieces this way with no words exchanged. I ended up with a nice Han dynasty terracotta horse's head and a Han funeral figure. Among many other things, my friend bought the remaining 18 funeral figures after assuring that mine was the finest. My cost was $60.

We did little buying on our European tour, with the exception of maps and prints. As luck would have it, when I walked down the street to the Metro on Boulevard St. Germain, I had to pass two of the best antique maps and prints shops in the city. I spent many quiet hours on rainy days poring through folios, always making a few purchases. Although I stayed mostly focused on Asian subjects I did occasionally buy prints relating to Hawaii, Alaska, and the Pacific Northwest of America. Perhaps the most interesting item of what I found is a 1752 map of the voyages of Admiral de Fonte that purported, incorrectly, to show the Northwest Passage linking the Atlantic with the Pacific. The map now hangs on a wall in our dining room surrounded by other antique Asian maps. One of them only 20 years newer than de Fonte's map is a map of the same area from the great Captain James Cook. The main difference is Cook's map is accurate.

I made a major purchase by chance. Just outside the town of Ste. Mère-Eglise where paratroopers from the 101st Airborne Division landed early on June 6, 1944, I passed a *brocante* shop, a dealer in secondhand goods, one step down from an antique shop. Outside stood a beautiful 19th-century pine sideboard. I bought it after a short negotiation, which included its delivery to Paris. The price was less than half the Paris price.

I saw Burma, Southeast Asia's "hidden pearl," as my last shot at serious collecting. Despite harsh military rule and bitter ethnic conflicts, life was unchanged for millions of Burmese, heirs to a rich and ancient culture that produced lacquer ware, tapestries (*kalaga*), silver, ceramics, textiles, and painting. Rangoon didn't have many antique shops. For decades Augustine—the man to know—had a virtually monopoly on the antique trade with foreigners. This soft-spoken, ethnic Tamil of Indian extraction and a Roman Catholic miraculously produced treasures great and small. One wrinkle in dealing with Augustine was his disquieting habit of calling all male customers "Master" despite pleas to desist, a throwback to colonial days when such behavior was tolerated if not expected. He also kept very limited office hours: three hours a week from 0900 to 1200 on Saturdays. With time and patience, I established a close rapport, which resulted in Augustine holding pieces for me that he knew I would buy. I learned much from Augustine while buying quantities of lacquer offering bowls, Burman and tribal textiles, silver betel boxes, and Shan swords. I bought a large, finely worked silver bowl. When I found a bigger and better one, I traded up. I did this three times until I found the one I wanted. It sits on a golden-teak coffee table in the living room.

Burma has a rich tradition of painting in watercolors. We made friends with Ma Thanegi, one of my favorite Burmese water-colorists. A very talented lady who not only paints but is also a leading writer and translator, she once served as private secretary to Aung San Suu Kyi. She spent some time in prison with The Lady when they were fighting for democracy for Burma. Some say Thanegi was even tougher

Burmese artist U Sein Myint at work in his studio in Mandalay.

than her boss and I am inclined to agree. My guru for all things cultural and culinary in Burma, she collaborated with me on an article on pottery for the magazine *Arts of Asia*, and later on a book titled *Myanmar Architecture: Cities of Gold*. She wrote the text, I took the photos. Among the paintings I collected by Ma Thanegi are sketches of our sons. I particularly like a simple but arresting small work depicting the intricate iron grillwork on an old colonial building. When I bought it Thanegi could have been jailed for painting this innocent watercolor. The paranoid military regime might be offended at the iron bars, which could suggest the repression of the regime. To me, it exemplified her toughness in daring to mock the military through her art.

Since 2010, with the glacial shift towards democracy, the arts have flourished. An example is the Mandalay-based artist U Sein Myint who excels in two art forms: painting and weaving. A self-taught painter who works in acrylic or watercolors he portrays traditional Burmese cultural themes. He is also the leading designer of tapestries that depict traditional scenes of life in Burma. Charming young ladies patiently and quietly labor in teams to bring life to his designs staff his workshop. I have a watercolor of a tiger puppet by Sein Myint and a larger collection of his tapestries, including a large representation of the one hundred lives of the Buddha as seen in the Buddha's footprint.

Perhaps the most avant-garde art produced in Burma came from the workshops of French designer Patrick Robert and his Shan wife, Claudia Saw Lwin Robert. They took traditional arts and crafts in new directions and to heights never seen before. Sometimes serious, often whimsical, their art brought Burma new attention on the international art scene. I am proud to have a few pieces in our collection. I am particularly fond of an oil painting of a consort of the Chinese emperor Qinglong (1735–96). Only the face of the painting has been changed. It now shows BJ's face; she looks much better than the original model.

One of the finest artists we have collected, almost by accident, was the Swiss artist Theo Meier, best known for paintings from Bali before World War II when he was one of the few Western artists who made their homes there. I first met Theo in 1963 in Chiang Mai, Thailand, when I working there as stills photographer on the film *Tarzan's Three Challenges*. I was with Tarzan (played by Jock Mahoney) when we were taken to meet Theo, the city's most eminent foreign artist. Theo and I became friends. I now have an oil painting of my sister, Jenny, two sketches of me at age 19, and a sketch each of BJ, Theo's Thai wife, Laiad, and a Balinese dancer. Theo taught me a lot about the important things in life, and kindly allowed me to photograph his charming open-air Chiang Mai house on the banks of the Ping River for my first article in *Architectural Digest*. Some of our Theo Meier treasures, along with photos I took of Theo, appear in the book *Theo Meier: A Swiss Artist Under the Tropics* by Didier Hamel.

As I look back, I see that the real fun is in the collecting of art, not in the owning. The passion comes from the hunt. There is also great pleasure in knowing some of the artists who have enriched our lives. Many of the art objects we have collected we could not afford to buy at today's prices. But there is always new art and new artists on the scene, so every generation has its chance. I did not start out viewing art collecting as an investment but in retrospect I probably should have. In street value, our collection has far outstripped real estate and stock market gains over the years. Today, as I sit in front of a fire in our Kirkland, Washington, home and look around the room at my favorite friends I fondly recall the good times we had getting together. Each piece has a story.

***

I must add a few words about BJ. After I was commissioned in the Marine Corps after receiving my BA from the University of Washington in 1967, it was pretty clear where I was headed. Already, some of my friends from Naval ROTC had gone to war, and a few had been killed in action. I had one thing to do before heading to war; get married. BJ and I had been together for a few years and watching how she handled her father's bout with tuberculosis when she graduated showed me that she had grit. I thought she could handle the dreaded knock on the door from a uniformed Marine officer bearing bad news. We had a typical wartime wedding at Quantico just after my Officer Basic School class graduated. The base chapel was busy; there was one wedding every 15 minutes. Bob Peterson played the dual role of best man and photographer, while his wife, Lynn, was the bridesmaid. No family was present, regrettably, as I was under orders to Vietnam and time was short. My AP mentor, Hal Buell, gave the bride away. A sword arch of my classmates gave the occasion a touch of Marine Corps tradition. Then I went to Vietnam while BJ taught high school in Seattle and coached the girls' tennis team to a state championship.

After being a Marine wife for three years, BJ probably expected a normal life of a wife who would pursue a career of her own at the same time. Wrong. I entered the CIA thrusting BJ into a new role as a spy's wife, which proved to be sometimes more dangerous than being a Marine's wife. The constant moving from one country to another made it difficult for her to continue her own career as a teacher. And the wife of a CIA case officer brought new and different stresses. For one thing, if I made an operational error, or a target declined recruitment and reported my "pitch," I could expect to be expelled from the country within 48 hours. This can be very disruptive for familial harmony.

BJ surmounted every challenge, including my first one, another separated tour. Most overseas tours are accompanied by families but with Cambodia at war no spouses were permitted at post. "Safe havened" in Bangkok where I would visit every month for a long weekend, BJ taught English, learned Thai, and made friends fast. She came to Phnom Penh to see me during school breaks. That ended the day a rocket hit the roof of a house across the street from my villa strewing shrapnel into the garden. BJ was reading on the verandah at the time and returned to Bangkok the next day unharmed.

The Agency did not require spouses to entertain, but it did expect all case officers to do so. Even when BJ was teaching or working in other positions, she usually hosted one sit-down dinner party per week while we were posted abroad. They were invariably of a very high quality; BJ was a Michelin-star quality cook. She expanded her considerable talents by attending Cordon Bleu courses. In Seattle, she founded a catering company with my sister, Jenny, and did very well. Scott Carsberg, a James Beard-award winner and a top Seattle chef, calls BJ one of the best cooks in Seattle. I agree and have the waistline to prove it.

BJ played a crucial role in my success as a recruiter of clandestine sources for the CIA. A great "reader" of people, BJ watched the "development" of assets

BJ enjoying lunch at the Pushkin Café in Moscow in 2015.

and I would not make a "pitch" until BJ said he (or she) was ready. Recruiting spies is not a business in which a .500 average wins prizes. This isn't baseball, it's life and death. In my case, I "batted" 1,000 percent. BJ worked for the State Department. During one posting, she served as the embassy's Community Liaison Officer (CLO), a sort of an ombudsman position. People with problems would go to the CLO, and BJ would sort the matter out. She conducted culture and shopping tours for embassy personnel, and was very popular among the large embassy staff. When Vice President Dan Quayle visited Jakarta, BJ was designed the official "greeter." Within the embassy community, I was known to many as Mr. BJ.

While doing all this, BJ found time to bear and raise two sons: Seth and Brendan. That they both turned out to be out-going, well-educated, polite, and successful is due in very large part to BJ being a superb mom. She put up with a lot over the years from the US Marine Corps, the Central Intelligence Agency, the Department of State, and from me. On November 30, 2018 we celebrated our 50th anniversary. That's a good start.